Transfeminist Perspectives

Edited by
ANNE ENKE

Transfeminist Perspectives
in and beyond Transgender and Gender Studies

TEMPLE UNIVERSITY PRESS
Philadelphia

TEMPLE UNIVERSITY PRESS
Philadelphia, Pennsylvania 19122
www.temple.edu/tempress

Copyright © 2012 by Temple University
All rights reserved
Published 2012

Library of Congress Cataloging-in-Publication Data

Transfeminist perspectives in and beyond transgender and gender studies /
edited by Anne Enke.
   p.   cm.
   Includes bibliographical references and index.
   ISBN 978-1-4399-0746-7 (cloth : alk. paper)
   ISBN 978-1-4399-0747-4 (pbk. : alk. paper)
   ISBN 978-1-4399-0748-1 (e-book)
   1. Women's studies.   2. Feminism.   3. Transgenderism.   4. Transsexualism.
I. Enke, Anne, 1964–

   HQ1180.T72 2012
   305.4—dc23   2011043061

Printed and bound in Great Britain by
Marston Book Services Limited, Didcot
061212P

Contents

Acknowledgments   vii

Introduction: Transfeminist Perspectives   1
A. Finn Enke

Note on Terms and Concepts   16
A. Finn Enke

PART I   "This Much Knowledge": Flexible Epistemologies

1 Gender/Sovereignty   23
Vic Muñoz

2 "Do These Earrings Make Me Look Dumb?" Diversity, Privilege, and Heteronormative Perceptions of Competence within the Academy   34
Kate Forbes

3 Trans. Panic. Some Thoughts toward a Theory of Feminist Fundamentalism   45
Bobby Noble

4 The Education of Little Cis: Cisgender and the Discipline of Opposing Bodies   60
A. Finn Enke

PART II   Categorical Insufficiencies and "Impossible People"

5 College Transitions: Recommended Policies for Trans Students and Employees   81
Clark A. Pomerleau

6	"Ain't I a Woman?" Transgender and Intersex Student Athletes in Women's Collegiate Sports *Pat Griffin*	98
7	Training Disservice: The Productive Potential and Structural Limitations of Health as a Terrain for Trans Activism *Christoph Hanssmann*	112
8	Transnational Transgender Rights and Immigration Law *Aren Z. Aizura*	133

PART III Valuing Subjects: Toward Unexpected Alliances

9	Elusive Subjects: Notes on the Relationship between Critical Political Economy and Trans Studies *Dan Irving*	153
10	Reclaiming Femininity *Julia Serano*	170
11	What's Wrong with Trans Rights? *Dean Spade*	184
12	When Something Is Not Right *Ryka Aoki*	195

Notes	203
Bibliography	233
Contributors	249
Index	253

Acknowledgments

One of the greatest things about collaborative projects is that at the outset and for a good bit of the way through, no individual—even the editor of a collection of solicited articles—can quite envision the process or predict the outcome. I did not take this project on lightly, but thanks to the many people who generously contributed their time and wisdom, this has been an exceptionally rewarding experience. Through it, I have had the opportunity to meet and learn from a great number of inspiring people and to simultaneously develop a deeper appreciation for the ways that our everyday lives as well as local and global political contexts fuel our work. First and foremost, I must express my gratitude to the eleven other contributors to this collection: Aren Aizura, Ryka Aoki, Kate Forbes, Pat Griffin, Chris Hanssmann, Dan Irving, Vic Muñoz, Bobby Noble, Clark Pomerleau, Julia Serano, and Dean Spade. In addition to writing for this book, they have introduced me to others, shared resources, and in general have given meaning to the word "collaboration."

In some ways, this book began when Nancy Hewitt invited me to edit a volume of primary documents. It was a highly compelling invitation, and although I ultimately did not take it on, that invitation got me thinking seriously about where I wanted to put my post-tenure energies. That same year, the University of Wisconsin granted me a sabbatical that gave me the necessary time and space with which to imagine a transfeminist collaboration as one possible response to a pressing concern: namely, the mutually constituted but highly ambivalent relationship between Trans Studies and Women's Studies, and our need for new perspective on the ways that gender is disciplined and practiced in academic institutions and beyond. I also owe thanks to Jeani O'Brien, Rachel Buff, and Joe Austin, who, in very different ways, helped convince me that editing a collection can be enjoyable.

I am indebted to Janet Francendese, who, as editor in chief at Temple University Press, took an early interest in this project and has helped it sail smoothly along to its existence as a book. Not least, Janet lined up a stellar group of reviewers. Reviewing manuscripts is always "overtime" labor, but in the best of worlds, it is also part of what keeps our intellectual communities alive. I would like to thank Paisley Currah, Cris Mayo, and Susan Stryker for their generous and astute feedback at various stages of this project. All the articles individually, and the collection as a whole, have benefited dramatically from their critical acumen and deep knowledge of the interdisciplinary conversations in which this book takes part. Amanda Steele at Temple and Lynne Frost have also facilitated stress-free (at least on my end) production.

As is perhaps fitting in a book about gender and transgender, Temple has allowed some administrative navigations to remain or become visibly idiosyncratic. One such navigation is that my name appears on the book cover and title page as Anne Enke and on my contributions as A. Finn Enke. Much like gender, it turns out that names function at the confluence of personal histories, cultural categories, legal apparatuses, and marketing interests. Given these vicissitudes, it was my preference to keep all names available and accessible, though the reader will be aware that this poses some minor hazards of citation.

I owe heartfelt thanks to Susan Stryker for ongoing support and particularly for organizing the *Postposttranssexual: Transgender Studies and Feminism Conference* (2011), and to Sandy Stone, who, in so many ways, started it all. Kate Bornstein and Beth Elliott have also offered kindness, inspiration, and irreverent humor of the "without which" variety. I am grateful to Hans Scheirl for allowing me to use his paintings for the cover and for being an all-around mensch. Chris Hommerding and Faron Levesque worked on the compiled bibliography, sparing me some headaches. Shannon A. Thistle created the index and introduced me to the history and poetry of the indexing profession.

As always, Nan Enstad has been there to encourage this project from its first little spark of an idea; in fact, it seems quite possible that the first spark was hers. She helped me be patient during the long stage of not knowing what this would become, understanding my need to facilitate more transfeminist conversation. She also read and provided invaluable feedback on the parts that I wrote and offered suggestions related to the whole. She is thus an integral participant in this book and in my own sense of what transfeminist perspectives can offer.

A. FINN ENKE

Introduction

Transfeminist Perspectives

This book is born of the conviction that feminist studies and transgender studies are intimately connected to one another in their endeavor to analyze epistemologies and practices that produce gender. Despite this connection, they are far from integrated. *Transfeminist Perspectives in and beyond Transgender and Gender Studies* seeks to highlight the productive and sometimes fraught potential of this relationship. Feminist, women's, and gender studies grew partly from Simone de Beauvoir's observation that "one is not born, but rather becomes, a woman."[1] Transgender studies extends this foundation, emphasizing that there is no natural process by which *any*one becomes woman, and also that *every*one's gender is made: Gender, and also sex, are made through complex social and technical manipulations that naturalize some while abjecting others. In this, both feminist and transgender studies acknowledge the mutual imbrications of gender and class formations, dis/abilities, racializations, political economies, incarcerations, nationalisms, migrations and dislocations, and so forth. We share, perhaps, a certain delight and trepidation in the awareness that gender is trouble: Gender may trouble every imaginable social relation and fuel every imaginable social hierarchy; it may also threaten to undo itself and us with it, even as gender scholars simultaneously practice, undo, and reinvest in gender.[2]

Women's and gender studies have registered increasing interest in things transgender since the mid-1990s. Scholars have organized conferences on the topic, and numerous feminist journals have published special transgender issues.[3] This interest has been inspired in part by inquiry into the meanings of gender, bodies, and embodiment, by transnational and cross-cultural studies that address the varied ways in which cultures ascribe gender, and also by institutional practices that circumscribe or broaden the range of gender legibility. Interest is further inspired by the multiple arrivals and iterations of transgender in classrooms, playing fields, and political movements. As a direct result of these arrivals, the meanings associated with such terms as "gender," "transgender," "woman," "man," and "queer" have changed dramatically over the last two decades. Nevertheless, transgender remains institutionally marginal to gender and women's studies. As a well-established field, gender and women's studies may include transgender as an add-on, without fundamentally changing the theoretical articulations and material practices that all but ensure that the definition of "women's studies" will position transgender as something outside or other than itself. Gender and women's studies is one place where transgender studies has managed to make an institutional home (the other is LGBT studies), but it is as yet an ambivalent home. *Transfeminist Perspectives* suggests that trans might be central, not marginal, to gender and women's studies.

At the simplest level, *Transfeminist Perspectives* offers multidisciplinary models for integrating feminist and transgender theory, practice, and pedagogy. Its authors come from and teach in a wide range of scholarly disciplines, including English, history, cultural studies, zoology, evolutionary biology, psychology, public health, social justice, economics, law, sociology, sports education, sexuality and/or gender and women's and/or LGBT studies. These same authors also work as performance artists, bloggers, poets, musicians, administrators, grassroots activists, and nonprofit organizers. Although most articles primarily consider U.S. and/or Canadian contexts, transnational circulations and hierarchies are never completely out of sight and are sometimes central. With essays that focus on how gender is practiced (through scholarly disciplines, university administrations, athletics, law, public health, national border control, and other areas), we hope to make the conversation between feminist and trans studies more accessible and more relevant to scholars of gender in general.

If the affinity between transgender studies and gender studies is obvious, we recognize that it is not necessarily easy. Just about everywhere, trans-literacy remains low. Transgender studies is all but absent in most university curricula, even in gender and women's studies programs. For the most part, institutionalized versions of women's and gender studies incorporate transgender as a shadowy interloper or as the most radical outlier within a constellation of identity categories (e.g., LGBT). Conversation is limited by a perception that transgender studies only or primarily concerns transgender-identified individuals—a small number of "marked" people whose gender navigations are magically believed to be separate from the cultural practices that constitute gender for everyone else. Such tokenizing invites the suggestion that too much time is spent on too few people; simultaneously it obscures or refuses the possibility that transgender studies is about everyone in so far as it offers insight into how and why we *all* "do" gender.

But the problem runs deeper than the liberal identity-based values that continue to bring "marginalized others" into curricular relevance. Real conflict continues to separate transgender studies and feminist studies as arenas of inquiry. Our interests, vocabularies, and epistemological foundations can seem—and at times are—opposed. What do we variously mean by "gender" or "sex"? How is the body made to matter? Critically for us here, how do transgender studies and women's studies *each* make the body matter such that each field suspects the other of essentialized beliefs about which parts matter most? To whom, who gets to name them, and for what purposes? How do the environments we build and the visual, verbal, and institutional signs with which we build them reflect deep-seated attachments to the sex/gender status quo and all its hierarchies, contrary to our own theorizations? Given these tensions, we might characterize gender studies at the beginning of the second decade of the new millennium to be composed of disparate bodies differently freighting gender and sex while quizzically looking sideways—and occasionally winking—at each other. The sideways glance might be cautious, but it is surely born of a sense that, alone, neither *feminist* nor *trans* is living up to its most expansive vision and also that, at times, they fail us.

Transfeminist Perspectives critiques the constricting tendencies of disciplinary and identitarian investments. In this volume, the compound "transfeminist" arises out of a desire to see both "trans" and "feminist" do more flexible work; we would like to see them not only opening each to the other but opening broadly in all directions, as though they are *both* potential prefixes *and* suffixes that may modify and be modified by participants whose names we may not even yet know. Bringing feminist studies and transgender studies into more explicit conversation pushes us toward better translation, greater transliteracy, and deeper collaboration through which we may develop critical theoretical and methodological tools that will be relevant to all scholars within and across gender studies.

This book is organized into three parts based on three thematics that are central to feminist, gender, queer, and trans studies: Part I, "'This Much Knowledge': Flexible Epistemologies," considers the sources, proliferations, and contingencies of knowledge and authority; Part II, "Categorical Insufficiencies and 'Impossible People,'" tracks border crossings and somatic and definitional excesses as they become particularly concrete in the classroom and university infrastructures, public health, and even national border patrols; Part III, "Valuing Subjects: Toward Unexpected Alliances," considers the practical economies, violences, and desires that discipline gender and invites surprising—what we might call transfeminist—alliances in our academic and social-movement practices. The pedagogical logic of this ordering follows historical developments of feminist and trans theories and also transfeminist commitments to connect classrooms, social movements, and the world beyond. However, those for whom transgender is a relatively new arena might prefer an order that introduces trans issues. An introductory pedagogical ordering could start with Clark A. Pomerleau, who provides perspective on college policies generally, and Pat Griffin, who focuses specifically on athletics. The reader might then continue with Julia Serano's reflections on misogyny and trans-misogyny and Christoph Hanssmann's work on transgender trainings offered to health-care providers.

Gender and women's studies scholars regularly request glossaries of trans terminologies and "Trans 101" lessons. The request reflects the non-integration of transgender in gender studies thus far, but, perhaps equally, the fact that no standard lexicon exists; vocabularies and uses are invented and just as quickly challenged as we discover their unintended implications, exclusions, and limitations. It would be fair to characterize trans studies as a field peopled by those who will not rest content with the disciplining behaviors of language, and thus, intentionally or not, we nurture that other quality of language to be prolific and unruly. Some people even prefer the ensuing grammatical disasters, because they sometimes signify something profoundly accurate. In many locales, for example, "they" is a common third-person singular pronoun that some people feel is more flexible and "roomy" than the (over)determined and singular "he," "she," or even "ze." No single individual can keep up with the situational generation of new words across all communities, and published works are always already behind the curve: Glossary definitions in excellent trans studies articles published just one year ago may *now* seem (to some) to be mischaracterizations. The truth is, even within generally agreed upon lexicons, we discover that every term carries different implications for different communities.

That said, given the general unfamiliarity with trans studies, it is worth providing some trans social-movement perspective, addressing some common misconceptions, and offering some linguistic practices. A limited and provisional glossary, along with notes on usage, follows this introduction. Readers unfamiliar with trans lexicons may wish to read the "Note on Terms and Concepts" now or before delving into the chapters.

"Transgender" was coined in its contemporary sense in the early 1990s, when trans activist Leslie Feinberg used it to name a budding movement uniting all possible oppressed gender minorities. Although they did so in sometimes very different ways and in different communities, transsexuals, drag queens, butch lesbians, cross-dressers, feminine men, and masculine women all in some senses crossed, or transed, gender, and most modern "Western" societies took punitive measures to keep such crossings invisible or in check.[4] Transgender was thus first a social-movement organizing principle and came also to be the name of an identity that many people adopt to describe themselves. The ever-evolving list of trans-ing identities that now fit under the "transgender umbrella" may also include FTM, MTF, gender queer, trans woman, trans man, butch queen, fem queen, tranny, transy, drag king, bi-gender, pan-gender, femme, butch, stud, two spirit, people with intersex conditions, androgynous, gender-fluid, gender euphoric, third gender, *and* man and woman—and that list barely scratches the surface.

But the power of transgender does not depend on how many named categories we develop. Far more importantly, transgender is powerful because it names a politics stemming from a tri-fold awareness: First, binary gender norms and gender hierarchies are established and maintained through violence against those who visibly deviate from them; second, many humans—in their gender identities and/or gender expressions—do not conform to conventional gender expectations or moral judgments about what kinds of gender "go with" what kind of body; and third, this gender variation itself is intensely valuable as one facet of the creative diversities essential to wise and flourishing societies. This tri-fold awareness is the foundation of trans alliances that ideally cut across nuanced identity labels to make life more livable for people who trans gender, particularly those who are most vulnerable to institutionalized punitive systems, such as incarcerated people, homeless people, poor people, unemployed and underemployed people, undocumented people, youth, and people of color.

In keeping with trans's work as a prefix meaning "to cross," the most expansive definitions of transgender emphasize movement away from the culturally specific expectations associated with the sex one is assigned at birth and a movement toward gender self-determination.[5] By this expansive definition, most feminists should be seeing feminism as a transgender phenomenon: Some version of gender self-determination and resistance to binary gender norms and oppressions has always been central to feminism. Transgender phenomena are also created through the accusation of gender deviance, and this accusation is part and parcel of what maintains social hierarchies and the appearance of binary gender. Historically, not only feminism but also lesbian and gay desires and embodiments have been regarded as transgender phenomena: In a sexist and homophobic culture, feminist claims and gay and lesbian desires are all gender-crossing, gender-variant, and gender-deviant. Trans-gender policing has been one node of racialization and the maintenance of class hierarchy, reflected in the practice of calling a grown man "boy" or pretty or fairy, or deeming any woman too masculine or too sexual, too strong or fast, domineering, emasculating, or "castrating" of men. Transgender perspective thus includes political awareness of the ways that social institutions and built environments train all people to pass as a single, consistent, legible, and acceptable gender; simultaneously, that we speak at all is owed to recognition of the ubiquity of gender variance.

In practice, transgender is usually used less expansively and is often reserved for people with significant cross-gender identification, including people who were assigned female at birth and visibly identify and/or live as men (people on a female-to-male spectrum, trans men, and people on a trans-masculine spectrum) and people who were assigned male at birth and visibly identify and/or live as women (people on a male-to-female spectrum, trans women, and people on a trans-feminine spectrum). Reserving transgender for this kind of gender crossing recognizes the particularities of the experience of significant cross-gender identification; it also acknowledges that legal, medical, and social institutions specifically target gender transition and transsexuality with extreme forms of gender oppression that make it difficult to use public accommodations, public services, and many public spaces, and to do anything that requires legal identification documents.

At the same time, limiting the definition of transgender this way may perpetuate the marginalization of trans by reinforcing the misconception that "trans" describes a very small number of visible people who (by definition) are not everywhere. It may constrict trans itself by requiring certain conformities of people who would take up the name. And, most dangerously, restricting trans to its MTF and FTM manifestations may inhibit alliances by signaling investments in the *relative* normativities and privileges accorded to "less" gender-transgressive phenomena (e.g., being a feminist, being a lesbian, being a masculine woman); such investments avoid and sometimes actively refuse the possibility that trans issues *are* feminist issues and are *within*, not beyond, the scope of feminism.

The belief that trans is rare comes in part from the common misconception that transgender and transsexuality will be visible and obvious (i.e., "You can tell by looking"); therefore, if someone appears to be a woman or man, that person surely is not trans. In truth, the vast majority of people with significant cross-gender identification are not visible as such, and they are not likely to come out as trans whether or not they are living in their gender identity. Many trans people do not have any connection to, and are thus not even known to, trans- or LGBT or queer organizations; this includes many trans students even on campuses that do have trans activist and support groups. It is therefore accurate to assume that we know nothing about other people's gender histories and identifications. We are meeting, working with, learning from, and teaching trans people all the time.

The other common misconception that shrinks awareness of trans presence is that transsexual identifications are based on surgery. For some people, surgeries are one deeply important aspect of gender self-determination, but it is not surgical status that defines people as transsexual. In fact, the vast majority of transsexual people and people with significant cross-gender identification will have no genital surgeries: Many trans people have no access to medical care, surgery may not be appropriate for many, and many do not want it.[6] The transgender-liberation movement seeks to improve access to all forms of health care and recognizes that body modifications are vital to many people's gender self-determination. With health care and gender self-determination as core goals, the movement resists being *defined by* the medical establishment that actively excludes the majority of people and pathologizes transsexuality and gender variance. Departing from surgical definitions, a recent study by the University of California found that .3 percent of people (1 in 333) in the United States experience significant cross-gender identification. Many more experience a degree of gender fluidity or gender nonconformity that makes the expectations associated with a binary gender structure profoundly alienating. Along with feminist, queer, disability, and critical-race theories, trans studies recognizes that *all* bodies are made, one kind of body no more or less technologically produced than the other.

Feminist and trans pedagogies begin by honoring this variation regardless of whether it is visible to everyone. Learning not to impose gendered assumptions on others and learning to use language that resists binary gender whenever possible helps. (For examples, see the glossary and usage guide.) "Getting the pronouns right" is not always central to people's life chances, but it might be a barometer that measures the extent to which an environment is respectful and inclusive.[7] It should be no more difficult to address people by their preferred names and pronouns than it is to comply with the name changes that some people adopt when they marry. However, many people—even people who otherwise work to deconstruct gender binaries—feel uncomfortable calling someone "he" unless that person conforms to cultural expectations of what a "he" looks like. Closely related, some people may assume that he should use the women's bathroom because he "still looks like a woman," and therefore that is where he belongs. At the very same time, people on a trans-feminine spectrum (for example, a person who is assumed by others to have a penis and who wears women's clothing and may identify as a woman or as trans) are often pointedly unwelcome in the women's room.[8] These cultural habits continue to structure campus and classroom climate; they also prevent the majority of trans people from making their trans identities visible. When efforts are not made to break these habits, it signals disbelief in gender variance; it also suggests that there is no place for trans people. Not least, it tells us precisely where feminist ethics and gender and women's studies draw lines in the extent to which they can tolerate nonbinary sex/gender, and it suggests that trans identities cross that line into some other inscrutable or impossible form of existence.

In the unruly generation of new language, it is no accident that people are discovering such terms as trans*, Tiresian, and so forth to name new possibilities and to rename the binary-resistant ontologies that exist within and beyond our grasp. Not surprisingly, many authors in this collection take a moment to reflect on how they are each making trans, or trans-, or trans* *work*. Bobby Noble writes of trans "not [as] transgression through gender and/or national, cultural crossings, necessarily, but trans as a modality for reformulating institutionalized and bounded disciplinarities. . . ." Many reiterate the queer-activist and queer-theory call for an anti-identitarian politics. Aren Aizura, for example, argues that we need "a trans theory that not only acknowledges its debts to feminist theory and incorporates feminist critiques of heteronormativity but turns 'trans' in an anti-identitarian direction." *Trans-* emphasizes its work as a prefix. It is possible that the asterisk in *trans** functions as a truncation symbol the way that putting an asterisk after a word or fragment works in many library search systems. The tension here is that we cannot be claiming to signal literally *all* possible things that could follow trans-: We do not always or equally mean, for example, transpire, transverse, Transylvania, transform, transduct, and transport (although sometimes we might). Once, in an impulse to connect and to leave open simultaneously, I attempted to type *trans*feminist*. As I typed, I discovered that my computer reads these asterisks as commands to bold whatever they surround; thus, what my computer types is not *trans*feminist* but rather **trans**feminist*. This would carry its own set of implications—not what I had in mind, but possibly worth considering. The prefix dash and the asterisk each force us to know *trans* as modification and motion across time and space. It is not simply a noun. With its mobilities, it modifies; it is a motion anticipating a second; it enacts, it continues with a question, and a star.

"This Much Knowledge": Flexible Epistemologies

In a 1991 article often credited with helping launch the field of transgender studies, Sandy Stone asked whether and how it is possible for the transsexual to speak: "To attempt to occupy a place as a speaking subject within the traditional gender frame is to become complicit in the discourse which one wishes to deconstruct."[9] Feminist theory and trans theory have each concerned themselves with ways of knowing, and they have elaborated critiques of the ways that universalizing discourses become authoritative by making other ways of speaking and knowing impossible. Central to this critique is consideration of the *site* of knowledge production. What counts as "knowledge," and how are legitimacy and authority dependent on the location of its production? What is "experience," and what role does it play in the production of authoritative and marginalized knowledges? Who can speak, and from what subject position?[10] These questions have infused feminist theory with anti-identitarian, transgender potential, as realized in the work of such philosophers as Monique Wittig and Judith Butler. Transgender studies historian Susan Stryker draws on these and also Michel Foucault's concept of subjugated knowledges to assert that "experiential knowledge is as legitimate as other, supposedly more "objective" forms of knowledge, and is in fact necessary for understanding the political dynamics of the situation."[11]

Transgender studies could emerge as an academic field only when transsexuals began to produce themselves through counter-discourses and those discourses began to find slender footholds in the academy. Prior to this emergence in the 1990s, experts in various medical specialties, such as endocrinology, psychiatry, and surgery, had produced "the transsexual" and written volumes on transsexuality, and a few feminist scholars had advanced their own gender theorizations on the backs of transsexuals. Sandy Stone's pathbreaking "The Empire Strikes Back: A Posttranssexual Manifesto," produced in 1991 with the encouragement of her adviser, Donna Haraway, is one of transgender studies' first anchors. Stone's arrival in the academy interrupted a discourse on transsexuality produced entirely by people who had little or no connection to trans lives. More specifically, her arrival as the author of her own story and "posttranssexual" theorizations offered a transfeminist alternative to the explicitly transphobic attacks (against Stone and others) that was then passing as feminist theory.[12]

Feminist and trans studies depend partly on "experiential knowledge," because social hierarchies keep certain knowledges marginal to the academy. Until recently, the overwhelming majority of scholarship building the field of transgender studies was produced by people who worked outside, or in marginal positions within, the academy: activists, graduate students, and people in temporary positions. The balance is only beginning to shift (but not yet tip), with an increasing number of scholars who have secure (tenure-track and tenured) positions in academic institutions, and a number of scholars just completing advanced degrees, some of whom will—we hope—remain in the academic labor force. Even as a sizable handful of colleges offers postdocs and temporary teaching positions that include trans studies as a sought-after specialization, every year universities deny tenure to trans* scholars for reasons that are not evidently based on quality of scholarship, teaching, and service. The regulatory mechanisms of academia are part of what makes it necessary for transfeminist studies to continue to fuel the vital connections between academics and the larger world of justice activism.

The title of Part I, "This Much Knowledge," comes from a documentary interview with Christopher Majors, an African American man who is reflecting on growing up as the child of Miss Major. "It's wonderful having her as my dad. . . ." Smiling, Christopher holds his arms wide apart and, his voice soft with emotion, says, "with my dad, I got this* much* knowledge*."[13] Miss Major, as people often say, "has been there longer than any of us can imagine."[14] By this, they mean that she was transgender in the 1950s, before transgender had a name; she was among the "street queens" who fought back against police harassment in the 1960s; and, in the complete absence of public resources and organizations, she helped keep trans youth and trans people of color sheltered and as safe as possible. In Bobbie Jean Baker's words, "she has so much knowledge," and the community (loosely defined) depends on precisely this.[15]

The academy, slow to pick up on the knowledge produced by the most marginalized members of society, knew nothing of Miss Major until recently. But transgender studies has never been far from named and unnamed organizations serving marginalized populations. Now, Miss Major is searchable on the Web, a public-health activist who has worked for countless resource and justice centers in California; she currently serves as the community organizing director for the Transgender, Gender Variant and Intersex Justice Project, which seeks to end human-rights abuses committed against transgender, gender-variant, genderqueer, and intersex people in prisons. Among the most excluded from dominant social institutions, such as medicine, academics, and law, she is simultaneously among the most articulate critics of the medical, legal, and criminal-punishment systems. Trans-produced documentaries, such as *The Believers* and *Diagnosing Difference,* now make Miss Major's acumen accessible to a wider audience.[16] Transfeminist studies needs "this much knowledge," and more, if it is to work from what Dean Spade and others have called "trickle-up" models of justice and education that start with the most vulnerable among us.

The epistemological flexibility of transgender studies is reflected in the breakneck pace with which we adapt and adopt new vocabularies and linguistic practices. But *Transfeminist Perspectives* situates naming in a much broader context of imperial power and anticolonial politics. The collection opens with

Vic Muñoz's reflections on "transing pedagogies." As a Boricua/Puerto Rican professor-activist-blogger "trapped in the wrong classroom" at an American college built on still-contested Cayuga Nation Territory, Muñoz confronts the "racism, classism, sexism, heterosexism, ableism, transphobia, and language structure that constrain everything I do as an educator" and imagines a "gender sovereignty" grounded in larger decolonizing projects. Chapter 1, "Gender/Sovereignty," opens with a consideration of naming, quoting Linda Tuhiwai Smith: "What happens to research when the researched become the researchers?" This is necessary, but it is also a power that bears terrible responsibility. Continuing with Paulo Freire, "To exist, humanly, is to name the world, to change it." These two quotes frame the heart of our epistemological challenge. As Muñoz asks, "What happens to feminist pedagogy when feminist transpeople of color name the world?" To imagine gender/sovereignty requires not simply a critique of dominant institutions, such as the medico-legal system that named transsexuality; it requires placing the production of gender identities within a "broader framework of antiracist and decolonial struggles." Along with Muñoz, *Transfeminist Perspectives* begins by asking how the *site* of knowledge production itself actively contributes to assumptions about what knowledges matter, how they matter, and to whom they matter.

In Chapter 2, "'Do These Earrings Make Me Look Dumb?' Diversity, Privilege, and Heteronormative Perceptions of Competence within the Academy," Kate Forbes addresses feminist epistemological conflicts head on. Because she is trained and teaches as an ecologist and environmental biologist, lay people grant Forbes excessive authority to answer questions not only in her own area of specialization (ladybugs) but also about birds, weather, and virtually everything imagined to be "science." *Within* the still male-dominated worlds of the sciences, however, Forbes (along with probably most feminine people in higher education) is aware that "looking like" an authority rarely entails femininity. And finally, in gender studies, Forbes is not the researcher, but the researched. As a trans woman, she is "a primary source" in a world that privileges secondary-source knowledges. *Transfeminist Perspectives* critiques the extent to which credentialing (including tokenizing) continues to be gendered in every possible way and joins Forbes in her call for a more ecological model of "diversity" in the academy.

Just as we may ask *how* we know, since its inception, women's studies has rightly asked *what* we should know: What is our subject and appropriate purview? The category "women" has been challenged from multiple sources, beginning with de Beauvoir and Wittig, who questioned the efficacy of organizing under the name "women" when abjection is inscribed into the category itself. Women's studies has also struggled with and against the question of whether "women" is the foundation and universally defined subject of women's studies. If this "women" is a subject produced through colonizations, racializations, class hierarchies, homophobias, ableisms, and transphobias, then who gets to be a woman? In conditions of compulsory heterosexuality, Adrienne Rich suggested that all women exist on a lesbian continuum, while Wittig suggested that lesbians are not, in fact, women. Although Joan Nestle tackled the problem of being (not quite) woman from a working-class femme perspective, Gayle Rubin explicitly addressed the historical contingency of any "line" between butch and trans and—by extension—between woman and man.[17] *Transfeminist Perspectives* highlights these tensions and insecurities by, as Bobby Noble puts it, "critically trans-ing" women's studies at the level of its epistemologies, disciplinarities, methodologies, and even its institutionalizations. In Chapter 3, "Trans. Panic. Some Thoughts toward a Theory of Feminist Fundamentalism," Noble considers the ambivalent presence of trans entities in women's studies. This proximity itself tweaks at the longstanding contratrajectories inherent to gender studies between stabilizing the fields and subjects (such as "woman" and even "women's studies") that maintain our own institutionalizations on one hand and "undoing" these very same fields and subjects on the other. Perhaps we open gender studies by "undoing" ourselves and—as Butler suggested—letting ourselves be undone, even as we may never fully escape the capitalist structures of our own production.

If naming is a productive action, it is so always in relation to place. In Chapter 4, "The Education of Little Cis: Cisgender and the Discipline of Opposing Bodies," A. Finn Enke elucidates the passage of the neologism "cisgender" from a social-movement context to a campus context, where it politicizes and confirms most identities as "not-trans." As a disciplinary tool, "cis-" erases gender variance among all people while dangerously extending the practical reach and power of multiple normativities. What investments may account for the appeal of cis- in our classrooms, and what happens to trans* in the process? Resisting the regulatory function of this binary, *Transfeminist Perspectives* picks up on Sandy Stone's suggestion that we see gender as genre and on Wendy Brown's suggestion that gender studies should function as a "genre of inquiry" that sustains gender as "a critical self-reflective category rather than as a normative or nominal one."[18] Only in this way can we reorient away from identity- and oppression-based politics toward a broader transfeminist vision of education and justice.

Categorical Insufficiencies and "Impossible People"

If we can become speaking subjects only by occupying legible nodes within institutional structures—that is, by having a name, performing a recognized demographic category, and so forth—we also reckon with the fact that we exceed every possible legible node ... sometimes so much so that the institution literally has no place for, or violently *mis*-places, such subjectivities. We may be, in Dean Spade's words, "impossible people."[19] Most social institutions make medico-legal definitions and genital status the criteria for spatial and social organization: Restrooms are the most ubiquitous example, but also shelters, prisons, crisis centers, treatment programs, and dorms. The structure of most colleges and universities makes this all too concrete. As Clark A. Pomerleau explains in Chapter 5, "College Transitions: Recommended Policies for Trans Students and Employees," application forms, e-mail addresses, dorm assignments, and even class rosters may only permit potential students to identify according to their "legal sex," which may have nothing to do with how they perceive themselves or how others perceive them; athletic facilities and restrooms that are sex segregated may be completely inaccessible to students, faculty, and staff who do not conform to conventional gender expectations or who do not identify with the gender that others might assume them to be; curriculum and instruction may proceed as though sex and gender are binary, static, and obviously legible; emergency support services, health services, and rape crisis services may only acknowledge clients by their legal or genital status and may even explicitly discriminate against those who do not conform to common gender expectations. Academic institutions thereby discipline gender for *all* participants, and those who will not be disciplined very likely will not be participants at all unless these institutions change.

Arenas such as bathrooms, dorms, and athletics that sex segregate based on the (presumed) physical body make most obvious many people's investments in binary sex/gender habits and biases. Although feminist theory has long engaged in deconstructing gender, it has often done so by preserving sex as a more stable and knowable foundation (the insights of Butler and others notwithstanding). This habit of thought presumes that there is a knowable difference between male and female bodies, and that is why (for example) athletics are sex segregated; it presumes that patterns of socialization (aggression, sexualized objectification, and so forth) are built on these physical differences, and that is why (for example) restrooms and dorms must be segregated. In North America, restroom segregation is legitimized by both ideologies together: Many people see urinals and stalls not as cultural structures built to facilitate two different styles of urinating but actually as mimetic representations of bodies with penises and bodies with vaginas. (It should be very confusing, then, to be in countries in which restrooms consist simply of rooms with drains in the floor. Curiously, most North Americans visiting such countries are able to make the adjustment without facing an ontological crisis; curiouser, that making such an adjustment is all but unthinkable once we have urinals and stalls to *organize* gender.) In truth, even as various sciences authorize the appearance of binary sex, they could not simultaneously make it more clear that there is *no* definitive measure of maleness and femaleness; human bodies and psyches are all over the map. Moreover, *all* bodies and psyches are subject to technical engineering and social manipulation. As Susan Stryker puts it, "Sex, it turns out, is not the foundation of gender.... '[S]ex' is a mash-up, a story we mix about *how* the body means, which parts matter most, and how they register in our consciousness or field of vision."[20]

Athletics is an arena heavily invested in efforts to keep male and female bodies distinct while continually confronting the impossibility of doing so. Athletics is one of the most common examples used by lay people to "prove" that males and females are "really" (materially and therefore truly, unquestionably, and consistently) different. Enter transgender and gender-nonconforming athletes and athletes with intersex conditions. Title VII, Title IX, and the principles of educational equity require that all students have the opportunity to participate in school sports. Investments in binary sex/gender foreclose this opportunity for many and belie the multiple factors that contribute to varying abilities *within* as well as across sexes. Pat Griffin's essay "'Ain't I a Woman?' Transgender and Intersex Student-Athletes in Women's Collegiate Sports" (Chapter 6) addresses epistemological and philosophical barriers to full participation and suggests models to optimize fairness, feminist, and transfeminist principles.

While gender and trans studies have maintained a strong sense of connection between the academy and the world outside the academy, health care is an arena in which these connections are most vital and also most obviously strained. Trans health provision and provider trainings geared at improving the quality of care available to trans and gender-nonconforming people offer a critical lens into the competing epistemological frameworks guiding institutional practices. In Chapter 7, "Training Disservice: The Productive Potential and Structural Limitations of Health as a Terrain for Trans Activism," Christoph Hanssmann details the challenges of offering trans-health education to medical institutions that shape curricula *before* trans enters the picture. "Trainers [Hanssmann among them] struggle to teach information and strategies that are relevant, useful, and legible to providers, while simultaneously feeling quite troubled by the ways 'trans health' is not teachable in the ways that are most broadly available for us to teach it." Specifically—as will be familiar to many in undergraduate gender studies classrooms—"cultural competence" models frequently deploy "community members" or trainers to sit on LGBT panels for one class out of an entire semester. This common curriculum suggests that simply becoming aware that "diverse" (i.e., marginalized) people exist and are human will somehow translate into better, more-accessible, and less-discriminatory service provision. The training structure leaves no possibility of understanding that "trans"—if it might be considered a demographic at all—is vast, complex, and infinitely diverse across every other possible demographic; much less does it permit educating about the structural factors themselves—including the reproduction of the institution—that contribute to marginalization and lack of access to basic health care.

Transfeminist Perspectives participates in anti-identitarian theorizations by noting that educational curricula may follow liberal political strategies that view "rights" as something to be earned by naming, gaining successive recognition for, and belonging to marginalized or "left-out" populations. We see identity-based categorizations reinforced also at national borders, where people are made to perform as a passing (and documented) demographic, as Aren Z. Aizura forcefully argues in his essay "Transnational Transgender Rights and Immigration Law" (Chapter 8). While acknowledging that "transgender is an identity category whose subjects' access to freedom will be divided along the cuts of affluence, racialization, gender, and citizenship, we also need to look at where and how bodies escape or act clandestinely outside of those categories—and at moments in which the categories of immigrant, transgender person, man, woman become incoherent and inconsistent." When gender, along with so many other signifiers, is a central feature of identity documentation, its legibility must be seen to be contingent on and produced by global movement and border control.

Valuing Subjects:
Toward Unexpected Alliances

The many examples of institutional efforts to spatially organize bodies (restrooms, identity verification, national borders, and so forth) provide lenses into the ways that bodies are not self-evident material, and they also serve as reminders that so-called "cultural" and "material" realms are inextricable. Although this idea is not new to feminist, queer, or trans theory, Dan Irving points out that our pedagogies and epistemologies often continue to be based in systemic logics that "create distance between . . . the purview of political economy and the construction of recognized trans identities and political organizing." In Chapter 9, "Elusive Subjects: Notes on the Relationship between Critical Political Economy and Trans Studies," Irving critiques strategies used by Canadian trans activists to gain access to provincial health insurance plans. Making political claims based on the "fitness" and entrepreneurial potential of trans people may bolster the very structures that create the conditions of oppression. Irving asks, for example, "How does the marketing of trans workers to potential employers contribute to the formation of 'proper' or 'deserving' trans subjects? What are the implications of such knowledge for sex/gender-variant people who remain chronically unemployed or employed in criminalized sectors of the economy?" Liberal logics present some bodies—masculine, white, educated, and/or legal bodies—as having greater intrinsic value and potential than others, simultaneously maintaining the marginalization of feminine, poor, criminal, and/or undocumented bodies.

Although most dominant political economies continue to prioritize and to privilege masculinities, even feminist economies may participate in misogynies. In Chapter 10, "Reclaiming Femininity," Julia Serano provides greater nuance to the misogyny that judges all expressions of femininity as artificial, frivolous, manipulative, and less valuable. *Trans*-misogyny, more specifically, delegitimates trans people who are on the trans-female/feminine spectrum of gender identity and expression. In feminist and many queer contexts ranging from alt femme conferences to privileged institutions, such as the Association for Women in Psychology, trans women are shunned as "doubly artificial, because we are trans and because we are feminine." Serano suggests that *all* femme- and femininely identified and feminist people need to develop alliances around the value and power of femininity even while challenging the compulsory femininity that confronts virtually all people assigned female at birth. Trans-misogyny is an essential element of misogyny in general; by the same token, trans-misogyny is not specifically a "trans" issue but, more broadly, a feminist issue. Rather than being outsiders, people on trans-feminine spectra are inherent and necessary to the "community" invoked in the name *feminist*.

Feminist, queer, and trans scholars and activists have long charged that the distinction between political issues and personal issues is a false one. The decision by lawmakers, states, and other institutions to frame certain issues as "personal" is itself a political act intended to obscure what are actually organized violences and injuries against marginalized groups. Nevertheless, many activist organizations continue to organize through "rights" discourses that reify the belief that justice can be served by gaining privatized or individualized entitlements. In "What's Wrong with Trans Rights?" (Chapter 11), Dean Spade analyzes the common twin prongs of trans rights (law reform) and hate-crimes legislation and details the structural reasons why neither improves the life chances of those they purport to protect. Neither model eliminates bias, prevents discrimination and marginalization, or deters violence. We need, therefore, to shift our framework away from a trans-rights model. Instead, Spade calls for "critical trans resistance" that will center our social movement strategies in mobilization against sites of violence and prioritize "those living under the most severe forms of coercive violence." This is not easy, and Spade acknowledges that it requires every bit of creativity, humility, bravery, self-reflection, and perseverance we can muster.

Activists (and, probably even more so, academics) are not always known for our humility; nor is self-reflection always held up as a powerful tool of resistance and social transformation. And yet, without these, as Ryka Aoki points out in her essay, "When Something Is Not Right" (Chapter 12), we are destined to keep making the same mistakes over and over. "Once," Aoki admits, "I imagined art was my savior." But she learned otherwise through two encounters she had while touring with the Tranny Road Show in North Carolina and Colorado—each terrifying in its own way. It turns out that art—and I would say also academics—can only heal when we are open to the most surprising and unexpected alliances: the connections that shatter our preconceptions about each other, and also about ourselves. It is in this spirit that the authors of this collection share our transfeminist perspectives.

A. FINN ENKE

Note on Terms and Concepts

The terms and concepts here supplement this volume. This is not a glossary of all terms relevant to transgender studies, trans histories, and trans lives. It would be impossible to be exhaustive here, as the list of terms related to cultural and community-based gender practices is literally infinite. Neither is it definitive: Meanings and uses change across time and place.

Language itself is a social activity; words, phrases, and uses effectively communicate only within a community that grants rough consensus to that particular expression. At the same time, language adapts around cultural changes and may be open to new words and new grammars; in the same measure, communities and individuals do learn new languages all the time. Since the 1960s, the concept of "gender-inclusive" language has gone from referring to the once-radical practice of saying "people" instead of "men," "person" instead of "man," and "he and she" instead of just "he" to today, when "gender-inclusive" might refer to language that does not impose binary gender and honors the actual gender diversity of human lives.

The English language imposes binary gender, and, in many cases, it requires work to circumvent this imposition. In contrast to many languages, English does not gender all nouns or attach gender to the first person singular ("I"). However, most singular pronouns ("he," "she") are gendered, as are some familial terms (e.g., "aunt," "uncle"). In many cases, English provides a neutral choice (one can say "child" rather than "son" or "daughter"), but speech customs may make certain options feel awkward. Workers in many service-sector jobs are taught to greet customers as "ma'am," "sir," or "ladies"; this is an entirely gratuitous gender imposition that may feel polite and even friendly to some people, but to others it may feel irritating if not violent.

Transliteracy suggests the following:

- Become more aware of when the language, culture, or simply one's own habits of speech are imposing gender.

- Consider one's own attachments or intentions with such speech.
- Learn to use alternatives.

These are ways to begin to change cultural consensus in language. This does not mean doing away with gender-specific language; it means developing additional fluencies to respect the complexity of gender.

Gender-Inclusive Pronouns (often called gender-neutral): ze/hir/hir; they/them/theirs (subject/object/possessive, respectively). Gender-inclusive pronouns are not associated with a specific gender and thereby do not ascribe gender. In English, the plural "they" is an example. The singular "they" dates back to the fifteenth century and is common in some parts of the English-speaking world, but in most places in North America, the singular "they" is less familiar. For the singular, our most common options ("he" and "she") are specifically gendered. Trans-aware communities developed the use of ze/hir/hir as gender-inclusive alternatives. In more recent years, they/them/their is becoming even more popular as a singular pronoun.

Usage considerations: For many trans people who identify as men or women, use of inclusive pronouns can feel like an offensive refusal to recognize their gender identity. At the same time, the fact that many people identify with one of the binary pronouns does not preclude using inclusive pronouns as a *general* practice for all people, conveying that we do not know how other people identify their own gender and also that some people do not identify with either of the binary options. In some communities and classrooms, "ze" and/or "they" are used universally and with complete fluency. However, these options have yet to circulate through mainstream culture, and thus their use must be considered political and pedagogical.

Sex: From the perspective of evolutionary biology, human sex is conventionally classified in two categories (female and male) according to whether a body produces eggs or sperm. Associated with this characteristic are others, such as genital morphology, chromosomal makeup, and genetic factors that affect secondary sex characteristics (body hair, breasts, and so forth). The variety of factors involved and the natural variation in all of them have led to greater acknowledgment of the fact that humans exceed sexual dimorphism (that is to say, male and female are not neatly distinct) and also that it would be theoretically possible to group humans into more than two sex categories.

Legally Recognized Sex Status: People's legal existence in the United States is accompanied by the requirement to have a legally recognized sex status, but in practice, sex status is indicated by multiple and at times competing factors. Legal sex is designated on such documents as birth certificates, passports, Social Security cards, and state IDs. Because such documents are purportedly used for identification, institutions place great weight on whether a person "looks like" the sex indicated on the document. In the absence of federal law, the ease with which identity documents may be changed varies according to laws established at the state and/or local level and according to bureaucratic idiosyncrasies. For these reasons, a person's identity documents may not all have the same sex designation, and the concept of "legal sex" itself is a bit of an oxymoron.

Intersex Conditions: More than thirty variations in sexual development fall under the category of intersex conditions. Some of these lead to ambiguity in genital morphology, others to secondary sex characteristics less commonly associated with genetic sex, and so forth.

Usage considerations: In recent years, medical institutions have come to favor the term "Disorders of Sexual Development" (DSD). Some people with intersex conditions prefer this term over "intersex"; others identify as intersex, or as persons with intersex conditions, and many feel that DSD is pathologizing and depoliticizing.

Gender: Gender results from cultural practices of ordering or organizing different types of people according to bodies and behaviors. Social gender has mainly to do with a combination of the expectations assigned to one's sex and the role one plays in one's society. Because each culture establishes its own categorizations of norms for genders, gender conformity and gender crossing are necessarily culturally specific. In many societies, production, reproduction, consumption, and distribution are infused with and constitute gender.

Gender Identity: One's sense of one's self as a gendered person (e.g., as man, woman, both, neither, or some other configuration of gender). A person's gender identity may or may not match the sex assigned at birth or current legal sex as indicated on any of the several documents indicating sex, and it may or may not conform to conventional expectations of maleness or femaleness, including expectations of what a man's or woman's body looks like.

Gender Expression: How people express, wear, enact, and perform gender through behavior, mannerism, clothing, speech, physicality, and selective body modification.

Transgender: The term "transgender" incorporates three distinct but overlapping arenas of social organization. "Transgender" may be used as:

- The *name of a social movement* that insists on the right of all people to determine for themselves their own personal and legal gender statuses (gender self-determination), freedom of gender identity and gender expression for all people, and civil and social rights for all people regardless of gender identity, gender expression, and body type.
- An *ever-expanding social category* that incorporates the broadest possible range of gender nonconformity for the purposes of movement building, organizing, and social-service recognition. In the United States and Canada, this may include transsexuals, transvestites, cross-

dressers, female and male impersonators, persons with intersex conditions, butches, studs, femmes, fem queens, drag queens, drag kings, feminine-identified men, masculine-identified women, MTF, FTM, trannies, gender variants, genderqueers, boi dykes, trans men, trans guys, trans women, bigender, two spirit, intergender, neutrois, pan gender, third gender, gender fluid, and so forth. People who place themselves in any of the above categories may or may not identify with the collective term "transgender."
- An *identity* that some people embrace for themselves. *Transgender identity* may include a gender identity that differs from the sex assigned at birth; a gender expression that differs from that conventionally expected of people according to their bodily sex; and/or a desire for alteration of the body's sex/gender characteristics.

Usage consideration: Many people who do trans or have transed their culture's gender expectations do not identify with the term "transgender."

Transsexual: Medical and popular term describing persons with significant cross-gender identity. Due to varying life circumstances, transsexuals may or may not live in their gender identity some of or all the time; depending on medical access, legal options or restrictions, financial means, physical appropriateness, and desire, transsexuals may or may not change bodily characteristics and/or achieve legal sex reassignment through hormonal and surgical means.

MTF (Male to Female, also MtF, M2F): A trans spectrum indicating movement from male (assignment at birth based on perceived physical sex) to female (gender identity); it includes personal and sometimes social recognition of feminine and/or female identity; MTF may or may not include hormonal and/or surgical modifications and/or sex reassignment.

FTM (Female to Male, also FtM, F2M): A trans spectrum indicating movement from female (assignment at birth based on perceived physical sex) to male (gender identity); it includes personal and sometimes also social recognition of masculine and/or male identity; FTM may or may not include hormonal and/or surgical modifications and/or sex reassignment.

Usage consideration: MTF and FTM are often preferred as adjectives modifying a noun, such as "person" or "spectrum," rather than as a noun substitute. For example, just as one is a "transgender person" rather than "a transgender," one might prefer to be considered an "MtF person" or "person on an MtF spectrum" rather than "an MtF."

Trans (trans-, trans*) and Trans People: At this time, "trans" is an inclusive and respectful term available for use by people outside trans communities as well as by those who identify with or as trans; as a general term, it avoids the subcultural specificities and alliances that require specialized knowledge for appropriate use.

Usage considerations: "Transgender," "transsexual," and "trans" are words that have institutional recognition in many English-speaking countries, but many people who would be included under the "transgender umbrella" do not identify with them. For example, some people with trans histories reject being considered trans-(anything) but instead are men or women, period. Furthermore, identities are generally community-specific and thus may also be specific to class, race, nationality, location, age, and so forth. For example, a person who has a penis, wears feminine clothing, and has a feminine name may consider herself a queen or gay or *bakla* and not identify with the term "transgender." It should also be noted that "transgender" is part of a universalizing dominant discourse; gender-variant people in many parts of the world may not identify with the concept or with the political regimes that disseminate its logics.

Cisgender, Cissexual: From the Latin prefix "cis," meaning on the same side or staying with the same orientation, "cisgender" and "cissexual" name the characteristic of staying with or being perceived to stay with the gender and/or sex one was assigned at birth.

Cis- privilege: The privilege and power accorded to people who are perceived to follow the norms associated with the sex they are perceived to be and assumed to have been assigned at birth. People who trans gender as well as people who do not may receive cis-privileges, and people who do not intentionally trans gender as well as people who do are denied cis- privileges if they fail to pass (or pass enough) in the sex/gender they are expected to be.

Sexual Preference (or Identity or Orientation): Sexual identity and gender identity are two different things. Sexual identity (or preference) has to do with sexual, erotic, and/or emotional attractions, interests, and orientations. For each person, sexual identity may have nothing or everything to do with gender identity and body type. Like all people, trans people may be gay, bi, lesbian, straight, asexual, pansexual, queer, and so forth; similarly, people across all sexual identities may or may not be trans.

A Note on Transgender and Intersex: These two categories are distinct but may overlap and form alliance. As with the general population, some people who have intersex conditions are trans-identified; in addition, some trans people may consider their trans-ness itself to be one form of intersex condition. Politically, distinct movements have formed around dramatically distinct histories that transgender and intersex have with medical and other powerful social institutions. Trans and intersex movements achieve alliance based on the overlap (some people occupy both categories), especially on the shared goal of sex/gender self-determination and the right to respectful medical care.

I

"This Much Knowledge"

Flexible Epistemologies

1

VIC MUÑOZ

Gender/Sovereignty

What happens to research when the researched become the researchers?
—Linda Tuhiwai Smith

To exist, humanly, is to *name* the world, to change it.
—Paulo Freire

What happens to feminist pedagogy when feminist trans-people of color name the world?

In an earlier work, "Trapped in the Wrong Classroom: Making Decolonial Trans-Cultural Spaces in Women's Studies,"[1] I began to think about relationships between pedagogies of critical consciousness[2] and transing[3] as a praxis for decolonization.[4] I took the master narrative about trans-people "being trapped in the wrong body"[5] and thought about the classroom as a colonized and colonizing space, for trans-students and trans-educators, which needed to be transformed to become a place of dialogical practice.[6] I began to imagine a space for dialogue that did not trap—colonize—my body and experiences as a trans- Boricua[7] professor of psychology and gender studies. Different from the metaphor of being trapped in the wrong body, what I felt was that I was trapped in the wrong classroom in my displaced/diasporic body.

To be "trapped in the wrong classroom," for me, is to be aware of but not to take action against how colonization, racism, classism, sexism, heterosexism, ableism, transphobia, and language structure and constrain everything I do as an educator. It is to be dehumanized through a process of forgetting, denying, and being made invisible.

In this chapter, I attempt to narrate a decolonizing pedagogy of transing that might create spaces for trans-, for sovereignty, and for gender: what I think of as gender/sovereignty spaces. This involves a process of remembering, critical reflection on where I am located, and a desire for and praxis of education as a process of humanization, social justice, and liberation. This chapter is an account of my pedagogical transitioning.

All learning, in this country, takes place on Indigenous lands that were stolen through the removal, destruction, and colonization—the systematic genocide—of Indigenous peoples. Against this continuing colonialism, Indigenous peoples struggle on a daily basis to recover, to heal, and to create peace and justice. The Indigenous people of the land where I teach are the Haudenosaunee. Specifically, the college where I teach is situated in Cayuga Nation Territory.

When I write that pedagogy must be grounded, I do not mean that as a metaphor. What I mean is that non-Indigenous educators, scholars, academics, and activists have to educate ourselves in the history and present struggles of the lands with Indigenous peoples who are hosting our visits. From this point of view, I teach as a long-time guest in Cayuga Nation Territory. As a guest on stolen and contested lands (see the Onondaga Land Rights statement[8]) and as an educator, I have the obligation to make connections between the denials of rights to Indigenous people, trans- and queer people, and those who are all the above.

Transing pedagogy, for me, is grounded in a struggle for decolonization and transformation that starts by remembering and honoring where I am located.

This project frames trans- and feminist classrooms as historical spaces where simultaneous realities are generated, contested, and lived within the past, present, and future against the continuing processes of colonization and imperialism. This means, for me, that pedagogy must be grounded in place, past, present, and future in addition to race, class, gender, sexuality, dis/abilities, language, and ethnicities. To create trans- cultural decolonial spaces for social diversity and justice, all the above (and more) are needed.

Gender/sovereignty is an approach that contests the Eurocentric medicalized model of trans- identities by placing gender identities within a broader framework of antiracist and decolonial struggles. It is an attempt to create spaces for gender that are self-determined and that can negotiate the interminable tensions that exist between heterosexism, Christianity, colonialism, and homophobia for Native LGBT people and trans- people of color.

But first, I need to locate myself within this project.

At the 2008 American Educational Research Association annual conference, I attended symposia sponsored by the Indigenous Peoples of the Pacific Special Interest Group (IPP-SIG). I immediately saw relationships between the ideas presented and my own Boricua history.

One was the idea presented by Laiana Wong[9] that to speak Hawaiian was not enough to support anticolonial Native Hawaiian education if the language was learned as a translation of thinking in English. Rather, Wong proposed that it is crucial to, in his words, "Speak Hawaiian in Hawaiian." This argument is one that runs deeply through my history as a Boricua. My grandmother, Inés María Mendoza, a school teacher, testified in English before the Commission of Inquiry on Civil Rights in Puerto Rico (the Hays Commission). The commission was investigating *la massacre de Ponce*.[10] My grandmother requested a chance to testify in these hearings on behalf of what she called "the massacre of the mind of Puerto Rican children"[11] that would occur through the imposition of teaching all Puerto Rican children in English.

She was granted a hearing on Friday, May 21, 1937. Excerpts of her testimony follow:

> *Mr. Arthur Garfield Hays:* Can you explain any connection between this language question in Puerto Rico and civil liberties?
>
> *Answer:* Education serves politics in all countries of the world. It serves it in Germany, in Russia, in the United States. The same thing happens also in Puerto Rico, but as we are not a people with the sovereign responsibilities of its government, as we are a colony, we face the tragedy of our people whose education is at the service of a colonial policy imposed on us by force, the result being that our schools do not exist to promote the interests of our own culture and our nationality but to serve the purposes and interests of a very indefinite colonial policy.
>
> *Mr. Hays:* What point of civil liberties is involved in this language question?
>
> *Answer:* When a people is free to constitute its government, it is free to determine what education it wants for its children. The root of this question lies in our own system of government. Under the colony, education will always be deficient. You, Mr. Hays, you have been able to witness at these hearings how men behave themselves in a colony. The Attorney General in person declared he was two persons in one: a general prosecutor on the one hand and a man on the other. This is a painful disintegration of man's higher values of character and spirit and the result is a clear duplicity in ideas, concepts, attitudes, criteria—that can easily be explained by the fact of our centuries of colonial life.
>
> *Mr. Hays:* That also happens in free countries.
>
> *Mrs. Palacios [married name]:* Yes. This is true, but chances are greater in the colony.[12]

Alison Jones presented another idea based on the work that she and co-researcher Kuni Jenkins have been collaborating on: a book project that investigates Maori-as-Maori[13] and Pakeha[14] relationships. Jones projected on the screen the famous rendering of Samuel Marsden's sermon on the beach in 1814 at Rangihoua in the Bay of Islands.[15] The quotation under the image reads, "Behold I Bring You Good Things of Great Joy." In her presentation, she focused on the Marsden sermon and raised the possibility that events "*did take place and* that they *did not*,"[16] depending upon whether one is Maori or Pakeha. This reading of history unsettles temporality (when something was said to happen) and meaning (what exactly happened?). In the paper upon which the presentation was based, Jones writes:

> *There was no sermon.* There was a political meeting, again organized and choreographed by the leading chiefs of the area, within which Ruatara got to speak about the strangers now coming to live permanently—at his

behest—in this place. Remember, Marsden, preaching from St. Luke, did not speak *te reo Maori,* and the people aside from Ruatara, and one or two others, *did not understand English.*[17]

A contemporary example of something taking place and not taking place is discussed in the article by Kuni Jenkins and Leonie Pihama[18] in *Feminism and Psychology* titled "Matauranga Wahine: Teaching Maori Women's Knowledge alongside Feminism." The piece was initially invited to be written as a "response" to an article by Jones[19] titled "Cross-cultural Pedagogy and the Passion for Ignorance," which appears in the same issue and addresses power dynamics and tensions that occurred in a course that all three had co-taught.

Jenkins and Pihama disrupt the meaning of what a "response" to an article should be by discussing their own experiences as Maori women teaching about Maori women. In other words, Jenkins and Pihama rewrite the event—in this case the course that was co-taught—not as a response to Jones but as an investigation of their own experiences as Maori women. There was not, in fact, one course taught, but many courses. Or, perhaps, there was no course at all for the Maori women students; instead there were displays of Pakeha power dynamics in a classroom.

Jenkins, Pihama, and Wong offer positions from which Indigenous knowledge not only unsettles colonizing histories but revises what really happened through Indigenous points of view. This is *not* multicultural education, a place where each culture supposedly takes an equal place at the pedagogical table.[20] It is not where each culture has its place on a continuum of difference and a week or a month to celebrate each. Decolonizing approaches *revision* and *rewrite* Western history through Indigenous thinking and lived experience.

Continuing with Jones:[21]

> If we are to *abandon* the idea that we can find the "truth" here about *what was actually happening* in December 1814, and if we *cannot* place the two contrary realities *alongside each other* in a "rich bicultural understanding," or "a celebration of diversity," what becomes possible?
>
> All that becomes possible is tension. Contradictory and irreconcilable realities sit in interminable tension with each other. And in the *tension* between contradictory realities is the *ake ake ake,* the endless struggle—to know, to read, to understand, to work with, *to engage with,* others.

Places of Interminable Tension

What are the colonial encounters taking place today that are called "education"? How are these colonial encounters possible sites for trans- formation?

If you drive along Route 90 in Cayuga County in central New York in Haudenosaunee lands, you will see big signs that say, in red, white, and blue, "*No*

Sovereign Nation. No Reservation!" These signs, printed, paid for, and placed along what is officially a "Scenic Byway" in central New York State, are the result of the group United Citizens for Equality. The signs make their views plain regarding the Cayuga Indian Nation Land Claim. Reflecting the legal battles that have been ongoing since 1980, these signs are so common that they have become part of the landscape.

A few years ago, the signs were upgraded from handmade ones—spray paint on barns and cardboard—to printed ones nailed to pressure-treated wood and dug into the ground. They are now permanent signs. Because Route 90 is a designated "Scenic Byway," these signs should not be placed along the road, but that is the political climate in Cayuga County with regard to sovereignty for the Cayuga Nation. This is where I teach.

As a Boricua living in diaspora in the United States, I look at these signs every day on my drive to work. I think about how lands are taken and people are forced to leave, sent to school to learn a history that never happened that way, and taught to forget. Central to the colonial project globally is the process of forgetting and in its place remembering a history that never happened that way.

In Boriken, we are taught that we are descendants of the Taíno, African, and European. We are a blend of cultures and histories. We were the ones who greeted the Spaniards. We thought that the Spaniards were gods until a Taíno drowned one to see whether it were true. After that, it was a more Earthbound battle, although still unfair, with the Spaniards having firearms. Later, anthropologists would declare that no Taínos were left; "decimated" and "extinct" were and still are the terms used to describe what happened after Agüeybana greeted Ponce de León.

Today, as Boricuas continue to remember and to investigate our own history from our own historical perspectives—that is, from decolonial perspectives—we are beginning to document that, although the brutal decimation carried out on the Indigenous peoples of the Caribbean is irrefutable, the anthropologist master narrative of Taíno extinction is a myth.

The popular (white colonial) imagination contains within it a Caribe of cruise ships, beaches, surfers, hotels, and golfing in gorgeous tropical climates where everyone can wear shorts and flip-flops all day and, because it is so hot, not think about much at all. The stark contrast of the tourist in Boriken, Culebra, and Bieke with the experiences of Boricuas who *do* think in hot weather and *do* wear shoes repeats the earliest of colonial encounters on a daily basis.

Issues of sovereignty run deeply through the psyches of Boricuas, who, after so many years of colonialism, have as an identity marker which political party they belong to and the status of sovereignty or lack thereof for which they vote: Commonwealth, Statehood, or Independence. But these designations of identity, literally along party lines, obscure a more complicated history; indeed, they pull economic resources and time away from daily grinding issues of poverty and lack of health care. It is a kind of delusion that keeps the mind away from remembering how we, as a people, got here.

I want to remember.

Every academic semester begins with my resistance to containing learning within a syllabus. I worry about what should be taught. It is not a case of being "prepared" as a teacher or of feeling as if I am "in control" of the material. It is an ambivalent feeling of not knowing what will be learned—no matter what or how I present "the materials."

What did I learn as a Boricua that now is being undone?

My own life experiences tell me that I have rarely been prepared to learn something new. It has usually taken me by surprise. I have not been poised with the pen, expectant, listening, knowing I will learn something. I think about what to teach, what I should say, what materials to present, what to put forward, in relation to what might be remembered.

What did my Abuela not tell me so as to create a story of progress even as she knew better?

What is of value to know, and to whom? For me, these are moral and ethical questions that elicit complicated responses, responses complicated further by my position as a visitor displaced from home and now standing on someone else's stolen lands.

If I cannot remember my own history, how can I remember someone else's?

Abuela, help me remember. You grew up a Jíbara but didn't want any of us to be Jíbaros.

You were my best teacher.

Decolonial Transing

What does it mean to disappear a people and then act like it never happened? What connections can be made between colonization and trans- and feminist pedagogies?

Gender is also a site of colonization. Through alliances with land rights and Indigenous rights, trans- becomes more than just another area of white studies.

Reading evaluations for a psychology course, I see that several students wrote that adolescent development involved more than race, ethnicity, gender, sexuality, and class and that they wanted to learn psychology. This is an interesting position to consider; social identities and intersectional approaches in psychology[22] are not, in white students' minds, a psychological study. The reference point is Western (white) psychology, so in that way they are right; this is not Western psychology.

Another student wrote that a "textbook approach" was what was expected in a psychology class. Clearly, I am a disappointment. I refuse to use racist, classist, sexist, Eurocentric textbooks, the same textbooks that forget on whose land we teach, textbooks that teach to forget what happened here.

As a follow-up to feeling that there was too much emphasis on young people of color, several more comments were offered:

- Why is everything about race, class, and gender?
- There is nothing about white adolescents. We have problems, too; it should be equal.

There were, in fact, many readings focused on white adolescents. But this white student felt forgotten in the process of learning about adolescence through the social identities of race, class, sexuality, and gender. The two statements stand in contradiction to each other. On the one hand, "everything [is] about race"; on the other hand, "there is nothing about white adolescents."

One student wrote, "The class was not structured around adolescent development!" This student went on to advise, "Professor M, I really liked your class—when we actually learned about adolescents, it was great. Please focus in on more or offer a class about minorities instead."

To go into memory and to find different truths from what we have been colonized to think is conflictive and unsettling space; it is tense and contentious. What kinds of dialogue can take place here, at what Gloria Anzaldúa[23] conceptualized as *la frontera*? At these contested places, the borderlands, accessing knowledges in their wholeness and allowing *world*views and *word*views to emerge is a struggle for land, a border struggle.

Contradictory and irreconcilable realities sit in interminable tension with each other. And in the tension between contradictory realities is the ake ake ake, *the endless struggle—to know, to read, to understand, to work with, to engage with, others.*[24]

Claiming space for education as a practice of freedom[25] rather than a practice of forgetting "*sit[s] in interminable tension with each other.*"

Maybe there was a course on adolescent development. Maybe there was not. Maybe there was a trans- feminist course on youth.

Greetings.

I try to teach within the possibilities of psychology, women's and gender studies, and trans- studies without closing my eyes to the uncomfortable truths that emerge when one truly starts to learn what a free mind might actually bring one to think about.

I take heart from anticolonial educators,[26] Maori educators,[27] and Pakeha educators[28] in Aotearoa/New Zealand, who have taken on the project of centering Maori education and creating schools that are for Maori following Kaupapa Maori.

I take heart from the work and research of Stephanie Waterman (Onondaga) and her sister, Freida Jacques (Onondaga), who are educators working with Native students at the elementary and higher education levels.

I take heart from the writings of Troy Richardson (Tuscarora) on Indigenous diplomacy and the possibilities of Indigenous philosophy and education.

I take heart from the many students of color, LGBTQ students, and allies who courageously participate in antiracist and antiheterosexist dialogue and examine white and heterosexual privilege.

I remember.

Women's, gender, trans-, and feminist studies demand this kind of investigation into what has been covered over by colonization all over the United States and all over the world, not just in places where there are clear land claims and open struggles for sovereignty, as is the case here in what is called central New York State but is really Haudenosaunee land. The map should read, from east to west, Mohawk, Oneida, Onondaga, Tuscarora, Cayuga, Seneca.

What are the colonial encounters taking place today that we call "education"?

The route that the Sullivan/Clinton Campaign[29] followed to reach Goi-O-Gouen (Cayuga Castle) was the Great Iroquois Trail, which runs north-south along Cayuga Lake. Renamed the "Gansevoort-Trail" in honor of Colonel Peter Gansevoor, who was part of the Sullivan/Clinton Campaign, this is the route they took to destroy the Cayuga villages, to burn the fall harvest, and to destroy the Cayuga and Tuscarora territories in 1779. This same route, today called State Route 90, is not just a scenic byway but also a place of murder.

Look at the signs by United Citizens for Equality and the monuments erected by the State of New York and the New York Education Department. They each tell the lies about when the Cayuga and Tuscarora—the word carved in the monument is—"departed."

The struggle for land continues today by the Cayuga Indian Nation, but this time there are no crops to burn. There is a gas station owned by the Cayuga just a few miles from where Goi-O-Gouen was destroyed. The lines of cars are often long, just off Route 90, just off the old Great Iroquois Trail.

The Sullivan/Clinton Campaign helped defeat the English and bring about the creation of the United States and freedom from the British colonizers. It is through the genocide of Indigenous peoples that the United States came into being.

What do you see?

I would like to conclude this section with two quotes that speak with each other across time about decolonial education and freedom. Here is testimony from my maternal grandmother on the importance of the vernacular and not teaching in a foreign language and writing on the dialectic of freedom by Maxine Greene. First, my grandmother:

> When learning is carried out in a language foreign to the child, it confuses his mind. If the Department of Education imposes teaching in the

schools in a language foreign to the child, it will bring about the deterioration of the child's mind and will destroy and render impossible the integrated formation of his character—and hence the integrated formation of our people.[30]

Maxine Greene:

I want to explore some other ways of seeing, alternative modes of being in the world; and I want to explore implications for educating at this moment of "reform." My focal interest is in human freedom, the capacity to look at things as if they could be otherwise.[31]

Gender/Sovereignty

Karina Walters et al.[32] write:

The term two-spirit is used currently to reconnect with tribal traditions related to sexuality and gender identity: to transcend the Eurocentric binary categorizations of homosexual vs. heterosexual or male vs. female; to signal the fluidity and non-linearity of identity processes; and, to counteract heterosexism in Native communities and racism in LGBT communities.

The Maori word "takatapui"[33] is similar to the term "two-spirit" in the ways it makes space within the Maori Nation for diverse sexualities, gender identities, and connecting culturally with being Maori. At the same time, the word distinguishes Maori from the Pakeha LGBT communities in Aotearoa/New Zealand.

Both terms, takatapui and two-spirit, are decolonial approaches to sexual and gender identities for Indigenous people in the United States and Aotearoa/New Zealand. There are many other examples of terms that work in similar ways in Cree, Osage, Dakota, Blackfeet, Anishinaabe, Dine, and Zapotec.[34] These words make cultural spaces for negotiating sexualities and gender identities within Native communities as well as create spaces for gender sovereignty for Indigenous people against the prevalent racism of white and Eurocentric LGBT communities.

For examples of Indigenist LGBT research—that is, research done by Indigenous researchers with Indigenous people—that engage decolonizing approaches with Native LGBT people, we can go to the work of Wesley Thomas and Sue-Ellen Jacobs[35] in their co-authored piece, ". . . And We Are Still Here: From Berdache to Two-Spirit People." We can also read Sabine Lang's collection of writings in the text *Two-Spirit People: Native American Gender Identity, Sexuality, and Spirituality*.[36]

We can learn from Walters et al.[37] in the piece, "My Spirit in My Heart: Identity Experiences and Challenges among American Indian Two-Spirit Women." Walters's work with her co-authors importantly highlights the lack of research with American Indian women who identify as two-spirit. The majority of writings on two-spirit people are actually about two-spirit men.

We can read the writing by artist Adrian Stimson, "Two Spirited for You: The Absence of 'Two Spirit' People in Western Culture and Media":

> With the recognition and reclaiming of Two Spirit people comes the opportunity to further explore aboriginal ideology or ways of being. Integrated connections that once existed for aboriginal people may again be acknowledged and valued. Two Spirit people are playing a role in changing paradigms.[38]

What the words "takatapui" and "two-spirit"—among many others—do is claim the right to frame one's self in relation to histories, cultures, languages, spiritualities, gender, sexuality, and ways of being within the traumatic experience of colonization. These words are negotiations with cultures and histories, families and communities, psychology and society. These are ways of being that change the paradigm of gender needing a cure and move forward in new ways to consider what it means to recover from colonization.

These are forms of gender/sovereignty, approaches that describe and reflect upon the lives of trans- people as processes of psychological self-determination, as processes of gender self-determination within historical and cultural contexts.

Embedded in all these stories and research are the historical and contemporary experiences of colonization. Language recovery as a response to the colonial attempts at annihilation has also been crucial to recovering ways of being trans-, to becoming two-spirit. Traditional Indigenous Knowledges take contemporary shapes and blended practices,[39] creating new negotiations of gender identities and roles as well as sexualities.

These are approaches that decolonize trans- and feminism[40] through a fierce devotion to sovereignty in all its forms. Decolonial negotiations of gender identities and sexualities counter the Christian/Western project of reducing the multiple ways of being gendered and having sex to single letters in the English alphabet (i.e., LGBTQ).

What happens when transing as a culturally grounded and decolonizing approach is included in feminist and trans- pedagogies?

Overlapping places, for me, are in the ways Indigenist terms support decolonial negotiations that make space for antiracist and decolonizing pedagogies for Native LGBT people as well as trans-people of color. These negotiations of identities, culture, desire, gender, sexuality, family, communities, language, and spirituality compose what I think of as a process of gender/sovereignty.

Gender/sovereignty, for me, is a way of transing feminist pedagogies, gender and LGTBQ studies, and psychology as part of the ongoing struggle for decolonization and trans- formation.

What happens to feminist pedagogy when feminist trans-people of color name the world?

The capacity to look at things as if they could be otherwise.
  The integrated formation of our people.
    Places of interminable tensions.
      Learning to remember. This is Indian Country.

2

KATE FORBES

"Do These Earrings Make Me Look Dumb?"

Diversity, Privilege, and Heteronormative Perceptions of Competence within the Academy

Power and credibility are not evenly distributed in societies, and this includes the academy. I am a transsexual woman, an academic, and a scientist; the disconnect between many of my personal and professional experiences is jarring. On the one hand, I'm a scientist—people are very willing to trust me as an expert on many topics. On the other, I don't have the academic credentials to speak as an "expert" on gender, even when that gender is my own. The fields of women's and gender studies are not universally open to trans perspectives on gender. However, cissexual gender theorists are not even the ultimate keepers of the gender orthodoxy. In many respects, that honor goes to medical professionals and, ironically for me, scientists. It is important to remember that not all scientists are equal; in my experience in the academy, there is an idealized vision of what a scientist should look like. Although this vision potentially puts me at a professional disadvantage, transsexuality is not necessarily the lone, or even largest, strike against me. Rather, like people in most professions, scientists perceive various personal traits (such as masculinity, to name one example) as signs of competence. Although the academy needs to progress in how it treats trans- and gender-nonconforming (henceforth, simply "trans*") people, it simultaneously needs to address how it views feminine people and all individuals who do not mirror the dominant paradigm. That is, the academy needs to develop a critical lens into the ways that culturally grounded perceptions of competence create pressures to "cover." My fellow ecologists spend a great deal of time addressing diversity as it applies to flora and fauna. I suggest that were the academy to devote similar amounts of thoughtful consideration to human diversity, it would be a different and better place.

Gender in the Academy

Like many trans* scholars, I have plenty to say about how the academy deals with gender. However, unlike many (perhaps most) of this volume's contributors and readers, I am not trained as a social scientist or a humanist. For the past decade, I have been a student and now a faculty member in the natural sciences. I even had a lab coat in my last office (although I have no idea how it got there). Knowledge of gender is not part of my professional credentials but a byproduct of my life. Because I am not a "gender professional," I worry that, much like people outside higher education, I have very little say about how the academy deals with me and many of my friends.

Mainstream social arenas extend a certain amount of privilege to me and other members of the academy, and we are glad to accept it. Professors get to lead discussions related to their expertise and, in some cases, indulge in telling the world "the way things are." However, talent and motivation are not the only determinants of who accesses, completes, and facilitates higher education.

Although it is hardly revolutionary to contemplate the connection between the academy and power, as an insecure thirty-something faculty member who just completed her Ph.D. dissertation, I find society's sudden deference to my shiny new credentials disconcerting. I work at a diffuse, unorthodox institution where most students seek degrees in areas that have nothing to do with theoretical ecology, population biology, agriculture, entomology, or any other subject tangentially related to my thesis. I am the only faculty member in my building with credentials in science. Although my colleagues (many of whom are in similar situations) understand that I do not possess knowledge equivalent to dozens of departments at land-grant universities, the experience can still be a bit unnerving. Colleagues turn to me as someone with expertise in "science." Students look to me as someone with an advanced degree, a professorship, and all the answers. Certainly, I do know *something,* just not as much as others might assume.

The social life of a young scientist can be just as bizarre. Casual acquaintances expect me to be able to identify bird species I have never seen. Life-long gardeners ask for my advice on how to improve their harvests. I suppose I could make them a model, but I don't think that's what they are going for. In short, like many young faculty (particularly, I suspect, women), I struggle with "imposter syndrome."

Sometimes U.S. society turns to the academy for guidance. Yes, there are times (say, during discussions of global warming) when the public may not want to hear what we have to say. Still, people look to us as professors (and, furthermore, as scientists), for solutions. It's not the stupidest thing society could do. I spent seven years studying ladybugs, something that in most universes qualifies me as something of an expert. My concern is not that lay people consult professionals who have devoted their careers to understanding and expanding upon specific sets of knowledge but that society can misplace this reverence. Have a question about ladybugs? Try me. Need help identifying an unusual bird? You would do better to talk with a retired bus driver with a passion for bird-watching.

Colleges and universities are, to some extent, aware of the value of knowledge gained outside the academy. My college is a leader in the assessment of prior learning, whereby academic institutions award credit to students who can demonstrate that they have learned "college-level" material outside the confines of a classroom. Assessment of prior learning is a burgeoning field within a subset of the academy. However, this assessment still takes place within the context of institutions run by trained experts in the business of conferring merit upon individuals' experiences. Useful as such nontraditional credentialing programs are, they work in opposition to the premise that individuals' experiences are valid in and of themselves and do not require approval from external "experts."

I am a transsexual lesbian woman; I've learned a great deal about gender and sexuality during my life. Regardless of my credentials, I have been gathering information on the subject for as long as I can remember. In my early twenties, when I finally learned that trans* people existed outside the narrow confines of talk-show narratives, I found myself doing a lot of thinking about who I was and what gender meant in the very specific context of my life. Being an academic, once I began to actively contemplate gender transition, I did a ton of reading, a ton of listening, and even a bit of talking. After most people began to recognize me as a woman, I had to reconcile the small changes I had made with the small and jarring changes in the ways people interacted with me. Again, this involved more reading and more listening.

Being a femme lesbian has provided me another set of opportunities to gather anthropological data. The amount of information on gender and sexuality that I have taken in, coupled with the amount of time I have spent processing it (and, yes, my personal experience), makes me something of an expert on the subjects, regardless of my lack of formal training.

Thus, the primary tension I see between my personal life and the academy hinges on the distinction between theory and primary data. I *am* the primary data. As such, my experiences do not really care for theory. Although it is nice to see my life put into a larger context, it is not my job to fit my life to theory, but rather the other way around.

My relationship with the field of gender and women's studies is strikingly like that of many of the adult college students I work with. Just as they have often accumulated vast arrays of knowledge throughout their lives, I have learned all sorts of things about gender—but not in the classroom. To the extent that I have not been wholly immersed in the reading canon (although to some extent, I have), I lack a sense of the vocabulary of gender studies and of the formalization of theories that I live with on a daily basis. As a result, I'm not in a position to routinely be an active participant in academic discussions on gender—and this means that I cannot easily contest the exclusion of my life from a club I'm not necessarily qualified to join.

Now, as always, is a good time to consider who is part of women's studies and the like. I am reminded of Judith Halberstam's concept of "queer time."[1] I find it intriguing to consider whether queer people's priorities cause them to live their lives in spatial and temporal spaces that are less marked by or that resist heteronormative accounts of social structure. However, to me, it is as troubling as it is obvious to note that the academy does not run on queer time. The academy runs on a fictive middle-class trajectory in which a high school graduate leaves home for college, soldiers through graduate school (with no more than a minimal interruption between the two), writes a thesis, takes some sort of academic apprenticeship, becomes an assistant professor, and then goes on to a clearly marked seat of authority, that of tenured professor. Any number of things can break this chain, making one a less-desirable candidate (for example, children and/or economic realities have a notable habit of throwing one off course[2]). I don't see many signs of queer input in the construction of this map.

Being trans* makes the path to tenure harder to walk. Queer youth are at risk of bullying by peers, parents, and teachers, with poor (or non-) performance in school as a possible result.[3] Being in the closet or coming out brings great stress. Undergoing gender transition takes time away from studying and research.

Putting aside issues of stress and diminished efficiency, transition may involve a great deal of time out of the office. For instance, for some trans* women, facial hair removal may involve hundreds of hours of electrolysis. Therapy takes a good deal of time, and standards of care may force trans* people to endure more than they would like. Because of systemic prejudices within the medical community, the nearest medical providers may be hours from one's home and work, even for trans* people residing in large cities. The cost of all this medical care may make it necessary to take on additional employment (if one can find an employer willing to hire a visibly trans* person). Although scholars have written about the constraint that parenting (notably, mothering) places on academics' career trajectories, the academy has not yet acknowledged the difficulties associated with queer personal matters. This failure precludes the possibility of actually rectifying the inequality trans* scholars face.

A design insensitive to the aspirations of queer young people is not the only impediment to the inclusion of trans* voices in academic discussions of trans* lives. Early in graduate school (often age early- to mid-twenties), one chooses a career path. Although coming out prior to this point may largely take tenure off the table, scholars who come out after this stage may have already made themselves effectively ineligible to become part of women's studies writ large. Although not all trans* academics wish to be part of gender studies, I worry that personal and professional timelines hinder greater collaboration between those who study gender and those of us who have the greatest stake in the discussions.

I'm not here to pick a fight with academics who study gender. There are scholars who, given the appropriate opportunity, would likely be willing to listen to and to *value* my perspective. These scholars may have access to additional narratives that are unavailable to me. They are in positions to use their professional training to sift through all this information and use any number of lenses to make sense of it. Like all people, social scientists and others may treat me as a research subject. This is not necessarily a bad thing.

Unfortunately, as a research subject without proper credentials, I find myself in the bizarre position of being a primary source in a secondary-source world. I have my own lens, through which my life makes perfect sense. It is foolish to ignore this perspective. The world outside the academy trusts gender professionals more than it trusts first-hand accounts when it comes to explaining transsexual people like me. However, *I* am the ultimate authority on me. Degree or not, I am in a position to point out when others' theories fail to explain my experience.

Many cultures do not place trans* people in a position to claim and to defend their own identities. This is a tragedy for all of us but is particularly surreal to someone who, like me, is privileged enough to be taken seriously in professional endeavors. While I was teaching a course in behavioral evolution at the University of Wisconsin, a medical professional at an academic institution eight hundred miles away confided to my in-laws that I was likely a gay man. To my students, I was an expert on how mating systems have evolved, yet elsewhere, I was merely a subject, unable to defend myself against charges that I knew neither my gender identity nor sexual orientation. I also work with several colleagues with credentials in gender-related fields. As far as social hierarchies are concerned, I am not even the biggest expert on my identity in my own hallway: When the State of New York needed "proof" that I was a woman, I had to go two doors down from my office to get a credible opinion.

I am sure many of my readers in women's studies and related fields notice a certain inharmoniousness in my analysis. I am arguing that trans* voices are relatively underrepresented in relevant academic departments and that trans* people often find other people speaking for us in academic circles. This is not the same as arguing that Women's Studies departments are at the root of trans* people's problems, regardless of the existence of past and present tension. Women's and gender studies professors are not society's final arbiters of what "gender" means. On the contrary, as I understand it, women's studies arose in part as a result of society and the academy's prejudices against women.

To the extent that trans* people are marginalized in the academy, they are within the context of other marginalized groups. To the extent that mainstream society privileges learned professionals' narratives of trans* people, scientists and doctors write the book. More often than not, that book is the *American Psychiatric Association's Diagnostic and Statistical Manual of Mental Disorders (DSM)*,[4] much to the consternation of the majority of trans* people.[5]

I do not have the space to discuss all the flawed work on trans* people that researchers have put forth as science. However, as a practicing scientist, I feel compelled to echo other authors' critiques. Scientists are quick to search for explanations of traits that they deem abhorrent while leaving traits that they accept as normal unmarked and unexamined. Researchers create taxonomies *a priori* and ignore or dismiss phenomena that do not meet these predetermined criteria. The discredited theory of "autogynephilia"[6] presents an extreme version of this and is discussed by other writers elsewhere.[7]

Trans* people feel compelled to conform to cissexual narratives of trans* lives for treatment, falsely confirming researchers' biases. Indeed, the modern history of trans* women obtaining medical treatment is replete with stories of women forced to tell versions of the same story as a prerequisite of receiving medical care.[8]

Researchers in all fields have a wonderful way of finding exactly what they are looking for at the expense of alternate possibilities. Particularly in medical settings, practitioners frame trans* as pathological without examining the multiple assumptions required to reach that conclusion. Studies of gender and sexuality in nonhuman animals are not exceptions in this regard.[9] Despite the plethora of critiques from other scientists and scholars (sadly, these criticisms almost invariably come from scholars who share the cultural trait that scholars have erroneously superimposed onto their subjects), the scientific establishment and, in turn, broader society often accept the work of the "experts" who reflect societal prejudices.[10]

When it comes to gender, sexuality, or other normalized traits, I honestly do not think that most scientists are aware of the biases in others' works (let alone their own)—willful ignorance creates and reinforces privilege. Most of us don't get out much. Certainly, scientists tend to be selective in what we read and what we comment on. My former professional society, the Ecological Society of America, has more than ten thousand members, and, as the name implies, it mostly comprises American ecologists. Any one person can only read a fraction of this body's work, much less the work of all American scientists or all ecologists or scholars worldwide. Scientists (and, I suspect, other academics) tend not to contest work far from scholarly backyards lest they find themselves in over their heads or, worse yet, find themselves with an unnecessary number of new critics. Thus, when a psychologist says something troubling, most other physiologists are not rushing to comment.

Although it is somewhat understandable, the isolation of many academics is a problem twice over. First, wearing blinders is a huge luxury. For example, I spent the time devoted to my Ph.D. thesis examining the population dynamics of two ladybug species. I find the subject fascinating, but whatever other ecologists might say about this work, most of it admittedly is not that central to society. For me to completely ignore the world outside ecology and entomology in favor of highly specialized research would mean ignoring key issues in social justice. I am a femme lesbian transsexual woman, partner, and mother living in a racially diverse, environmentally degraded, mixed-income neighborhood in an economically depressed region. Devoting my life to "pure science" seems foolish (if not impossible) when other issues arise that demand my personal and, in some cases, professional attention. Of course, I can do "pure science," but I should not be expected to do exclusively "pure" (i.e., supposedly apolitical) research to the exclusion of other personal and profession endeavors. I am one of many people who cannot simply blow off issues of bigotry, inequality, and injustice as someone else's problem—the structure of the world around us requires us to fight these battles daily.

Second, scholars need to speak up when they see something that is askew: in a just world, there's no such thing as "not my problem." Many scientists are loathe to take "activist" stances, as if doing so would compromise their positions as unbiased discovers of "truth." This attitude is (1) based on false assumptions about how impartial science is,[11] (2) based on being privileged enough to find one's self in a position where one need not worry about defending one's self against unjust attacks, and (3) irresponsible. Regardless of your professional affiliation, if you hear someone claiming that fish of certain genders are "sneaky" and "mimics,"[12] that bisexual men do not exist,[13] that women are innately bad at math,[14] that trans* people are mentally ill,[15] or that a certain gender or sexuality is "alternative,"[16] you should speak up. These phrases are all too common. Given mainstream culture's (and particularly corporate media's) tendency to embrace "expert" opinions that confirm existing biases, it is vital for other "experts" to step forward to challenge flawed and frequently bigoted research. Part of being a member of the academy involves having confidence in your own mental capacities. We should all be able to recognize the difference between technical mistakes in each other's fields and inexcusable personal biases. Failing to speak out and, yes, to listen to "other people's" complaints is not acceptable—it is nothing short of enabling injustice.

I think the biggest reason that so much flawed work on transgenderism and transsexuality goes relatively unchallenged is the same problem that compromises the ability of the academy to reach its full potential—the startling lack of diversity in colleges and universities, particularly in the ranks of faculty. Whereas questionable research on transsexuality may contribute to my inability to receive adequate medical care, to find a job, or even to live safely, non-trans* faculty often have the privilege of not needing to think about issues surrounding trans* lives. To the extent that the composition of the academy is skewed toward heterosexual people, white people, affluent people (or at least not the economically disadvantaged), men, or other demographics, one can predict holes in the academy's ability to work in the public's interest.

Perhaps the biggest difficulty in criticizing the academy for having a dearth of meaningful diversity or misplaced priorities is that the academy has been a traditional ally of the center-left. More than once, trans* and/or lesbian acquaintances have reminded me that, as a queer person, the academy represents one of my best opportunities for meaningful employment. Being better than bad is not necessarily good, however. Which queer people does the academy accept, and in which contexts?

Additionally, it is quite possible that being enlightened when it comes to some oppressed groups does not preclude having deep-seated biases against others. Horizontal oppression is a Saturday-morning sport in social-justice circles. Participants in movements for gender or racial justice frequently forget about (or minimize) the realities of women of color.[17] Gay and lesbian people have been known to forget about the existence of bisexual and trans*[18] people, and so on. Likewise, being a progressive academic does not guarantee that one is fighting for social justice. This is an important point, because one person's sport is another's fight for survival.

Re-viewing the Search Image

Although I can only speak to my own disciplines (primarily ecology), academics are no different than other people in their tendency to conflate a set of personal traits with professional competence. In ecology-speak, this is the idea of a "search image."[19] In other words, just as an eagle looking to find a mouse might be looking for oblong shapes with long tails, ecologists tend to have something particular in mind when they are looking to find another ecologist. Just as I imagine that most people imagine a middle-age or older white man when they hear the terms "lawyer," "doctor," or "senator," some personal traits appear to be more "ecological" than others. This is not a secret—I have joked with more than one colleague about this.

A proper ecologist should be wearing sandals (preferably dirty ones) coupled with tangled hair and a cheap T-shirt. Admittedly, this is a glib and rather sarcastic way of putting it. The bottom line is that, for obvious reasons, ecologists frequently look and act like people who like to spend large amounts of time working outside, large amounts of time inside and alone at a computer, or both. There is nothing particularly wrong with this image, except for the implications that people who like to do to any of those things should look or "be" one way and that this is somehow correlated with job performance. Do people of color enjoy camping? Do people who wear makeup enjoy computers? What hobbies does a "good" ecologist enjoy? These are all (hopefully) offensive questions, and I sincerely doubt that any academic would ask them, except perhaps to make a point.

"Covering" is a succinct way to describe the act of hiding traits related to disadvantaged groups in order to appear more acceptable to a dominant culture. As Kenji Yoshino points out, people do not necessarily consider covering when they think of discrimination.[20] Requiring trans* people to play the "good queer" to be taken seriously is discrimination, even if equality of opportunity theoretically exists for all people willing to conform to an oppressive standard. In other words, many people recognize that it is wrong to treat women, gay people, members of religious groups, people of color, or members of other groups worse than they would treat some individual with the optimally privileged profile. However, insisting that individuals hide marginalized traits is a form of discrimination. It is still discrimination to insist that women not be feminine or that people of color not be so "ethnic." People are, in fact, different from each other, yet this difference does not justify the creation of a pecking order. Viewing people who possess certain irrelevant traits as better, more natural, or more competent than others creates a demand to cover, and it is wrong.

The major biases that I see in the academy are not as overt, and, as such, many scholars refuse to take them seriously. Academia is filled with unequal relationships, cliques, and the like. Such dynamics seem inherent in an institution built on the premise of experts teaching students, who, under the right circumstances, go on to become fully credentialed scholars in their own right.

People studying the same topics may come from the same labs and may well find themselves evaluating the work of friends. These academic cliques reinforce the need to cover and the failure to properly evaluate work for bias with negative implications for diversity.

The lack of (and/or disregard for) appropriate practices in human relations reinforces the academy's insularity. Experience tells me that this is the case—not because of malice on the part of scientists but rather due to indifference and obliviousness. I have seen countless job interviews during which, in the name of being welcoming (often to old friends), dinner and wine have been served. I can recall scientists dismissing the work of visiting scientists (including at least one job candidate) not because of its quality but rather because of the mannerisms of the speaker. How is it that in a discipline where some practitioners view social ineptitude as a virtue, failure to strike up an appropriately jovial conversation over pizza is considered a fatal flaw? How is it that I have found myself as an overnight guest in the house of a potential employer rather than, as is the expected practice, being put up in a hotel? Presumably, my host did not consider that a woman in my circumstance (or *any* circumstance, for that matter) might find it unsettling to find herself as a guest of a strange man. Looking back, many of my personal experiences as well as those of colleagues on the job circuit read more like bad dates than job interviews.

All this is emblematic of a systemic failure. Often, as part of our devotion to our craft, we blur the lines between our work and our social lives. Professionally, we spend long hours together, and we want to find colleagues that we can get along with. We are nice people, and we want to be hospitable to people in our field we have not yet met and spend time catching up with old friends whenever the opportunity arises. Unintentionally, this leads to a world where some people may be more welcome than others. When I say that some people may be "more welcome," I am also implying that certain people are more likely to suffer discrimination than others.

Based on my experience, I am inclined to agree with Julia Serano's assessment that it is often hard to differentiate between the dismissal of trans* women and the dismissal of femininity.[21] When a potential employer spent an extended period of time questioning my ability to perform fieldwork (owing to, well, I'm not sure what exactly), I did not know what to make of it. At the time, I was clearly a nonpassing transsexual woman. Was he subconsciously (or consciously) giving me a hard time because I was trans*, because I was feminine, or because I was a woman? Is there a difference? If I were a tomboy, would I have encountered a similar problem? What can those of us who stand out due to our "activist" stances on issues, our physical or personality traits, or incorrect and arbitrary paperwork do to gain equal access to the academy?

I worry about how stereotypes of trans* women and tokenism may impact my career as a scientist. However, the albatross in the room is still the treatment of feminine women in science. A lot of writers have addressed the issues facing women scientists—namely, that our colleagues are much less likely to take our work (and our lives) seriously than that of our male colleagues.[22] However, it is important to note that not all women (or members of any demographic) are the same, and, certainly in the sciences, femininity itself is often a liability.

For me, one of the more jarring lessons of gender transition is that, as a woman, I still have to put a lot of thought into how I dress and how I carry myself. Sadly, this is not so much a "trans* thing," as it is a "woman thing." More to the point, in the sciences, it is a "covering thing." I recall a colleague asking a bunch of my fellow graduate students, "Do these earrings make me look dumb?" It was before an important committee meeting for her, and she followed her (female) adviser's advice and replaced the offending hoops with something of a "more-intelligent" size. What is telling is the number of women I have run across who have admitted to thinking twice before daring to don makeup, skirts, or (shudder) heels at their science-related jobs. It is simply not healthy for any professional endeavor that such a large pool of potential employees is made to feel unwelcome. Who knows how many potential scientists have chosen different career paths because they did not see places for people "like them" in the academy? Without diverse role models, members of younger generations may come to depressing conclusions about which career paths are truly open to them.

As a rule, most of U.S. society does not deal well with diversity, and the academy does little better. Rather than thinking about what diversity might truly mean and why it might matter, we resort to measuring it the only way we know how—with crude categorizations and numbers. Although this sorting satisfies the logic of the law, this census approach to diversity strikes me as academically dishonest.

Within ecology, we debate the meanings of various measures of diversity.[23] For ecologists to address diversity, we need to know why diversity is important in a given situation. To ecologists, diversity has two primary components. Richness tells us how many types of organisms we have present (e.g., how many categories exist). Evenness tells us about the relative commonness of these types (e.g., how individuals are distributed between the categories). There is no universal way to measure either richness or evenness. A measure of richness may lump together all trees as interchangeable, or it may set the boundary at all maple trees, all members of the same species of maple tree, or all trees with the same genetic makeup. Besides, what *is* a species, anyway?[24] Different measurements have different implications; a tree filled with five different species of warblers is the same as and different than a tree filled with *warblers*. The issue is that in creating a category, we are designating all members of the category as equivalent. This is a necessary evil, but it is important to consider which approximations are reasonable in which situations.

Different measurements of diversity give different weight to species' evenness. A stand of trees containing lone spruce, oak, and maple trees among acres of pine trees is identically rich to a stand containing equal amounts of all four types of tree. However, the second stand is much more even, and as such, more diverse. How much more diverse is it? How important are rare species? Does the presence of a couple of honeysuckle bushes change everything? Nothing? Obviously, the answer depends on why one is asking the question.

We need to apply the lessons of ecology to discussions of human diversity. Counting the number of people who belong to various federally protected groups is easy, somewhat informative, and legal to boot. However, this method builds tokenism right into the measurement. It is safe to say that not all women are interchangeable, nor are all people of color, nor are all people of a certain age. This method of accounting allows us to maintain the fallacy that the most competent academics should share the same basic traits. In other words, it does nothing to prevent the pressure to "cover" rare or exceptional traits. If all the faculty in a Women's Studies department have similar backgrounds, do they really represent all women? What happened to intersectionality? Is it fair to view race or gender as trivialities when, in reality, scholars may be bringing something to the table precisely because of who they are rather than in spite of it? Ultimately, we need to address why diversity matters. Diverse groups of scholars are likely to consider a broader range of ideas and, in short, to facilitate engaging and critical dialog about a wider range of issues.

If we (the academy, social institutions, the culture at large) were to truly embrace diversity, we could come closer to realizing some of the things that I dream of for future generations. I want to see a world where trans* people are not pathologized. Ideally, an increasing number and range of role models would be available to young trans* people. Medical support would be readily available and obtainable by all people wishing to transition. Discrimination and violence against trans* and *all* LGBTQ people would stop, along with violence and discrimination against all people. No person, regardless of economic status, sex, race, gender, gender identity, ability, or anything else, would feel limited in what could be achieved.

It may not be scientists' first job to champion the fight for such a future, but this does not mean that trans* people should be dismissed as yet another identity group with its own special issues. The very things that will strengthen the academy are those that will promote its diversity and, in turn, the state of the larger world around us. Trans* people's issues are not other people's issues, because there are no such things. A world where everyone is allowed to reach their full potential is a world that reaches its own full potential.

3

BOBBY NOBLE

Trans. Panic.

Some Thoughts toward a Theory of Feminist Fundamentalism

> While women's studies once served to legitimate and support, in a positive way, feminist scholarship across the academy, it would now seem to legitimate it negatively by allowing feminist scholars in other disciplines to tacitly define themselves and their work *against* women's studies. Women's studies has come to be perversely useful to some academic feminists as "the other" against which respectable feminist scholarship is defined.[1]

As I sat down over the first few months of writing this chapter, some of those months overlapped with one of the longest, most devastating academic strikes taking place at my university. One of York University's largest unions representing casualized academic labor—graduate teaching assistants, contract faculty, and research assistants—held a strike that lasted almost three months. It is now a substantial period of time past the day that local union CUPE3903 was legislated back to work and we all resumed something of the extended academic session to complete that school year. The university senate suspended all classes for the duration of the event, meaning that all instruction at York had come to a complete standstill. Given that CUPE3903 is a large union representing more than 3,400 research assistants, teaching assistants, and contract/sessional faculty members who, as ghostly workers, do more than 50 percent of the teaching work at my school, full-time tenured and tenure-stream faculty members like myself, it must be noted, continue to perform research in an increasingly class-based corporate climate deeply embedded within haunted capitalist corporacies (a form of late capitalism governed by the corporatization of labor, among other things) and their imagined relations as meritorious, egalitarian, and (vis-à-vis national location) democratic.

In memoriam—Sharon Michelle Rosenberg (1964–2010); in honor of JD, CK, and TL; and in recognition of the labor of love and remembering.

Such a reconceptualization of the university as imagined academic and knowledge inside an "ivory tower" to a site of haunted academic and epistemological labors, with their attendant gender, race, class, politics, and corporatization, is vital to the argument and questions I ask here. These questions seek to elaborate the stakes of reconceptualizing women's studies through transfeminism inside what we might now think of, through the work of Andrea Smith, as an academic-industrial complex:[2]

> If we understand epistemology as rooted in the commodification of knowledge, then it is apparent that the academy becomes the site where knowledge is bought and sold in the academic marketplace. In this sense, we can identify the existence of an "academic-industrial complex," a synergistic relationship between capitalist accumulation and academic knowledge production and dissemination. The academic-industrial complex is the site where intellectual labour is alienated from peoples and communities, and is thus constitutive of capitalism.[3]

It is clear to me as a result of the strike that such practices of capitalism certainly structure and saturate the kind of work accomplished by what Smith identifies as the academic-industrial complex. In a chapter in the same book as Smith's, I deploy the term "educational-corporate complex" to resonate with Smith's argument but to out the increasing corporatization of academic institutions as a form of corporate capitalism. As such, then, I situate this argument about the necessity for transfeminist epistemologies within the growing critique over the last thirty years of the category "woman" within liberal capitalist democracies. Feminism and its work through such categories is equally embedded within, not transcendent of, the manufacturing, indeed, active, labor of producing identity and identity politics within modernity itself.

One of the many things students asked me about the labor disruption in our school, beyond a very real concern for their tuition monies and the protracted nature of "make-up classes," was the "appropriateness" of such an action in the first place. If campuses were unionized, so their logic argued, then that means there are workers, bosses, and products to be carried to the market place. "Are we the product?" they asked, attempting to discern exactly what was the product of such labors inside this institution.[4] The act of conceptualizing universities in the context of labor relations, workers, markets, alienation, products, and strikes produced, after a while, an interesting kind of dysphoria (defined by the *Oxford English Dictionary* as "a state of unease or mental discomfort") for many of my students who could not reconcile (some never did) the breakdown of conceptual paradigms that such a strike initiated. Although not *"trans"*—if by this term we mean a minoritized reduction to identity-based practices of transsexual and transgender—such conceptual dissonance certainly is *transed* if we rethink the term as the critical crossings and mobilities of previously categorically fixed territories. Susan Stryker, Paisley Currah, and Lisa Jean Moore pose what I frame here as a fundamental question about *trans* so reconfigured in what has formerly been identified as women's studies: "What kinds of intellectual labor can we begin to perform through the critical deployment of 'trans-' operations and movements? Those of us schooled in the humanities and social sciences have become familiar, over the past twenty years or so, with queering things: how might we likewise begin to critically trans- our world?"[5] In particular, how might we begin to critically *trans* our women's studies worlds? With Stryker, Currah, and Moore, this article seeks to retrace the shape of women's studies by *transing* its epistemologies, disciplinarities, and methodologies.

To elaborate such a *trans* reshaping, I must first posit several conceptual, pedagogical, and epistemological axioms. One major conceptual truism has to be that there is always much more to a university campus/corporate site, its disciplines, and its byproducts—what we imagine to be self-evident knowledges based on equally imagined self-evident experiences of "women"—than what we can see (or not see, as it were) on the surface. My second premise, by inference, then must be that by the second decade of the twenty-first century, we now need to assume that "women's studies" is a vastly different signifier across its reiterations if not, by now, a completely empty one. My university has a School of Women's Studies with dozens of lines (both 100 percent and cross-appointed across two campuses, one French, one English). Ask any random ten or so of these academics what "women's studies" means, and you will hear at the very least answers, narratives, histories, methodologies, and so forth; this is the case at the women's studies council that governs the school (made up of a press, a library, an undergrad and grad program, a bridging program, sexuality studies, and so forth). There is intense acrimony over what these words do, should, can, and might mean. We must presume, then, that women's studies will mean different (?) things to universities and colleges across any province, across the country, and then comparatively, again to schools and states in the United States, England, and so on.

To stay with this example, I want to append a context-specific hypothesis: If I were to ask any ten feminist academics in and across my home university whether *trans* bodies are present, or should be, as *trans* bodies in women's studies—that is, bodies not reducible to the sex binarized hegemonic and clinical imperatives of "male" or "female" (that is, in this clinical grammar, as bodies that cannot possibly have histories as both and neither, exclusively)—I cannot help but worry that the answer will be a quiet or completely dumbfounded no, even in the face of my hire. Wars have been happening inside feminism for a very long time; these have survived the shift from "activism" to "institutional location." As large-scale global-political shifts occur, such shifts recalibrate what we have in the past called "radical" feminism. This is no longer what it imagines itself to be, especially if we are measuring by consequences and not intentionalities, and, again, its consequences do violence. One small example: an insistence on using female pronouns in all documents regarding grad students (documents all faculty members see but students do not) even as the same program (but not the same people) regularly and rightly accepts *trans* men and cisgendered men. Curious though is the reality that there have been almost no MtF *trans* women who have applied for admission to our graduate program. One further example: The undergraduate introductory course I teach is still called "On Women," even as I step up to the podium to teach it, very much not a "woman" and not teaching "on women" in any disciplinary sense. There is a level of intransigence that generates very high stakes, often quite unwittingly. At the very least, such intransigence places undergraduate and graduate students in structurally manufactured *trans* and race panics, often with faculty members who have also put their own minds, bodies, and intellectual labor on the line building "women's studies" programs in the first place. What seems abundantly evident, then, is the need for a conceptual mechanism with which such labors of epistemological "innocence" (the kind that sounds like "we are just trying to protect women" or "whatever happened to the 'women' of women's studies?") might be discerned, acknowledged, theorized, contemplated, and reckoned with.

I write "innocence" in premise number two to secure the work of premise number three. *Trans* bodies have always been present in feminism as a social movement, even as those bodies have been ghosted by a belief that such bodies have never been a part of feminism or women's studies. Sandy Stone's broken tenure at Olivia Records, producing the "sound" and "feel" of feminism through the 1970s and 1980s, is a case in point. This spawned one of the most visible of the early wars over *trans* inside feminism. Stone's response, "The Empire Strikes Back: A Posttranssexual Manifesto" (1987), is often hailed as launching transgender studies but is rarely considered integral to women's studies.[6] We might historicize the current incarnation of *trans* wars as feminist history repeating itself, because it did not reckon with the issues as an identity-based (and deeply invested) practice. These debates are happening in women's studies, and they have always happened in feminism. But the fact of their occurrences and reiterations cannot and should not be read as their "success," given such easily forgotten histories. Instead, their reiteration suggests that the field is haunted, forever grappling with the exclusions it self-generates. Such exclusions, as hauntings, support the argument made by Avery Gordon that epistemological ghosts return because they are what we relegate to the outside even as they are deeply central.[7] This chapter seeks to name the violence of these occlusions, disavowals, and denials as part of a disciplinary but also historical and ideological imaginary. They have, in other words, normalized what Raymond Williams identified as a "structure of feeling" in women's studies where such challenges from within are met with the same acrimony as antifeminist misogyny.[8]

A transfeminist reconceptualization of women's studies seems vital. To that end, I offer the term "*trans* entities," borrowing from two queer-identified *trans* FtMs of color—Wil and Papí—who are the subjects of one of the most interesting docu-porn films of late, *Trans Entities: The Nasty Love of Papí and Wil.*[9] Wil and Papí coin the term "*trans* entities" as a way to describe themselves, noting the need for such descriptions given the often binarized options made available through such language as female-to-male, male-to-female, transsexual, and so forth. Arguing that such binarized options are themselves products of clinically regulated medical-diagnostic technologies, Wil and Papì—both of whom, at the time of filming were also nonoperative (for these same reasons but also as an intervention in the class politics of sex reassignment) and identified as "trannydudes" who had gay sex with each other—also carefully note the way that such languages, their clinical grammars, and their practices of identity formation are inherently racialized at best (and most likely racist in consequence) and certainly function to colonialize the space of *trans* as white in the service of whitesupremacist scientific racism. Their use of the term "entities" instead of "-gender," "-sexual," or "-national," for that matter, signals one reconfiguration of the labor it takes to live on a day-to-day basis with the undoing accomplished by clinical and binarized language systems not one's own and that create little possibility for practices less discursively overdetermined.

But my use here of *trans* reconceptualizations also attempts to signal the conceptual and disciplinary limitations—indeed, intransigent failed labors—of women's studies as an institutional project. One of this paper's questions: Where in such an epistemological or institutional deployment of the term "women" is there space to theorize the work that subjects like Wil and Papì accomplish undoing racially gendered capitalist categories? To frame this question differently, in *Undoing Gender,* Judith Butler rigorously reads the complexities of "trans-gender" when she argues that "to flourish as a bodily being ... not only does one need the social world to be a certain way in order to lay claim to what is one's own, but it [also] turns out that what is one's own is always from the start dependent upon what is not one's own, the social conditions by which autonomy is, strangely, dispossessed and undone. In this sense, we must be undone in order to be ourselves."[10] The specificity of Butler's "we" notwithstanding, this is a map to the territories that *trans* entities must labor to undo even as that same map guides their unmapping.[11] This is all the more so when such undoings occur inside institutional spaces that have as their *raison d'être* the securing, fixing, stabilizing—indeed, the very labor of doing—one version of what has been done: documenting the experiences of "women" (meaning a shared demographic with enough commonality based upon biological femaleness to function as such an empirical demographic in the first place). These contratrajectories—between stabilizing (and the active labor of "doing") fields and the labor of "undoing" foundations—seem permanently caught in a tension that cannot be resolved. Hence, my interest here is as much *what has been done?* as *what to do?* when competing forces such as these collide on *trans* bodies, all the more so in a women's studies department and/or program. What occurs, I suggest as part of an answer, is a sometimes productive and other times violent dislocation where the labors of such disparate dislocationing and their outcomes are unequally shared across bodies subject to "women's studies" as an academic discipline and day-to-day practice.

Although a rhetoric of openness and inclusivity has always saturated women's studies as an institutional practice—indeed, so much so that a quiet lament over the changing face of women's studies is audible within corridor conversations—the opposite is true as epistemological and methodological practices where some women's studies scholars and practitioners remain *trans* illiterate and deeply fearful of the remarkably productive work that *trans* entities can accomplish. "Integration" of the *trans* body—presuming such a thing becomes possible and deemed valuable—necessitates the productive structural and conceptual shifting of the ground of the women's studies project as it has functioned in many places to date. Practices of *trans* illiteracy condition folding that *trans* entity into a noncritical binarized sex system in which that body can only make sense as either a male or female body. For that body to access the institutionalized program *qua transed* would mean that the conceptual ground of gender in women's studies would need to be rethought as radically interdisciplinary, indeed, *trans* disciplinary. As such, a *trans* feminist reconceptualization is often met with a series of complex but contradictory disavowals: On one hand, the rhetoric and historical practice of women's studies as a discipline self-mandates—in the form of a gender-panicked, sometimes tearful plea over "what's happening to the women of *women's* studies"—an unproblematic and unmediated focus on the lives of women where we understand "women" to mean biologically born women.

On the other hand, a *trans* feminist logic necessitates a profound challenge to the ease with which that "woman" is conceptualized and exchanged as an essential truth. Critical *trans* perspectives should be making it much harder to make truth claims about the universalizability of "women"—experientially or otherwise—without at least using it with much more precision to identify a relation to "woman" no longer reducible to the female body or the nefarious "women's experiences." If *trans* as critical mobilities across or as undoing of categorical terrain (again, not to be reduced to the clinical transsexual body) accomplishes its work, especially in women's studies, then the universality and territorialization of the term "woman" should be problematized somehow, beyond the additive and tokenistic practice that includes writing "women and *trans* people" but making no consequential conceptual, curricular, epistemological nomenclatures or modifications day-to-day modus operandi transformations of practice (such as the exclusive use of female pronouns to refer to faculty and students). Doesn't the gender-panicked imperative to "remember the women" mark an unequivocal gender fundamentalism, where such fundamentalisms themselves—not unlike those of nationalism, military-state, white-supremacist, or Christian, to name only a few—function to ground a feminist imaginary and its methodology of social, moral, and biological coercive normalization? By "fundamentalist methodology," I borrow from *Contesting Fundamentalisms*: "The fundamentalist methodology involves re-imaging the past and invoking an authentic community with deterministic social characteristics. In doing so, it produces a paradox—the fundamentalist simultaneously engages in nostalgia for the past while displaying historical amnesia about a system of living that never existed."[12] *Trans* entities have always been present inside feminist spaces; to make a claim to the contrary would be to fly in the face of at least thirty years of writing and debate about the presence of *trans* bodies "on the front line." The degree to which those *trans* entities remain *located within* or *dislocated from* actively renarrated pasts as well as academic and disciplinary communities and their nomenclatures is precisely the stake to be won or lost.[13]

Such a stake, between the knowledge-producing field of women's studies as a field always concerned about the truths and experiences of women and the contradictory place of *trans* bodies in that field, is, as Robyn Wiegman points out in her introduction to the collection *Women's Studies on Its Own*, symptomatic of a self-generating, discipline-sustaining, and disciplining epistemological practice (2002). With the ironic title *Women's Studies on Its Own,* this important collection outs the circularity with which such field mapping and narrating often functions. If my own premises here are correct, then so is Wiegman when she suggests that not only does "feminism's own self-narration as an agent of liberating women" need to come into critical view, but so too must the stakes of its own temporalities within modernity. Such an examination of feminism's boundedness with the hegemonic privileges of modernity, she argues, marks feminism "itself [as] historical (and not, as our own celebratory narratives often have it, as a revolutionary agent of history's making), with all its complicit and resistant ties to modernity, capitalism and various forms of patriarchy."[14]

Self-authorizing practices of storytelling are themselves the effect of modernity and humanism, all the more so given the hegemonic dominance of positivist, antitheoretical, and social-science methodologies and their open hostility toward and dismissal of theoretically complex deconstructions of such methodologies in the first place. It behooves one not to register the deep skepticism toward critical theory, psychoanalysis, anti-Empire and postcolonial theory, poststructuralism, deconstruction, and, sometimes, queer theory, and the charges leveled against these forms of knowledge as equally "abstracted" and not always immediately "relevant" to "women's" lived experiences. Wiegman answers these self-generating, self-justifying, and "heroic" narratives with a call for radical rethinking of such methods as deeply embedded in humanist histories:

> Such a call for making Women's Studies the institutional domain for critiquing the convergences as well as the differences between historically constituted feminist discourses and "woman" has critical effects that reverberate. . . . Certainly it calls into question the field's own imperative to produce positivist knowledge accounts of the life experiences of diverse women, because it raises *as a question* the equation of humanism's construction of the self-authorizing subject as feminism's political destination. It also asks us to rethink the imposition of the subjective as the critical domain within which feminist scholars can know their objects of study, "women."[15]

To move beyond the self-generating subjective and its attendant methodological disciplining requires calling into question the very assumption with which women's studies began its disciplinary work: Knowledge production has been inadvertently biased and so must be countered with another identity-based paradigm—one speaking the "language" of women's subjectivity instead. But Wiegman is uncategorical in her historical evaluation, arguing that the success of intersectional critiques of faulty universalisms has produced the need for new sets of bodies, identities, political acts, and critical practices—indeed, "new objects of study." I want to hail these new objects of study as *trans*:

> Functioning now as the critical content of the category *gender*, these new objects of study (alternative masculinities, transgender identities and identifications, transsexuality, intersexuality) and the subjects that might be said to mirror them (gay men, straight men, transsexuals, the transgendered) are by definition referents for *women's* faulty universalism—that is, they function implicitly to claim identities as women's other. As a collective of new identity claims, their incorporation into feminism's field imaginary displaces onto *gender* the optimistic hope that a relationship of compatibility, if not consistency, between field formation and its object of study can (finally) be won.[16]

Wiegman is not uncritical of the dangers of paradigms shifts from *women* to *gender*. In fact, she is quite clear to carefully map the troubles with gender studies via the trajectories of queer theory and women's studies. But what she offers instead is a location of the gender studies versus women's studies debate in and as history itself, marking also the shift from a minoritized field of study to one universalized:[17]

> The sudden shift from sexuality to gender that marks the transition between Women's Studies and gender studies demonstrates the end of gender's critical mobility to signify outside and beyond the domain of specific identities, becoming instead the collaborative term for new identities that need to be given representational visibility. It is at just such a moment that *women* takes on a most patriarchal signification, becoming the referent for the particular in a dynamic that reduces it to the normatively literal domain of sexual difference. Why feminism would want to author such a reduction of women is perhaps not immediately clear.[18]

What Wiegman calls "patriarchal significance," I call "fundamentalism." Hence the full irony of the collection's title: To parse this out, women's studies, *on its own,* is embedded inside the capitalist and colonial educational corporate complex, and without a clear sense of its own historical production, it too duplicates the master's house (the problematic of modernity's temporalities and identity formation as its effect). But, moreover, *women's* studies on its own fails to mobilize the critical capacities of its own incoherencies when it maps itself as imperative onto a construction of a referential and fundamentalist coherency to the exclusion of subjects attaching themselves to its criticalities (the problematic of field and categorical formations and proper objects). In addition, women's *studies* on its own enables a fantasy of itself as a field with epistemological and methodological coherence, but when clustered with department status and disciplinary force segregated from what Wiegman calls "the sexual division of knowledge" across the university, it becomes complicit with—but also arrogant about—the uneven development of feminist knowledge in the university itself, where "women's studies" is imagined to be the *only* site of feminist knowledge production (the problematic of institutionality).[19]

Again, it bears reiteration that Wiegman is not making an overly simplistic claim to *substitute* gender for women, nor does she advocate against such shifts. Instead, she is doing precisely the kind of work that I suggest *trans* feminist practices can do—that is, *trans* one categorical territoriality against, across, and through the other to produce the "space of connection and circulation between the macro- and the micro-political registers through which the lives of bodies become enmeshed in the lives of nations, states, and capital-formations."[20] Wiegman seeks an intervention, one not, as she puts it in an interesting circumvention of grammar's modernist mythologies of temporality, "late enough":

> I want to intervene in a critical moment—a moment of critical analysis—that seems to me to have come too early, in part because we are not late enough in our thinking about how to avoid dyadic rubrics and build critical vocabularies that make possible the intersectional imperative that we believe we believe in.[21]

Curiously, then, Wiegman calls not for a new wave; such a construction would remain fully compatible with currently existing feminist presentist narratives as they already exist. But she is also extremely careful to infer that, although how we conceive of feminist knowledge production is a work in progress, feminism has neither completed nor quite begun its institutional work. What she calls for, without fully articulating this, is a deterritorialization of the temporal sequencing of feminist self-narrations and a reconciling of those critical territories with the rhetorics of what I offer as *trans* feminist imperatives. In other words, Wiegman seeks a critical *trans* formation; what is this if *not* a turn to the paradoxical crossings induced by *trans*?

Wiegman's *transing* of time across, within, and over feminism's praxis itself does to feminist consciousness and historicities what *trans* does to bodies and to their attendant subjectivities. There is, at the very least, a doubling of consciousness where both—indeed, all sides of consciousness—exist in a profound complex relative to time and to what haunts temporal modernities as one of the ingredients in subject formation. Where *trans* subjectivities must be, as Butler notes, enabled by "individual choice" proven to be "dependent from the start on conditions that none of us author at will," so, too, admittedly is feminism's institutional materialization a practice none authors at will.[22] Wiegman's argument that critical interventions in feminism are coming too early *and* not late enough similarly identifies these modernist operations of history as the discourse that has produced feminism but also the obstruction that now constrains it.

To put this into different terms, any institutional materialization of an identity-based practice must also take shape around the mandates as well as the limitations of the "truth-telling" disciplinary imperatives of the educational-corporate complex. Such disciplinary imperatives, as Brown notes in the quotation with which this chapter opens, have not been without their costs as well as their very ironic and paradoxical hauntings. There can no denying that the permanency and tenaciousness of the wars inside feminism for at least a century, and for as long as feminism has been institutionalized as "women's studies," indicate that "women's studies" remains a haunted discipline as well as signifier and referent. Such hauntings are, as Gordon tells us, a permanent condition overdetermining the epistemologies of modernity wherein that which must be excluded for truth and epistemological regimes to function returns as a "seething presence" that haunts the present and the presentist.[23] "Hauntings," Gordon notes, "are a constituent element of modern social life. It is neither pre-modern superstition nor individual psychosis; it is a generalizable social phenomenon of great import" demarcating the "zone that somewhere every culture has . . . for what it excludes."[24] Such zones of exclusion—to which *trans* entities have been relegated—have always already constituted discourse about "difference" in feminism (discourse and difference each identified as nefariously as "the sex wars," "the race wars," "the moral panics about transgender bodies," or "the porn wars") and so marked feminism's simultaneous and self-generative hauntings and failures. Yet despite the siege mentality that seems to be the condition of possibility for women's studies in its institutionalized form, there can no measuring its capacities for a diagnostic criticality without a modality for calibrating its own embeddedness within the truth regimes of modernity.

Gordon elaborates such a modality by noting a couple of seemingly simple axioms that ground a paradigm through which to read and to reckon with what I have been identifying as *trans* ghosts. The first states "that life is complicated is a fact of great analytic importance . . . and while this may seem like a banal expression of the obvious, it remains perhaps the most important theoretical statement of our time."[25] Why? Gordon answers, because despite our best scholarly and epistemological efforts, the power relations that characterize any historically embedded society and social formation are never as transparently clear as the names we give to them imply. Power, social formations, and something Gordon identifies as complex personhood will always exist in excess of our nominalisms. As such, what remains excluded, unnamed, and nonreckoned with haunts as a present absence of *trans* bodies with histories in excess of a binarized gender truth regime.

Gordon's second axiom: If axiom one is true, not only do ghosts of our social formations precede our entry into it, we ourselves, as effects of our social formations, are always already haunted as women's studies remains. Ghosts exist culturally, historically, and institutionally beyond what our complex or sometimes-not-so-complicated methodologies and epistemologies can discern. These seething presences remain actively invisibilized even as we fetishize in an era of, at the very least, postmodernity, the hypervisible believing that all that could ever be seen has already been seen and, therefore, named and known. Again, zones of unreality and extremely precarious nonpersonhood are the conditions upon which mechanisms of truth and knowledge production depend.

Gordon's paradigmatic remedy for reckoning with hauntings is directly relevant for the argument I have been making here for the work of *trans*. Although I remain cautious about this argument, it still begs to be asked: In what ways might we now begin to talk about a relation between identity-based practices of epistemological and methodological disciplinarity and the boundaries it imagines outside itself? To frame this differently: Can any formal, coherent field of scholarship with a self-delimited proper object, a methodology of approach, a body of experts and experts in training, canonical texts, and huge corporate publishers claim and aggressively defend a space of "outsider" status while building a home inside one site of public authority, credibility, authority and legitimacy? If there are complicated hauntings in our practices, then does not women's studies, defined as such, not produce the very thing it imagines to empirically discover?

If Gordon is right in her argument that more complex social relations and formations exist than what we can name, then with what presumptions and methods can we begin to name that which cannot be named? Gordon argues, and I would agree, that our first caution has to be one decidedly against the truth-producing practices of our *trans* resistant disciplinary imperatives, something I have been calling disciplinary and methodological fundamentalism (for instance, women's studies deals with "women"; sexuality studies with the body and its biological but socially organized impulses; postcolonial studies with coloniality; English with fiction; and the social sciences with truth). And so we rightly counter disciplinary fundamentalism with the language of interdisciplinarity as one way to calibrate against the disciplining imperatives of our various institutions.

As a sociologist, Gordon offers interdisciplinarity as partial remedy, although, as with most remedies, caveats and cautions abound. The mistake that too many *inter*disciplinary scholars might make is thinking that one way of managing this impossibility is to attempt to make already constituted disciplines wiggle over a bit to make room for each other and for our something "new." Citing poststructuralist literary theorist and semiotician Roland Barthes, Gordon offers *trans* (-disciplinarity): *transing* modalities that can begin to reckon with the ghosted subjectivities and spaces of women's studies, and also with the discursive and social machineries producing subjectivities as fixed, static, singular, and imagined as immobile in the first place: "'Interdisciplinary work . . . is not about confronting already constituted disciplines (none of which in fact is willing to let itself go). . . . [I]t's not enough to choose a "subject" (a theme) and gather around it two or three sciences. Interdisciplinarity consists in creating a new object that belongs to no one.'"[26] In constituting or reckoning with such a new slippery object, one then discerns rather than disciplines its meaning into existence by tracking its ghosts, not its so-called certainties.[27]

This kind of unmooring—"creating a new object that belongs to no one"—is precisely what is at stake in a *trans* practice and methodology unmoored from identity.[28] *Trans* (-disciplinary) modalities discern by attempting to see that which must be withheld for an identity-based discipline to accomplish its work. That is, one begins an epistemological and/or methodological practice not simply with "the vocabularies themselves" (in this case, for instance, with albeit necessary questions, such as *what is a woman?* Or *how is the category racialized?*) but instead proceeds with "the constellation of historical and institutional effects that make a vocabulary a social practice of producing knowledge."[29] Perhaps, to push this one step further, one no longer debates whether the master's tools will dismantle the master's house; one learns to reckon with the persistent and troubling *trans* ghosts in the house instead.

I want to posit that this is where we might begin to elaborate a complex, mobile, fluid, and deeply nuanced object of *trans*—not transgression through gender and/or national, cultural crossings necessarily but *trans* as a modality for reformulating institutionalized and bounded disciplinarities, ways of producing truths about the social overlay where history and subjectivity meet. In my monograph, *Sons of the Movement,* I suggest that "trans as a prefix functions most potently when signifying its own discursive histories . . . [a]s well as spaces of movement across, through and beyond national affiliations and identifications as well. . . . Transwork is the work of de-construction."[30] This argument has company in the work of Susan Stryker and others. As Stryker, Currah, and Moore put it, "it is most certainly time to critically trans- our world: to 'burst trans-open' as a framework with which to interrogate the ghosted, the disciplined, the bounded and the policed."[31]

Such ghostly circumlocutions of modernity's categories—temporality, scopophilic, sexed, national, and embodied, to name only a few—against their own imperatives of linearity and truth are *trans* reconfigurations worked perversely also against the feminist generational metaphors frequently passing as the "pesky" never-ending debate between "second-wave feminism," "third-wave feminism," and "post-feminism." Such wave-frameworks represent extremely problematic constructions of history, time, and temporality. *Transing* temporalities instead productively works against such seamless temporal narratives of progress as "second wave," "third wave," or "post"; at the same time, such circumventions are also part of what Leslie Heywood and Jennifer Drake identify as the lived messiness of consciousness in, at the very least, a post-second-wave-feminist moment: "This is a contradiction that feminism's third wave has to face: an often conscious knowledge of the ways in which we are compelled and constructed by the very things that undermine us."[32] Their caveat that such knowledge is "often conscious" is vital for discerning the imperative to undo history and its attendant subjectivities in the first place.

Hence, the absolute necessity for theorizing *trans* in the imperative feminist case and as perhaps a formulation coming, of course, too early but not yet late enough. In the first instance, such disproportionate relations of knowingness dictating the need to undo feminism with such an intervention are themselves the measure and sign of the very instabilities within identity categories that are self-evident as a politic, or not. In this case, such a working of *trans* (-gender) has come far too early, especially when erroneously hailed as the downfall or end of feminism. But in the second instance, coming not late enough, *trans* (-national) continues to be the central pillar around which critiques of second-wave feminism have been organized since, at the very least, *This Bridge Called My Back* began performatively and theoretically to codify the *trans* national theory and practice that have always constituted feminism, despite white feminism's occlusions of such *trans* entities as derivative, minoritized, or not constitutive of feminism *proper*. The latter (race panic) and former (gender panic) are telling of the limits of feminism as it has been institutionalized, something detailed in all the collections under discussion here and in a profoundly significant field of antiracist, postcolonial, decolonizing body of feminist work. However, remove the panic, and these *trans* hauntings of feminist theory and knowledge production have been significant and successful. What difference, if any, might it make to forge a strategic convergence between them? What kinds of labor (for white *trans* subjectivities) and/or utility (for troubling the hegemonic fundamentalist female nation) might be extracted from such *transings*?[33]

I am aware that the question I am attempting to ask here is one deeply embedded within its own histories. As *trans* entities slowly fight their way into institutionalized feminist spaces, and as tenure-stream faculty members, several interesting questions emerge: First, to what degree is white supremacy operational as part of the machinery enabling such mobilities? And second, to what extent might the categorical imperative of "female at birth" be operational as *trans* men seem to find a way into institutionalized feminist spaces that draw far fewer *trans* women? I offer these as tentative, speculative questions, but they are telling of the larger problematic I have been articulating here: To what extent has the institutionalized practice of women's studies enforced the disciplinary coherence of "woman" functioning as racialized but also as sex-binarized?

Again, these are not the same thing, nor am I attempting to superimpose them onto each other. But if these speculations are at all tenable, then thinking feminism through *trans* bears productive fruit and also, more importantly, potent interventions. What would it take to theorize the productive hauntings of women's studies by conceptually linking the *trans* of *trans* national and the *trans* of *trans* gender? I am aware of the pernicious and complex ways that white subjectivity can play ethnicity cards, sexuality cards, class cards, age cards, and transsexual cards as ways of declaring clemency from white supremacy and its privileging of white-skinned bodies. Still, as I read accounts of the field of women's studies, I see work that stops abruptly short of a elaborating a full *trans* disciplinarity, with some responding instead to what Wiegman calls the apocalyptic narratives of old feminism:

> That these apocalyptic narratives, as I call them, always find the specter of feminism's political end in the academy is one of the paradoxical features of "old feminism" today: it has come to define itself against the very project of institutional intervention it inaugurated and hence against those women who inherited from it a feminism animated by the questions, contradictions, and complicities of academic feminism's relationship to both politics and knowledge.[34]

My draw to such critiques, as well as to the potentialities of *transing* feminist knowledges and disciplinary boundaries, is certainly set into motion by my own embodied *trans* disciplinarity, which itself is in part a response to fundamentalisms.[35] Holding the possibility that the bodies of *trans* entities can fold these diametrically opposed categories through each other seems a sheer and very dangerous impossibility, one not unlike being stuck with one's arm trapped between a rock and hard place. In the best of all possible feminist worlds, the day-to-day language and practice of pronouns—in my case, *he*—offers a form of recognition that, in the best-case scenario, initiates a form of respect in its reiteration. At other times, the *he* is a response of violence to the conceptual terror induced by the presence of a body that is *he* and *she* at the same moment while being neither one nor the other enough to stop the incoherence from traumatizing foundations. Welcomed as the *he* might be, its hauntedness in the context of women's studies is easily likened to leaving a part of one's flesh unbearably trapped behind a boulder.

Here, Sharon Rosenberg's arguments in *Troubling Women's Studies* about the places of trauma are vital: Trauma persists, Rosenberg suggests, in the inescapability of its belated impact; as such, the task might be to contemplate rupture and to learn to live with the unbearable.[36] Calibrating the traumas of death and in particular of violence, of the Montreal massacre, Rosenberg's words signal a process of attempting to respond to what seems like an unbearable interruption of business as usual, the ruptures and tears to the every day that a *trans* body potentially induces. And, in return, such calibrations figure the ruptures that such an every day does back to the *trans* body; how do I bring to bear on my everyday world a productive haunting, something rendered in excess of the visible post-transition—that is, an almost-thirty-year butch-lesbian history that I do not disavow across transition but that is now housed invisibly in what is, for all intents and purposes, perceived exclusively as a man's body? What might it mean for a "women's" sociality—academic or otherwise—to attempt to come to terms with these *trans* ghosts in its house? And much like the stories of unioning that I begin this chapter with, how are such academic, social, intellectual, and affective labors to be shared across an institutional and identity-based discipline so haunted by impossibility in the first place?

This is ghostly laborious rupture, interruption of the body *as trans* body, as incoherent discontinuity for which few mechanisms of comprehension exist. But what is also true is my hope that modalities of *trans* disciplinarity might also want to calibrate ways of conceptualizing and, indeed, practicing *trans* whiteness with a similar cognizance of the need for rupture. What kinds of daily *transing* institutional practices are necessary to ensure that such productively traumatizing ruptures "succeed" or not as needed, and when? Cathy Caruth phrases this much more eloquently when she writes, "In trauma, the greatest confrontation with reality may also occur as an absolute numbing to it."[37] Caruth cites Dori Laub again in yet another attempt to write it—"trauma precludes its registration"—and as such we might well need to recognize that part of the resistance to *trans* lies perhaps in its tearing at the fabric of certainty around the referent of "women's studies." But the incessant repetition of panic over *trans* entities in the house of feminism tells another story. Is the turn to anxious foundationalism with its embeddedness in fundamentalisms one mechanism of disavowing the registration of traumas in the social and, by implication, epistemological and methodological?

As I am wondering about it here, this is indeed one of the most precarious tests of a *trans* entity—asking it to transition across the "homes" whiteness has carved into and *as* colonial spaces of nation and institutional spaces violently traumatizing. At the very least, might this reconceptualization of such *trans* whiteness itself as haunted address a crisis of coherence in practice? Or will "women's studies" itself develop further symptomologies of those hauntings in new ways? The *how* of this to me has already been signaled by Rosenberg's conclusion that perhaps what is necessary is a "marker in which to become lost rather than a category of knowledge presumed secure."[38] Is the sometimes-fundamentalist labor of making "women" a home *found,* one that refuses to be productively lost and, in so refusing, takes up a place within the very modernity that has produced it? Are such ironic and disavowed losses fundamentalist products of an anxious and melancholic self-reflexivity securing a field around its insecurities or relocations of a neoliberal discipline correcting itself? Presuming yes to both, might it be time, again, to declare the project permanently haunted?

4

A. FINN ENKE

The Education of Little Cis

Cisgender and the Discipline of Opposing Bodies

I am trying to assess campus climates for the transgender community. . . . Issues of interest are transphobia, hostility, general knowledge and understanding, attitudes of the queer community and cisgendered people, etc.
—Dana Leland Defosse, 1994

I just kept running into the problem of what to call non-trans people in various discussions, and one day it just hit me: non-trans equals cis. Therefore, cisgendered.
—Carl Buijs, 1996

In other words, it's the opposite of transgender. . . . So why are y'all tripping, cisgender people? Cisgender isn't an insult.
—Monica Roberts, *TransGriot*, 2009

Things change when a neologism moves from a social movement context to a classroom context. On one hand, our ability to keep classrooms relevant depends on this movement, this perspectival and practical exchange between academic and activist worlds. And theorizations that take place in the classroom can provide sustaining energy to social concerns. On the other hand, meanings do change when words cross from one medium to another. Academic contexts—perhaps a bit slow on the uptake—can simplify, ossify, and discipline otherwise queer terminologies while authorizing, legitimating, and institutionalizing their use.

The neologism "cisgender" has long been associated with a kind of stasis, based on the Latin root "cis-," which prefixes things that stay put or do not change property. Biologist Dana Leland Defosse is generally credited as the first to put the term "cisgender" into public circulation in 1994, using it in a Web-based call for research on campus climate and transgender subjectivities. At that time in Minneapolis, Defosse and I talked a lot about "trans-" as a prefix, and Defosse explained why cis- might serve as a linguistic complement to trans-. Within molecular biology, cis- is used as a prefix (as in cis-acting) to describe something that acts from the same molecule (intramolecular) in contrast to trans-acting things that act from different molecules (intermolecular); in organic chemistry, cis- refers to substituents or groups that are oriented in the same direction, in contrast to trans-, wherein the substituents are oriented in opposing directions; also implied in cis- are things that do not change state as they contact certain media. Defosse—followed by others—saw the potential of cisgender to describe the condition of staying with birth-assigned sex, or congruence between birth-assigned sex and gender identity. Now, in common usage, cisgender implies staying *within* certain gender parameters (however they may be defined) rather than *crossing* (or trans-ing) those parameters.

But cisgender does not stay put. It is even now traversing contexts, and—like genders and many other substituents—it is changing in the crossing. Cisgender did not hit the ground running upon its introduction in 1994, and it is still only sparsely used in trans* communities across the country.[1] Nevertheless, the word is seeing new life on college campuses, particularly within student orgs and classrooms that critically interrogate the categories of gender. Cisgender's migrations can tell us a great deal about the power of language to transform gender politics and queer alliances in and out of the classroom, for better or worse. Specifically, the term appears to encourage investments in a gender stability that undermines feminist, trans*, queer, and related movements.

Feminist, queer, and trans studies all pull hard on the seams of conventional sex/gender nomenclatures. Between the mid-1990s and around 2008, my undergraduate courses (at state universities in the United States) were frustrated by the problem that "women" and "men" acted as normativizing categories in contrast to "trans women" and "trans men": Once we have "transgender," the unmarked quality of "woman" and "man" reinforces the highly problematic conviction that most women and men (those whose female or male medicojuridical designation and social status have been consistent over a lifetime) are *naturally* women and men. I offered the terms cisgender and cissexual as conceptual tools, but these had too much of a subcultural "insider" feel to be democratically adopted in the classroom at that time.

I was surprised, then, around 2008, when an increasing number of queer-savvy students began to casually toss "cis" (as a noun or adjective as well as a prefix) into their classroom comments. They used such phrases as "she's cis," or, "the cis man in the film said . . ." or, "as a cis woman, I. . . ." Required to explain for the benefit of the class, they typically defined "cis" along these lines: "Cis is short for cisgender, which is non-trans." A more elaborate explanation often included, "You are cisgender if your gender identity matches your sex, the sex you were assigned at birth."[2] Subsequent conversations occasionally problematized such definitions but rarely led to doubt about the *use* of the word. On the contrary, even critical conversations about cisgender had the effect of educating students who had not known the word in how to become disciplined users.

What role is cis playing here, and how can we understand its market value in this context? This deserves some explanation, not least because the term does have its share of detractors. In 2009, *TransGriot* blogger Monica Roberts suggested that it is people who are not transgender who object to the word; in her analysis, "cisgender people" feel insulted by the word "cisgender" because transgender (i.e., stigmatized minority) people dare to name and to *other* them.[3] It is also clear that many people object to being interpellated as cis because cis is generally conflated with normativity, and they do not think of themselves that way. More recently, trans* people have become the most vocal critics of cisgender.[4] It is all the more pressing, then, to analyze the campus and classroom context, because it reveals troubling contradictions behind the adoption of cis.

Although trans activism initiated discourses of cis, the word's broader uptake may be an effect not of trans activism in itself but rather a particular expression of ally desire. In the classroom, people bring cisgender into being as a performative ally-identity, explicitly reserving the term "trans" for others. In its association with normativity, cis turns out also to be a racialized status. White students who identify themselves as trans *allies* (some of whom may also identify themselves as queer and/or gender-queer) are the most likely to refer to *themselves* with that term through such phrases as "as a cis woman I. . . ." The use of cis in the classroom allows us to see these other aspects of its discursive power, including its paradoxical appeal.

Queer, trans, and feminist theory have not talked about cisgender, but they do provide ample basis for skepticism about its ontological nature. Riki Wilchins once wrote about trans, "Trans-identity is not a natural fact. Rather, it is the political category we are forced to occupy when we do certain things with our bodies."[5] I am sure that the very same is true of the categories "woman" and "man," although the manipulations required to produce them are naturalized and mystified. Without overlooking the vast social inequities meted out by transphobia, we do know from Simone de Beauvoir to Monique Wittig to Judith Butler to Riki Wilchins that "woman" and "man" are not natural, that they are coercive and compulsory, and that their power is built into institutions that structure what we do with our bodies, among other things. Cisgender must fall under similar theorization.

Just what kind of category is cisgender? What manipulations are required of the body and psyche of the so-called cisgender person? Exactly which signifiers of gender cannot be "crossed"—and exactly which borders between "male" and "female" cannot be "crossed over"—for one to perform cisgender? If cis is equated—and it usually is—with gender normativity, in what ways does its achievement depend on class status, ability, whiteness, and the maintenance of racist and nationalist hierarchies? Given the tendency of all things to change across time and place, can anyone be cis- anything? And, most pointedly, *what happens to trans and everything else* through the embrace of cis and the positing of cis and trans in binary relation to each other?

In this article, I first elucidate the discursive uptake of cis, emphasizing its use within social-movement contexts and the queer-studies classroom.[6] I offer a critique through the lens of trans, queer, disability, and feminist—what I call transfeminist—theory and politics. The performative uptake of cis should invite questions about its cultural value not just to classrooms but to the multidiscipline of gender and women's studies as a whole.[7] Cisgender may hold appeal for maintaining gender and women's studies as an arena that produces and disciplines "women" and "men" as self-evident categories, contrary to gender and women's studies' more radical potentials. How troubling: Just when queer and trans theory remind us that gender and sex are made and have no *a priori* stability ("one is not born a woman"), cisgender arrives to affirm not only that it is possible for one to *stay* "a woman" but also that one *is* "born a woman" after all.

The Genealogy of Cis

The history of cisgender begins with transgender activism. Transgender and transsexual activism has a long history in North America, but in the early 1990s, a transgender liberation movement by that name came into its own with a groundswell of concerted action that had momentum and staying power. At that time, "transgender" was most broadly conceived to encompass "the whole spectrum" of gender non-normative practices, communities, and identities.[8] The transgender liberation movement was to recognize and to address the connections among many different forms of gender-based oppressions and the economic, nationalist, and racist structures that buttress those oppressions; simultaneously, it would forge alliance among *all* the diverse gender-variant communities and identities that arise out of such oppressions.[9] Transgender signaled dissident politics and a positive embrace of new possibilities. As Currah, Green, and Stryker put it, transgender

> was meant to convey the sense that one could live non-pathologically in a social gender not typically associated with one's biological sex, as well as the sense that a single individual should be free to combine elements of different gender styles and presentations, or different sex/gender combinations. . . . [I]t represented a resistance to medicalization, to pathologization, and to the many mechanisms whereby the administrative state and its associated medico-juridical-psychiatric institutions sought to contain and delimit the socially disruptive potentials of sex/gender non-normativity.[10]

Transgender also emerged as a politicized identity category, as activists sought to collectively instantiate social viability for gender variant persons. Transgender furthermore described individuals by what they *do*, as in Susan Stryker's articulation of transgender as "people who move away from the gender they were assigned at birth, people who cross over (trans-) the boundaries constructed by their culture to define and contain that gender."[11]

The term "cisgender" arose in the context of this groundswell, articulated most often by people who visibly crossed normative gender signifiers and/or experienced significant cross-gender identification. This naming made visceral sense, as the world indeed seems divided between trans and non-trans epistemologies. Within trans activist circles, non-normative gender variability is normalized: The array of things we do with our bodies, pronouns, names, and histories is a necessary (in measures both joyful and coerced) aspect of being human in a gendered society. In the 1990s, collectively attempting to clear a wider path while faced with the inflexibilities of most social institutions confirmed that "the public" was (and still is) an explicitly and often violently trans-exclusive and disenfranchising space. People who reject medico-juridical determinations of sex at birth or who in any other way occupy a less legibly male or female sex/gender comportment can attempt to buy access to social arenas: We can supply specific narratives to garner specific diagnoses to attempt to win a legal status that will allow the most privileged among us access to sex-segregated spaces, jobs, housing, and health care.[12] We need the exact right combination of *visible* "difference," passability, *and* nonvisibility (a combination assisted by whiteness, abledness, legal citizenship, employment, and noncriminal status) to hope to be granted authenticity, transparency, and belonging within a chosen gender.[13]

The distinction between living a life in congruence with static medico-juridical determinations of one's sex/gender and living a life in defiance of that congruence is a highly consequential one, because our social institutions are structured to uphold and to privilege the former. It is hard to overstate how dramatically sex/gender congruence, legibility, and consistency within a binary gender system buy a privileged pass to social existence, particularly when accompanied by the appearance of normative race, class, ability, and nationality. The term "cisgender" was to name that privileged pass.

As the name of normative privilege, cisgender characterized the transphobic institutions and the everyday practices of a stunningly trans-ignorant and willfully normative public. Simultaneously, it purported to challenge the naturalization of "woman" and "man" by making visible their rootedness in the interested achievement of social hierarchies, thereby also exposing the nonnatural privileges and exclusions gained by successfully performing them. The word "cisgender" spread as a strategy of social critique that resonated with feminism, critical race theory, whiteness studies, and dis/ability rights, among other arenas of radical politics. This theoretical and political intervention allowed cisgender to move outside as well as within trans communities. As Emi Koyama, an activist author who works for intersex, trans, disability, race, and class justice, put it in 2002:

> I learned the words "cissexual," "cissexist," and "cisgender," from trans activists who wanted to turn the table and define the words that describe non-transsexuals and non-transgenders rather than always being defined and described by them. By using the term "cissexual" and "cisgender," they de-centralize the dominant group, exposing it as merely one pos-

sible alternative rather than the "norm" against which trans people are defined. I don't expect the word to come into common usage anytime soon, but I felt it was an interesting concept—a feminist one, in fact—which is why I am using it.[14]

In 2002, Koyama did not expect the "common" adoption of cisgender "any time soon." But by signing the statement, "In Cisterhood," Koyama invited broader, allied use of the terms "cisgender" and "cissexual."

Related to all the previous factors, cisgender additionally emerged as a critique of the way that queer and LGBT organizations often define "queer" and "LGBT" by dissident sexual desires and *not* also by gender variance. The pointed use of the acronym "LGB *not* T" critically makes explicit the actual exclusions of purportedly "LGBT" arenas: Although LG(B) and queer groups may fetishize gender fluidity and non-normativity while tokenizing transgender people, very few embrace trans politics as an integral and essential priority.[15] In this context, cisgender became a way of distinguishing queers who do not have trans histories, identities, and perspectives from trans people who do. Koyama thus joined a small but growing movement of people who would make cisgender a political act that could be spoken by queer sympaticos of all kinds.

Cisgender (or cis) became a more common enculturated word and identity category, particularly among some activist communities that interface with academics.[16] Neoliberal rights discourses that feed on identity politics further promoted the sense that people are *either* transgender *or* cisgender; cisgender, that is, did not simply name privilege but could be used to describe individuals.

Widely accessible texts, such as Julia Serano's *Whipping Girl: A Transsexual Woman on Sexism and the Scapegoating of Femininity* (2007), also helped authorize cis identifications. Foremost a treatise on transsexual politics and the misogyny that undergirds transphobia, *Whipping Girl* is the first book to elaborate cisgender and cissexual privilege. Serano defines cissexual as "people who are not transsexual and who have only ever experienced their physical and subconscious sexes as being aligned"; cisgender more simply refers to "people who are not transgender."[17] If not lost, the distinction Serano implicitly draws between cisgender and cissexual allows nuance: People can be cissexual but not necessarily cisgender. One could feel congruence with one's assigned body sex and thus consider one's self cissexual but not identify with the gender that is typically associated with that sex and thus not be cisgender. Reading between the lines, gender-queer and transgender people who do not strongly identify with either part of the gender binary (maleness *or* femaleness) might not experience trans*sex*-ness or cis*gender*-ness, as *both* cisgender and transsexual suggest primary identification with one sex/gender in a binary system (male or female). In theory, this suggests variability within cis-ness, just as there is variation within trans-ness.[18]

Serano's critique of cissexual privilege, much like critiques of race privilege, ableism, and heteronormativity, successfully brings attention to the ways that people construct normative hierarchies through everyday behaviors. Her initial definition of cissexual privilege as "the double standard that promotes the idea that transsexual genders are distinct from, and less legitimate than, cissexual genders" names one fundamental root of the transphobia that undergirds most social institutions. Cissexual privilege is instantiated in part through the activity of "reading" and assigning male or female sex/gender to others. All people make assumptions about other's sex/gender, "whether we are cissexual or transsexual, straight as an arrow, or queer as a three-dollar bill."[19] But one privilege of cissexuality is that it performs as the arbiter of real, true, or natural gender. Cissexuality by definition is rarely required to but can always legally and socially prove itself; as such, it serves to judge the realness or legitimacy of all people's sex/gender. Cissexual privilege is authorized in part through connected practices: (a) assuming everyone is cissexual (erasure of trans existence), (b) demanding that trans men and women come out as trans rather than simply as men and women, and, simultaneously, (c) requiring that transsexual men and women "pass" or "be believable to others as" the sex/gender they "claim to be" to make their trans-sex more palatable to people who feel that birth-assigned sex/gender is the only legitimate (true) sex/gender.[20] Serano's discussion effectively invites readers to see how the presumption that sex/gender is transparent naturalizes binary gender construction and pathologizes transgender existences; moreover, sexism and misogyny particularly pathologize all people on a feminine spectrum.

This is the kind of "eye-opening" that many students in a gender or sexuality course find satisfying: to see and to name systemic oppressions. In my experience, however, non-trans students assume the book is about someone else (transsexuals) who face an entirely foreign set of oppressions, and therefore it cannot also be about the very same sexism, misogyny, and binary gender system that they learn to analyze in Women's Studies 101. Neither do readers tend to see themselves in the generalizations about how cissexuals think and feel. But some—in effort to *not be* the kind of transphobic "cissexual people" critiqued in the book—may take up the ally mantle and "own" their privilege as "cis" people.

The uptake of cis among students in university contexts is also inspired by its use in community educational spaces such as Camp Trans, in part because such spaces confirm the word's subcultural authenticity. Camp Trans is a weeklong protest staged annually down the road from the Michigan Womyn's Music Festival (MWMF).[21] As a physical site comprising workshops, speeches, reports, performances, community-building activities, and direct actions, and as a generator of its own and related Web sites, blogs, and YouTube posts, its influence extends far beyond its temporal and geographic location.

Among the many productive outcomes of Camp Trans is that it began with insistence on self-identification, which was and is a fundamental tenet of trans activism; people's gender identity must be respected, regardless of how they may appear.[22] Camp Trans also generated some of the earliest articulations of the classism and racism embedded in the use of surgical status as a criterion for passable gender status. Emphasis on people's surgical status has frequently accompanied considerations of exclusion/inclusion policies in "women-only" community spaces; as the most well-known women-only space, MWMF occasioned some of the first critiques of the relationship among racism, classism, and transphobic definitions of women.[23]

Over the last decade, the term "cis" has gained platform at Camp Trans. The use of cisgender in this context, acting as it does in binary opposition to trans*, seems to cause an unfortunate amnesia of prior lessons about the relationship between binary gender and race and class hierarchies. The term "cis" has not generally been subject to race, ability, and class analysis; instead, its use reinforces gender as a self-evident, autonomous category.

As do many trans* spaces, Camp Trans makes explicit its intended constituency. Before elaborating the "Inclusion" and "Exclusion" policies, the Camp Trans Web site offers a "note on wording":

> Used on this page, please consider "trans" to be the broadest possible usage of the word, commonly written as "trans*" to include people who self-identify as trans, transgender, transsexual, transcending the gender binary, transvestite, and gender queer. . . . Similarly, as used here, "cis" is to be taken with the broadest possible definition, to include anyone not identifying under the umbrella usage of "trans."[24]

The suggestive list following trans* is meant to be elaborated into "the broadest possible" range of trans identities. Cis is identically broad, perhaps ironically, as seemingly none of the above.

The Inclusion/Exclusion policy disciplines by positing cis people as the sole agents of cisgender privilege. According to the Inclusion policy ("who is camp for?"), "Camp is secondarily a place where trans and genderqueer people are centralized. This does not mean that cis people are not allowed at Camp at all, but it does mean that Camp is not set up to play to the privilege cis people experience."[25] The Exclusion policy ("who shouldn't come to camp?") states, "A cis person who wants to learn about trans and genderqueer people. A cis person who does not understand concepts of gender privilege and oppression. Please note that this applies to cis partners of trans people coming to Camp as well."[26] These statements have been important to the preservation of Camp Trans as a space for trans organizing. Furthermore, such guidelines instruct insiders and outsiders in basic respect for Camp Trans as a trans-centric space that gains its vulnerable efficacy from its education and outreach mission, its proximity to MWMF, and its high profile to people seeking "real-life" queer classrooms.

Such statements contribute to the appeal of cis as an ally-identity in college classrooms: They offer a certain cultural capital to those who are close enough to trans contexts not only to imbibe vocabularies but also to be able and willing to address gender privilege and oppression outside trans-literate contexts. But we must see that the compulsion to name cis (as that which is not trans) demonstrates that the difference between trans and non-trans mobilities is far more concrete than the rather elastic distance between male and female.

In an effort to restore nuance, Defosse generously reentered the fray in 2006: "As a biologist, I simply used the prefix cis as the complement to that of trans. In the simplest interpretation, cis means on the same side and trans means across. *Cis and trans are not just where something is, however; they extend to the realms of their respective effects.*"[27] Here, rather than being fixed in identities, cis and trans describe locations and effects. This is a critical point. Trans studies scholars have noted the extent to which trans invokes a person's (or body's) orientation in space and time.[28] Cis theoretically must also be *effected through* time and space, despite the presumption of stasis. Furthermore, cisgender's value from a social-movement perspective comes from the recognition and denaturalization of its powerful *effects*.

Notwithstanding claims that cis is simply "the opposite of transgender" in some neutral way, its effects are inextricably associated with transphobia. Monica Roberts's claim in *TransGriot* that calling people cisgender "is not an insult" thus rings rather untrue; it seems that the best cis can hope for is ally status. Cautionary reminders about the costs of identity politics have held little sway, as cis becomes a subject position in the performance of allyship. In the process, cis and trans both shrink, in exactly the way living things do when they desiccate and ossify.

Enter the Unmarked Cis-Ally

From its social-movement origins, cisgender and simply cis wound their way into gender and women's studies hallways, where they found audiences eager to understand and to confess their places in a world of hierarchies, violences, and privileges. Here, further organizing comes in the concept of ally and the practice of allyship education that is increasingly popular on college campuses and elsewhere. Related to antiracist education, allyship education speaks to the desire of some members of "majority communities" (e.g., white, heterosexual) to solve rather than to participate in the oppression, stigmatization, and marginalization of "minority communities" (e.g., people of color, gays, lesbians). Inherent to the concept of allyship is acknowledgment of the relative privilege of being seen as part of majority communities and also of the relationship between that privilege and the perpetuation or redress of injustice. Ally is a paradoxical identity, however, claiming simultaneous proximity to and distance from those of whom one becomes an ally. This is perhaps nowhere more obvious than when it resides in the embrace of trans ally.[29]

Increasingly popular trans-ally trainings depart from antiracist and antioppression education in several respects.[30] As Vik DeMarco, Christoph Hanssmann, and others have rightly observed, although white antiracist and antioppressive education emphasizes learning about and taking responsibility for one's racism and racial privilege, trans-ally trainings tend to take the form of "Trans 101," in which participants learn (usually in the space of an hour or two) about the plight of the mysterious others we call transgendered and are virtually never asked to consider their own transphobia and passing privilege.[31] Defining, tokenizing, and fetishizing transgender individuals according to their greater oppression, such education suggests absolute and *discernable* difference between trans and "everyone else," the presumptive majority. Trans ally confirms not-trans identity by investing in a definition of trans as *someone else,* a more oppressed other. In just the way that "LGBT ally" effectively marks one as straight, "trans ally" is a discursive practice that resecures some portion of normativity.

With remarkable efficiency, the cisgender trans ally campaigns for the exceptional ontological stability of non-trans gender in several ways. It reinforces the assertion that we can accurately read and assign gender identity, not least by presuming that everyone is cis unless they come out as trans. Regardless of the gender identity of the observer, this has the paradoxical consequence of simultaneously invoking and erasing trans presence. For example, to signal alliance with trans people as well as to interrupt what is otherwise a routine lack of awareness of trans existence, we might completely replace "man" and "woman" with "cis-man" and "cis-woman." To wit, "the cis-man in the film said . . . ," "as a cis-woman, this author thinks . . . ," and so forth. This marks the speaker as trans-literate but removes trans presence and variable gender from view. The only way to restore this presence is for trans and gender queer people to come out as such, thereby reauthorizing the stability of cis.

The concept of cisgender *privilege* provides a necessary critique of structural hierarchies built around binary sex/gender, and it has the potential to intervene in the "Trans 101" model of allyship. However, such phrases as "as a gender-queer cis-woman I . . ." or "the cis-man in the film said . . ." don't so much acknowledge as reinforce this privilege by enacting a distinction between cis and trans. Such speech invokes trans by its absence; and this absence is predicated on a definition of trans as a rare but visible embodiment of "cross-sex" identification, or as the most institutionally recognized form of sex-crossing. When cis is taken up as an admission of privileged identity, it is cis- privilege itself that reifies trans as most oppressed—so oppressed, in fact, that it cannot speak out of character.

And finally, one of the most repercussive limitations of the discursive production of cisgender is the lack of attention to the *multiple* hierarchies on which cis status depends. Although trans studies increasingly acknowledge the extent to which sex/gender is constituted through class hierarchies, racializations, nationalisms, ableisms, and so forth,[32] cisgender has thus far remained impervious to theorizations of the multiple dimensions of dominance inherent to its privilege. Cisgender privileges are surely most commonly conferred and achieved when the appearance of normative race, class, and ability are also achieved, along with a host of other normative mobilities. Scholars have shown that gender normativity is all but dependent on and reserved for whiteness, legal citizenship, and normative ability. David Valentine, Dean Spade, and others have also shown that the institutionalization of the term "transgender" inheres a history of race and class hierarchies and violences.[33] Cisgender then necessarily plays out as a normatively racialized ally status confirming its privilege through association with whiteness, legality, and ability. Can this be part of its appeal, even as people use the term in an attempt to critique systemic hierarchy?

The coincidence of trans erasure and cis's enactment of whiteness is nowhere more apparent than in classroom discussions that might otherwise focus on racialization and ethnic or racial identities. I offer here an illustrative example, only one of many that students and faculty from several universities in the United States have shared with me as friends, colleagues in gender studies, or students seeking support.[34] A mid-level course on women and literature included a Crow narrative attesting to non-binary gender systems. In this context, the professor saw fit to talk about Native American "transvestites" and "trannies." A trans-identified student in the class later initiated an e-mail exchange with the professor to express discomfort, to explain why those terms are considered stigmatizing, and to request that the professor use more respectful terms, such as "two spirit" (if appropriate) or, more generically, "trans person." The professor responded appreciatively, apologized for the offense, admitted she had not thought about the implications of using words she had heard trans people use, and offered to bring it up in a subsequent class. The student then requested that the professor also actively teach about being respectful of subcultural or "reclaimed" terms, such as "tranny." Displeased with the professor's response, the student sent me the entire e-mail exchange with an explanatory note:

> i also wrote a little bit about reclaimed words. i said that if she was using these words in front of a class of people who don't know much about gender studies (as she said), then they wouldn't know what were appropriate words to use for trans people, and that it wouldn't be ok for cis people to be using those words. she sent me a response email and seemed kind of mad at me because she thought i was saying that she was cis. she said she didn't identify as cis because it really upset her when she felt expected to wear really girly clothes. she kept reiterating how much of a trans ally she is.

In this exchange, the cultural complexity of gender in general, as well as the diverse gender ideologies within various indigenous nations, completely fell to the wayside.[35] In its place, cis took center stage and did so as an essential, transphobic, and racially unmarked subject. The student, feeling marginalized and exposed as the only person willing to speak as a trans person, could see no common ground in the professor's own potentially complex history with gender and with race. The professor, feeling wrongly associated with cis, objected to the assumption and asserted her trans ally intentions.

The exchange constituted "cis" and "trans ally" as mutually exclusive. This is not as paradoxical as it first sounds. Trans* has historically played a "dissident" figure as part of an identity-politics strategy that pushes against normative policing systems and hierarchies. In opposition, "cis," whether it is taken up as a self-referential identity *or* rejected as an interpellation of one's self, can never do the same. But far more dangerously, cis and trans ally—like whiteness—are suddenly freed to function independently of ethnic literature, other cultural processes, and racializations. In turn, the trans ally can only be so as a normative, racially unmarked subject, covering the tracks of the racism and transphobia on which its own authority depends.

Identity politics thus authorized, how do we learn to recognize our own participation in transphobia, misogyny, and sexism no matter what sex/gender identities we may inhabit? And how do we challenge the structures that make identity politics seem attractive and even necessary for survival in a neoliberal and still transphobic world?[36]

Will the Real Cis Please Stand Up?

How do we determine the distance between cis and trans, and at what point in time should this distance be measured? As someone who peed standing up as a child, who spent more than twenty years terrified that someone would discover that I was "really" male, and who passes almost consistently as a woman, I would hate to rely on the American Psychiatric Association's *Diagnostic and Statistical Manual of Mental Disorders* (*DSM*) to answer that question. For most of my lifetime, the *DSM* has used "rejection of urination in a sitting position" or "desire to urinate from a standing position" as one criterion toward the diagnosis of Childhood Gender Identity Disorder, but only when it occurs in children with vulvas; neither the desire nor the behavior are diagnostic when they occur in children with penises, because such children presumably *naturally* urinate standing up.[37]

In the summer of 2010, out of curiosity, I let my light beard grow in, and I was not sorry to find that it has thinned over the years. Writing now, I pause, because I know that all parts of that statement can signify a lot of different things depending on one's political persuasions, what one thinks of the relationship between beards and genders, and, more specifically, what is assumed about my body and my history. But as a historian, I want to say that history making is a highly suspect business. Particularly when it comes to identity confirmation, narratives do their work by selectively collapsing time and place into the present through the use of undisrupted signifiers.[38] What must stay the same and what must change to determine the distance between cis and trans? Or, is it not the fact of changing but rather the *method* by which one changes that distinguishes cis from trans?

As an adolescent, I secretly began to interfere with my body's endogenous hormonal balance to inhibit certain (gender-laden) body changes and to encourage others—and I did so at some cost to my health. After five years, others ferreted this out, and I submitted (under duress but not force) to medical authority's technique of using exogenous hormones to "restore" a more stereotypical sex/gender endogenous hormonal balance (this, too, at some cost to my health). In my late twenties, I dispensed with the conventional medical program. I became a lesbian, and, for the first time in my life, I lost most of the fear that someone would discover that I was "really" male and thereby forever deny me whatever moments of self-determination I had won. Alongside the joys of those liberations, I wince whenever I am called "ma'am" or "sir" (which is nearly constant, because in most places, gendering others is considered polite rather than violent).

Or perhaps the cis/trans distinction depends most on place and privilege.

During my grade school years in Michigan, I imagined myself becoming a monk to live and work in a monastery that I loved to visit. In addition to the sublime silence, I felt my gender "matched" that of the community, and it was one of few places I could imagine being a viable adult self. Forty years later in Wisconsin, I work as a tenured professor. Here, I wear a braid and men's clothes, and I pass as locally legible: The combination of locale, the deference accorded to my race and class status, my job security, and a workplace culture formed by a prior generation of feminists all contribute to the common interpretation of my appearance as a white, middle-class, lesbian-woman academic, which, after all, is a category of person that earlier won a place in this institution. Such interpretation projects onto me a history that erases uncertainty and secures my legitimacy as "woman" rather than as trans-woman, trans-man, cross-dressed trans-woman, or "unknown." My birth certificate and passport match this interpretation; I pass security checks and cross borders—uneasily and often under scrutiny, but the law is on my side. Crossing the threshold to the women's room still gives me the willies; I don every item of privilege, entitlement, and history available to me every time I enter.

I offer these selective disclosures with skepticism, not about the veracity of the points but about the ends they might serve. I could be coming out as something or other. I could be asserting my right to belong in some space built around politicized identity categories. I could be anticipating interrogation—who am I, after all, to be writing on this topic? I do not seem to be claiming my own transparency (relying on the privileges available to me, I can afford to obscure signifiers), but might I want self-representation?[39] It would be easy to narrate a true history of gender consistency across my lifetime, and it would be equally easy to narrate a true history in which my expressed and/or perceived gender has changed dramatically across time and place. Critically, I could show how being read as male or female at various times and places was not about gender alone; in fact, it was at least as much my race and class privilege, my perceived age, and my perceived mobility and ability that have served as the functional cues leading to people's interpretations of my sex/gender. What narrative signifiers are most important to maintaining a cis/trans distinction?

In the summer of 2010, my department of Gender and Women's Studies moved from one building where we had an almost wheelchair-accessible, single-occupancy restroom to a renovated building with wheelchair-accessible, multi-stalled restrooms that have mutually exclusive signs on the doors. I go there, braided and bearded, and am furious to discover the options. Workplace bathrooms acknowledge that workers are biological beings; the signs, on the other hand, suggest that some bodies—most pressingly in this moment, mine—somehow need not be biological. The signs provide social messages, too, telling other people that they should defend this territory that is clearly marked as *theirs*. But I also know that here, due to my relatively high status in the university's hierarchies, I can walk through *either* door, and I will not be physically or verbally assaulted. I enter the one that says "women" and, at a sink that is too high and set too far back to use from a wheelchair, I splash my face with cold water. I am not using a wheelchair. And I am white, and I am a professor, and, actually, no one is looking. I kick the door as hard as I can on my way out. Do I make the signs impossible, or do they make me impossible?

Despite the fact that the majority of transsexuals will have no transition-related surgeries in their lifetimes (due to lack of access or desire), medico-juridical transition continues to be a defining feature in the constitution of trans as a category, and never more so than when trans is elicited by cis. By announcing its own sex/gender consistency, cis makes the *across* (n.) that trans *crosses over* refer to the "line" between "male" and "female," as though we agree upon what and where that line may be as well as on what constitutes male and female.[40] Doing so effectively asserts the naturalness of medico-juridical determinations of and control over trans existence.[41] At the same time, cis further distances from trans by establishing its own relative normativity.

As trans-studies scholars emphasize, trans theoretically inheres movement and change, or space and time. But when we posit cis in binary opposition to trans, cis and trans *both* must erase their temporality and location. At precisely what point in time do trans-ness and cis-ness depart from each other? I think a lot about Dr. Marci Bowers, a surgeon and gynecologist who offers sex reassignment surgery (SRS—also known as gender confirmation surgery) and one of the more famous women with a transsexual history. Practicing in Trinidad, Colorado, she is willing to use her status to create publicized platforms for education around transgender issues. Dr. Bowers seems to enjoy her notoriety as SRS's "transsexual rockstar."[42] But she tells me to "get the *nomenclature* right": She does not think of herself as a transsexual or a transsexual woman; "that's all in the past; I am a woman."[43] While not rejecting transsexuality, Bowers marshals several entitlements to successfully reject the *abjection* that neoliberal discourses of oppression cast upon transsexuals. This strategy is available to few people, and it may leave most others (poor and unemployed people, people for whom surgeries are not available, people of color, and so forth) disenfranchised.[44] But if we take Bowers at her word—and I think we must—her perspective suggests that at an *earlier* time, perhaps but not necessarily including when she was living as a boy and later as a man, Bowers was a transsexual woman. Then—also "in the past"—she transitioned: She became a woman and *now* is a woman. One might say she is a cisgender, cissexual woman. This suggestion flies in the face of most assumptions that attend the cis/trans binary, not least of which is that a transsexual history makes one forever trans and precludes cissexuality at *all* points in time.[45] Cis's peculiar ontology erases location and effects through time and space: To preserve the stasis of cis as non-trans, trans must never have been or become cis but instead be consistently trans across all time and in all spaces.

Bumping into Walls

Trans studies and disability studies together provide compelling insight about movement and change. Movement is integral to trans studies, but disability studies may do a better job of recognizing that bodies, abilities, and core identities change. For example, disability studies will not reify ability as a static *condition*: cis-abled?! Impossible. Although people with disabilities constitute 20 percent of the population, only 15 percent of people with disabilities (roughly 3 percent of the whole population) were born with disabilities; the other 97 percent of the population is likely to enter the status of disabled at various times and places even though they may presently feel securely abled. Moreover, built environments reflect social normativities and biases, and thus, by design, they also constitute dis/ability. Moving from one context to another, an individual may be abled then disabled then abled again. Disability and ability, along with identity and subjectivity, are situational, temporal, spatial, and culturally constructed; barriers are in the same measure social, physical, and psychological—which is to say, always political.[46] Bringing transgender studies and disability studies together, we can see that physical movement and habits elicit ableist judgments and social gendering simultaneously.[47]

Trans, queer, and disability movements suggest that we should not assume anything about a person's gender identity, sex, desires, abilities, personal history, *or* future. Trans-ness, for example, more often than not is nonvisible to outside observers regardless of how queer-savvy those observers may be. But positing the existence of the cis-normative subject seems to encourage the assumption that the people around us—our peers, coworkers, and students as well as "the man in the film"—are cis unless they provide visible and narrative proof of trans-ness.[48] Alternatively, knowing that trans-ness is among us regardless of whether it shows itself as such makes it impossible to assume that anyone here is non-trans.

Social spaces that depend on identity categories—as most do—are constituted through the constant surveillance and policing of those within. The presence of "difference" from the operative identity category is simultaneously invoked and erased: Social spaces suggest that all people within them *pass* as *really being* members of the social category that the space thereby helps produce.[49] Thus, normative social spaces are structured around the presumed absence of disabled, queer, trans, and other marginalized subjects, which is to say that such spaces inscribe exclusion.[50] Disability and trans theories insist that we challenge this cultural logic, a logic that believes that "the physical body is the site of identic intelligibility."[51] How can we interrupt the erasures enacted by normativity? The strategy of identity politics believes that if we first *get in* (accept the pass granted by the presumed absence of queer, trans, and/or disabled subjects), we can then perform or make visible our own non-normativity by *coming out* as disabled, and/or queer, and/or trans. However, such solutions underwrite visibility politics and attendant discriminatory practices as well as hierarchies between those who can pass and those who never will.[52]

Critiquing visibility politics, disability and queer studies scholar Ellen Samuels has argued that dominant social institutions *and* resistant social movements require "difference" to be made visible, and most especially visible *on the body*. This "focus on specularity and visible difference" fuels a culture of surveillance and policing. Drawing on Michel Foucault's notion of the Panopticon, in which "the Panopticon's power is to 'induce in the inmate a state of conscious and permanent visibility that assures the automatic functioning of power,'" Samuels explains that dominant cultural institutions render nonvisibility—what some call "passing"—tantamount to fraud. However, institutions also reify a narrow or stereotypical range of recognition: Disability, for example, may be legible to outsiders only if performed with a wheelchair or by bumping into walls. Samuels states, "Thus many nonvisibly disabled people may feel that our choice is between passing and performing the dominant culture's stereotypes of disability."[53] Marginalized communities, too, often render nonvisibility as normativity, reifying the demand to perform one's marginalized status and legitimating one's belonging in the marginalized community through scripted disclosures.

For trans* subjects, trans visibility and the achievement of gender legibility are vexed, because they invoke the exact nexus of power among medical, legal, and other social institutions that confirm or deny people's right to occupy virtually every kind of space and cross virtually every kind of metaphoric or geopolitical border. Moreover, as trans scholars and activists have noted, normativity maintains itself in part by ensuring that only people who do *not* trans (v.) some boundary of sex/gender can be the experts on the trans subject's sex/gender.[54] Within this hierarchy, the role of the trans subject is to display stereotypical physical markers for scrutiny, to supply a scripted narrative of transsexuality or transgendering, and to submit to the most intrusive questions about our bodies and what we have done or want to do with them. All this further reinforces the outside observer's sole power to assess the trans subject's true sex/gender and confirms the belief that cissexuality and transsexuality are readable and readably distinct.

These dynamics have clear Foucauldian implications. As Serano points out, *everyone* participates in conferring and benefiting from cissexual privilege by sharing in the assumption that we can accurately assign "sir" and "ma'am" to those around us. But any benefits come at the price of further submission to the hierarchies of normativity even as we rail against them. We do not win the right to authorize our own existence by coming out as trans while managing to *be read as* our chosen genders; doing so does not interrupt the assumption of cissexual universality but instead authorizes its hegemony.[55]

Despite their binary opposition, cis and trans are not functionally equivalent or parallel figures. The presumption of cis as non-trans will continually effect the marginalization of trans existence, requiring trans to appear through an ever narrower set of signifiers. Cis, meanwhile, never needs to prove itself. To draw on Evelynn Hammonds's metaphor of black (w)holes, we can only know the existence of cis by the effect that it has on bodies around it.[56] It might be tempting, then, to attempt to disrupt the normativity of cis, to dis-cover the cis subject, to define its borders and limits, to authorize its distinctive narratives and its distinctive specularity, and to force it to prove itself. But to do so is to invest in all the policing functions and powers of the Panopticon. Surely we can find better friends than that.

The effects of cis make clear that we cannot simply add trans to the list of "differences" covered in our classrooms without launching a simultaneous critique of the impulse to name cis as trans's absence. Wittingly or not, gender and women's studies derive disciplining security from the embrace of cis: This occurs in the presumption that "women" is not "trans" and in the presumption that "trans" is limited to a relatively small fraction of human existence that does not intersect with habituated definitions of "gender" in the title "Gender and Women's Studies."[57] As cis circulates, it renders "woman" and "man" more stable, normative, and ubiquitous than they ever were. In the very same gesture, the cis ally reduces "trans" to the most oppressed and institutionally defined object fighting for recognition within a framework of identity politics and additive "rights." Whatever else it may accomplish, cisgender forces transgender to "come out" over and over through an ever-narrower set of narrative and visual signifiers. This erases gender variance and diversity among everyone while dangerously extending the practical reach and power of normativity. That is to say, little cis and its step-cister ally can only rediscipline gender.

As so much feminist, queer, and trans theory has suggested, the compulsion to identify and even to posit a cis/trans binary in which people are either cis or trans is an effect of neoliberal politics in which identity categories are crafted to maximize a share of normative privilege. Feminist and queer theory and gender and women's studies as a whole have therefore been challenged to develop perspectives on lives, power, and oppression that do not require speaking as or speaking for the next identity category to be "included." This challenge has helped produce our best resources. Recalling Sandy Stone's charge that "passing means the denial of mixture," we might take greater pause at the constrictions wrought by cis.[58]

As a teacher and activist, I am humbled by the extent to which we exceed the English language. Words fail utterly, as do all conventions of naming the variety of ways we live with gender. In one sense, this underscores how powerfully most communication reinscribes binary gender. We make up pronouns and prefixes—languages change, after all—and then we wrestle with how to use them, because they do not escape systemic gender policing. We inevitably cloak ourselves in paper suits of biocertification, all the while tearing at the seams.[59] But perhaps it is in this very wrestling that we can find hope and be changed. Otherwise, to paraphrase Ryka Aoki, our classrooms may only encourage us to make our mistakes more eloquently.[60] As a transfeminist teacher and activist, I have a vested interest in keeping the categories woman, man, and trans* wide open, their flexible morphologies blending into one another and becoming accessible in more ways than we can even imagine.

II

Categorical Insufficiencies and "Impossible People"

5   CLARK A. POMERLEAU

College Transitions

Recommended Policies for Trans Students and Employees

Overview

During the last two decades, U.S. media have run exposés on anti-LGBT harassment's devastating consequences, including the murders of Brandon Teena and Matthew Shepard and the spate of youths who were bullied to the point of killing themselves in 2010.[1] After twenty years, the U.S. Department of Education's Office for Civil Rights has supported calls to reduce bullying in schools. The office asserted that harassment based on perceived gender or sexual orientation violates Title IX of the Education Amendments of 1972, because such harassment includes sex-stereotyping that constitutes sex discrimination.[2] Framing LGBT harassment as discriminatory sex-stereotyping opens the way for serious enforcement, but schools need a clear understanding of what actions and policies are discriminatory. This chapter focuses on constructing best practices to prevent sex discrimination against university students and personnel who are trans and/or gender diverse.[3] A small but growing literature addresses how American universities can change policies to support full inclusion. University personnel benefit from the fact that most of this literature is accessible online and responsive to changing conditions. This essay assesses what trans activists and legal advisers consider the best practices in place for (1) safety, (2) access to information and resources, (3) people's ability to control knowledge about their own trans status, (4) traditionally single-sex accommodations, and (5) programming. It uses the experiences of four white, trans students as an illustrative and instructive lens in making this assessment.

Safety

Students Arrive from a Context of Prevalent Bias and Harassment

Universities reflect the diversity of values within our society and are affected by broader societal trends. The prevalence of anti-trans bigotry and harassment due to gender expression in lower education raises concerns about how that affects college students and employees and how university personnel can differentiate the college level from rampant gender bias in lower education. The Gay, Lesbian, and Straight Education Network (GLSEN) has documented discrimination and violence that students face based on gender expression and sexual orientation since 1999. In its 2009 survey, 39.9 percent of the 7,261 lesbian, gay, bi, and trans sixth through twelfth graders surveyed "felt unsafe because of how they expressed their gender." Their concern was part of a larger problem of policing gender expression, in which 62.2 percent had heard negative remarks at school that someone was not acting "masculine enough" or "feminine enough" often or frequently, and 59 percent had "heard teachers or other staff make negative comments about a student's gender expression at school."[4]

Students can be harassed for their gender expressions regardless of their sexual orientations or gender identities, but rates of harassment have been highest for students who identify as trans, genderqueer, or androgynous. In the 2009 GLSEN survey, 63.7 percent of all the students "had been verbally harassed because of their gender expression" in the past year, "and 25.6 percent reported that it happened often or frequently." The overall rate of physical harassment due to gender expression was 27.2 percent, and "12.5 percent were assaulted at school because of how they expressed their gender."[5] The 2007 GLSEN survey reported that more trans students reported "sometimes," "often," or "frequently" experiencing verbal harassment (89.8 percent of them), physical harassment (56 percent), and physical assault (37.9 percent) than all other students, including racial and religious minorities.[6] As a result, 76.3 percent of trans students and 52.9 percent of those who chose "Other Gender" felt unsafe because of their gender expressions.[7] These rates have remained steady over the course of the 2001, 2003, 2005, 2007, and 2009 GLSEN surveys.[8]

Accounts from students who shared their experiences for this chapter diverged sharply based on whether they identified early as LGBT and were labeled as such by school staff. Julia[9] was the only one who had not identified with a non-normative gender until partway through college and had no memory of unsafe conditions for herself or others in high school. Sam, who had "expressed the gender non-conformity . . . by combining masculine and feminine fashion statements" at an arts high school had the second-least experience with harassment. The "very liberal arts" high school had "lots of queerness going on and diversity that had to be accepted in order to thrive in your art." Staff at Sam's high school enforced respect for diversity by suspending students who made fun of Sam's trans boyfriend in the only incident Sam remembered.

In marked contrast, Mary and Nick were labeled gay and lesbian respectively in sixth grade. Mary's guidance counselor told her parents Mary was "gay" after she had confided to female friends that she was "a girl trapped in a boy's body." Rumors spread in Nick's school that he was lesbian after he started dating a girl he met elsewhere. Both students were aware of being trans in early adolescence. Nick rejected lesbian identity and being labeled female. The summer before high school, he researched "Gender Identity Disorder" after doctors mentioned the term. Nick would explain to those who said he was a lesbian woman:

> "Yeah, I was biologically female"—and I'm a kid doing this; nobody ever told me how to explain it. So I would tell them, "I'm not male because physically I'm female. But I'm not a female because I'm just not a female." And they would understand that I wasn't female because I never acted like one of the girls. I was never one of the girls. So I always told them I was a slash in between the "fe" and the "male." And so they kinda got it.

Mary and Nick experienced extreme but representative harassment and violence due to hostile school climates, and each found a different way to cope without having recourse to parental support. Mary remembered:

> Junior high is when things started to get really sexually violent. I couldn't walk down the hallways without being called faggot. In the gym room they used to grab my head when we were changing and shove it down to their crotch and pass me around like a mock gang rape. I was diagnosed with post-traumatic stress syndrome this fall of 2008. My parents weren't supportive of me being gay.

In response, at thirteen or fourteen, Mary changed her persona to be a stereotypically macho straight guy. She benefited from media coverage of the Columbine High School shooting:

> Columbine really helped me because I fit the profile. . . . At the time it was obvious I was suppressed. I was getting made fun of. I made the grades. I was in all advanced classes. I was out about being an atheist. Things that really don't work well in a conservative Christian environment. I really used that to my advantage a little, and people just stayed the fuck away from me. And you know I had a reason to be angry. No one fucked with me. . . . I was [correctly] labeled a suicide risk by my middle school.[10]

Mary and Nick were very aware that their teachers and administrators were mostly antigay and unsupportive. Mary recalled incidents where she or other students stood up against antigay harassment of other students; the principal did nothing, and a teacher claimed the student "[brought] it on himself." This reinforced her determination to "play up the straight male part" and actively work not to be attracted to men. She characterized herself as "a complete asshole . . . the most offensive person on campus" from 1999 to 2002. At sixteen, Mary encountered a Queer Liberation Front table that affirmed it could be cool to be queer. She also shifted from the metal music scene to the punk scene's more flexible male gender presentations. She became an ex-ex-gay and participated in bringing a national student event called "Day of Silence" to her "really conservative high school" to raise awareness about LGBT issues. High school was less violent than middle school for Mary, because she "had friends [she] could call up to kick your ass." First she hung out with "meth-head friends," and then—as she started to shed her "[self-]creation out of *Spinal Tap*" for a combination punk scene/debate team identity—she cultivated friendships with female debaters and popular athletes in her advanced classes. She also found one LGBT advocate teacher who stood by her when she came out again as gay to her parents in 2004, recommended Kate Bornstein's *Gender Outlaws* to help Mary understand herself, and also answered her questions about which colleges would be safe.

At Nick's high school, other students who were LGBT or questioning sought him out for advice, because he was visibly and vocally queer. He challenged his school by complying with his principal's requirement that he get five thousand signatures before students could hold a Day of Silence. Nick and his friends went beyond the school's three thousand students and fulfilled the petition requirements to start the yearly event. He also got "in a lot of fights" on behalf of students who told him they were being harassed.

Unlike Mary, Nick was not able to cultivate protective friendships to counter abuse. Nick related that in his junior year, five members of the varsity football team attacked him from behind with a metal baseball bat when he was eating lunch alone and hit him in the head. He saw the school varsity jacket as he fell to his knees before he lost consciousness due to the beating. A friend called authorities and had him helicopter-lifted to a local hospital, where he says he was in a coma and then recovery for six months. Nick claimed that the principal covered it up and attributed the motive that the principal "thought it was just a permanent solution to the problem that I was. He was really angry when I came back to school." When I asked about his parents' response, he explained that his parents had emancipated him at age fourteen, because they disagreed with his "lifestyle." He had been living in an apartment with an older girlfriend and never talked to his parents. He chose to return to the high school to finish in half a year "to prove that you couldn't hold me down. I wanted to prove that you couldn't take me down just because I was different. You can't silence what's different. You have to see it."

Mary and Nick's experience of apathetic or hostile teachers and administrators conforms to nationwide findings. The frequency of reporting negative remarks on gender expression to GLSEN has not changed in eight years of surveying. Although LGBT students were more likely to report biased language than the general population of students, 62.4 percent did not report harassment or assault to staff, and 54.9 percent did not tell any family member. Of those who told family, only 25.5 percent "said that the family members ever addressed the issue with school staff."[11] More than a third of students did report an incident, but 33.8 percent said staff did not respond.[12] Reports of having heard homophobic, sexist, racist, and religiously biased remarks or experiencing victimization—including sexual harassment—were highest from students in the South and the Midwest. Southern students reported the lowest rate of teachers and staff intervening against bigoted language and the lowest rate of reporting these incidents themselves to authorities compared to students in the West, the Midwest, and the Northeast.[13] Trans youth and young adults experienced higher rates of discrimination and violence than gender-conforming peers and were more likely to turn to substance abuse and thoughts of suicide. The majority of states have no antibullying, antiharassment, or antidiscrimination laws that protect students based on gender expression.[14] Compared to the general student population, the grade point average of students who experienced severe "victimization based on their gender expression" was almost half a grade lower, their rate of absenteeism was three times higher, and 13.6 percent of them did not plan to go to college, compared to 8.9 percent of students who did not experience frequent physical harassment.[15]

Not only do these results indicate that universities are losing otherwise capable students due to the trauma they have sustained at school, but they show that the other 86.4 percent of highly harassed LGBT high school seniors who do intend to go to college come to campuses with reason to fear for their safety and assume that school authorities will not help them. Nick put it succinctly:

> Honestly, anywhere I go and anything I start, I automatically assume there's going to be problems just because of my high school.... It causes me severe anxiety because I'm afraid of what's going to happen, but I'm going to do it because it's what I want to do.

People like Nick and Mary and students who have observed transphobia in middle school and high school but have not yet self-identified as trans may enter college affected by the prevalence of bigotry in their youth in the ways they think about themselves, care for themselves, and relate to others.

Being sensitized to transphobia and homophobia also may lead to researching schools with that in mind. Campus Pride, which has developed a Campus Climate Index since 2007, reports that "more and more LBGT high school youth are making life decisions on the college that not only best fits their academic needs, but also a college where they can live and learn openly in a safe and welcoming environment."[16] Mary and Sam actively researched which colleges would be safe and supportive of LGBT students. Mary asked her LGBT-friendly teacher. Sam looked at prospective schools' Web site lists of student organizations for LGBT and trans-specific student groups and attended meetings as soon as he came to campus. Nick, who expected problems and did not try to assess LGBT climate, started at a trade school so he would have a license and job with which to get through a four-year college. He was lucky to be at a trade school with understanding employees. A staff person connected him with another trans student, and the registrar issued their identifications with their preferred names and genders.

Social Transitions Often Occur in College

For many students, self-acceptance of trans identity will occur after matriculation. College is increasingly becoming a key time when people transition. News reports of preschool and elementary-school children whose parents advocate for them to be able to live in the gender they know themselves to be document that the age at which people in the United States first continuously assert their trans or gender-diverse identities has decreased substantially since the 1950s.[17] However, it is more often the case that students' parents are not aware or supportive. College represents a major increase in autonomy, offers more information on gender variation, and may be a space where gender-questioning students explore their gender identities through their presentations.

Nondiscrimination Policy and Hate-Crime Policy

An important first step toward supporting safety for trans students and employees is implementation of a nondiscrimination policy that includes actual or perceived gender identity and expression. Out of more than 4,000 colleges and universities with physical campuses, 363 American colleges had such nondiscrimination policies at the end of 2010. An explicitly trans-inclusive hate-crime policy and clear information on how to report and handle a hate crime could be a further step in written policy.[18] Trans activists and policy makers universally recommend trans-awareness training, availability of information, and policies that give trans students and employees control over who knows their trans status.

Emergency Funding

Given that parents are not always supportive, trans students, like LGB students, risk their parents' disowning them and cutting off their college funds if the students come out. This was an issue for three of the four students who spoke with me. If universities expanded their emergency-funding programs to include disowned LGBT students, trained staff to recognize that situation as an acceptable reason for needing funds, and let students know that emergency funding is a possibility, they could expect to see better retention rates.

Access to Information and Resources

Trans-Awareness Training

More than 220 colleges and universities have formal training sessions to teach people how to advocate for LGBT people.[19] Safe Zone or Ally Training programs should give an overview on trans and gender-diverse issues to attending staff, faculty, and students and provide written information. It is not uncommon for students to initiate programs on their campus. Trans-awareness training can also come from energetic undergraduate LGBT-queer-and-questioning groups. For example, Julia, Mary, Nick, and Sam had all participated in a yearly trans Q&A panel organized by a non-trans program coordinator for an LGBT group. Ally Training or Safe Zone attendance may be voluntary, or it could be compulsory for types of front-line staff, such as residence hall advisers and counseling staff, or other school employees. Extant literature recommends compulsory trans-awareness training for faculty and staff but has not addressed backlash that could occur based on the subject matter and time taken away from employees' other duties. Before shifting LGBT-sensitivity training from voluntary or targeted audiences to all faculty and staff, an institution needs support from higher administration and a nondiscrimination policy that includes actual and perceived gender identity and expression.

Information and Services

Universities have organized their online and hardcopy information about trans and gender-diverse policies and programs numerous ways. They have created separate Web pages; presented material at on-campus workshops; housed the information with already-existing LGBT student groups, Ally Training/Safe Zone Programs, Women's Centers, or Disability Accommodations; or relied on an ombudsperson to have trans competency. The University of North Texas's (UNT's) expanding diversity mission for its Multicultural Center presents a unique opportunity to avoid the problems inherent in tying trans to queerness, femaleness, or disability. The problem with such linkages is embodied by the heterosexual male trans man who does not feel affinity with LGB people or women and who balks at having his route to manhood portrayed as a disability that needs a clinician's disorder diagnosis. UNT could create a "best practice" if trans and gender-diverse resources become available through the Multicultural Center and programming emanates from the Division of Institutional Equity and Diversity. The benefits of that policy would be buy-in from the highest levels of administration and locating trans and gender diversity within broader diversity instead of isolating it.

Ally Training/Safe Zone is important, because students will seek information from a variety of campus divisions, depending on how trans or gender-diverse status relates to the issue at hand. When an office for Equity and Diversity is known to advocate for LGBT issues, students may call to ask how they can change their names after they find that the registrar requires legal name changes. Sam sought help from four campus services. He asked student legal services about a family dispute over the execution of a will that occurred after relatives learned about his transition. He sought on-campus counseling sessions that are prerequisite for hormone supplementation and surgery. He asked whether the health center could oversee hormone supplementation. Sam also asked the career center's LGBT specialist about trans-related issues in looking for a job.

All the people with whom Sam spoke needed to be knowledgeable about trans issues to help him, and when a division did not provide services (e.g., a gender counselor and enough counseling sessions or someone qualified to prescribe testosterone), they needed to be able to refer Sam.

Too often, universities have not gathered the information for referrals. In such cases, students turn to individual peers or university employees they know or to the Internet. Mary had researched hormone supplementation online but rejected advice she got from a peer to buy estrogen illegally. She was unsure where to turn to start her process until a student mentioned that her teacher was a trans man. Having access to one local person can open the way to information about area counselors, doctors, and support groups. When students lack a contact, it can be difficult to wrest the information from online sources. Nick had little success until he got a job at a gay bar and learned about the LGBT community center. Minority students, broadly speaking, benefit from having role models at college. As universities have sought to increase diversity in their student bodies and staff, minority faculty frequently find that they need to spend time helping students who approach them based on common identities. Although minority professors often are happy to help, they can become disproportionately burdened if they are the token representative of a type of diversity and employees across campus are not trained to address diversity-related questions.[20] This is why vibrant Safe Zone/Ally Training programs and continuing diversity education that relates to specific units are crucial to student services.

Self-determination through Preferred Name

Names and Interacting with Students, Faculty, and Staff

Explaining their name was a major issue students discussed. Because legal names appear on class rosters, identification cards, and e-mail addresses, faculty, students, and staff can see the legal name of trans people who attend or work for universities. Sam recalled:

> I've had some very awkward situations with other students when roll was called. At this point, I'm over that, and if someone doesn't get it, I'll just be like, "I used to be a girl. Get over it." But when you don't have that level of self-confidence in being trans, it's very distressing.

Julia had the unusual good fortune to have parental support for a legal name change and hormone therapy. She has only had to explain her name change to one foreign-language professor with whom she continued to study. She says, "Everyone I've run into seems to be very supportive." Mary, Nick, and Sam have had to approach each new professor or let themselves be misgendered. They have generally found faculty supportive. All three students suggested that a key reform would be for universities to allow preferred names and genders. Sam noted that this was doubly important for professors who pass around attendance sheets or have online components in their lesson plans. Unless professors edit their rosters, the attendance sheets use legal names. Likewise, online components require university-issued e-mail addresses that often force the use of legal names.

Preferred Name and Gender to Prevent "Outing"

Because the names and gender pronouns people use for themselves validate their identity, people show disrespect when they intentionally and repeatedly call others by names against their will or misapply "he" or "she." The main way students and employees can hope to control who knows they are trans is by deciding how their names appear on university forms, identification, rosters, e-mail accounts, and other online media. Forcing trans students and staff to wait until they have completed costly and time-consuming legal-name and sex-marker changes before others address them by the names and pronouns they know are correct for themselves puts them at risk for discrimination and harassment from unsympathetic teachers, staff, and students. In most cases, the people interacting with a trans person do not need to know that someone was given a gender marker at birth that is inappropriate to the person's current gender. Forced delays also increase the unease trans people feel in their daily lives.

Applications

The need for recognition of a preferred name may occur from the time people apply to be affiliated with the university or may develop as their trans identities solidify during their studies or work on campus. Having to write down name and gender designations that are antithetical to one's identity and that will follow one is an impediment. Nick described the process:

> It's like an anti-name barrier because I'm sitting there trying to write it, and it's fighting me because I don't want to write that name. . . . And then it gets to that part where it says, "Gender: Male or Female." And here I did what I normally do. I circled Gender because . . . I can't legally say I'm male. Not yet. So I circled Gender because I'm not circling that F. Won't do it. And the school gave me problems when I enrolled because [the registrar said], "Well, you're female right?" And I'm like, "*No!*" "But your transcripts say female." But I'm like, "No, but I'm male!" "You're female!" And I argued with them, and finally I was like, "Fine, I'm female. I'm female for now." . . . It bugged the crap out of me with everything saying my female name.

Universities can develop systems that have preferred-name and gender sections on applications to study or to work at the universities. Such a system would cover trans people as well as all other people who use nicknames or middle names or otherwise do not go by their legal first names. Most universities conform to federal legal standards that prioritize concern about fraud and ability easily to match applicants' names with Social Security numbers (Social Security records list legal names and sex markers). Universities that choose to prioritize applicants' privacy can create systems that correlate preferred name and gender identity with Social Security information and federal financial-aid accounts without revealing the federal information to acceptance boards and hiring committees. Sam noted that being able to put FTM, MTF, intersex, or other on applications, housing forms, and health-center forms "automatically" would explain "why my name is different and why my presentation is male" and could tip off health-care professionals about specific medical issues. Self-identification would give students and prospective employees the greatest autonomy. The University of Michigan and the University of Massachusetts, Amherst, let students supply preferred names for course rosters and other systems without having their names legally changed.[21] As of 2006, seven campuses that had nondiscrimination policies allowed self-identification of gender on forms for admissions, housing, and/or health care. These forms either specified "Gender: Male, Female, Transgender" or "Gender: male, female, self-identify: ____" or asked students to write in their genders.[22]

Legal Vulnerabilities

In most states, legal name change for reasons other than marriage or divorce are up to the whim of the judge after the petitioner has paid around $300 in filing fees and fingerprinting costs. If successful on the first attempt, the process will likely take at least a month or two. Changing the name *and* sex marker requires proof of an "irreversible surgical change" that "permanently changed [the petitioner's] sex characteristics and should qualify [him or her] to be legally considered" male or female depending on whether transition was from female to male or male to female.[23] States frequently leave unclear which and how many surgeries applicants must have to "qualify" legally as the opposite gender. Trans people do not seek clarity, because genital surgery options are prohibitively expensive, receive mixed reviews on their results, and are not desired by all trans people. The phenomenon of trans identity disproves the idea that the body's appearance determines gender identity. There is a strong history of judges in some states being unwilling to accommodate trans petitioners regardless of whether petitioners conform to a legal assumption that genital surgery validates gender identity. Cases of changing the sex marker in hostile legal climates have generally occurred with the intervention of lawyers. Due to the fact that students typically have not entered careers to have earned their own savings and, instead, often are financially dependent on their parents, students rarely are able to afford surgeries or major court costs, even if they want them.

Protecting trans students and employees from having their birth names and sexing at birth revealed against their will looks out for the well-being of members of the college community. Failure to do so could result in harassment and legal challenges to university policies. A 1999 Supreme Court ruling interpreted Title IX to argue that schools have the responsibility to provide a harassment-free environment.[24] The Department of Education's 2010 letter specifically warned that harassment based on sexual orientation and gender expression falls under the scope of Title IX. In an example, the letter argued:

> The fact that the harassment includes anti-LGBT comments or is partly based on the target's actual or perceived sexual orientation does not relieve a school of its obligation under Title IX to investigate and remedy overlapping sexual harassment or gender-based harassment. In this example, the harassing conduct was based in part on the student's failure to act as some of his peers believed a boy should act. The harassment created a hostile environment that limited the student's ability to participate in the school's education program....
>
> By responding to individual incidents of misconduct on an *ad hoc* basis only, the school failed to confront and prevent a hostile environment from continuing.[25]

A great challenge at the policy level is that, unless those who craft the policy apply constant pressure, policies can get detained for years as they wind through upper administration or languish in a university's legal department. Failure to sign off on inclusive nondiscrimination policies acts similarly to a pocket veto. One can hope that the Department of Education's support will help administrators recognize the liability they face if they do not protect their students.

Preferred Name and Gender Accommodation

A procedure for transitioning students and employees to change their preferred names and sex markers online is the preferred method for avoiding the financial burdens and delays related to the court system. The University of Vermont, American University, and the University of Illinois, Chicago, allow trans students who have not obtained legal name changes to have identification cards either with different first names or with the initials of their first names and updated, gender-appropriate pictures. The University of Maryland allows students to change their names and genders on record with letters of support from mental-health professionals. A policy like Maryland's would vastly reduce changes and eliminate concerns about students' changing names for fraud or fun, but it has the disadvantage of delaying students by forcing them find therapists and to pay for the number of sessions their therapists determine is necessary.[26]

Single-Sex Accommodations: Restrooms, Dorms, Locker Rooms, Health Care

Restrooms and Changing Rooms

In addition to being called by an appropriate name and pronoun, trans, gender-diverse, and nonconforming people face impediments to their safety and ability to attain gender-appropriate accommodations from single-sex design. A daily problem is restroom use. The ability to relieve one's self in peace is crucial. Restrooms are a frequent site of violence against gender-diverse people. Julia has not had trouble, but Mary stated, "I'm just worried that some person will notice and start asking questions when I'm using the restroom, which is kind of demeaning. Safety—I just kind of worry about a few things." Like Julia, Sam got to a point in transition where he was not mistaken for the wrong gender. Before then, he "just mostly avoided using public restrooms." Nick, who has not yet been able to afford hormone supplementation while working two jobs to put himself through college, said, "I've never really [used the restrooms] on campus unless it's like an absolute emergency. . . . And I still get nervous walking into the guy's bathroom, because obviously there are still some feminine traits about me that show, and people will just see me as a big old dyke." Given that harassment often conflates a perception of gender deviance with being gay or lesbian ("big old dyke"), Nick was nervous about being misgendered as a woman in a men's room and facing a homophobic as well as misogynist response.

Trans students who are concerned about restroom safety often are more aware of the possibility of circumventing single-sex construction. Single-occupancy unisex restrooms are open to people of any gender and can be used by trans people as well as families, people with disabilities who have attendants of different genders, and anyone else who wants more privacy. More than 150 universities provide at least one gender-neutral restroom.[27] In a survey of twenty-five colleges that had adopted trans-inclusive nondiscrimination policies before 2005, nearly half had failed to construct any gender-neutral restrooms. Structural changes to buildings may seem more costly than policy and programming changes but are absolutely essential. Having one or two individual restrooms on a campus with more than one building is inadequate and leads people who are concerned about whether others will misrecognize their genders either to use a restroom despite their fear or to wait for hours before they find a safe restroom. Constructing private changing rooms, locker rooms, and shower stalls in student recreation centers would provide safety and comfort in ways similar to restrooms. They would also circumvent the possibility that a culture of sports-related trash talk and teasing becomes a cover for transphobic, homophobic harassment. In one study of twenty-five four-year institutions, only seven offered these privacy options.[28]

Housing

Trans and gender-diverse undergraduates who live in residential dorms often cannot escape tensions around their genders by retreating to their rooms, because most dorms assign roommates by gender and may place students on specific wings or floors by gender. At best, this situation increases unease at being misassigned. Nick mused:

> If I'm dating a girl, and she understands that I'm male but still technically female, when we get back to that dorm, and she's like, "Well, you're male. Shouldn't you be on a male floor?" "Nope, they put me on the female floor." It's just uncomfortable. . . . I couldn't even live on the female side. I can't imagine what it's like in the dorms. . . . They all share a bathroom [averts and shields his eyes at disrobing]. I couldn't live with that many females. It's the man in me. I can't go through your purse. I can't live in the same room as a female, because that would just be awkward.

At worst, students may face hostile roommates. Trans students are becoming increasingly savvy about the possibilities, and Nick and Mary suggested the policy employed by about a dozen Residence Life departments. Wesleyan University; University of California, Riverside; University of Pennsylvania; and other institutions have gender-neutral policies that allow students who agree to be assigned to or to choose their roommates regardless of gender.[29] Implementing a gender-neutral policy reconfigures existing space instead of requiring new construction. Alternately, Residence Life can allow students to be housed by their own gender identities and to use the restroom appropriate to their gender identities if that conflicts with what their Social Security records or birth certificates say. As a make-shift solution, universities have given trans students single rooms at the same price they would have paid to room with someone. A few universities have considered constructing a dorm for LGBT, queer, questioning, and ally students. Not only do these efforts tend to garner negative sensationalist national media coverage,[30] but segregating students based on their sexual orientations or support of queerness is a questionable policy. It does accommodate students and show institutional support, but it also marks students' sexual orientation, gender identity, or sympathy to gay rights by their physical location. Some trans students are heterosexual, and some have normative gender identities as women or men. Gender-neutral floors or dorms avoid labeling students. The National Student Genderblind Campaign's 2008 report lists the housing accommodations of thirty-eight universities that have committed to gender-neutral rooming.[31]

Health Care

Students and employees who are distressed by their gender variances or people's reactions to their gender presentations can benefit from crisis hotlines and individual counseling. These services are sometimes crucial to preventing or alleviating depression, feelings of hopelessness, and suicidal thoughts that people are at risk for when they live in a society that claims something is fundamentally wrong with them. Counseling also remains a mandatory prerequisite for attaining hormone supplementation and access to surgeries some trans and gender-diverse people use to make their bodies more recognizable to themselves and to others as the genders they know themselves to be. University counseling staff could obtain training from gender therapists in private practice. Alternately, university mental-health coverage could extend beyond campus facilities to private practitioners. On-campus counseling would alleviate the problem of a scarcity of therapists who specialize in transition and the related issue that students who have no vehicles have trouble seeking services beyond walking distance.

Physical health care can be perilous for trans and gender-diverse people, especially when they have encountered harassment or disrespect from health providers. Patients and their providers must recognize the importance for preventative care of wellness checks on body parts not usually associated with their genders. Insurance plans frequently exclude trans-specific coverage and may balk at covering wellness checks that do not match the patient's legal gender marker. Both issues can lead health problems to reach life-threatening stages while people seek providers who will care for them and challenge insurance companies that reject the claims. Since 2004, the University of California system's health insurance plan has covered psychotherapy, hormones (and presumably intramuscular syringes), and surgeries for employees, their spouses or domestic partners, and their children.[32] Increasingly, universities' student health insurance plans cover hormones and surgeries for transitioning undergraduates. The pharmacy at the University of California, Santa Barbara, also provides hormones to transitioning undergraduates.[33] When patients can make confidential appointments on Web-based programs, ensure that staff will call them by their chosen names and pronouns and use that name on campus-pharmacy prescription labels, use gender-neutral restrooms, and get genital exams outside women's health clinics, they can reduce dreaded questions about whether they are in the right place for genitally based health care. Sam related:

> I've passed this point where I'm okay with telling anybody that I'm trans if they see that my name's weird. But I know that most college-aged trans people aren't at that point. And I've experienced a little bit of awkwardness, and I know other people would experience more awkwardness like at the counseling center, the health center, whatever, when they call your name to figure out who's coming up there. Because how many trans people experience this whole, "I don't want anyone to know that I was something other than I am now." So if you're sitting in a waiting room with three other people and they call Samantha Who-

ever, and you're like, "Uh." I'll stand up, and they look at you, "Samantha?" And you're like, "Yeah [in depressed tone], that's me."

It is helpful for campus health centers to include reproductive health care based on genital body parts as New York University does rather than subsumed under "gynecology," "women's health," or "men's health."[34]

Programming

Universities committed to getting rid of policies and mind-sets that disadvantage gender diversity typically revise their nondiscrimination policies and increase programming, because these methods of change do not require the degrees of monetary investment involved in changing buildings and record-keeping software. Programming has been a way of assessing how trans-friendly campuses are, as with the prevalence of Ally Training/Safe Zone programs and the inclusion of trans issues in student LGBT groups, such as Q&A sessions, or participation in the Transgender Day of Remembrance to commemorate people who have been murdered in the past year due to transphobia. Events that address a number of issues simultaneously help normalize and integrate trans. For example, UNT hosted former *MTV Real World: Brooklyn* participant Katelynn Cusanelli. This well-attended event drew people interested in media, reality shows, and popular culture. Cusanelli talked about a range of issues, including her trans-woman identity. This event is indicative of how programming can extend beyond LGBT groups and capitalize on popular culture to include trans and to be multifaceted.[35]

Two concerns about making programming an indicator stem from what students' needs really are and what is not measurable. Sam gave the opinion that "extra programming is failing in general for the most part, because I've been to maybe four or five extra event things like that, and usually they're not very well attended." He admitted that as a commuter student, he neither read the constant stream of e-mail announcements for programs nor wanted to hang around campus beyond his classes. Nick, who retained apprehension about transphobic violence and was also a commuter, avoided whole areas of campus, including the student union, because when students pulled away, questioned him, or teased him, he said, "It makes me uncomfortable, and it makes me go home and question why are they looking at me different? What can I do to change me, so they stop looking at me different? And I don't like that." He mainly stayed off campus. Campuses and opportunities in the surrounding communities vary widely, but students may not always want to use their leisure time on school-sponsored lectures, discussions, movies, and the like.

One of the things programming does not measure is how open groups are to trans people; these four students have been involved in groups on and off campus. Julia, who also identified as lesbian, considered members of the LGBT group to have a "shared common experience." Seeing "people in different stages of self-confidence and self-acceptance . . . and creating programs" heightened her sense that pushing for LGBT rights was important. Mary found all the student organizations she joined very supportive of her. She listed the LGBT group and the AIDS activism organization as encouraging and got the strongest support from the feminist group in which she was an officer. As an activist, the feminist group merged her interests in reproductive rights and gay rights. Nick overcame apprehension about being judged and went to the LGBT group at his girlfriend's prompting. He made friends there and saw it was "easier to be proud and to have people around you than it is to not have anyone and stand alone and still be proud."

In addition to finding people with common interests and support, membership in groups gives people opportunities to develop leadership skills.[36] All four enjoyed offering education about being trans formally or informally. After he participated in the trans Q&A panel, Nick related:

> I realized that it made me a lot more comfortable, and it made me proud and happy and filled me with a sense of good, because we all sat down there, and they got to ask us questions, and we all got to give our point of view, and we got to educate people that otherwise wouldn't know and would keep questioning and would probably never know and be able to approach someone and ask those questions. And so it filled me with a really big sense of pride. . . . And I would be more than happy to educate in any way I can to help people understand that we're just like anybody else.

Although Sam felt that groups off campus influenced him more than student organizations, he too saw his role in the LGBT group as being a positive, personal representations of trans: "I think no matter where you are, it's always good for people to see that, 'Oh, this person's a transsexual, and he's a normal friendly person. I like him.' And so they associate that identity, that status, with someone they actually like—with a real person." Mary, who was the most active, took on the role of officer and planned and executed such events as a performance of *The Vagina Monologues,* a merchandise sale, and passing out of condoms. She has appreciated how much the feminist group taught her before transition when she worked as a male feminist: "You have to worry about cooptation when you're a guy helping out with the feminist cause. . . . Of course, I probably screwed up once or twice. I reflected, became a better activist." Inclusion and affirmation from welcoming non-trans students gave trans students opportunities to contribute to organizations and to develop their skills.

Concluding Suggestions

Students advocated for group and one-on-one support in addition to policy and physical changes to universities. Julia and Nick suggested that campuses set up mentoring systems or small support groups. Julia thought mentoring would help alleviate the problem that "there's a lot of transgendered people that obviously don't have the self-confidence and the support systems that some of us have. And I think there's a lot who are scared and nervous about themselves and what's going to happen to them when they come out—especially living on campus." Nick stressed that support needed the options of anonymity and informality. Rather than a big room with a circle of chairs, he suggested online and in-person places where students could vent, maintained by volunteers who would respect the venters' privacy.

Structural and procedural changes to traditionally same-sex facilities and services and continued trans-inclusive programming can complement less-formal support to provide a superior campus experience. Campus staff can make forms inclusive; name and gender change easier; gender-neutral restrooms, locker rooms, and housing an option; and trans counseling and hormone prescriptions on campus to give trans students and employees equitable experiences of school and work.

Ideally, students and university employees in the United States will have comprehensive legal protection at the state and federal levels. But with or without federal and state laws, universities can and should go much further to implement comprehensive diversity statements and antiharassment/antidiscrimination policies that include actual and perceived gender expression, gender identity, and sexual orientation; clear reporting procedures; and accountability for staff response. With accountability comes continued training for employees, which, in turn, should foster access to supportive information and resources.

6

PAT GRIFFIN

"Ain't I a Woman?"

Transgender and Intersex Student Athletes in Women's Collegiate Sports

The title of this chapter is borrowed from Sojourner Truth's powerful demand that white feminist abolitionists in the nineteenth century expand their awareness to include the needs of black women in their fight for race and sex equality. Her question, "Ain't I a Woman," seems fitting for the twenty-first century also with regard to the inclusion in women's sports of transgender women and men and women who have intersex conditions. Increasing numbers of athletes who are transgender or have intersex conditions are challenging gender boundaries in sports as they insist on their right to participate according to their self-affirmed genders. Recent controversies surrounding the eligibility of South African runner Caster Semenya to compete in women's events and the participation of transgender athletes, such as George Washington University basketball player Kye Allums and professional golfer Lana Lawson, challenge the traditional boundaries of sex and gender in sport.

This chapter explores how the gender and sex binary assumptions upon which the organization of sports competition is based can create problems when people whose gender identities or variations in sexual development do not conform to these assumptions assert their right to participate. I discuss how transgender and intersex athletes challenge assumptions about the essential nature of the category "woman." At the same time, I show how sexist and heterosexist stereotypes converge to affect the gender performance of all women in sports, with a particularly limiting effect on people whose gender identity, gender expression, biological sex, and/or sexual orientation do not conform to cultural norms.

After a description of relevant language related to this topic, I review selected historical events describing concerns about women athletes' sex, femininity, and heterosexuality. I then explore how these concerns and the gender-binary assumptions undergirding them affect policies governing the eligibility of transgender and intersex athletes to participate in women's collegiate athletic events. I conclude the chapter with a discussion of current efforts to provide transgender and intersex athletes with opportunities to participate in school-based women's athletic competitions.

A Word about Words

The language of sex and gender can be confusing and complicated. Many of the concepts feminist scholars and gender activists use challenge conventional notions about gender and sex. Moreover, the language is evolving, and many feminist scholars and gender activists disagree about how the language should be used. For example, the terms "sex" and "gender" are used interchangeably by some writers, while others find it useful to provide specific and separate definitions for each of these terms. I find it helpful, at least on a conceptual level, to define these two key terms separately.

According to Gender Spectrum, an education and advocacy organization for gender-variant children and teens, "sex" is biological and includes physical attributes, such as sex chromosomes, gonads, sex hormones, internal reproductive structures, and external genitalia. At birth, individuals are typically categorized as male or female based on the appearance of their external genitalia. This binary categorization ignores the spectrum of biological sex characteristics that confound attempts to fit everyone neatly into either male or female categories. The term "gender" is similarly complicated. According to Genderspectrum.org, "Along with one's physical traits, it is the complex interrelationship between those traits and one's internal sense of self as male, female, both or neither as well as one's outward presentations and behaviors related to that perception." I find it helpful to make this differentiation, especially when discussing these terms in relationship to sports, where physical attributes are integral aspects of the discussion.

Gender is not inherently related to sex. A person who identifies as transgender has a gender identity (an internal sense of gender: being male or female, trans, or other gender sensibility) that does not match the sex (or gender) they were assigned at birth based on an inspection of their physical characteristics. A transgender woman or girl may be born with a body identified as male and, on the basis of that body, assigned to the gender category "boy," even though she identifies as a girl. The reverse is true for a transgender man or boy. Transgender people choose to express their genders in many ways: changing their names and self-referencing pronouns to better match their gender identities; choosing clothes, hairstyles, or other aspects of self-presentation that reflect their gender identities; and generally living and presenting themselves to others consistently with their gender identities. Some, but not all, transgender people take hormones or undergo surgical procedures to change their bodies to better reflect their gender identities. Transgender encompasses a vast range of identities and practices; however, for the purposes of this essay, I use the term "transgender" more specifically to refer to women who have transitioned from their assigned male gender at birth to their affirmed gender as women and to men who have transitioned from their assigned female gender at birth to their affirmed gender as men.

People with intersex conditions may be born with chromosomes, hormones, genitalia, or other sex characteristics that do not match the patterns that typify biological maleness or femaleness. Many intersex people are not aware of their intersex status unless it is revealed as part of a medical examination or treatment. People with intersex conditions are assigned a gender at birth; many live and identify with that assigned gender throughout their lives, although many do not. In this essay, I use "intersex women" to refer to women with intersex conditions who have always identified as women (for more information about intersex conditions, go to www.accordalliance.org).

The participation of transgender and intersex women poses related but different challenges to gendered divisions in sports. Transgender women and intersex women are viewed by many sports leaders, women competitors, and the general public as men or as "not normal" women whose participation in women's sports threatens the notion of a "level playing field." In the context of sex-segregated women's sports, these athletes' bodies are viewed as male, and they are often perceived to have an unfair competitive advantage over non-intersex or non-transgender women athletes. But trans and intersex visibility and participation belies the myth of the level playing field and the myth of binary gender on which it rests.

Sports and the Gender Binary

Although some school athletic teams, such as sailing, are composed of men and women who compete without regard to the sex or gender of participants, mixed-sex competition is the exception at all levels of sports. In most sports that women and men play, schools sponsor separate men's and women's teams—basketball, volleyball, swimming, track and field, lacrosse, or soccer, for example. This sex division is based on the assumption that sex-separate competitive opportunities are the best route to equal opportunity and fair competition for all. Title IX, the 1972 landmark federal legislation prohibiting sex discrimination in education, includes guidelines for providing comparable school-based athletic opportunities for girls and women and boys and men on sex-separate teams to provide equal participation opportunities (Brake 2010; Hogshead-Makar and Zimbalist 2007).

Dividing participants into sex-separate teams is based on two assumptions: (1) Sex and gender are binary and immutable characteristics, and (2) salient physical differences between males and females substantially affect athletic performance to the advantage of males in most sports.

Rather than a binary of athletic performance based on sex, it would be more accurate to describe sex differences as a spectrum, with females and males occupying overlapping positions. Although it is fair to say that most adult male athletes are bigger, taller, and stronger than most adult female athletes, some female athletes outperform their male counterparts in sport. So, even among athletes who are not transgender or intersex, sex-separated teams do not always adequately accommodate the diversity of skill, motivation, and physical characteristics among female and male athletes. Some boys or men might find a better competitive match competing on a girls' team, and some girls' athletic performances are more comparable to those on a boys' team.

Some girls and boys have been allowed to participate on teams designated for the other sex, particularly if a school only sponsors a team in that sport for one sex. For example, girls sometimes compete on boy's wrestling or football teams, and boys sometimes compete on girls' field hockey or volleyball teams. However, cross-sex participation on sports teams is always an exception and is often greeted with skepticism by other competitors, parents, and fans. Even among prepubescent girls and boys where size and strength are similar or where girls are often taller, stronger, and faster than boys, sports are typically divided by sex. Such is the entrenched nature of the belief in a static and immutable gender and sex binary in sports.

For most athletes whose gender identity is congruent with their gender assigned at birth or whose physical sex anatomy is congruent with their sex assigned at birth, the answer to the question of which team to play for is simple. However, for athletes whose gender identity does not match the gender they were assigned at birth or for athletes with differences of sexual development, the separation of sports into participation categories based on binary sex has often resulted in humiliation and discrimination. Transgender and intersex athletes challenge the gender binary in sports and force sports leaders to reflect on how and where to draw gender boundaries for the purposes of identifying on which teams an athlete is allowed to compete.

Because women athletes have always challenged the hegemonic notion of athleticism as a masculine trait and because sports participation has historically been a male privilege to which girls and women were not entitled, the fight for equal sports opportunities for women is ongoing. Gendered expectations for girls and women have not comfortably included such characteristics as "competitive," "athletic," or "muscular"; as a result, women athletes have always had to prove their "normalcy" based on socially constructed assumptions about femininity, heterosexuality, and an unquestioned acceptance of a gender binary. Women who excel in sports *and* whose appearance, behavior, and/or identity does not conform to traditional notions of who is a woman, how a woman should look and act, and who a woman should be sexually attracted to are viewed with suspicion and as illegitimate participants in women's sports competitions (Cahn 1994; Festle 1996; Griffin 1998).

History of Gender Anxiety in Women's Sport

During the early twentieth century, women participating in athletic competitions were subjected to white middle-class criticism from medical doctors, media commentators, psychologists, and others who warned of a range of catastrophic effects of athletic competition they believed would cause physiological and psychological damage. Based on the belief that white women were physically and psychically frail, sports participation was viewed as dangerous to their health and well-being. The prevailing medical and social perspective was that women who did compete in sports were subjected to a number of "masculinizing" effects on their appearance, behavior, and sexual interests that would prevent them from living as "normal" women whose proper roles were wives and mothers. Thus, the early seeds of gender suspicion about women athletes were planted. Advocates for women's sports participation and women athletes themselves often responded defensively to these criticisms by highlighting their femininity (according to racially white heteronormative standards) and heterosexual interests, and by portraying their sports interest as a complement to their focus on motherhood and marriage (Cahn 1994).

These fears are best illustrated in public reaction to Babe Didrikson, a multisport athlete who won Olympic medals in track and field and played baseball, basketball, and tennis before later focusing on professional golf. Didrikson was a well-known cultural icon whose brash manner, quick sense of humor, and competitive fire always made for a good story. Unfortunately, Didrikson was treated as a gender freak and ridiculed for her lack of femininity, her "masculine" appearance, and her athletic prowess. Called a "muscle moll" and worse, it is no wonder that by midcentury, Didrikson initiated an intentional public-relations campaign to reassure the American public that she was a "normal" woman after all, despite her athletic achievements (Cayleff 1995). She began wearing dresses and talking about her love of cooking, and, to seal the deal, she married wrestling champion George Zaharias. These efforts succeeded in quieting the concerns of male sports reporters and the general public about Didrikson's femininity and heterosexuality.

As women's competition in Olympic sports and professional golf and tennis became more visible in the 1940s through the 1970s, another wave of suspicion about the gender and sexuality of women athletes prompted some women's sports advocates and athletes themselves to take an apologetic stance by focusing on disproving sexist assumptions about the "masculine" lesbian women who lived in the sports world. These efforts included the institution of feminine dress codes, instructions about makeup application and hair styling, and direction of media attention to the "pretty ones," who served as goodwill ambassadors who contradicted the unsavory image of "masculine" women athletes (Gerber, Felshin, and Wyrick 1974).

These fears, coupled with the belief that women are inherently athletically inferior to their male counterparts, caused increased gender suspicions about outstanding athletic performances by female athletes. These questions were raised in the 1964 Olympics by Russian hammer-throwers and shot-putters Tamara and Irina Press, whose muscular appearances and medal-winning performances provoked suspicion that they were actually men posing as women.

In 1976, Renée Richards, a transgender woman, was denied entry in the Women's U.S. Open by the U.S. Tennis Association (USTA) on the basis that she was not a "born woman." The New York Supreme Court ruled against the USTA and enabled Richards to compete in the women's event. Despite this court ruling, the Ladies Professional Golf Association (LPGA) maintained a "born woman" requirement for membership until 2010; when faced with a lawsuit by transgender woman golfer Lana Lawson, the LPGA dropped its prohibition against transgender participants. Transgender women, such as Richards and Lawson, are viewed by some suspicious tennis players and golfers as illegitimate women who have male bodies that confer an unfair competitive advantage when competing against so-called "natural" women.

In 1966, in response to fears of male cheaters competing as women, the International Olympic Committee (IOC) instituted mandatory "gender" verification testing of all female competitors. (The tests were called "sex tests," and their purpose was to confirm that competitors were female-bodied and, later, that their chromosomal makeup was female.) The first such tests required all Olympic competitors entered in women's events to appear naked before a panel of "experts," who, by visual inspection, determined whether the prospective competitors were eligible to compete as female.

Not surprisingly, athletes and other sports observers criticized this humiliating process. Medical experts also criticized the process, because, in addition to the invasive and voyeuristic nature of the "gender test," it was also a crude and ineffective means of determining whether a competitor was female.

Eventually, more "scientific" procedures were developed in which women athletes were subjected to buccal smear tests in which mouth swabs yielded cellular samples from which the chromosomal makeup could be identified. Athletes whose chromosomal makeup was other than XX were determined to be ineligible to compete as women. Women who "passed" the test were given "certificates of femininity" and allowed to compete.

These supposedly more-scientific tests also failed to achieve their intended goal. Rather than identifying male imposters, the only competitors who were ever disqualified were women with atypical chromosomal makeup who had lived their entire lives as women and were not attempting to gain an unfair competitive advantage. The resulting traumatic and public shaming that followed their identifications as "not women" not only terminated their athletic careers but damaged their personal lives as well.

Current Policy Governing the Participation of Transgender and Intersex Athletes

These "gender" tests revealed the folly of identifying a simple and fair, not to mention respectful, means of determining who is a woman. Nonetheless, although mandatory "gender verification" testing was discontinued prior to the 2000 Olympic Games, individual women athletes who trigger suspicions about their sex are now tested on a case-by-case basis. Unfortunately, these sex challenges are typically triggered by such ambiguous and culturally biased gender criteria as short hair, small breasts, preferences for "masculine" clothes, deep voices, muscular physiques, and excellence of athletic performance. Thus, the challenge of identifying who is and is not a woman for the purpose of determining eligibility to compete in women's sports events continues to be controversial.

During the 2009 Track and Field World Championships, South African runner Caster Semenya astounded the international track establishment with her gold-medal performance in the women's eight-hundred-meter run, leaving her competition far back on the track. Semenya was identified as a female at birth, has always identified as a woman, and is accepted as a woman by her family and friends. However, unconfirmed speculations are that she has an intersex condition. Immediately following her victory, some of her competitors and race officials from other countries filed challenges to the International Association of Athletics Federation (IAAF) under the IAAF's case-by-case "gender-verification" policy. (Mirroring the IOC, the IAAF policy had replaced mandatory "gender" verification testing of women athletes in favor of a case-by-case process.)

After months of subjecting Semenya to medical examinations, public speculation about whether she is a woman, public humiliation, and egregious breaches of confidentiality by the IAAF, she was allowed to keep her gold medal. Eleven months later, after secretive IAAF deliberations, she was cleared for competition in women's events. The IAAF released this decision without an explanation of its process, criteria, or reasoning. When Semenya won her first two races after returning to competition and finished third in another, some of her competitors again began complaining that they were unfairly forced to compete against a man or, at the very least, a "woman on the fringe of normalcy," as one competitor described Semenya.

Whether being intersex confers any performance advantage is open to speculation. No scientific data are available to indicate that it does or does not. However, Semenya's competitors assume that she is a man or not a "normal" woman and that she has an unfair competitive advantage that should disqualify her from competing in women's events. These objections to Semenya's eligibility to compete as a woman are based on her margin of victory over the other women in the 2009 World Championships and on her "masculine" physical appearance, clothing, and deep voice. All these characteristics challenge the gender binary upon which sports competition is based as well as binary assumptions about who is a woman and therefore eligible to compete in women's events.

In 2004, in a surprisingly proactive decision by a typically conservative organization, the IOC adopted a policy outlining criteria enabling transgender athletes to compete in IOC-sponsored events:

- The athlete's gender must be legally recognized on official identity documents.
- The athlete must have completed genital reconstructive surgery and had his or her testes or ovaries removed.
- The athlete must complete a minimum two-year postoperative hormone treatment before she or he is allowed to compete.

The IOC policy is the first attempt by a mainstream sports organization to identify specific criteria governing the participation of transgender athletes. However, transgender-rights advocates criticize the policy, noting the class and sex bias built into the policy as well as problems related to privacy and medical confidentiality. Moreover, some transgender medical experts have provided some data indicating that a one-year waiting period is adequate for the athletes' hormonal levels to be within the range of non-transgender women and men. To date, no transgender athlete has competed in the Olympic Games under this policy.

Despite its considerable flaws, USA Track and Field, the U.S. Golf Association, and a few state high school athletic governing organizations have adopted the IOC policy (for example, those in Colorado, Connecticut, and Rhode Island). The participation criteria identified in the IOC policy would make it virtually impossible for transgender student athletes to compete in high school sports. The requirements of genital reconstructive surgery, mandatory sterilization, and changing the sex indicated on official identity documents impose financial and legal burdens that even many adult transgender athletes cannot or choose not to pursue. The two-year waiting period is not supported by medical data and is not practical in school sports, where a student athlete's eligibility is already limited to four or five years.

As of 2011, no national governing organization for high school sports has adopted a policy concerning the participation of intersex athletes in school-based sports events. However, in 2008, the Washington State Interscholastic Activity Association (WIAA) adopted the most progressive policy to date governing the participation of transgender student athletes on high school sports teams. This policy requires neither surgery nor change of identity documents. Transgender students can participate in their affirmed genders after appealing to the state interscholastic activities association and providing written documentation of the student's gender from the student and parent/guardian and/or a health-care provider. To date, the policy has been used successfully to enable transgender students to participate on sex-separate teams.

At the collegiate level, the National Collegiate Athletic Association (NCAA) released a statement in 2004 clarifying that the organization does not prohibit transgender student athletes from competing in NCAA-sanctioned events but that student athletes must compete in the sex identified on their official identity documents. NCAA legal advisers believed that this provision was a simple solution to addressing the question of transgender participation in NCAA athletic programs. Because of significant differences among state requirements for changing the sex indicated on official identity documents, however, this requirement is discriminatory and creates complications when athletes from different states compete against each other. More recently, the NCAA has recognized the need for a more nuanced and inclusive policy. In 2011, it adopted the first-ever national policy regarding transgender athletes in collegiate athletics; the policy allows transgender athletes to compete in sex-segregated sports if, and only if, their hormonal treatment is consistent with current medical standards—standards that themselves suggest different treatment requirements for trans men and trans women (Lawrence 2011).

As of 2010, only two collegiate openly transgender student athletes had competed in NCAA-sponsored events. Keelin Godsey competed on the women's track and field team at Bates College and in the Olympic trials in the women's hammer throw. Allums currently is a member of the George Washington University women's basketball team. Godsey and Allums are female-bodied transgender men who are not taking testosterone so they can continue to compete in women's events. Because they are not taking testosterone, an NCAA-banned substance, and are competing in the sex identified on their official identity documents as specified by the NCAA and IOC, Godsey and Allums are eligible to compete on women's teams.

Whether the perceived threats to women's sports are identified as male imposters, transgender women, transgender men not taking testosterone, intersex women, butch-looking straight women, or lesbians, protecting the boundaries of women's sports from these gender transgressors by upholding the gender binary has become increasing difficult as the myth of the gender binary and the myth of the level playing field have been exposed.

The Myth of the Level Playing Field

Just as some people view lesbians as threats to women's sports because they fear association with the stereotypes of lesbians as unsavory, so, too, do many athletes and the general public view transgender and intersex women athletes with particular suspicion. Although lesbians may be viewed as women who look or act like men, some people view transgender and intersex women as actually *being* men, in most places making them ineligible to compete in women's sports. The most-often-cited concern about the participation of transgender or intersex women in women's sports is that they threaten a "level playing field." Many competitors, coaches, and parents assume that transgender and intersex women, because of their male bodies, have an unfair competitive advantage over women who are not perceived to be trans or intersex.

Even without the participation of transgender or intersex women in women's sports, the playing field is hardly level. The entire focus of sports competition is to gain a competitive advantage, as long as that advantage is defined as being within the rules. Training hard to gain a competitive advantage is fair. Taking performance-enhancing drugs is not fair. Competitive advantages in women's sports come in many different forms: social, economic, environmental, psychological, and physiological, to name a few. Some women grow up in cultures where girls' sports participation is supported by social norms. These girls have a competitive advantage over other girls whose cultures restrict female athleticism. Girls whose families have the financial resources that enable them to train with the best coaches, to use the best equipment, to have access to good nutrition and health care, and to compete with the best athletes have a competitive advantage. Girls who live in places with clean air and water and safe streets have a competitive advantage. Girls who have inner resources of mental toughness and competitive drive have a competitive edge over physically talented but less mentally tough opponents. Some women have competitive advantages over opponents in their sports because of their genetics. Even some genetic conditions, such as Marfan syndrome, which results in unusual height, can be a competitive advantage in some sports where being tall is an advantage. All these competitive advantages are viewed in sports as fair and part of the game. All these advantages expose the myth of the level playing field even among women who are not transgender or intersex.

Why then is it that all these competitive advantages are accepted as fair variations among women athletes that can account for athletic-performance differences, but the competitive advantages that may or may not be enjoyed by some transgender or intersex women are viewed as unfair and threats to a level playing field warranting banishment from women's competition?

Competitive advantages assumed to be conferred by perceived maleness or masculinity are viewed as unfair competitive advantages. Transgender women, intersex women, or any women who do not conform to social expectations of femininity and heterosexuality are threats to the image of athletic women as gender conformists. As long as women athletes can be cast as feminine, heterosexual women, they do not pose a threat to the dominance of men in sports and male privilege in sports. This is the price of acceptance that women in sports have had to pay since the early twentieth century, when they began participating in sports in large numbers.

Gender Binary Meets Transgender and Intersex Athletes: What Is the Way Forward?

Women who by their inability or refusal to conform to binary gender norms in sports also challenge the mythical gender binary altogether. Given that athletics as an institution has been built on sexist assumptions about the natural superiority of men's sports performance over that of women and that the gender binary forms the basis for how sports are structured into sex-separate participation categories, how should women's sports address the question of including transgender and intersex athletes?

Policy development designed to address this question can take several forms: (1) Protect the gender binary by using sex-verification testing to exclude "non-women," (2) address challenges to the gender binary on a case-by-case basis, (3) eliminate gender as a sport-participation category, and (4) expand gender categories to include participants whose bodies and/or gender identities do not conform to the gender binary.

Protect the gender binary with mandatory sex-verification testing of all female participants. This policy has been discredited as impractical, discriminatory, invasive, and ineffective. The IOC abandoned this policy in 1999, and nothing suggests that any improvement of testing procedures will bring it back as a mandatory process.

Use sex-verification testing on a case-by-case basis as challenges to individual female participants arise. This is the IOC/IAAF policy now in effect. The controversy surrounding the challenge to Semenya's eligibility to compete in women's events illustrates many of the problems with this policy. The criteria for challenging an individual athlete's gender are based on a combination of sexist assumptions about female athletic performance and bodies, socially constructed gendered expectations for appearance and behavior, and a selective belief in the level playing field in sports in which some competitive advantages, particularly those based on genetic differences, are viewed as fair while others are not. Testing on a case-by-case basis eliminates the impracticality of testing all competitors entered in women's events and avoids the mass anxiety inherent in the process. However, the sex testing of individual competitors on a case-by-case basis is based on myths about gender and a level playing field that subject the athletes who are targeted to an invasive and humiliating, and often public, process. The effects of these tests are questionable given the arbitrary nature of determining when a woman's physiological makeup crosses a socially constructed line to become "too" male to qualify to compete against other women.

The IOC policy for determining the eligibility of transgender women athletes on a case-by-case process includes criteria that require surgical intervention and legal documentation of transition that create insurmountable obstacles for most transgender people. The policy also requires an excessive waiting period once hormone treatment has begun that is not supported by current medical research.

Eliminate sex and gender as sports-participation categories. Some LGBT legal advocates believe that eliminating men's and women's sports in favor of other criteria for determining sports participation is the only way to address the complexities and challenges of including transgender and intersex athletes. These advocates argue that dividing sports participation on the basis of a sex and gender binary is inherently unfair. Some feminist legal critics of Title IX believe that the law, by assuming that sex-separate teams are the best route to equality for women in sport, has enshrined sex inequality and relegated women's sports to a permanent second-class status. Their assumption is that Title IX establishes a "separate but equal" goal even though this legal concept has been discredited in lawsuits challenging racial and disability discrimination (McDonagh and Pappano 2008).

The logic and goals of such legalistic arguments for the elimination of sex-separate sports as a way to address the myth of the gender and sex binary, inequality in women's sports, and the inclusion of transgender and intersex women athletes are appealing in some ways. Dividing sports by such performance-related physical criteria as height, jumping ability, or weight might be a reasonable strategy to eliminate discrimination based on sex and gender identity. Using actual performance in sports, such as running or swimming speed, agility, balance, points scored, or batting averages, also provides alternatives for dividing competitors into teams to level the playing field.

Although is it true that the gender binary creates a questionable division between the athletic interests, talent, and performance of men and women, it is also accurate to say that, for adults, most male athletes are bigger and stronger than most women athletes. As a result, dividing school teams by such "nongendered" criteria as physical characteristics and athletic performance at this point in the history of women's sports would likely result in most athletic teams consisting of men and a few select women (including trans and intersex athletes). Second teams, if school chose to field them, would probably consist of men and women in more equal numbers (including trans and intersex women). Third teams, in the unlikely event that schools chose to expand their support for more than two teams per sport, would probably consist of mostly women (including men and some trans and intersex athletes) and some men.

It is also questionable whether these performance-based criteria are really non-gendered. Many of the physiological differences between male and female bodies do give men a competitive advantage over women, depending on the sport. However, gendered social and cultural expectations still encourage and reward male athletes more than they do female athletes. Sexism in sports still limits women athletes' access to sports and the resources that support athletic teams. Much like the rationale behind affirmative action as a way of correcting past race and sex discrimination, sex-separate sports enable women to overcome past sex discrimination in sports. Studies documenting the impressive increases in girls' and women's participation in sports and the increasing quality and quantity of women's sports experiences since the passage of Title IX demonstrate the law's undeniable positive effects (Carpenter and Acosta 2004). At the same time, despite these successes, resistance to Title IX compliance and persistent sexism are still obstacles to full women's equality in sports.

I worry that eliminating women's sports in favor of "non-gendered" sports opportunities will, at this point in the development of women's sports, relegate the majority of women athletes either to the junior varsity or to the sidelines. Sport is gendered by social and cultural expectations. Even criteria meant to be "gender-free" are still embedded in historical and contemporary societal structures of sex inequality that disadvantage female athletes while advantaging male athletes. I keep imagining an incredibly talented athlete, such as the University of Connecticut women's basketball player Maya Moore, sitting on the bench for a varsity college team made up of mostly taller, stronger men or starting on a junior varsity team that receives less attention and fewer resources than the varsity team. Moreover, Moore is an exceptional athlete. How does the elimination of women's teams benefit the majority of college women athletes (including trans women and intersex women) who are not as talented as she is?

Expand gender categories to include participants whose bodies and/or gender identities do not conform to the gender binary. I believe that, despite compelling criticisms of the problems posed by dividing sports participation into sex-separate participation categories, this structure is the best way, at this point in women's sports history, to achieve sex equality in sports. Sex-separate sports teams provide the most participation opportunities for the most girls and women. Title IX, although not perfect, has demonstrated that, when opportunities are available, girls and women come to play in increasingly larger numbers with every successive generation. I do not believe that this would be so if girls and women were competing not only against each other but also against boys and men for these opportunities.

If sex-separate sports are indeed the best route to sex equality, the question is how can we expand our criteria to include competitors in women's sports who challenge the rigidity of the gender binary? Can we respect the self-affirmed gender identities of transgender athletes and the differences of sex development in intersex women by including them in our definitions of "woman" so their right to participate on women's teams is also protected?

Current Efforts to Create Inclusive Collegiate Athletic Policy Governing the Participation of Transgender and Intersex Athletes

In October 2009, the National Center for Lesbian Rights and the Women's Sports Foundation co-sponsored a national think tank titled "Equal Opportunities for Transgender Student-Athletes." The attendees were legal, medical, athletic, and advocacy leaders with expertise in transgender issues. The think tank's goal was to develop recommended policies for high school and collegiate athletic programs. The report from this think tank, *On the Team: Equal Opportunities for Transgender Student-Athletes,* includes a comprehensive discussion of issues, policy recommendations for high school and college athletics, and a list of best practices for sport administrators, coaches, student athletes, and parents (Griffin and Carroll 2010).

The following guiding principles served as a foundation for the think tank's discussions and the policy recommendations included in the report:

1. Participation in interscholastic and intercollegiate athletics is a valuable part of the education experience for all students.
2. Transgender student athletes should have equal opportunity to participate in sports.
3. The integrity of women's sports should be preserved.
4. Policies governing sports should be based on sound medical knowledge and scientific validity.
5. Policies governing sports should be objective, workable, and practicable; they should also be written, available, and equitably enforced.

6. Policies governing the participation of transgender students in sports should be fair in light of the tremendous variation among individuals in strength, size, musculature, and ability.
7. The legitimate privacy interests of all student athletes should be protected.
8. The medical privacy of transgender students should be preserved.
9. Athletic administrators, staff, parents of athletes, and student athletes should have access to sound and effective educational resources and training related to the participation of transgender and gender-variant students in athletics.
10. Policies governing the participation of transgender students in athletics should comply with state and federal laws protecting students from discrimination based on sex, disability, and gender identity and expression.

To maintain the integrity of women's sports while including transgender and intersex women athletes on women's sports teams requires that sports-governing organizations at all levels develop policies enabling women who challenge the gender binary to play. These policies must be focused on providing equal opportunities to a broad spectrum of women and be based on current medical and legal information rather than on unchallenged acceptance of the gender binary, female athletic inferiority, and a selective view of what constitutes a level playing field. This endeavor will require confronting our anxieties about blurring gender and sexuality boundaries and recognizing the arbitrary manner in which we define who is a woman to maintain a comfortable but oppressive understanding of gender and sexuality. We must recognize that the enforcement of exclusionary definitions of who qualifies as a woman denies some students the opportunity to play on school sports teams. We must understand that enabling transgender and intersex students to participate on women's sports teams is an important step toward greater equality for all women and strengthens women's sports in the same way that addressing the needs of lesbians, women with disabilities, and women of color strengthens the broader social movement for women's equality.

Most colleges and universities include as part of their education missions commitments to equality and fairness. As reflected in nondiscrimination statements and educational programming focused on social justice and diversity, schools endeavor to invite students and staff to think more critically about privilege and disadvantage based on social and cultural identities. Policy development in collegiate athletics should reflect the broader goals and values of the schools they are part of and not allow competitive goals or financial gain to shape policies (Buzuvis 2011). Policies governing the inclusion of transgender and intersex student athletes must be based on a commitment to providing all students with equal opportunities to participate on school sports teams, while at the same time protecting the integrity of women's sports as the best strategy for achieving sex equality in sports.

7

CHRISTOPH HANSSMANN

Training Disservice

The Productive Potential and Structural Limitations of Health as a Terrain for Trans Activism

This essay focuses on health-provider trainings and their relationship to activism around transgender health. Sometimes referred to as "Trans 101," "Transgender Health," or "Transgender Awareness" trainings, these provider trainings are often delivered to health-professional students or as continuing education to health-care providers.[1] I aim to show that although transgender health activism is a productive and necessary site of activism within transgender and gender-nonconforming communities, the over-reliance on provider trainings actually limits the potential and reach of the trainings themselves as well as of trans health activism and advocacy broadly. I also highlight the opportunities that transgender health advocates have to expand the effectiveness of such work, including building conceptual and concrete linkages with feminist health advocates.

I write this essay as a health educator who has conducted transgender health trainings and as a public health researcher who has studied their effectiveness. As a trainer, I experienced firsthand the sense of which messages resonate (and fail to resonate) in an educational setting. As an evaluator, I have traced the course of those messages beyond the site of training to gain a sense of how providers translate these teachings into practice, to encouraging and deeply disturbing ends.

The following experience well typifies the common dilemma. Recently, I was invited to present with a colleague to a class of university graduate students in various health-professional fields (nursing, medicine, dentistry, social work, public health, pharmacy, and others) about health care in underserved communities on the topic of LGBT health. This was a weekly, student-run class, and the organizers were expected to arrange a series of volunteer speakers who could lecture to a variety of health-professional students. One week of the quarter focused on LGBT health, and we were invited to speak for half the three-hour class session. The organizer let me know that there simply was not time to instead devote one session to LGB health and one to trans health. Prior to the lecture, I asked whether the organizer had a specific focus in mind or whether the class had any questions that we could speak to. In reply, the organizer said, "Maybe just help students understand how LGBT communities are actually underserved." It was a deceptively simple charge.

We could have chosen from among a multitude of possible approaches. We needed only to share morbidity and mortality data or data from health providers and health-professional students revealing widespread homophobia and transphobia toward patients and clients. Alternatively, we could use film clips or stories—exemplaries include *Southern Comfort,* a documentary that follows a trans man who dies of ovarian cancer after doctors refuse to treat him; Leslie Feinberg's personal account of a frightening medical encounter published in the *American Journal of Public Health*; and the case of Tyra Hunter, who died as a result of injuries sustained in a car accident when paramedics withdrew treatment after learning she was trans, is another brutal cautionary tale. We could talk about institutional and interpersonal violence in queer and trans communities and about the relationship of this violence to health and health-care access. We could tell students about how trans people in prison, detention, or foster care are routinely denied access to appropriate health care, let alone gender-appropriate clothing or residence. We could discuss intake forms and scripted patient interviews and point out the areas where they fail to reflect many queer and trans lives and realities.[2]

As my colleague and I ruminated over what approach we would take while preparing the presentation, I thought about how painfully easy this question is yet how inadequate. When I train, one of my goals is to actively engage participants. I want to focus on issues that are relevant to them, to offer strategies that they feel will help them in practice, and to speak directly to their questions. I want them to feel motivated to seek out more information, more resources, more teachers, more connections with communities. I felt quite confident that we could speak in the training to the ways in which queer and trans communities are "underserved" and that we could effectively direct students (at least some of them) toward a continued engagement with queer and trans health. I also felt that we could effectively speak to the problematic tendency for "trans health" to be collapsed into a corner of LGB health, even as we operated under this constraint.

I felt markedly less confident that, in the hour and a half we had to speak, we could demonstrate how the structure of their education up to this point had neglected to answer, or even to pose, this question. I wanted to clearly communicate that "LGBT" had already been present, although probably unmentioned, as an aspect of the lives of people within each of the "populations" that they had studied up to that point. For example, homeless health care, adolescent health care, and immigrant and refugee health care are also sometimes queer and trans health care. Most critically, how these very overlaps and elisions interact to exponentially exacerbate the degree to which individuals, flattened into members of so-called populations, are underserved. I wished to share that, in fact, the term "medically underserved" is historically specific and that it carries its own set of acronyms, designations, and numerical qualifications that may bend and flex with social, political, geographic, and cultural movements and pressures.[3] More broadly, I wanted to discuss how population health itself is concerned with the management of populations, and how the role of the clinician is inextricably tied up in this project.[4] I wanted to talk about the ways in which this manifests in medicine's restrictive definitions of transgender being taken as authoritative in questions of legislation, administrative regulations, and policies that shape (and usually damage) trans people's lives.

My confidence here flagged, because I knew that training health professionals can be challenging. Our objectives were that students understand that a medical model does not and should not define trans or gender identity, which is in direct conflict with the dominant messages of their ongoing socialization. According to Mary-Jo DelVecchio-Good et al., physicians in training are quickly socialized to be "most caring of patients who are willing to become part of the medical story they wish to tell and the therapeutic activities they hope to pursue."[5] In addition, DelVecchio-Good and colleagues argue, time, efficiency, and speed are highly valued. We wanted students to build skills to cope with ambiguity and also to understand that, although identity is frequently a poor predictor of behavior, it can be a predictor of marginalization. In addition, we wanted them to grapple with the ways in which medicine often takes an inappropriately invasive and authoritative role, and how its authority flows into and interacts with a variety of other institutions in ways that maintain social and economic inequity. None of these messages mesh well with medical models of gender and sexuality, and none of them lend themselves particularly to efficiency or expedience. How would we communicate these messages to students who were presumably already steeped in the very medical model that we wanted them to question? And how would we be able to accomplish that before our ninety minutes were over?

Furthermore, given that providers are hungry for "personal contact" with trans people, how would we—myself, a generally passing, white trans man, and my colleague, a non-trans woman of color—situate ourselves within the training? This was a particularly thorny question, because providers tend to draw drastically inaccurate, representationalist conclusions about trans people in general based on what they perceive about trans or gender-nonconforming trainers.[6]

This conundrum illustrates the way that the institution of medical practice (or, in this case, health-professional education) shapes a training curriculum before trainers may even begin to develop it. It is important, as trainers, to push up against these boundaries. To do this with a strong consciousness of maintaining engagement requires finding a set of links to the formulas, scripts, and expectations of medical education. Trainers (myself among them) struggle to teach information and strategies that are relevant, useful, and legible to providers, while simultaneously wondering whether the concepts of trans health that we seek to teach will translate in the venues that are available to us. I describe some of the specific ways that this plays out in a subsequent section. Truly engaging with trans health greatly exceeds the narrow space of a single lecture, and its reach extends far beyond a single "population."

Trainings

Provider trainings have been a popular means through which to educate providers and to disseminate clinical information about trans and gender-nonconforming communities. The goal of such trainings is to increase the ability of providers to deliver high-quality care for these individuals as patients. Most trainings offer a mixture of information designed to improve clinicians' "clinical competence," or their aptitude for understanding and delivering clinically appropriate care to patients, and their "cultural competence," or the behaviors, attitudes, and policies that guide them in providing compassionate care to trans and gender-nonconforming patients. It is assumed that this combination increases trans and gender-nonconforming individuals' ability to access high-quality care and minimizes or at least reduces some of the barriers to doing so.

In the past decade, needs-assessment studies have documented the gaps in and barriers to accessible health care for trans and gender-nonconforming individuals. A frequent recommendation of these studies has been to conduct trainings with providers to increase their ability to deliver high-quality care to their trans and gender-nonconforming patients. Frequently, these trainings are developed and facilitated by members of trans and gender-nonconforming communities. The growing availability of such trainings reflects the increased demand by organizations and agencies to improve their cultural competence and health-care delivery.[7]

Similar trainings are also widespread outside health-care settings, in student organizations, classrooms, nonprofits, public agencies, corporations, and so on. Although these do not have an emphasis on health-care provision, they share many of the same elements of the clinical trainings that I describe here. Generally, the emphasis is on terminology and definitions, and they often utilize panels comprising a few trans individuals to discuss their experiences. The focus is usually on tolerance and cultural competence. Most begin with terminology and then move into personal narratives and discussions of differences between sexual orientation and gender identity. By and large, they presume audience members to be non-trans.

Cultural-competence training in the context of health-care provision has been a point of entry for instigating material changes in biomedical practice and education. In many ways, this has been a successful strategy: In some cases, members of marginalized and pathologized communities have had the opportunity to speak for themselves and to take positions of authority and expertise in instructing health providers about how best to serve members of their communities. In other ways, the existence of such trainings has underlined the ongoing nonattendance in health-professional education to issues of transgender and gender nonconformity and how they pertain to health.[8] The conspicuous absence of these topics in health-professional curricula persists,[9] and rather than include and integrate these topics into regular teaching, institutions instead tend to devote a short amount of time to trans health as a "special topic" or to include it within a single lecture (often in the midst of a session about lesbian, gay, bisexual, and queer health).[10] In addition, the individuals who conduct trainings must shape them in such a way that they fit within the context of medical education more broadly. This may serve to significantly limit the focus, message, or goals of the training. It also functions to erroneously cast health care and medicine as a neutral (or potentially neutral) practice.

Cultural-competence trainings have gained traction in medical education in the past two decades. The choice to mold trans-health trainings to such frameworks has probably enabled them to be integrated as broadly as they have been, given the familiarity of the model in clinical-education settings. As a result, many more providers have been exposed to topics concerning trans health than might have been otherwise. However, the limitations imposed by "fitting" trainings into health-professional education and using cultural competence as a foundation for education have shaped content and delivery of trainings in such a way that reduces complexity and focuses primarily on a particular transgender narrative or experience. This strategy has also resulted in a failure to join with other health advocacy projects that struggle against sexism and other forms of marginalization. Medicine has a long history of authoritatively and problematically managing not only gender but also disability, poverty, race, age, and so forth.[11] Scholars have therefore analyzed the detrimental effects of the ways in which medicine produces and maintains normalizing categories.

Individual health-care providers are not generally ill-intentioned individuals who set out to control the lives of marginalized individuals. Nevertheless, as part of larger institutional structures, providers act as gatekeepers, repetitively producing norms through disciplinary power to enforce gendered conformity and compliance.[12] This also depends on the recirculation of the medical model of transsexuality by patients, which is, for some, a strategic choice. To interrogate this production of knowledge, we must examine the ways in which the medical management of gender nonconformity "has resulted in a governance of trans bodies that restricts our ability to make gender transitions which do not yield membership in a normative gender role."[13] Although cultural-competence training approaches appropriately do not vilify health-care providers, neither do they do nearly enough to interrogate the crucial roles that providers play in producing and reproducing these harmful norms.

Cultural-Competence Frameworks

The concept of cultural competence was originally articulated as a single strategy within a broader systemwide approach. Initially, Cross et al. defined it as "a set of congruent behaviors, attitudes, and policies that come together in a system, agency or among professionals and enable that system, agency or those professions to work effectively in cross-cultural situations."[14] Two decades later, the term is much less broad in scope, centering primarily on the clinical encounter between providers and patients.[15] Despite the lack of evidence that cultural competence makes a difference in practice, it has been incorporated with enthusiasm into medical education.[16] In some states, continuing medical education (CME) in cultural competence or "multicultural health" is required for renewal of medical licensure. New Jersey, California, and Washington have introduced mandatory legislation. Several other states have introduced but not yet enacted similar legislation.[17]

As the breadth of cultural competence has changed, so has the message. Rather than focusing on social and income disparities, it now centers on notions of culture based flatly on race or ethnicity.[18] The framework was originally intended to create a structure to foster institutional shifts that reduce service disparities, but in recent years it has tended toward an essentializing "cookbook" approach. Although guidelines usually stipulate that individuals do not always behave congruently with "their culture," they tend toward the reductive, with chapters that instruct providers (usually tacitly presumed to be white and seen as culturally neutral) in how to behave in a clinical setting given the "culture" of African Americans, Asian Americans, Native Americans, and so forth.[19] Most detrimentally, cultural competence is now seen as a sufficient strategy to reduce disparities on its own; it does not generally include or see itself as working in concert with analyses of community embeddedness and social disparities of health.[20]

Critiques of cultural competence argue that it tends to offer a notion of culture that is one-dimensional, reified, universal, essential, and static and that it oversimplifies the concept of "culture" by equating it with race and assuming fundamental differences between ethnicities.[21] Sakamoto asserts, "Perhaps the greatest limitation of cultural competence is its overwhelmingly apolitical or de-political nature," and he describes the ways in which cultural competence, without an analysis of systems of oppression, allows these systems to "disappear into the background."[22] Biases and prejudices are seen as personal flaws for members of dominant culture (white people, non-trans men, straight people, gender-conforming people, and so forth) to overcome rather than as a reproduction of institutional dynamics of power.

G. Pon describes cultural competence as "ossify[ing] culture as absolute" and as too inflexible to register the mutability and fluidity of culture.[23] The cultural-competence framework's ability to comprehend culture is limited to the extent to which it varies from an ostensible (and unarticulated) "center." In the case of cultural competence in health-care delivery, that center is medical practice, which is cast as neutral rather than as a complex and multilayered culture unto itself.[24] In addition, the reductive approach to conveying culture prevents multiplicity or intersectionality from being made intelligible.[25]

It excludes or glosses over multiple or shifting notions of political and social memberships and identities. Cultural competence can only comprehend one vector of "culture" at any given moment, severely limiting its ability to consider the compound effects of marginalization.[26]

Medical providers have appropriated cultural-competence frameworks in an attempt to improve patient-provider relations, often at the encouragement of trans and gender-nonconforming advocates. In so doing, they have adopted an educational strategy that does not interrogate the sexism and transphobia inherent in the pathologization of gender nonconformity that pervades the culture of biomedicine.[27] In addition, in its inability to navigate multiplicity, cultural competence is not equipped to advance a concept of gender identity that may be shaped by race, ethnicity, disability, religion, geographic location, citizenship, class, or other factors that mutually constitute positionality, experience, and identity. Nor is it able to capture the ways in which these singular or multiple factors may be in perpetual flux or the ways in which intersections of memberships may generate complex, contradictory, and context-specific manifestations of gender and identity.

The Consequences of Adopting a Cultural Competence Framework for Queer and Trans Health

Although cultural-competence frameworks may occasionally allow for trainers to scratch the surface of institutional limitations, these do not provide the tools and support necessary to take up entrenched inequities at the level of the institution. For example, many trainings attend to the presumptuous structure of intake forms that ask patients to respond to a question about "sex" or "gender" without including options for gender-nonconforming or trans individuals who do not consider themselves to be simply "male" or "female." However, trainings do not frequently attend to the ways in which politics of gender anxiety, far more than ethics of care, inform medical and health establishments' decisions about delivering and covering trans-specific medical care.[28] Changing an intake form is an easier fix than changing institutional oppression; it is only a singular symptom of the longstanding ownership that medicine has taken in managing, monitoring, and controlling sex and gender.

Cultural-competence frameworks have little capacity to foreground the dispersed and damaging effects—in law, policy, and beyond—of medical management of transgender identity.[29] Without a means to attach the underlying misappropriation of authority to its effects (such as exclusionary intake forms or blanket exclusion clauses in insurance coverage), we can expect any resulting shifts in medical culture to take place only at a correspondingly superficial level.[30] The surface-level changes do make a difference in trans and gender-nonconforming patients' ability to better access care, but they do not attend to some of the central problems of medicine's role in managing gender and the ways these often have deeper and longer-lasting effects on trans and gender-nonconforming people's lives. Just as importantly, failing to attend to the sexism that underpins medical management of sex and gender precludes trans-health advocates from creating alliances with feminist health advocates that have long advanced such critiques of health care and medicine.

Trainings about transgender health, although by no means uniform, have a number of common features. Besides clinical recommendations, these often include (1) offering definitions for terms used frequently in trans communities, (2) distinguishing between sexual orientation and gender identity, and (3) sharing experiences or narratives of trans or gender-nonconforming people. In the realm of cultural competence, this is "knowledge-based" pedagogy, or strategies to help providers understand what it is, what it means, and what it is like to be trans. This approach has three major problems.

The first problem with this knowledge-based approach is that in offering up definitions and specific linguistic distinctions, we limit the ability of providers to cultivate their skills to establish trust with patients and to elicit important information rather than offering "answers" or concrete metrics by which they might categorize their patients (with or without their patients' participation or complicity). Accordingly, we also limit the possibility of trans or gender-nonconforming patients to describe and to define themselves for providers to the extent that doing so may be pertinent to care.[31]

The second problem is that terms, definitions, and narratives are all local knowledges associated with a vast range of meanings, contradictions, assumptions, and sources. Although important to the sustenance and survival of our communities, they are not as a whole vital to our health care. The attempt on the part of providers to understand us can distract from a focus on eliminating barriers, and it can also obscure the ways in which barriers to care for trans people are related to barriers to care for many other people as well.[32] Further, the ways in which these local knowledges are mobilized may tend to prioritize or to centralize certain members of communities over others, and, in the context of trainings, these "most-common" or "loudest" experiences rise to the top.

The third problem with the narrative or experiential approach in particular is that although "humanizing" the issue may be a powerful and effective move, it is also a potentially fetishizing one. And although it may be pedagogically appealing to present stories "in our own words" to providers, this approach may lend itself to a reductive "representational" message: the circulation of a myth that a prototypical trans person exists.

Trans people have often articulated medicalized narratives in the context of clinical care to obtain the interventions they need that may not otherwise be available to them because of restrictive medical requirements. For this reason, narratives are already perilous territory for trans people in the context of medical care, and offering them up within trainings (particularly if the participants are resistant to the conventional medical model) could have a variety of consequences.[33] These might be positive: Perhaps in registering the extent to which the "trans experience" cannot be reduced to a universal set of psychiatric symptoms, providers might argue for a relaxation or removal of the strict criteria for access to medical interventions. They might also be damaging: Providers may take this as confirmation of widely held stereotypes that trans people are frauds,[34] that trans and gender-nonconforming individuals are prone to lie or exaggerate in general and about themselves, and therefore require *more-* rather than less-restrictive regulation of treatment.

In either case, without context of how trans people's experiences are embedded in and materially affected by exclusion, lack of access, and other forms of marginalization, trans narratives are vulnerable to being universalized, co-opted, or otherwise used against the interest of trans access to quality health care. Even if such context is included, the degree to which dominant trans narratives[35] have been articulated within a category of assimilation and productivity has exacerbated the marginalization of trans people of color, those with disabilities, those who do not pass, queer trans people, undocumented trans immigrants, and trans refugees, among others.[36] Within cultural-competence frameworks, those who vary least from the biomedical "norm" of gender variance are the most likely to benefit, because, for this group, the "one-vector" approach is not as off the mark as it may be for many other marginalized trans and gender-nonconforming individuals.

I do not intend to imply that training providers about caring for trans and gender-nonconforming individuals is a worthless endeavor—quite the contrary. In fact, Vivian Namaste notes the great success of trans people having moved from a position of being objects of pathologization to subjects of scholarly inquiry.[37] Continuous with this move toward subjectivity, the fact that some trans activists and advocates have taken positions of expertise in educating health providers is a profound shift, particularly considering the uncontested dominance of medical opinion in shaping the lives of trans people in the recent past.[38]

However, the ways in which this "expertise" has been taken up by trainers and curriculum developers has not resulted in an equitable distribution of or increased access to quality health care for all trans and gender-nonconforming people. Inequitable distribution is in part a function of the cultural competence framework and its limited applications. Medical education has allowed only a very narrow space for discussion of delivery of care to trans and gender-nonconforming individuals and little to no room for institutional transformation. Lastly, the professionalization of LGBTQ activism and the forces of assimilation at work within this have given disproportionate voice and presence to educated, professional-class individuals as trainers.[39] The confluence of these factors leads to a scenario in which providers are informally given the message that knowledge about transgender patients is "special" (and therefore optional or extraneous) knowledge, and that trainers, especially when they are themselves trans or gender nonconforming, are largely representative of trans and gender-nonconforming communities as a whole, although this is distinctly not the case.

Although providers may not wish to damage trans and gender-nonconforming individuals, most operate in a biomedical context that rests on a set of erroneous assumptions about gender nonconformity. Alternative trans-affirmative models do exist, such as Arlene Istar Lev's work and others.[40] These models—those of self-determination, wellness-based medicine, and administrative policies that do not depend on medical interventions, for example—would pair much more productively in trainings with information about clinical conduct and guidelines about primary and specialty care than the current information about terminology and narrative trans experiences.[41]

Practicing Training and Evaluating Effects

What happens after the training can be surprising and alarming, as it reveals some of the profound limitations of the cultural competence–based training approach.[42] In the course of a community-based evaluation research project I completed with community research team members, I conducted a number of interviews with health-care providers who had participated in training administered by a nonprofit LGBT health organization.[43] Some of their comments and reflections were affirming and exciting. For example, a number of interview participants had without probing or suggestion taken on advocacy roles in their clinics and institutions with regard to trans health. However, other reflections were disappointing and unsettling. For example, a number of interview participants latched on strongly to the aspects of the training that covered terminology or that included one or two experience-based narratives from trans trainers or panelists. These sections were frequently named as being the most memorable or most important part of the training. A number of providers discussed the ways in which they felt that the terminology section of the training had helped them to *more accurately categorize their gender-nonconforming patients.* Given the rapidly changing and community-specific quality of language in trans and gender-nonconforming communities, this focus is bound to lead providers to apply terms to people who do not necessarily use the same terms to describe themselves. Other providers felt that the narrative sections had helped them get better pictures of "who trans people are" and "what they look like."[44] Given the enormous variation within trans communities, this was a highly reductive and potentially harmful effect of this strategy.

One of the most disturbing examples of the misappropriation of terminology was a provider who not only incorrectly recalled the definitions as they were discussed in the training but also described how she could now use these terms to distinguish between "transgender people" and "transvestites" among her patients:

> [A transvestite] either identifies themselves as female or feels female sometimes, [but is] a male . . . has male genitalia. And so then, either lives most of their life or part of their life dressed up as a female. Or vice

versa. As opposed to a transgender person who I guess I see . . . as someone who's taking more steps by taking hormones or doing surgeries or really transforming the physical nature of their body to be like the gender that they think they are.[45]

Comments such as these are rather chilling. Not only had this individual misunderstood the trainer's message, she did so in a way that was likely to harm rather than to improve the quality of her delivery of care to some trans and gender-nonconforming individuals.

In fact, many trans individuals do nothing to "transform the physical nature of their body." Many of these individuals would not identify as "transvestites" and might respond quite strongly to being labeled as such. It should also be noted that in the training, the term "transvestite" was introduced alongside the term "cross-dresser" and was mentioned as a term that people do *not* frequently apply to themselves. Moreover, the cue that might cause this health provider to call upon any "transgender health" skills that she may have gained in the training is the degree to which a trans patient passes or has sought gender-specific medical interventions, such as surgery or hormone treatment.[46] Because these are expensive interventions, it is likely that the patients for whom she will tend to draw on these skills will be those who have chosen and who can afford these interventions. This group falls disproportionately along lines of class, race, age, and other factors that favor people with greater degrees of privilege.

Even if providers recall terms with more accuracy, the "single-lecture" model allows for only very limited discussion and correction of errors and does not lend itself to synthesis or to contextualization within a larger frame of healthcare provision to marginalized communities. Furthermore, in offering concrete, specific, and bounded words and definitions, providers are likely to want to use them in practice, even if trainers explain that these are not universally used or acceptable within communities. This drive likely originates from a well-intentioned desire to facilitate comfort for patients by demonstrating knowledge and expertise. And, indeed, using such bounded terms and definitions with trans patients who subscribe to a medical model or whose self-definitions align with the terms put forth in the training may have this result. However, for those whose use of words or definitions differs or departs significantly from taxonomies that are promulgated in trainings, it may have the opposite effect and may close rather than open a space for discussion with providers.[47]

In his book *Imagining Transgender,* David Valentine describes the origins and uses of the term "transgender" and the ways in which the least enfranchised, including low-income people of color, have resisted this as a meaningful term and as a category of self-identification. He describes "transgender" as a category that hinges on an articulated separation between sexuality and gender that "unintentionally reproduce[s] other social realities, in particular, historically situated structures of class, racial and gender differences."[48] The strength of the term "transgender"—namely, its malleability—is at the same time a liability:

"The very flexibility of transgender, its strength as a tool of political organizing ... makes it possible to use without specifying who is being invoked in particular instances."[49] In his ethnographic work, Valentine speaks with a number of informants who, although recognizing that they are understood by social-service providers as "transgender," do not align themselves with this term. Related to the problems I have discussed with circulating bounded terms, Valentine's work demonstrates the ways in which the very categories and conceptual separations (as between "sexuality" and "gender") that are advanced in trainings may not be widely accepted, even by those who would benefit in a variety of ways from the competent, quality care trainers attempt to inculcate in providers.

As a trainer, I have struggled with the predicament of building a training curriculum that fits the constraints imposed by those requesting it while still holding to on to the challenges of discussing a "community" that is by no means singular, aligned, or uniform in its needs.[50] Oftentimes, one must fit topics into an impossible timeframe—sometimes no more than an hour or two. A trainer must also strike a balance between using a pedagogical approach that will be effective for those immersed in medical education with an approach that demands a paradigmatic shift in the manner in which students approach not only gender but also the notion of "difference" more broadly. It is quite tempting to use such a convention as offering a concrete set of terms of definitions, because this seems to give providers a chance to feel as if they have learned something important. It also may give a trainer the sense that they are helping providers demystify a set of concepts and better comprehend the existence of trans individuals, which seems a logical first step to improvement in quality of care. Similarly, when a trainer is transgender or gender nonconforming, it may seem to make sense to use one's self as an example. These moves, however, can have unexpected consequences. Many times, some of those teaching strategies that seem to be the most effective during trainings directly depart from the intention or objective of the message when translated in practice.

Health-Care Provider Trainings: Potential for Change, Actuality of Limitations

Although it is difficult to ascertain how great a role trainings have played in this, it is clear that there has been some movement in medicine and public health to improve health-care provision for trans and gender-nonconforming patients and communities. Trainings may play significant roles in prompting changes to gender markers on intake forms, contesting blanket insurance exclusions, and revising some of the harshest and most unreasonable and coercive features of the World Professional Association for Transgender Health (WPATH) standards of care, such as the "real-life experience" phase or "real-life test."[51] In short, they may afford an opportunity to make specific and concrete recommendations to providers about how to structure practice that makes substantive (if not foundational) changes in the experience of health-care delivery. And once again, they do important work to shift the position of "expert" with regard to knowledge about care provision to transgender and gender-nonconforming patients.

Trainings almost certainly serve to foreground a discussion that otherwise rarely, if ever, takes place in medical or continuing medical education.[52] This alone can be viewed as a success in raising into relief a set of patient needs that is otherwise not attended to. However, although it is understandable that trans advocates have utilized cultural-competence frameworks as sites from which to mobilize projects to improve the quality of health-care delivery to trans and gender-nonconforming individuals, this choice has come at a cost. As mentioned, relative privilege among trans individuals has tended to replicate itself as a result of using these approaches as a strategy for educating providers. This is in direct conflict with the hopes and intentions of trainers and trans activists and advocates in general.

Health-care provider trainings offer one example of the ways in which transgender-health activism has brought greater benefit for those trans individuals who have the greatest access to privilege and/or are most closely aligned with medical models of transgender. We should be further analyzing how transgender-health activism has at times inadvertently supported the misdistribution of benefits. In addition, it will be important to continue the project of developing and refining theories and frameworks that will facilitate the redistribution of benefits such that marginalized trans and gender-nonconforming individuals are considered to be primary recipients. The goal should be to facilitate material changes to people's lives and life chances; it may also serve academically to develop a notion of transgender studies that is engaged more broadly and deeply with feminist practice and theory.

The terrain of health as a site of trans activism continues to gain traction. In 2004, the National Coalition for LGBT Health published a set of transgender health priorities with a focus on eliminating health disparities. In addition to the various transition-specific standards of care, Vancouver Coastal Health has developed guidelines for primary care. Trans-identified individuals now sit on the WPATH board and have played roles in modifying the most-restrictive aspects of its standards of care. A variety of studies has established (with the empirical weight required by federal funding agencies) the preponderance of marked health disparities in trans communities. The scope of the conversation about trans health has grown dramatically in the last decade, and it will likely continue to expand.

Many strategies might be undertaken to increase the reach and effectiveness of trainings. It is first necessary to broaden the existing pool of trainers and to decentralize the professional, class, and race privilege within this group. Trans and gender-nonconforming people who are most affected by multiple vectors of marginalization have unique vantage points regarding which issues might be most critical to discuss with providers. Leadership in curriculum development and training strategies should be shifted to those who are most affected by varied and overlapping health disparities. Leadership development and "train the trainers" sessions could support this and also serve to build skills across the entire pool of trainers (who many times do not have teaching or training backgrounds). This change in leadership would serve in part to mitigate some of the concentration of privilege among those who develop and administer trainings. This would also shift the direction of trainings away from "trying to understand the cultural other," as Izumi Sakamoto put it, and "towards interrogating the power-laden contexts in which the process of othering occurs; towards naming and subverting the dynamics of power that allow for the culturally different to be deemed as 'other' in the first place."[53] In general, this requires problematizing static notions of culture and politicizing the frameworks through which patient-provider dynamics occur.

A number of factors make it very difficult to effect broad change within the practice of medicine, but it is a challenge to which many people and groups have risen. Moving forward, it will be critical to take stock of which changes have taken hold, the people or groups who are leading these, and how these have affected our communities as a whole.

Strategies to Bring about a More-Expansive and Inclusive Trans-Health Movement

Thus far, I have discussed some of the limitations in the dominant approaches within trans-health activism to create changes in medical practice. I would like to conclude by mentioning some current innovative approaches that have the potential to benefit trans and gender-nonconforming individuals in a manner less disparate than the gains offered by other, less-inclusive approaches.

Samuel Lurie and Ben Singer are two individuals working within the field of public health and health education. Both have conducted extensive trainings with health-care providers. Singer has also conducted ethnographic work with providers on this topic, and Lurie has conducted educational-needs assessments and evaluation. Both individuals compassionately recognize the constraints inherent in health-care provision and the socialization that limits providers' ability to engage in supportive, nonpathologizing, and affirming ways with trans and gender-nonconforming patients. However, they also recognize the potentially productive moment of pushing providers to grapple with the infinite possibilities and manifestations of transgender and gender nonconformity, inoculating the providers they train against the "singular representational" model.

Lurie's trainings move providers from a familiar "Traditional Binary Gender Model" through a "Continuum Gender Model" to what he terms a "Revolutionary Gender Model."[54] The latter includes an expansive set of possible combinations of sexuality, gender expression, and bodies. Although Lurie utilizes some of the language and structure of cultural-competence frameworks, he departs from these in a variety of ways, using terminology as a jumping-off point to create what one might call "useful confusion" through positing his

"Revolutionary Gender Model." In addition, instead of using a formulaic approach, he works with providers to determine their questions, assumptions, and gaps in skills and knowledge to develop useful content and approaches to trainings.[55] Further, unlike many trainers using a cultural-competence approach, he employs regular evaluation of trainings sessions.

Singer, who has also used Lurie's model in his own trainings, relishes this moment of engagement with what he calls the "transgender sublime":

> It is my hope that by seizing the moment of sublime recognition of the limitless possible bodies, genders and sexualities in trans worlds, and by confirming the potential terror of being faced with the great unknown, that a more ethical way to relate to trans people can emerge in the training of medical service providers. To deny or try to eliminate the sublime aspect of trans-health is to miss an opportunity to create strategies that accommodate both the needs of providers and the needs of those accessing care. The paradigm shift from a medical pathology to a trans-health approach provides us with a context for such ethical relationships to emerge.[56]

Singer's proposed health-care "paradigm shift" from a "pathology model" to a "trans-health model" is an attempt to shift from the "medical gaze" of pathologization toward a means of self-determination for trans and gender-nonconforming individuals. He offers, as a rough model of what such a shift might look like, a variety of possible alternatives to the medical model of transgender: Instead of institutional regulation and gatekeeping, he proposes harm reduction, advocacy, and informed consent. Instead of medical "experts" and providers being in control of decisions, he instead suggests peer expertise and community partnering. As an alternative to the Gender Identity Disorder (GID) diagnosis, he offers "Non-disordered Gender Complexity." It may be somewhat difficult to imagine precisely how these would be mobilized within the significant constraints of medical education and practice. Nevertheless, it is refreshing to think through a possible way to reconceptualize the pathologization of gender nonconformity in a way that could benefit health-care providers and trans and gender-nonconforming individuals.

The Sylvia Rivera Law Project (SRLP) in New York City offers a variety of trainings, including trainings about health care. Unlike many other organizations, it offers trainings for trans and gender-nonconforming community members as well as for service providers. Trainings for community members are conducted as "know your rights" sessions and are designed to assist low-income trans and gender-nonconforming individuals in particular to navigate a complex and at times contradictory health-care system. Trainings for service providers focus primarily on barriers to trans and gender-nonconforming individuals' accessing a variety of services, including health care, public benefits, and other social and legal services. In presenting health trainings through a lens of access,

SRLP utilizes a variety of training tools to show the links between disproportionate poverty, homelessness, incarceration, and deportation and illuminates the role of inadequate health care, education, and other factors within this broad set of social determinants of health. Trainers also facilitate discussion that includes developing "strategies for addressing gender identity discrimination through [service providers'] work and providing exceptional services to communities in crisis because of gender identity discrimination."[57] The breadth of this approach allows trainers to advance with the concept of "health" as something more expansive than the clinical encounter and to implicate providers as agents in fighting the effects of gender-identity discrimination rather than simply being responsible for providing "competent" care." Also notable is the choice in language to avoid "competent care" in favor of "exceptional" care, sidestepping problematic associations with a cultural-competence framework and simultaneously raising the bar in terms of demand for high-quality and effective care provision.

In addition to utilizing the medium of trainings, a variety of groups and organizations have taken up trans health as one aspect of broader, multi-issue campaigns or projects to eliminate barriers to survival and well-being for trans and gender-nonconforming individuals. TransJustice, a group of trans and gender-nonconforming people of color, is part of the Audre Lorde Project (ALP) in New York City.[58] It works on a multitude of issues, including job access, housing, education, health care, HIV services, and resistance to various forms of institutionalized and anti-immigrant violence.[59] This group, along with several other organizations, including SRLP, Housing Works, and Queers for Economic Justice, formed a committee in the fall of 2008 to fight transphobic discrimination in New York City's Human Resources Administration that prevents low-income trans and gender-nonconforming people from accessing public benefits.[60] This work is an example of multi-issue, grassroots organizing–based work that is inclusive of issues of health access but takes a broader approach to reducing barriers. Its potential gains are centered among trans and gender-nonconforming individuals who encounter the most precipitous barriers to health and survival, which has not generally been the case in cultural competence–based training.

Other practitioners, activists, and advocates who work more squarely within clinical practice have done work to effect broad change for health-care providers. Recognizing the lack of knowledge as a problem for general and specialty providers, and taking into account providers' anxiety about how much they needed to know, the Vancouver Coastal Health's (VCH's) Trans Care Project, in concert with the now-defunct Transcend Transgender Support and Education Society, developed a set of standards for transgender primary and specialty care.[61] This was a particularly significant project, because prior to this, standards and guidelines of care were specific only to gender-related medical interventions. Although the Transgender Health Program continues to see trans and gender-nonconforming patients, the Trans Care Project is complete. The resources it produced are linked on its Web site and are available for order from VCH.[62] Among these resources are seven sets of clinical guidelines, seventeen consumer-information booklets, and several training frameworks. Although the specialty guidelines for gender-specific medical intervention parallel those of the WPATH (previously called Harry Benjamin International Gender Dysphoria Association, or HBIGDA), they also focus on the limitations and flexible application of these and emphasize a harm-reduction and informed-consent approach to these interventions.

Across the Borders of the Academy

Trans- and genderqueer-identified scholar activists, such as Susan Stryker, Jin Haritaworn, Dean Spade, and Namaste, accomplish a critical project in acting from their multiple memberships within and outside the academy. In this historical and academic moment, gender and sexuality studies scholars have at times used the category of transgender as a vehicle for critical inquiry without necessarily engaging with the lived realities of trans and gender-nonconforming individuals. In addition, some scholars have approached trans studies by placing the onus of a politic of gender transgression on trans and gender-nonconforming individuals, overlooking the ways in which gender-conforming individuals also have profound roles to play in the politics of gender transgression and obscuring the ways in which some trans and gender-nonconforming individuals explicitly do not align themselves with such politics. The scholars that I have named instead present a set of theories and approaches to looking at the category of transgender that lends itself to application and that offers a nuanced critique and political analysis. At the same time, these scholars remain involved, active, and rooted in the communities in which they study.

One of the ways that many scholars (trans and non-trans) have accomplished this simultaneity of engagement across the borders of the academy is by employing such research methods as community-based participatory research (CBPR), which has at its center an expectation of community members' playing active roles in shaping, taking part in, and benefiting from academic research.[63] This approach to research serves in part to decrease the separation between academic production and dissemination of knowledge and concepts and provides a means to establish shared agreements about what research has relevance and will benefit the set of communities at the center of research. It demands, or at least begins to demand, a redistribution of what counts as valuable knowledge and takes up the question of how that knowledge will travel within, through, and beyond the context of the academy.[64] Health-professional work will continue to benefit from taking this approach to research and to building sustainable partnerships with trans and gender-nonconforming communities (including, but also beyond, organization-based communities).

A number of research projects that have taken this approach use complex and multi-issue lenses to examine health disparities within trans, gender-nonconforming, and queer communities. Researchers who take into account overlapping marginalizations are better equipped to identify, in partnership with communities, the range of complexities that affect health and social issues in these communities.[65] In addition, these projects contextualize health problems with the effects of marginalization, and, instead of flattening communities into a category of "vulnerable populations," they identify and leverage support for community strengths.

One such study in San Francisco was successful in helping gain funding to create changes in health- and preventive-care services for trans and gender-nonconforming individuals, including making changes to gender markers on data-collection forms throughout the San Francisco Health Department.[66] Currently, the HONOR project carries forth this strengths-based model among urban LGBTQ and Two-Spirit Native Americans and Alaska Natives, as it works to develop a model of coping with stress and trauma that incorporates cultural resilience and links health outcomes with historical trauma.[67] The Trans PULSE project in Toronto, Ontario, is studying problems identified by local trans communities with access to health and social services.[68] The research team is looking specifically at the ways in which transphobia, social exclusion, and cisnormativity affect health.[69]

In planning projects to improve health and health access in trans and gender-nonconforming communities, it helps immensely to orient projects toward contextual approaches to health (historical and forward-looking), models of strength and resiliency, leveraging funds and sharing resources, and formation of sustainable partnerships to foster health. Doing so demands that researchers and scholars create, against the geometry of inequitable distribution of resources shaped by institutions, an increased degree of equitability within and between academic and nonacademic communities.[70] Distinct from a fetishization or false idealization of communities, this instead calls for a sustained engagement over time with the complexities, contradictions, and challenges as well as the rich sources of knowledge that exist in nonacademically affiliated community settings.

One of the strengths of CBPR as an approach, in contrast with cultural-competency work, is its political engagement. Although these approaches are far from cohesive, most researchers who bring this orientation to their work seem to consider the terrain of health to be an extremely broad one. This makes a great deal of sense, given researchers' sustained engagement with the communities with whom they work, as health issues rarely occur in a vacuum.

Unfortunately, a number of projects that might be much more far-reaching and that would directly and immediately affect trans and gender-nonconforming people's lives have been left to languish while resources have been concentrated in cultural competence–based training and in legal-reform strategies. For example, a great deal of resources have been used to fight for employment inclusion, although few have been used to increase trans and gender-nonconforming people's access to health insurance that covers gender-related medical interventions.[71] In addition, voices advocating for single-payer or universal health care through a lens of access for trans and gender-nonconforming individuals have been notably absent from town-hall discussions and other discourse around health care–reform movements.[72] Given the degree to which consumerist health care seems to shape the wealth-privileging character of trans health care, particularly gender-related surgeries, this is a profound absence. Trans voices would complement, overlap with, and enrich a number of the arguments that have been issued by proponents of disability rights, women-of-color feminists, reproductive-rights activists, and others in the course of the health care–reform debate over the last two years. The same has been true of Medicaid reforms and cuts, particularly given that private insurance companies tend to follow the lead of public agencies when it comes to decisions about health coverage.

Expanding the Scope of Trainings

Utilizing trainings is a potentially useful strategy, when used in concert with others, to increase quality and access to health-care services for trans and gender-nonconforming individuals. It is not a strategy that will work alone, however, nor is it one that will benefit communities equitably if it fails to expand its scope and reach. Writing of her experience in conducting work in an academic institution to document racism and to create race-equity policies, Sara Ahmed writes, "It is because colonialism, racism, and gender hierarchies continue to shape educational as well as social spaces that diversity matters."[73] Working to achieve diversity without an articulated connection to these larger contexts fails on a variety of levels. Similarly, cultural-competence approaches, in their failure to draw links to the variety of hierarchies that operate on and within trans and gender-nonconforming communities, will not accomplish what they set out to do: to improve health access and health outcomes for all members of these communities. Instead, that project requires a broad engagement with the social, political, and economic contexts of various trans and gender-nonconforming communities and must emphasize structural and policy change, sustainable and ongoing education and resource sharing, and elements of feedback from patients and people in these communities.

Although trans and gender-nonconforming individuals may encounter barriers disparately, depending on a variety of factors, it is most useful for trainers to focus on those who are most severely affected by barriers. As discussed earlier, most trainings tend to focus on those trans and gender-nonconforming individuals who align most closely to the medical model and who likely encounter relatively fewer barriers to health. More equitable and effective would be to use an approach of "teaching from the margins"[74] or to focus teaching on delivery of care to trans and gender-nonconforming individuals who encounter barriers that may be more numerous, profound, or constitutive of their daily lives.

In contrast to the standard cultural-competence framework, trainings must interrogate the ways in which the process of othering occurs—a critical orientation toward health and medicine that feminists have well explored. The pathologization of gender nonconformity reaches well beyond transgender in the culture of medicine, and illuminating these patterns serves to expose the coerciveness and normalizing forces of a variety of medical treatments and diagnoses, current and historical. Trainings would then have more potential to facilitate productive alliances with feminists and other activists struggling for self-determination in health care.

It is by no means necessary to abandon trainings as a strategy, but instead of focusing time and energy on terminology and background, it would be more useful to concentrate on information that will actually make a positive improvement in trans and gender-nonconforming people's experiences. In a clinical sense, this means giving knowledge-based information about clinical needs and offering reliable and less-coercive recommendations for care. It means emphasizing the inaccuracy of surgical status or other gender-based medical interventions as a marker for trans identity and discussing the limitations of "male" and "female" as gender categories, on forms and in general. In a broader sense, it means clarifying the internal discordance of how treatments are excessively regulated for gender non-normative treatment in contrast with the minimal regulation or ease of coverage for similar treatments when they are gender conforming and the direct consequences of submitting patients to violent and dangerous "treatments," such as the "real-life test." It means giving providers tools to care clinically for trans people and to understand the ways that medical culture creates barriers for trans and gender-nonconforming people within the context of accessing health care and outside this direct context, such as in the realm of identity documentation or in using or being subjected to sex-segregated facilities, such as restrooms, shelters, and jails or prisons. Lastly, it means giving providers a sense of the inappropriateness of their roles as gatekeepers and helping them minimize this position in the current context and work as agents to transform it as time goes on.

Conclusion

Doing this work is deeply challenging, and trainers are not in a position to easily transform the ways in which this information is conveyed to health-care providers. Trainers have already carried the burden of this work, using few resources and great ingenuity to fill in gaps that medical education leaves. In addition, the medical profession is generally not one that accepts change easily, adding to the difficulty of moving away from cultural-competence frameworks. Nevertheless, if trans-health activism plans to increase access broadly and to distribute its wins equitably, it is critical to take a broader approach. Without a change in strategy, trans-health activism will continue to benefit primarily the most-privileged sectors of trans and gender-nonconforming communities. Scholars and nonacademically affiliated activists can play important roles in broadening trans-health activism's engagement with social, racial, political, and economic justice. Scholars can advance politically and community-engaged scholarship, work collaboratively across disciplines, and develop frameworks that are theoretically rigorous and practically effective. Nonacademically affiliated activists (and, depending on context, scholars as well) can create alliances with people and groups that are similarly marginalized within health and medicine. All these changes will help us on a larger scale increase access and equity in health care.

8

AREN Z. AIZURA

Transnational Transgender Rights and Immigration Law

Imagining Rights

On a panel called Queer Necropolitics at the American Anthropological Association meeting in 2009, Sima Shakhsari related the story of Naz, a trans woman from Iran who was featured in a number of documentaries about transsexuality in Iran. In the global North, recent media attention to the situation of trans people in Iran has anxiously deliberated on the visibility of their "suffering." The symptoms of this suffering may include social and familial repudiation, difficulty finding work, and the seemingly odd juxtaposition of a sympathetic medical establishment and government that, simultaneously, imprison gays and lesbians. Such media portrayals explicitly beg a further anxious query of whether trans people in Iran are not simply gays and lesbians undergoing enforced surgical mutilation to live with their partners.[1] As Shakhsari pointed out, the rash of documentaries on Iranian trans people generally portray transsexual subjects as stuck in Iran as a repressive "elsewhere," juxtaposed with the ostensible freedom of queer life in the global North. Naz, however, did not remain in Iran. After the documentaries were filmed, she went to Turkey and from there applied successfully for asylum in Canada. A year after arriving in Canada, Naz committed suicide, alone in state-subsidized housing from which she would soon have been evicted.

What happened to Naz is neither uncommon nor unexpected. Immigrants to the "developed" regions of North America, Australia, and Europe are subject to a host of laws regulating their lives and racializing and criminalizing the undocumented. The reality of Naz's suicide acts as a counter-narrative to a familiar story in which an oppressed queer or trans person living in a developing country, a dictatorship, or a fundamentalist Islamic state immigrates to the "West" to encounter freedom, hope, and a better life. This narrative is a staple of feature films and documentaries about gender-variant and queer people immigrating.[2] This immigration narrative folds into the (often-mistaken) assumption that models for transgender rights are generally initiated in "Western" nation-states—the United States, Canada, Australia, the European Union—and will later spread to other, less-progressive "corners" of the globe.

Of course, models for transgender rights and citizenship *do* move, spread, and emerge, and often in locations that might seem unlikely. For example, the first International Congress on Gender Identity and Human Rights was held in Barcelona in 2010; but the agenda was not shaped by European or North American activists as much as by the presence of activists from India, Chile, Argentina, Thailand, the Philippines, Venezuela, South Africa, and a host of other locations. As gender-variant life has become more socially visible in particular locations around the world, concurrently more struggles are occurring to produce legislation, regulations, and administrative apparatuses that accord gender-variant subjects the privileges of citizenship (i.e., rights specific to gender-variant people).[3] What Paisley Currah calls a "transgender rights imaginary" are the arguments and counter-arguments, rights claims, and forms of law being deployed in these struggles.[4] Transgender-rights discourses are already contested: Many have critiqued the tendency to incorporate medicalized understandings of surgical transsexuality in the law or to enshrine a white, heterosexual, middle-class subject of rights as the "ideal" gender-variant subject. Yet the difficulty of survival for gender-variant people in the "developed" nations we champion as modern and progressive challenges this transgender-rights imaginary and begs a *different* question: What would happen if we thought about trans and gender-variant freedom outside and against the framework of the nation-state?

In this chapter, I intervene in emerging imaginaries of transgender rights and their usefulness in understanding and combating the global regulation of immigration and its effects on the lives of gender-variant people. In the realm of immigration, a transgender-rights imaginary can be seen emerging in several sites. One is a publication called *Immigration Law and the Transgender Client* (hereon referred to as *Immigration Law*), co-authored by the New York–based advocacy group Immigration Equality and the San Francisco–based Transgender Law Center. The only handbook available globally that addresses transgender immigration issues in detail, *Immigration Law* is intended as a practice manual for attorneys who represent gender-variant clients. Informally, this handbook also acts as a primer for gender-variant immigrants (or potential immigrants) to the United States on how to navigate different visa categories. Although it deals specifically with U.S. law, as a policy document it presages similar documents that may emerge in nation-states with a similarly high level of immigration and an exceptionalist image as the liberatory location in which people may live as trans without harm. Through a close reading of *Immigration Law*, I interrogate the limits of neoliberal-rights frameworks that produce gender-variant people as subjects who must perfectly perform regulatory procedures to gain access to rights. In this framework, political transformation is displaced onto individuals, who are asked to be visible as "transgender subjects" (hence also to conform to the nation-state's idea about what that means) for their cases to become part of the precedential law-making machine. In doing so,

Immigration Law exemplifies the limits and inconsistencies of a political practice oriented exclusively toward "rights."

Following this reading, I broaden the discussion to ask what work intersections between transgender studies, queer studies, and feminism can accomplish toward generating new strategies to prevent death. I argue that what we need is a trans theory that not only acknowledges its debts to feminist theory and incorporates a feminist critique of heteronormativity but also that turns "trans" in an anti-identitarian direction. Although it is important to acknowledge that transgender is an identity category whose subjects' access to freedom will be divided along the cuts of affluence, racialization, gender, and citizenship, we also need to look at where and how bodies escape or act clandestinely outside those categories—and at moments in which the categories of immigrant, transgender person, man, and woman become incoherent and inconsistent. This means taking on the lessons of particular feminist and queer antiracist work on intersectionality, and also challenging some of the limits of intersectional analysis.

It is neither new nor insurrectionary to write about borders in trans theory. With few exceptions until very recently, trans theory has examined those figural "borders" regulating traffic between genders rather than watching what happens to gender-variant people at real borders, appropriating the metaphor of the immigrant "without land or nation" to understand transgender experience without considering that many trans people are, in fact, immigrants.[5] For example, the slogan on the Web page of TransX, an Austrian transgender-activist organization, reads, "*Wir öffnen Geschlechterngrenzen* [We open gendered borders]." Even as TransX fights against the deportation of its asylum-seeker members from the European Union, the "opening-borders" metaphor risks annexing talk of the border to gender alone. Existing scholarly accounts of transgender immigration law often perform a similar error. Rather than analyzing discrimination against transgender immigrants as part of the broader immigration industrial complex that recognizes or misrecognizes different immigrant bodies using different tactics, case notes and reviews on transgender immigration generally begin with a critique of the legal mechanics of fixing the "truth" of gendered bodies (i.e., medico-legal interpretations of corporeal requirements to be recognized as transgender). With few exceptions, this critique is framed as though that were an end in itself, culminating in the argument that lawmaking should incorporate improved models of recognition.[6]

This chapter bypasses the task of "finding a better model." Rather, I probe how different regimes of gender definition regularly collide in a site where such collisions remain by-products of a much-more administratively violent biopolitics aimed at regulating national and racialized borders and directing labor flows. The differentiated recognition of gender-variant bodies has become just another part of the machinery of institutions that control geographic mobility, a new technique of control to modulate enclosure or opportunity.[7] Under these conditions, we need to look at the bigger picture. For such theorists as Dean Spade, this means resisting the move to frame law reform—particularly antidiscrimination and hate-crimes legislation—as the primary political goal of trans politics and remaining alert to how trans-political projects are mobilized toward neoliberal goals of inclusion, optimization, and incorporation.[8] Rather than framing queer or transgender as categories that are excluded or invisible within the *polis*, Spade investigates how the emerging inclusion and visibility of transgender and gender identity as legal and administrative categories are fraught, often producing "targeted insecurities and death" for those who are unclassifiable or misclassified.[9] Spade's focus on populations most at risk of death or lifelong precariousness—such as immigrants, the incarcerated, those who engage in informal economies, and people of color—is instructive here: These populations are also targeted for increased surveillance and regulation in the context of sustained, ongoing wars—on drugs, on terror, on immigration.

This chapter contributes to that project by situating the forms of power that produce and govern gender-variant bodies within a framework that looks beyond the nation-state (and especially beyond the United States). Gender-variant movement needs to be understood as part of global movement, and trans communities need to be understood as composed not of "citizens" but of people who are also undocumented, stateless, or constantly on the move. This commitment is both personal and theoretical. As an Australian citizen living in the United States, I encounter immigration systems regularly. However, my status as a white academic whose skills are in demand have thus far meant successful, if nerve-wracking, visa-application procedures (so long as I avoid presenting my female-assigned birth certificate alongside the passport that designates me as male, and possibly even then). As a scholar of transnationality, it is impossible for me to ignore how the majority of writing on queer and transgender studies and transnationality restricts critical attention to one nation-state or one diasporic community. This is not to say that we should make universalizing assumptions of generality at the expense of focusing on the local, acknowledging the specificity of juridical governmentalities, or acknowledging the specificity of differently racialized or ethnicized communities. What I sketch out here is a tactical commitment to approaching localized struggles as linked transnationally and politically, enabling us to grasp the contact points that bind gender-variant people into global migratory regulatory regimes regardless of which geographical regions they were born in, are traveling to, or are traveling from.

For a Biopolitics of Trans Migration

Despite the recent overuse of biopolitics as a conceptual tool, Michel Foucault's insight that modern politics deploys the optimization and extension of life to control its subjects does necessary work here.[10] To push against the assumption that the nation-state marks the perimeter of politics means tracing the trajectories of immigrants *before* they reach "destination" nation-states while recognizing that vectors of global-migration flow are modulated by many national borders acting as filters.[11] Not only national governments but international and localized nongovernmental organizations and institutions contribute to global/local "regimes of mobility control."[12] These regimes deploy a variety of contradictory mechanisms to optimize labor flows, to filter particular kinds of subjects into and out of territories, to secure those populations, and to manage popular political discourse around protecting nation-states from, or opening nation-states to, immigration.

Far from offering a perspective on immigration that privileges institutional calls for better "human rights," theorizing mobility control this way permits us to approach "humanitarian" and "nonhumanitarian" immigration laws as part of the same flexible set of assemblages, aimed at modulating the enclosures just in time, case by case. These assemblages include stratified visa categories (such as temporary-work visa categories, skilled-worker visa categories, partnership or family visa categories, or asylum-seeker visa categories); the detention and deportation of undocumented migrants or those who overstay their visas, often aimed at particular racialized populations; and transnational outsourcing of detention camps to nation-states located on migration routes to "developed" countries.

From this perspective, borders are not simply about exclusion. Rather, as Angela Mitropoulos puts it, "the regulation and transformation of the movements of bodies (become calculable, exchangeable) through space, the habituating of space as market and movement as commerce."[13] The words "calculable" and "exchangeable" here alert us to how encountering the border forces us not only to become legible subjects in stratified categories (asylum seeker, permanent resident, temporary worker, skilled worker, student, visiting researcher, "illegal alien," citizen) but also to reinvent ourselves as entrepreneurial subjects under contract with the nation-state. In exchange for permission to enter a territory legally, we agree to comply with visa requirements—to work or to not work, to pay the agreed-upon fees, to leave on time, to present ourselves as hard-working, responsible, or, in the case of queer or transgender asylum seekers, as the traumatized victims of "barbaric" third-world trans- or homophobia. The symbolic and material debt incurred in such an exchange ensures the pliability and self-surveillance of the immigrant herself.

In exchange for *not* entering legally, undocumented migrants clandestinely fill a growing need for domestic or unskilled labor in "modernized" nation-states. Yet the undocumented are also characterized as having broken a contract with the state and are thus subject to an illegalized existence at higher risk of detention or deportation and the inability to harvest the other contractual benefits potentially accorded to "good immigrant" behavior, such as health benefits, sick leave, or collective bargaining. Like the Schmittian exception that enables the sovereign to suspend democracy (thus, for Schmitt, defining sovereignty itself), the suspension of the contract is built into contractualism: "the failure of will to prevail over 'custom,' the non-identity of the contracting parties, the inability of certain people to 'control themselves.'"[14] At this juncture, racializing logics dictate that "those people" were never appropriate multicultural subjects to begin with and may be ejected forthwith. Calls for immigration reform often follow the same divisive logic, pitting "good" against "bad" immigrants. For example the now-demolished DREAM Act would have been the most progressive immigration-reform bill on the agenda in the United States, in that it would have entitled undocumented minors to permanent residence on the condition that they complete college or serve in the military. Populist support for the DREAM Act framed the U.S. government as benevolently excusing "innocent" children for the crimes of their undocumented parents.[15] Simultaneously, however, it must be acknowledged that those parents' low-waged labor is central to the survival of millions of American corporations and government bodies, so much so that, at least in Indiana, Democrats and Republicans alike condemned the undocumented criminalizing SB590 law as counterproductive for Indiana's (crisis-beset) economy.

Within this framework, the legibility or illegibility of subjects is paramount. Thus it should not surprise us that, for gender-variant people, negotiating borders is filled with risk and anxiety: the risk that one's documents will not match up with the gender read by strangers or immigration officials on the basis of appearance or the risk of being apprehended as being "in disguise" and therefore a potential threat. Recall the famous memo sent by the U.S. Department of Homeland Security in 2005 warning TSA guards to be on the alert for "cross-dressed" terrorists.[16] The new generation of airport X-ray body scanners picks up "inconsistencies" not by matching appearance with documents but by looking at the body's surface. Such biometric surveillance techniques complement skirmishes taking place at an administrative and legislative level, toward which I now turn.

Calculable under What Name?

> I can't find any information or guidance whatsoever, for transgendered people wishing to immigrate to the UK to be with their partner. There is no mention anywhere that I have found of how a trans person should properly apply, or under what visa category.[17]

This plea for assistance, written by a participant on the United Kingdom Lesbian and Gay Immigration Group (UKLGIG) online forum, appeared at the beginning of a thread entitled "Transgender visa application no help available." "It's as if Trans people do not exist," the post continued. A male citizen of the United Kingdom, the forum participant lived in the Philippines with his partner, a Filipina trans woman. They intended to return to the United Kingdom to live. Under the United Kingdom's relatively progressive partnership immigration laws, foreign nationals can obtain residency in the United Kingdom if they are married heterosexual partners, same-sex civil partners, or unmarried domestic partners of U.K. citizens. Unmarried partners must show they have cohabited for two years prior to immigrating, while civil partnerships or marriages do not have to provide evidence of prior cohabitation. The participant and his partner preferred to apply as a heterosexual couple—the author of the post considered himself to be a heterosexual male, and his partner identified as a woman. However, she was unable to obtain documents listing her gender as female in the Philippines. Because her documents designated her as male, it seemed that they must apply to the U.K. immigration authorities as same-sex civil partners. Once in the United Kingdom, she intended to gain legal recognition as a woman under the U.K.'s Gender Recognition Act (GRA), a process that would take two years of documented living as a woman. Neither party wanted to enter into a same-sex civil partnership as men—which would, at any rate, be dissolved once she was legally recognized as a woman under the GRA. If they applied as unmarried partners, the couple could not meet the requirements, because during their five-year long-distance relationship, they had not cohabited for two years. The forum participant could not decide how to proceed and found no helpful information in bureaucratic channels. Hence, he had turned to UKLGIG for assistance. "If anyone has a view on this, and can point me at the contact for immigration services in U.K. immigration, both myself and my as yet unmarried trans Fiancee would be very grateful," he wrote.

The dilemma in which this forum participant and his partner found themselves has all the hallmarks of a classical immigration story: faceless bureaucratic institutions, labyrinthine application procedures, a disconnect between the left and right hands of the body politic. It is a characteristic example of what transgender immigrants must contend with in nation-states that legally recognize either transgender persons' change of legal gender designation or same-sex partnerships but do not consider how one may contradict the other. Because the Gender Recognition Act and same-sex civil-partnership laws were passed by the U.K. Parliament in the same year, this example seems particularly farcical. The two forms of legal recognition seem plagued by discontinuity at precisely the point where an overlap would assist those who may be most in need of legal protection. At any rate, volunteer advisers in the UKLGIG message board offered advice regarding whether the length of time the couple had cohabited might "count" toward legitimating their unmarried partnership status but had no wisdom regarding the specificity of transgender immigration procedures. One moderator suggested the forum participant write to his member of Parliament, and there the exchange ended. UKLGIG's Web site still does not offer any advice for transgender immigration or asylum applicants. This episode illustrates how contradictory and complex immigration law may be for gender-variant people to negotiate. It also illustrates the need for comprehensive information about trans issues and the paucity of that information in purportedly T-inclusive LGBT immigration-advocacy work in the United Kingdom.

By contrast, the United States has quite comprehensive information available for transgender immigrants and their legal advocates in the form of a handbook, *Immigration Law and the Transgender Client*. Produced by Immigration Equality and the Transgender Law Center, the handbook articulates its target as two major problems that contribute to the increased marginalization, detention, and deportation of gender-variant immigrants to the United States: the misapplication of the law in cases involving gender-variant applicants, and the high prevalence of immigration attorneys offering transgender immigrants inaccurate legal advice.[18] It offers indispensable advice not only for immigrants seeking permanent residency but also for advocates acting for undocumented or criminalized immigrants in immigration detention.

However, a close reading of key chapters illustrates that *Immigration Law* requires its transgender "clients" to engage in precisely the form of neoliberal contractualism I critique above. Most of the advice offered deals with petitions for U.S. permanent residency through spousal and fiancée petition or asylum, because these are the categories of permanent-residency petition for which transgender status is perceived to have definite bearing on the outcome. To win permanent residency, the handbook insists, one must perform the correct legal maneuvers to gain strategic success within a system blatantly structured to filter entry exclusively to those who already have such skills.

Although Immigration Equality has worked extensively on lobbying for the Uniting American Families Bill to pass, which would open up permanent-residency petitions to binational same-sex partners, here the aim is more limited: to prevent the misapplication of the law and to quietly encourage law reform through precedent. Both policy initiatives address themselves to people who are already living in the United States, whether documented or undocumented. Advice is explicitly not provided for refugees—the refugee category under U.S. law designates those who apply under a humanitarian convention from outside the country, as opposed to asylum, which designates those who apply under a humanitarian category from inside the United States). These tactics may be the most immediately practical contribution either Immigration Equality or the Transgender Law Center can make with the resources at its disposal. Both organizations retain staff attorneys who represent trans and LGBT clients *pro bono*; the handbook's comprehensive "practice tips" demonstrate an ongoing familiarity with the logistics of negotiating lengthy application procedures. However, by focusing on how transgender immigrants can strategically negotiate immigration regulations with their attorneys through formalized case law, *Immigration Law* renders the struggle for freedom from harassment, discrimination, criminalization, and incarceration as an individual task. Although it is commendable that someone is doing this work at all, *Immigration Law*'s format relinquishes the opportunity to create connections between immigrants in a more networked or collective struggle to transform public policy on immigration or to assist those who prefer not to be outed as transgender or have the "correct" documents at all.

The key question here is whether changing one's administrative gender is more important than moving through an invasive permanent-residency application process with as little difficulty as possible. *Immigration Law* addresses itself to an attorney who is not familiar with transgender issues and offers a number of preliminary tips so the attorney can treat their client with respect.

These include suggestions that the attorney do the following: "narrow the issues" by steering away from discussing the client's gender identity if it will not affect the client's immigration status; permit the client to direct the attorney how to address and perceive them; refrain from making assumptions about the client's gender identity based on their appearance; and use the correct name, pronoun, and mode of address in all correspondence with the client. This should happen, the authors write, even if the client self-presents in correspondence or appointments using their legal name:

> Often, clients will tell their attorneys their legal name (i.e., their birth name) rather than the name they feel comfortable using. If your client's legal name clearly does not match his or her corrected gender, you should ask whether there is another name that is preferred.[19]

The authors also counsel that an attorney should see that the client makes all possible attempts to change their legal name and gender classification on documents. Ideally this should take place before an individual starts an immigration record. Thus, the authors advise attorneys that

> it is easier for your client to begin his or her immigration record with the name that corresponds to the gender identity. Therefore, especially for immigration clients, it is important to do all that you can to get your client's paperwork in order to file the application in the correct name. If your client has not legally changed his or her name, however, you will generally not be able to file in the name your client chooses. Nonetheless, it is best to explain in the cover letter to USCIS [U.S. Citizenship and Immigration Services] that your client is transgender and generally goes by a different name.[20]

It is clearly admirable to advise non-trans-"friendly" lawyers on how to be trans-friendly in their interactions with clients and to pursue whatever will make life easier for the client in terms of name and gender-classification changes. However, I want to trouble the final advice that an attorney should inform USCIS of the client's transgender status, *even when filing applications under the birth name*. The assumption here is that social, bodily, and administrative gender should be consistent. The corollary assumption is that a client will desire eventually to be administratively legible as the gender she socially identifies as and that name changes should be made before embarking on an immigration process that may take years. But must a gender-variant person always change their administrative gender? Depending on the state, it is not always possible or practical. In the United States, where a person might not need to change their gender classification on legal documents to access hormone therapy or surgeries, changing a legal name or gender classification may be unnecessary. This is not to say that the option to change legal identifiers should not be available—it should. Rather, I question the necessity of being visibly marked as transgender in a process that renders immigrants vulnerable to surveillance, discrimination, and violence. Being administratively marked as transgender may make a gender-variant individual vulnerable to harassment from immigration officials. This is particularly important, because (as the handbook reminds readers in the same chapter) gender-variant immigrants may think of themselves in ways that are not consistent with Euro-American understandings of transgender as exclusively about gender identity rather than sexual orientation.

The implicit project animating *Immigration Law*'s emphasis on transgender visibility becomes more clear in the chapter on spousal and fiancée permanent-residency petitions. To make clear the stakes of this reading, a brief summary of bureaucratic approaches to transgender permanent-residency applications is necessary here. In the United States, marriage-based petitions for permanent residency involving a transgender person are not officially "legal." But they can and have been approved by a mazelike process that exploits policy inconsistencies between different arms of government. Officially, USCIS's policy is to not recognize marriages between parties where one or both individuals claim to be transsexual, "regardless of whether either individual has undergone sex reassignment surgery, or is in the process of doing so."[21] (It is unclear whether this is because of common garden-variety transphobia or because officially allowing transsexual marriages might stray too near a perceived infraction of the Defense of Marriage Act, or both.[22]) After an application is first denied by USCIS, however, applicants are free to appeal. The Board of Immigration Appeals (BIA), administered by the Department of Justice, will often reverse the original decision and approve the petition. This approval dates from a 2005 case, *In re Lovo Lara*, what *Immigration Law* calls a "shockingly favorable precedential decision," which inaugurated a complex test to ensure the legality of a marriage.[23] The *Lovo Lara* requirements include the following: that it be proven not to contravene the Defense of Marriage Act, which stipulates that a marriage be between a man and a woman; that the marriage be legal in the jurisdiction in which it occurred; that the transgender individual (or individuals) obtain "complete" surgical gender reassignment prior to making the petition; and that the applicant's gender is recognized administratively through a corrected birth certificate.

In *Immigration Law*'s chapter on binational marriage petitions, the conflict between performing a legibly proper transgender identity and flying under the radar becomes even more explicit. Because around 25 percent of successful petitions for U.S. permanent residency each year are marriage-based petitions, *Immigration Law*'s chapter on marriage is deservedly extensive. (Advice on how transgender employees might negotiate employer-initiated sponsorship for permanent residency warrants two paragraphs, the assumption being that workers skilled enough to attract employer sponsorship do not require human-rights advocates). So-called "green-card" marriage is notorious for the resources the Immigration and Nationalization Service (INS) devotes to surveillance and interrogation of binational couples in attempt to ensure that these marriages are based on romantic love rather than convenience.[24] The authors offer advice on how to negotiate marriage-based petitions for permanent residency through all the permutations of transgender embodiment and foreign or national status, offering hypothetical situations to illustrate how the law works. For example, they advise that if a couple is married in a state that does not recognize such marriages, they should apply to have the marriage declared void and remarry in a state that *does* recognize the marriage. For couples who marry in a state that recognizes same-sex marriage, the authors stipulate that they should ensure they are marrying as a man and a woman, not as a same-sex couple (because, of course, same-sex marriages are not recognized federally).

A short section near the end of the chapter mentions cases involving a "Homosexual-Identified Couple but No Surgery." To quote the section in full:

> A lesbian-identified couple is comprised of Bette who was born anatomically female and Tina who was born anatomically male but identifies as female. Tina has had no surgery and has taken no steps to change her gender marker on identity documents. For immigration purposes, this couple should be able to marry as an opposite sex couple and succeed with a marriage-based petition. . . .[25]

In theory, this strategy might make the petitioning easier, because there may be no need to out one's self as transgendered or transsexual to U.S. immigration officials. For a gender-variant person who does not desire to change the gender recorded on their documents and is marrying a person recognized to be the "opposite" gender, this seems like the most common-sense way to negotiate the system. Why be visible as transgender at all if it is possible to fly under the radar? After all, the point of a successful marriage-based petition in this case is not to be outed as transgender but to obtain permanent residency for an individual who may not even be transgendered at all. In the following paragraph, the authors subtly undercut this logic. Many transgender-rights organizations, they point out, will not accept cases like this to represent—in particular, Immigration Equality and the Transgender Law Center, *Immigration Law*'s coauthors. "We feel uncomfortable," the authors explain, "advocating with DHS [Department of Homeland Security] for the position that a transgender individual who self-identifies as (in this example) female should be legally considered male simply because she has had no surgery."[26] The booklet offers some advice to private legal practitioners who choose to take on cases of this kind, however: the decision of whether to "pass" as a normal heterosexual couple or whether to disclose that one partner is transgender "but has had no surgery."

I could make a number of demurrals in response to this curious section. To begin with, the question of surgical status seems an incidental, not to mention euphemistic, way of putting it. What is being proposed is that a person pass as their birth-assigned gender to enter into a marriage that everyone but the state would regard as queer. Because "passing" takes many forms and is rather less concerned with embodied "reality" than appearance, the person's surgical status should not matter. Secondly, what "transgender" means is very particular here: To the authors, it evidently means an uncomplicated transition from male to female or female to male, in which (as I note above) social, administrative, and embodied gender all ought to be consistent. Finally, the comment that transgender-rights organizations would "feel uncomfortable" advocating that a person is non-trans when they are "really" transgender gestures subtly to a subtext of political expediency: *If we say you are non-trans,* the authors seem to be saying, *then the Department of Homeland Security will not recognize you when you say that you are trans. You cannot have it both ways.*

Of course, there may be additional political costs for legal advocates who admit they represent clients who pursue this strategy on paper. If it became public, it would be easy for INS and the Department of Homeland Security to claim transgender-immigration lobbyists were secretly pushing same-sex marriages through the back door, as it were. Given that queer and transgender foreigners embody a threat to heterosexuality and to the cohesion of the nation and that anxiety about defending marriage from homosexuality hovers spectrally about every transgender marriage case, it is unsurprising that lobbyists should desire their own cases to present watertight instances of heterosexual transgender people. It could also be argued that providing representation to couples who can access heterosexual privilege, however precarious, is not the concern of an organization dedicated to GLBT rights. (The perennial *ressentiment* of some gay and lesbian community members who perceive trans people to be "lying" about their correct genders to claim advantages must surely raise its ugly head here.[27]) However, given Immigration Equality's other policy focus on bringing about legislative recognition of binational same-sex relationships, a refusal of association with even the whiff of same-sex partnership seems odd.

Is this simply another case of Immigration Equality's investment in a "normative discourse on belonging," as Karma Chávez puts it in an incisive critique of the Immigration Equality publication *Family, Unvalued: Discrimination, Denial and the Fate of Binational Same-Sex Couples under U.S. Law*?[28] *Family, Unvalued* reports on nine hundred interviews with binational same-sex couples affected by the U.S. government's refusal to recognize same-sex partnerships under immigration law. Chávez argues that *Family, Unvalued* plays to a perceived middle ground on immigration issues by framing same-sex couples as homonationalist good citizens, with the same desires to unite in romantic fusion and reproduce the nation as heterosexual couples. Meanwhile, U.S. citizens' claims for rights to reunite their queer families via legal means deflect attention from undocumented immigrants—whose numbers are far higher, and whose criminalization and public demonization is far more serious, than legalized immigrants. Normative belonging signals a shift where the proper performance of citizenship offers a justification for legal reform rather than the ideal of universal rights.[29]

Reading *Immigration Law and the Transgender Client* as another, transgender-focused facet of the discourse on normative belonging seems apt. Yet I want to stress another aspect of the "normative" here. *Immigration Law* rewards those who have the capacity to be entrepreneurial and to decide in advance on the best legal strategy. One can safely assume that although the targeted readers are immigration attorneys, the "smart" gender-variant prospective immigrant to the United States will discover the existence of the handbook, pore over it, and arrive in a lawyer's office already familiar with the necessary procedures. In this sense, it calls into being a neoliberal entrepreneurial subject who is always and forever calculating her exchangeability.[30]

Intersectional Tactics

What political tactics might refuse the logics of neoliberal calculability? Does a theorization of calculability run the risk of evacuating an analysis of racialization and sexual normativities? For these techniques do, in fact, still perform important filtering procedures for who counts as a body to be embraced by the nation or expunged from it.

Queer, feminist, and pro-immigrant work that deploys intersectionality as a critical tool may be instructive here. To illustrate what I mean by this, I want to detour into a discussion of theoretical and activist critical work on links between queer and immigrant politics. Eithne Luibhéid's work on the interlinking of sexuality and migration in the U.S. nation-state historically frames immigration as the locus of control of sexuality and vice versa. In a reading of *Family, Unvalued*, Luibhéid refuses the homonationalist desire to gain queer rights through designating queer couples as "family." Rather than complying with the seemingly static categories of "legal" and "illegal," Luibhéid reframes these seemingly universal categories as processes of legalization and illegalization that are contingent and shift according to need. The inclusion of queer couples as a category recognized in permanent residency application, she argues, would mean that same-sex couples would be subject to the same surveillance as heterosexual couples. Luibhéid questions the biopolitics of intimacy that deploy couple relationships as strategies to reproduce good citizens through economic and social incentives. She concludes by arguing that we should address how "other cross-cutting social hierarchies also shape the production of il/legal status."[31] "Could the campaign be reframed to address the multiple, intersecting bases on which legal and illegal statuses are produced?" she asks.

A number of groups working on immigrant and queer issues have released statements arguing for an appreciation of the intersections between queer and immigrant politics. The New York–based group Queers for Economic Justice (QEJ) released a statement called *Queers and Immigration: A Vision Statement* in 2008; joint statements addressing measures against queer rights and immigration rights were made by the Arizona-based Coalición de Derechos Humanos (CDH) and Wingspan in the lead-up to and after the 2006 Arizona state election that included four anti-immigrant propositions and an antigay amendment to the state constitution. QEJ's *Vision Statement* makes a number of calls on issues that affect not only queer immigrants but also immigrants (in general) and queers: for example, repealing the ban on HIV travelers to the United States, refuting the proposed building of a U.S.-Mexico border wall, calling for an end to the criminalization of harboring undocumented immigrants, and so on. The statement ends with a resounding call for queer and immigrant-rights organizers to "address the intersection where we live and love and struggle."[32]

Chávez calls the political work these statements do a form of "differential belonging," in contrast to the normative belonging discourse of *Family, Unvalued*. For Chávez, these critiques reject normative inclusion by focusing on the connections between queers and immigrants (and other kinds of bodies) as threats to the nation and the focus of blame within nationalist discourse, drawing attention to the simultaneous homophobia, racism, and xenophobia of government: "At a fundamental level, migrants and queers are scapegoats that are easily blamed for a multitude of societal problems."[33] Thus, rather than focusing on the family as the mode of immigrant inclusion (which simultaneously excludes those who do not participate in recognizable family structures—i.e., queers), CDH, Wingspan, and QEJ "rhetorically craft a justification for belonging across lines of difference."[34]

What would an intersectional approach look like in relation to a transgender-rights imaginary? Such an approach might resist a rights framework that privileges those who already have access to the most economic resources and forms of social capital and who fit best into the dominant medico-legal understanding of male and female. Instead, it might address the dilemmas and needs of transgender people who are most vulnerable to violence, death, and discrimination. This might involve an analysis of how laws stigmatizing apparently unrelated populations, such as prisoners, sex workers, and undocumented immigrants, impact gender-variant people (who are statistically overrepresented in each of these categories). Many groups organizing on such principles already exist in the United States: For example, the Sylvia Rivera Law Project (SLRP) works to increase the political participation and visibility of low-income people and people of color who are gender variant. Its mission statement states that SLRP begins from the premise that "gender self-determination is inextricably intertwined with racial, social and economic justice."[35] It is clear that groups such as QEJ, SLRP, CDH, Wingspan, and others do very important work—work that is being done by no one else in the broader lobbying-focused political arena.

However, I want to challenge the assumption that an intersectional analysis is sufficient to harness a political project that desires to improve the lives of people who do not count as subjects at all under a national framework and paradoxically are also integral to that nation's economic stability. An analysis of intersecting oppressions and the corollary that different groups must work coalitionally across lines of difference assumes the coherence and stability of identity categories. As Jasbir Puar puts it, intersectional models of subjectivity "may still limit us if they presume the automatic primacy and singularity of the disciplinary subject and its identitarian interpellation."[36] Puar ascribes this insight to the affective turn within critical theory, citing Brian Massumi's resistance to positionality as gridlock as well as feminist and queer work on affect as the feelings or sensations that precede identity categories.[37] But we also need to challenge intersectional theories of politics that posit those who are excluded (strangers) as the groups who must form coalitions. If we accept an analysis of capitalist neoliberalism as relentlessly *inclusive* of bodies as long as they can present themselves as calculable (and even when they are not), we must also acknowledge that the imaginaries of liberal aspiration exhort us all to *become* calculable as the first step to self-improvement.

An analysis of gender-variant immigration that relies too heavily on intersectional politics risks reinstating terms such as transgender, queer, gay, person of color, immigrant, low-income, and family as uncontested or universal. When a person migrates through a number of different nation-states in which currency-exchange rates and what constitutes "poverty" fluctuate wildly, how does she come to know herself as "low-income"? When a feminine-appearing person who was assigned male at birth uses female pronouns but characterizes herself as *bakla, sao praphet sorng, waria, fa'fafine, travesti,* or *hijra* (or *gay*)—all non-English terms that denote different gender-variant embodiments and identities—from which U.S. support organization will she seek assistance if she needs it? If we assume that "the border" always means the U.S.-Mexico border, what transnational networks that see borders as interconnected and coterminous are lost? Or, to give an example closer to my personal experience, perspectives on what counts as "white" in Australia and the United States differ entirely: in Australia, close Greek and Italian friends are racialized as nonwhite according to the white Australia policy's shifting historical definitions, while in the United States, Greek- or Italian-American friends are now considered to be white. Their capacity to intervene in particular antiracist political debates thus changes according to geographical location (and contradictory racialized interpretations of the right to speak collide in transnational e-mail list and Weblog skirmishes). Intersectional political projects risk failure without an assessment of how transnational flows of people interrupt, transform, and resist these shifting lines of demarcation.

My final note on intersectional politics regards the symbolic burden placed on trans women of color, many times immigrants, to represent themselves consistently as victims of the most heinous crimes of transphobic violence. The Transgender Day of Remembrance (TDOR), which tallies a global list of transgender people murdered each year and commemorates their deaths with vigils and memorial services annually on November 21, offers a salutary example. Implicitly or explicitly, the statistics quoted on each nation-state imprint a shocking transnational sensibility on proceedings (nothing exemplifies this more ironically than watching mostly white Midwestern college students at a 2009 TDOR vigil in Indiana struggle to pronounce the "foreign" names of those on the list). Yet TDOR vigils often end in calls for nation-bound legislative recompense, such as national hate-crime laws, which would not help most of the people on the list of dead—not to mention that many seem to be vulnerable as sex workers or undocumented immigrants who are also subject to criminalizing anti-sex-work laws or the violence of numerous security agencies.[38]

A similar effect can be seen in writing on the global feminization of labor: As Neferti Tadiar puts it, writing on feminist critiques of globalization, "immigrant female domestic and/or sex workers . . . come to embody the material consequences of the gendered, racialized, and sexualized aspects of the normative logics of the capitalist economy."[39] Under this regime of representation, the subject "serves as the axiomatic form of human equivalence" who becomes the only player in moral-political narratives of dramatic suffering.[40] As with the story of Naz, whom I discuss at the beginning of this chapter, narratives about dead trans women of color too often mobilize suffering to support the exceptionalist lie that life is better in the center—except on those occasions when it is proved, after all, not to be better. The abstraction of these bodies into subjects of suffering also prevents the formation of a political model that might begin by understanding precisely how the privileges and freedoms of those who are documented, or not sex workers, or not transgender, are cosubstantial with and intimately connected to those spoken for, in ways we cannot anticipate in advance. These ways may not be about law reform, rights, representation, or belonging at all.

Exiting, Imperceptibly

Throughout this chapter, I offer examples of salutary moments in which legislative recognition or nongovernmental attempts at negotiating recognition of gender-variant people fail. The example of the poster on the UKLGIG message board illustrates how "gender recognition" and "same-sex partnership recognition" neither remove the necessity of demonstrating one's legitimate gender at all points nor remove the boundaries between same-sex and heterosexual partnerships. When it is impossible to verify gender transition, an unsurpassable gulf is created between subjectivation as a "same-sex partner" and a heterosexual "fiancée." My discussion of *Immigration Law* similarly demonstrates how even minimal, partial recognition of transgender immigrants within U.S. spousal permanent-residency petitions depends on the willingness of the gender-variant person to be administratively visible as transgender *and* to commit to a male or female legal identity. That discussion also illustrates how nongovernmental organizations can be compliant with and supportive of these conditions. Finally, I critique the assumptions of intersectional politics as reliant on the stability of categories of identity that clearly are not stable geographically.

If we are to take these failures seriously, we also need to acknowledge that the bodies we are dealing with in speaking of gender-variant immigration often do not desire visibility at all. It is a truism of transgender and transsexual community advice that the best way to obtain identity documents with the correct gender classification is to walk into any given bureaucratic institution and claim indignantly that the gender designation on the license or certificate is mistaken. One then relies on the embarrassment of the "customer service representative" one approaches to effect a quick, clandestine keystroke transforming one from M to F or vice versa. The same kinds of advice columns often recommend passing as the gender listed on one's documents while moving through airport security, even if one never does at any other time. That is to say, at times it is easier not to be visible (and vulnerable) as transgender—and there is no contradiction in working around the law to ensure one's safety. Undocumented immigrants, too, have a vested interest in passing under the radar. As theorists of migration and gender variance, it is our business to remain fidelitous to that need. In that case, it might be salient to reconceive of "the political" as designating exclusively representational and specular tactics. As post-autonomist theorist Yann Moulier-Boutang writes in an interview on the politics of flight, "It is the interpretation of the silences that interests me: to seize the silences, the refusals, and the flight as something active."[41]

In this final section, I challenge us to rethink gender-variant immigration as a form of flight, or exodus: a performance of politics without necessarily privileging visibility. This also means acknowledging that the mobility and flexibility of immigrants, and the "spread" of a transgender rights imaginary, may be convenient to capitalism. Emerging forms of transgender rights also bring into being new disciplinary mechanisms that operate transnationally. They depend on the capacity of bodies to be mobile in order to enclose them. This is not to downplay the efforts made by gender-variant activists and lobby groups to fight for transgender rights in an enormous number of jurisdictions across the globe. But it is to mark those struggles also as a way to bring gender-variant subjects into new networks of circulation that demarcate the political spaces in which "freedom" or "tyranny" are said to inhere.

For a forthcoming book, I researched the movements of gender-variant people: migrating to access health care if it does not exist in one's home; moving to access different forms of juridical recognition or laws about reassigning gender classification, marriage, work, and so forth; moving to earn more valuable currencies in the European Union or North America; and moving to take advantage of unfamiliar places as laboratories for tweaking with the intricate social interconnections that create, sustain, or shut down passing or identifying as any kind of gender. My research subjects lived in a number of locations across the globe and responded to my questions about their mobility in wildly differing ways. They all negotiated risk, danger, a desire for autonomy or mobility, and the incapacity to move. The desire of my informants to be mobile seemed be coterminous with a pragmatic and expert knowledge about how to negotiate visa restrictions, currency-exchange value, and transnational differences in expression of gender variance. Rather than consigning these tactics to the realm of the contingent, I regard them as politicized strategies of exodus.

Exodus gives one name to a political strategy that refuses to invest in the constitution of a state or in the affective and juridical forms of relation to statehood, such as inclusion or recognition. Exodus is an "engaged withdrawal," a refusal to participate, a means of flight.[42] Exodus is not necessarily passive, either: When Moulier-Boutang exhorts readers to view silences, refusals, and flight as something active, he asks us to reorient our conceptions of the political not only as recognition. Another name for similar strategies is imperceptible politics: the politics of the every day.[43] Imperceptible politics approaches immigration as a "constituent force of the current social transformation"—millions of people moving, sustained by networks of solidarity, cooperation, sharing resources, and knowledge of how to navigate without identifying one's self or how to best negotiate the filtering systems of multiple borders. This is a politics that is not quietist but quiet, not visible but disidentifying and invisible in the specular economies of representation and calculability inhabited by both nongovernmental organizations and the state. Such silences and invisibilities are not necessarily apolitical but trace the refusal of an easy dialectic between recognition and misrecognition, visibility and invisibility, or discipline and escape. Read collectively as tactics moving toward a form of exodus, the practices of gender-variant mobility might be understood as a desertion of the calculus of contractualism, marginalizing categories, classificatory systems, refusals of adequate health care, discriminatory institutions, and misrecognitions gender-variant people must contend with almost everywhere. Rather than contributing to a transgender-rights imaginary, contributing to this imperceptible politics demands the emergence of an *unimaginary*: not imagined and future-oriented but present-minded, oriented to real, everyday, and important tactics; not based on identity politics, but on seeing the cosubstantiality and intimacy of all bodies, all the time.

III

Valuing Subjects

Toward Unexpected Alliances

9

DAN IRVING

Elusive Subjects

Notes on the Relationship between Critical Political Economy and Trans Studies

As I elaborated a definition of neoliberalism to my Transgender Human Rights class, a student asked bluntly, "What does the economy have to do with trans rights?" Her classmates sat up with rapt attention, anxiously awaiting the answer. I responded by uttering a single word: "everything." I wish my tone had been more even to articulate the importance of considering political economy when theorizing trans identities and politics. It was not. Instead, the word reflected exasperation and trailed off. If the answer to her question was obvious, a single word answer may have been persuasive; however, the question begs a more detailed response—how does political economy relate to transgender identities and experiences?

That classroom moment indicates that dynamics of socioeconomic relations are not obvious considerations for students of trans theory and politics. To explain this lack of priority, we must problematize late capitalist political economic relations and ask: How is contemporary North American society ordered to create distance between what is deemed the purview of political economy and the construction of recognized trans identities and political organizing?

The insidious nature of many political economic relations is a significant factor accounting for this chasm. Identifiable economic relations are located primarily within sites of commodity production (i.e., "the firm or the factory") and consumption. Political economy tends to be reduced to the state, financial institutions, and trans/national organizations as well as individuals as managers, administrators, workers, and consumers. To move beyond narrow perceptions of economic spheres, we need to consider discursive constructions of economic relations.

The continuation of the split between realms deemed "cultural" and "material" within critical theory and among social movements is alarming (Butler 1998; Read 2009, 7). Issues concerning sex/gender, sexuality, race, and disability are classified as belonging to the former category, while the latter is reserved for spheres of commodity production, exchange markets, and state relations. What systemic logics produce knowledge of the economic as removed from the most intimate features of the self and lived experiences? What underlies the production of essentialist knowledge concerning trans identities as opposed to embodied sex and gendered performances commensurate with—but not reducible to—capitalist logics of productivity and consumption?

This chapter points to the relevance of applying political economy frameworks to trans and gender studies with the intention of opening space for further debate within this underresearched area. Focusing on the formation of trans subjectivities rather than individual identities fosters a greater comprehension of the ways that capitalism shapes trans experiences and politics. Here I show that critical approaches to political economy enable students to situate the active constructions of trans subjects in historical and contemporary material contexts. In so doing, they can explore how socioeconomic logics of capital inform the ways that trans identities become knowable and legitimized.

Analyzing subjectivities through a political-economy lens strengthens the transformative objectives of trans studies by offering additional grounds to disrupt homogenizing narratives of trans identities and communities (e.g., all trans people experience their sex/gender alterities similarly) and discourses of victimization (e.g., "trans people are the most marginalized and oppressed members of society"). These narratives that are present in trans-rights politics obscure the agency of trans subjects and the roles we play in the production of sex/gender-variant subjectivities and the subjugation of others. Focusing on the ways that neoliberalism contributes to the shaping of trans subjects fosters a keener understanding of the ways that trans individuals and communities are governed. Ultimately, I argue that this governing relation is based on specific notions of the active/proper/worthy/deserving neoliberal citizen, a construction that disrupts and further devastates the lives of trans people for whom the systemic barriers to emulating these ideals are insurmountable.

To make this argument, this chapter is divided into three sections. The first introduces two key arenas of critical political economic analysis—subjectivity and neoliberalism. In the next section, I provide examples that make room for further explorations of the ways that neoliberalism mediates the formation of trans subjectivities. Constructions of trans subjects through employment-rights discourses serve as the first example. I critique the educational efforts of trans-employment activists to create more opportunities for trans individuals at the hiring stage and to improve retention rates of workers who transition on the job. How does the marketing of trans workers to potential employers contribute to the formation of "proper" or "deserving" trans subjects? What are the implications of such knowledge for sex/gender-variant people who remain chronically unemployed or employed in criminalized sectors of the economy?

Second, I discuss the ways that female-to-male (FTM) transsexual subjects are constructed as worthy, valuable, and legitimate through unconscious reproductions of neoliberal socioeconomic and political discourses. Despite a history of pathologization, vilification, and marginalization, some trans men have achieved recognition as respectable citizens. How do neoliberal discourses mediate masculinities to enable select trans men to be assimilated into society while those positioned in the underlayers of the trans demographic remain abject?

The final section addresses dominant strategies used by trans activists to pressure the provincial government to relist sexual-reassignment surgery (SRS) within the Ontario Health Insurance Plan (OHIP). Their approach reveals the prevalence of comprehending access to medicalized transition procedures in terms of individual rights to sex/gender self-determination, cost-benefit analysis, human capital, and free-market competitiveness. Such rationale does not translate easily into a challenge of systemic power relations adhering to neoliberalism. In the context of neoliberal enterprise society, care of the transsexual self as a crucial right risks being eclipsed into a socioeconomic rationale positioning self-actualization as an entrepreneurial endeavor. How will such neoliberal logic alter the meaning of SRS, making it available to those demonstrating financial and moral fitness while augmenting problematic "at-risk" categories and denying those within these parameters opportunity to embody sexed identities?

Defining Critical Approaches to Political Economy

Materialism forms the basis of various critical approaches to political economy. Given the debt that progressive political economists owe to Karl Marx, it is fitting to draw upon historical materialism that prioritizes "human sensuous activity" or practices to explain the framing of social organization extending to the most intimate levels of existence. Marx asserts that "the human essence is no abstraction inherent within each single individual. In its reality it is the ensemble of the social relations" (Marx in Tucker 1978, 143–145).

Flexible and/or fluid boundaries have always been integral to the vitality of capitalism as a broad mode of production. Capital's transgression of borders has a long history of migrating "deeper into the social networks that produce and reproduce life" (Read 2003, 8). Therefore, trans/gender scholar activists cannot direct all our attention toward structural and visible manifestations of capitalism, such as the state and Wall Street or Bay Street, nor can we blame the media alone for the transmission of knowledge. We are not governed entirely by top-down forces that restrict our freedoms; instead, individual subjects play significant roles in (re)producing regulatory power relations. Critical political economic analysis fosters deeper understandings of the "micro-politics of capital" (ibid.).

The concept of subjectivity serves as the nexus between the capitalist mode of production, state policies, and the governing of our everyday lives. In keeping with the need to analyze the seepage of capital into all social arenas, it is important to comprehend the ways that individuals become socially intelligible subjects and are governed through such recognition. Subjectivity is derived from socioeconomic processes, such as relations of production, the construction of dominant knowledge, and class struggle; however, the formation of the subject is complex and multifaceted, because it exceeds these sources (Foucault 2001, 332).

Subjectivity has two defining features. First, individuals are located within social parameters regardless of their marginality, and individuals are subject to ruling relations. External structures and governing knowledge, such as capitalist logics of accumulation, play roles in subject formation. External pressures that are not of our choosing erect boundaries for our existences and direct our desires. Second, subjects are formed through self-knowledge. Power relations operate not unidirectionally but through mutual incitement and struggle (343). The constraints of systemic relations of dominance and individual freedom to maneuver contribute to the ways that people form themselves into subjects (327).

The relationship between the two defining features of subjectivity is complicated. Judith Butler explains that the subject is initiated into existence through submitting to power. Power has an internal life *within* the subject. The governable subject is the "effect of power in recoil" (Butler 1997, 3) whereby power resides in the form of *willed* self-identification (6).

The trans *subject* relies on systemic power relations to make sense of itself. As I demonstrate, the connection to external governing relations must not be severed through conceptualizing transgender/transsexual in terms of innate identities. It is important not to conflate the individual with the subject. As Butler puts it, the "subject is the linguistic occasion for the individual to achieve and reproduce intelligibility, the linguistic condition of its existence and agency" (11). Many trans individuals may understand themselves in terms of "neither/nor" or "both/and" regarding sex/gender; nonetheless, they must refer to dominant characteristics defining sex/gender categories to achieve the social recognition needed for the extension of rights.

It is necessary to define neoliberalism to further comprehend trans subjectivities. Neoliberalism, characterized in terms of the free-market economy, the minimalist state, antiwelfarism, and antiunionism, reflects the specific organization of socioeconomic and political relations that gained ascendancy in conjunction with global and national events during the 1970s and early 1980s (Saad-Filho and Johnston 2005, 2–3). This "regime of wealth accumulation" (Harvey 2005) extends beyond philosophy and policy through its functioning as a "political rationality" (Brown 2006).

Regarding subjectivity, the problem of neoliberal governance rests on how to take principles of the market economy and relate them to the art of government (Foucault 2008, 131). The logic of wealth accumulation stems from a mode of production and state policies exterior to individuals. However, economic strategies cannot have genuine effects *without* the cultural dimension of society (Butler 1998; du Gay 2001, 113). Linked to the need to remedy the falling rate of profit, economic growth serves as the foundation for social policy (re)shaping and regulating individuals: "Economic growth and only economic growth should enable all individuals to achieve a level of income that will allow them the individual insurance, access to private property, and individual or familial capitalization with which to absorb risks" (Foucault 2008, 144).

Neoliberalism links economic logics to cultural spheres largely through the production of the "enterprise society." It is here that the question of subject formation emerges, as we witness the shaping of neoliberal subjectivities according to enterprise and productivity (147). Naturalized neoliberal market relations emphasizing competition, economic growth, and hyperindividualism work to reconstitute a recognizable political subject. Entrepreneurial spirit, ingenuity, physical, emotional, and spiritual fortitude as well as independence are (re)constructed as personality characteristics, individual aptitudes, and qualities of the soul. The ideal "economic man" is not one who expects the protection and care from the state. A conversion must occur in the soul where individuals realize that their salvation rests on their own tireless efforts that will be realized through competitive market relations.

The most intimate effects of neoliberalism as it shapes subjectivity *qua* entrepreneurialism are observed here. Neoliberal subjects are

> incited to live as if making a *project* of themselves: they are to *work* on their emotional world, their domestic and conjugal arrangements, their relations with employment . . . to develop a "style" of living that will maximize the worth of their existence to themselves (Rose 1992, 149; emphasis in original).

Neoliberal discourses operate on intrapersonal levels, requiring individuals to become entrepreneurs of themselves (du Gay 2001, 119).

These techniques of the self contribute to the ways that entanglement of economic logic within cultural areas remains largely undetected. The construction of the human as entrepreneur ensnarls the individual into the "continual business of living" (du Gay 2001, 120). We seize the opportunities to preserve, to reproduce, and to reconstruct elements of ourselves as human capital. As CEOs of "Me, Inc.," we are responsible for managing our own advancement. We develop our worth through education, self-branding, and promotion.

The entrenchment of neoliberalism over three decades has shifted the meaning of human rights. Rights are not understood as the responsibility of a benevolent state; rather, rights are earned through individuals' *actively* demonstrating their worth. Those who have attained material "success" measured by one's participation in labor and consumer economies and demonstrate financial, physical, and spiritual fitness prove themselves deserving of rights. Success that affords the individual with increasing human capital is linked to one's innate aptitudes, character, and work ethic.

The inseparability between the economic and the cultural becomes increasingly evident when we analyze the devastating implications for subjects deemed irresponsible. They are targeted as immoral, criminal, and uncivil for their individual failing to measure up to neoliberal standards. Multiple power relations are naturalized through the slippage into the pathological "nature" of some (in)human beings, including welfare mothers, queers, prostitutes, and some transsexuals. Neoliberal entrepreneurial discourses rooted within competitive individualism have serious consequences, such as homelessness and underhousing, un(der)employment, denial of essential social services, and on-going discrimination, harassment, and violence.

The relationship between governance and freedom is a key consideration when analyzing the constitution of transsexuals as active neoliberal subjects deserving of rights. Trans theorists and political organizers stress the importance of individual autonomy to embody sex and to express one's gender identity freely. But sex and gender self-determination does not take place in a vacuum; instead, it is framed by neoliberalism and its manifestation within national and local contexts. In what ways is transsexuality constructed as an entrepreneurial project of the self? How does this particular manifestation of transsexual subjectivity facilitate the legitimacy necessary to achieve rights in late capitalist societies?

Critical Political Economy and Trans Studies

From its inception in the early 1990s, the objective of trans studies has been to engage with sex/gender as a binary system of power contributing to the social order. Similar to Critical Political Economy, transgender method exists as a three-tiered mode of engagement seeking to encounter, confront, and transform social relations (Halberstam 2005, 61). The stress trans studies places on boundary crossings supersedes the sex/gender binary. Commentators analyze the ways that the dualistic system of sex/gender is mediated by sexual, racialized, colonial, and nationalist power relations as well as the profound effects these systems have on sex/gender-variant communities. Few trans scholars apply a political economy analysis of trans identities and politics. (Exceptions include Leslie Feinberg [1996, 1998]; Dean Spade [2006a, 2006b]; Aren Aizura [2005]; and myself [2008, 2009].)

Most of the scholarship focusing on economic relations tends to emphasize the impact of capitalism on trans people's lives. Important connections are drawn between trans identities and race/gender/sexuality/nation as systems of power and class location. The extraordinarily high rates of poverty and its connection to criminalization, high rates of HIV/AIDS, homelessness and increased violence, harassment, and discrimination that includes accessing essential social services are stressed (Currah and Spade 2007; Gehi and Arkles 2007; Namaste 2005).

We need to extend critical analysis to the ontological implications of socio-economic discourses. How does neoliberalism as the regime of accumulation within late capitalism influence the constitution of trans subjects? Emphasis on subjectivity shifts focus from an understanding of economic relations as an external obstacle to the self-actualization of trans identities toward a fuller comprehension of the broad reach of capitalist logics within the subject.

A critique of efforts to gain trans employment rights that places subjectivity at the center illustrates the interior reach of neoliberalism. For many sex/gender-variant individuals, especially those who do not pass, un(der) employment is a dire issue. Although trans people occupy various class locations, they are overrepresented within service industries and other low-paying sectors of the economy (Broadus 2006; Hirshman 2001). It goes without saying that in neoliberal society, where Marx's quip that the only choice available to the non-owning classes is to "work or starve" is increasingly apt, securing access to the legal labor force is absolutely necessary. What is of concern, however, are the ways that discussions concerning trans employment rights leave unchallenged the connections between hyperexploitative labor relations and the reproduction of trans subjectivities.

Trans activists have addressed un(der)employment as well as on-the-job discrimination, which often pushes trans people out of the workplace. In addition to lobbying the state to secure economic rights through inclusion of trans people in the Employment Non-Discrimination Act, U.S.-based organizations, such as the Centre for Gender Sanity; trans-community publications, such as the *FTMi* newsletter and *Transgender Tapestry*; as well as scholar activists, such as Jillian T. Weiss and Phyllis Frye, seek to educate corporate management about transsexual identities, trans-specific struggles on the job (e.g., restroom accessibility, gender-appropriate uniforms, proper pronoun and name usage, and medical leaves and benefits regarding medicalized transition procedures).

Educational efforts aiming to cultivate a nondiscriminatory work environment for trans employees are not contextualized within class-based politics; instead, they appeal to capital's profit motive by asserting that adopting trans-positive human-resource policies makes good business sense. Trans people are represented as productive workers who are valuable assets to employers (Chambers 1990; Human Rights Campaign Foundation 2004, 8). This understanding of non-normative sex/gender identities meshes well with the "management diversity strategies" operationalized in the corporate sector. Further, it represents an entanglement of sex/gender identity and exploitative relations producing a particular trans subject.

The trans laborer as an active neoliberal subject is constructed in two ways. First, characteristics aligned with the enterprising neoliberal citizen are suggested to be intrinsic to transsexuals. Responding to the survey results of more than one hundred transsexual people who occupied senior management positions at the time of their transition, U.K.-based trans scholar activist Stephen Whittle (2009, 6) muses about their character:

> Is it that, predominantly, the *bright, articulate and able* transsexual people undergo gender role transition, rather than those less equipped. . . .

> [I]t may well be the case that being bright, articulate and able is an essential requirement so surviving [the] social stigma that still surrounds transsexualism and gives the best chance of being able to continue to earn a living.

The immense social stigma resulting from visible sex/gender alterity provides the backdrop for such engagements between trans-employment advocates and management. Western-based firms articulate their need to remain competitive globally and are explicit about their major concerns regarding trans employees being the possible negative correlation between non-normative sex/gender identities and their "bottom lines." To assuage such concerns, businesses have to be convinced that trans employees will not threaten the productivity of their workforce or offend their client-consumer base.

Judith Halberstam (2005, 18) and Susan Stryker (2008, 146–147) touch upon the connections between the fluidity and flexibility as character traits attributed to trans identities and the governing expectations placed on all members of late capitalist societies. Neoliberalism has ushered in increasing arduous economic times that have placed escalating pressures on the middle and working classes in the global North to adjust to the "dismantling of the welfare state" (McBride and Shields 1997) and economic restructuring processes that have resulted in increasing vulnerability. The post-industrial late capitalist economy has shifted the meanings of citizens' placing demands on individuals (women especially) to be flexible in the wake of economic changes and crisis as well as responsible for their individual well-being, the welfare of their families, and the vitality of their communities. Similar to flexibility and fluidity, attention must be given to branding of trans subjects according to the character traits Whittle stresses—brightness, being articulate, and ability. These characteristics exist alongside the physical, emotional, and spiritual fortitude that enables (some) trans people to endure the material consequences of social stigma and to use the lessons learned through adversity to render themselves not only valuable employees but capable of managing and directing big business. "Success" is a theme that runs through public discourses of transsexuality in which nothing separates the personal and the socioeconomic contexts that infuse transsexuality with meaning (Irving 2008, 2009). Surviving the often-brutal existence of living as non-normatively sexed/gendered and undergoing the difficult processes of medical transition are positioned as individual character traits, components of human capital, or property that one possesses. Such skills lend themselves to the production of a working transsexual subjectivity in the face of material consequences of neoliberal restructuring.

The second way that trans subjectivity is constructed according to exploitative labor relations relates to suggestions of the prospective potential of the transsexual employee should they be extended their rights to sex/gender self-determination. In her book *Transsexual Workers: An Employers Guide,* Janis Walworth (1998) presents medical benefits for sexual-reassignment surgeries and leaves as an investment in worker productivity (52, 54). It is through the realization of one's 'true self' through embodied sex and permissible gendered performance that transsexuals can be fashioned into loyal and hard-working employees (112). According to this rhetoric, transitioning sets sex/gender-variant individuals at ease, clearing mental, spiritual, and physical space to devote their energies to their jobs. Walworth assures management that "once a transition is completed, a transsexual employee is likely to become more productive than before . . . after transition transsexuals are less irritable, more cheerful, and easier to get along with" (54). Transsexuality becomes a threshold to be crossed on the way to normal functioning of the neoliberal citizen. This logic of latent creative and industrious capacity waiting to be unleashed is also evident within the mainstream print media's representation of select transsexual professionals in senior administrative and managerial positions. The *Toronto Star* has featured articles on successful transsexual women who may have transgressed the normative sex/gender divide but remain steadfastly tied to socioeconomic principles of competitiveness, industriousness, and individual autonomy (Kenna 1990, A1).

Efforts to raise the profile of trans people have often improved working conditions for transsexual employees. Although progress is slow, evidence suggests that an increasing number of corporations are recognizing the legitimate place that trans workers have in their workplaces. Trans issues are steadily becoming part of corporate diversity models as business concedes that acceptance of a plurality of gender-based identities boosts their competitiveness within labor and consumer markets. Paul Douglas, the vice president of TD Canada Trust, explains the benefits of a strengthened commitment to LGBT populations: "From a humanistic perspective, adopting a diversity agenda is the right thing to do. From a business perspective it's a necessity . . . [to] . . . avoid the fate of the corporate dinosaur. The strategic payoff in the end is business sustainability" (2007).

Trans subjectivities do not exist as preformed entities awaiting intelligibility. They are constructed through social relations and discourses, such as those marketing trans people as valuable employees. Given that power is a productive relationship, it becomes evident that trans activists and representatives from the business sector are producing meaning within neoliberal contexts. The dynamics between trans-employment activists and corporate management reveal "hegemonic bargaining" processes where deals are brokered for the advancement of some sex and gender-variant individuals based on trades within power relations (Chen 1995). If business is willing to invest in low-cost trans-health benefits and no-cost antidiscrimination policies, trans employees will demonstrate their capacities to be invaluable team players. Exploitative labor relations based on racialized, national, able-bodied power relations are obscured.

The significant role that neoliberal rationalities play in the cultivation of trans subjectivities extends beyond narrowly defined economic spheres, such as the labor market. An exploration of the formation of contemporary FTM subjectivities demonstrates the ways that neoliberalism is integral to constructions of proper trans masculinities. Such analysis challenges the naturalization of transsexuality either as a biological condition or as a metaphysical phenomenon, both of which are found in autobiographical and other personal accounts of transsexual men. Although biocentricity may be an effective strategy to gain rights, this reificatory approach does not address systems of power through which trans subjects are produced and governed.

Gaining legitimacy as a man depends heavily on physicality, given that "gender attribution" largely accounts for how sex is determined (Kessler and McKenna 1978). Nevertheless, physical attributes never quite secure one's position as authentic, because sex/gender functions through perpetuating symbolic ideals of masculinity and femininity. Sex/gender authenticity is illusive, with no fixed point of stoppage. One must always prove one's self to be a valid subject. Given the state of SRS, analysis of nonphysiological factors governing sex and gendered performances is possible. Phalloplasty remains undesirable for most FTMs due to aesthetics, lack of full functionality, and its exorbitant financial cost. Top surgeries, hormone-replacement therapy, and/or alternative "bottom surgeries" produce an alternatively sexed body. How do trans men demonstrate their worth within neoliberal enterprise cultures?

The prevalent theme of FTMs as self-made men within spaces of transsexual cultural production, such as autobiographies, Web sites, community publications, and mainstream media, reveals the wide reach of neoliberal governance. Situated within the perimeters of neoliberal enterprise society, certain FTMs can circumvent our sex/gender alterity and make claims to authentic manhood through aspiring to and performing hegemonic "business-class" masculinities (Connell and Wood 2005). The economic man as entrepreneurial subject is not contained within the workplace or market place. The neoliberal rationale of physical, moral, emotional, and financial fitness traverses all boundaries structuring all levels of society. One of the most insidious areas of its functioning occurs within the most intimate of locations—the subject.

Given the crisis of masculinity that has resulted from neoliberal socioeconomic restructuring, especially among middle- and working-class men (McDowell 2004; Skeggs 2004), trans and non-trans men face increasing pressures to prove themselves worthy citizens in spite of increasing financial stress and vulnerability. It is not coincidental that FTMs rely on dominant narratives of the self-made man to establish their validity due to the emphasis neoliberal policies and governing rationality place on hyperindividualism and the need for the individual to demonstrate autonomous, self-sufficient, industrious, innovative, strong, and flexible characteristics (Irving 2009).

Neoliberalism obscures social inequities produced through racial, colonial, imperialist, and sexual systems of dominance. It has become common sense for poverty, homelessness, illness, un(der)employment, and criminality, which under the welfare state were easier to discern as social perils, to be understood as individual character flaws. FTMs can establish themselves as valid and therefore valuable neoliberal citizens via the care of the self. As Henry Rubin explains of his FTM research participants, the need for "intersubjective recognition" rooted in the social propels trans men to aspire to societal norms: "Though FTMs ... are sympathetic to the types of negative effects wrought by normative ideals regarding sex, they are also aware of and thankful for the ways such beliefs can be marshaled for their own life projects" (Rubin 2003, 156). FTM spokespersons stress that in spite of their non-normatively sexed bodies, their character traits demonstrate their validity as men.

Similar to the preceding discussion of transsexual employees, the formation of trans-male subjectivities occurs through affixing trans masculinity to human capital. The making of the transsexual man and his existence post-transition demonstrates that he possesses the inner traits rendering him capable of contributing to the further advancement of late capitalist North American society. FTM's as "self-made men" represent a true entrepreneur of the self. They stood steadfast by their knowledge of self, which often became evident during their early childhoods. They weathered decades of adversity until they could capitalize on the opportunity to self-actualize. This reflects patience, intellect, strength, and independence while not wrestling into view whiteness (Noble 2006), economic locations (Spade 2006), and citizenship status (Aizura 2005), exemplifying some of the systemic power relations informing such gender performances.

Many illustrations of FTMs' entrepreneurial spirit represent them as productive workers located in blue- and white-collar professions. The autobiographies of British trans man Paul Hewitt (1996) and American FTM Dhillon Kholsa (2006) and the court transcripts of Michael Kantaras (a former guest on the *Dr. Phil* show whose custody case aired on Court TV in 2002) highlight skill sets, professional capacities, and earning potentials of transsexual men (Irving 2009). The mainstream media coverage of the pregnancy of Thomas Beattie softened this gender-bending act through representing Beattie as non-defiant. Situated within post-9/11 U.S. society rooted within late capitalist power relations mediated by whiteness and nationalism, Beattie may be a pregnant man, but he is not to be read as a queer or defiant figure (Puar 2007). Media exclusives take care to establish that this heterosexual trans man is only barely racialized and is seen as neither a racial other nor a gender terrorist. He is a good citizen who contributes to the wealth of the nation through owning and operating a small business as well as being a good consumer (Tresniowski 2008).

The significant role played by neoliberalism in the formation of FTM subjectivities is mediated by the politics of race and citizenship. The early photographic work of transsexual artist Loren Cameron featured in his book *Body Alchemy: Transsexual Portraits* (1996) illustrates the ways that these systemic relations of power are reproduced within trans-cultural production. *Body Alchemy* represents diverse FTM masculinities depicting racial, age, gender, and class differences. However, these photographic images and accompanying artist statements respond to unspoken questions posed within neoliberal society. Marked by the shrinking social-welfare system and a dwindling sense of public responsibility for the well-being of others, Cameron presents evidence confirming that trans men can assimilate into the category of all-American male. "Heroes" features Cameron himself gripping a large American flag that serves as the backdrop of the photo. This photo was intended to celebrate the courage and strength that trans men demonstrate throughout their daily lives within an intolerant society; however, it emerges out of a colonial, imperialist, and late capitalist context. During 1996, the United States and its allies were waging war on Iraq, while at home President Bill Clinton legislated the Personal Responsibility and Work Opportunity Act that made the receipt of welfare more stringent through workfare programs. Neoliberal American society declared war on its enemies within and beyond its national borders. To make a plea for acceptance for FTM transsexuality, trans men are presented as patriotic subjects in the book. While Cameron poses with national iconography, he presents other trans men—such as Chris, who works two jobs in the manufacturing sector—as extremely industrious family men. The viewing and reading audience is assured that the discipline demonstrated by Chase, a black body builder, is not only limited to his physique: Chase is also a student and proprietor of a small business. These representations not only work to placate non-trans audiences with assurances of normality but also to influence the ways the transsexual subject becomes intelligible within trans communities. Meanings constructed about proper transsexual masculinities exceed embodied sex and gender identity, as these are inseparable from expectations of character and behavior fitting of an active citizen as a social and economic actor. Given that Cameron's work is internationally renowned, what impact will the FTM as a self-made man have on those for whom reaching a close proximity to such an ideal is nearly impossible?

Critical Political Economy and Trans Resistance

Struggles by trans activists in Ontario to regain access to publicly funded trans health care also demonstrate the ways that transsexual subjectivities are mediated by neoliberalism. This section explores the efforts of grassroots political organizers to negotiate state recognition of transsexual subjects through reinstating SRS as an insurable procedure. Critical approaches to political economy lend themselves to the development of a more nuanced understanding of "transsomatechnics,"* or the technopolitics of embodied subjectivities in late capitalism. Marking the specific instances when neoliberal entrepreneurial spirit gets embedded within care of the self adds complexity to debates concerning trans body politics and gender performativity. Such instances reveal the ways that proper transsexual subjects are re/created on microlevels of community.

---

*This term is borrowed from a conference of the same name organized by Susan Stryker. Transsomatechnics was held at Simon Fraser University in Vancouver, British Columbia, in 2008.

Trans people's lack of access to health care is a long-standing problem. Within trans scholarship and community-based research, health care is usually approached in two ways. First, while it is acknowledged that many transsexual individuals face insurmountable barriers to transitioning medically due to discrimination based on racialization, citizenship status, criminalization, impoverishment, and/or ill health, a definitive component of transsexual identity is predicated on the desire to alter their physicality through medicalized transition processes to embody their sexed identities. Second, SRS and hormone-replacement therapies are viewed in terms of human rights. It is quite revealing of the character of contemporary trans political organizing that the rhetoric concerning trans rights is based mainly on the *right to sex/gender self-determination* and, to a lesser degree, the right to health care. Within neoliberal Canadian society, a focus on the latter would foster a wider critique of the increasing privatization of essential services that could produce broader relations of solidarity among marginalized groups.

Critical analysis of campaigns to reinstate SRS into publicly funded health care highlights the "paradox of human rights" (Brown 2002). Approaching trans-related health care procedures in terms of individual rights to sex/gender self-determination addresses the need to confront the systemic erasure of trans identities. The fact that transsexuality has been rendered socially unintelligible impacts trans people negatively. Recognition of the right to determine one's sexed embodiment as well as the right to gender expression extends life to transsexual subjects. Within liberal democratic contexts where interest groups appeal to the state for rights, framing issues of equal access to state-subsidized medicine through the inclusion of medical technologies that make sex/gender self-determination possible makes sense given that these technologies bring (transsexual) women and men into existence.

The right to sex/gender self-determination is paradoxical, because it creates governable subjects. Freedom in neoliberal democracy is a vexed and slippery slope. Trans activists lobby the government, make efforts to establish alliances with medical and psychological professionals, and engage with the judicial system to win the right to public coverage for trans-specific procedures that will enable the freedom to embody one's sex. Nevertheless, such freedom establishes parameters around the very category it ushers into being (Brown 2002; Butler 1997). Transsexual subjects must establish themselves as more than sexed bodies and gendered performances. They must demonstrate themselves worthy of such recognition from the state and society. It is precisely here that we can pinpoint the influence of neoliberal socioeconomic discourses on the formation of transsexual subjects. As demonstrated through preceding discussions of transsexual employment activism and the formation of FTM masculinities as self-made men, political activism concerning publicly funded trans-specific health care reveals the ways that enterprise factors into the production of transsexual subjectivities. To demonstrate their humanity and their deservingness of rights, transsexuals are pressured to prove they can assimilate into society and contribute to Canada's competitiveness in the global economy. This is done mainly through emphasizing the ways that accessing SRS will lead to the construction of productive bodies.

In 1998, the Progressive Conservative party delisted SRS from the Ontario Health Insurance Plan, meaning that this component of medicalized transition would be removed from Canada's publicly funded health-care system after thirty years of funding. This change was made in accordance with "Common Sense Revolution," the party platform that would entrench further neoliberalism throughout the province. This decision was challenged immediately through individual human-rights litigation and tireless lobbying efforts by community activists and organizations. In 2008, the Liberal government announced the relisting of SRS, stating that transsexual individuals who received an official recommendation from the Gender Identity Clinic at the Centre for Addictions and Mental Health (CAMH) would be eligible for funding. Given the decade of struggle preceding this favorable decision, the province's announcement was met with an exuberant response.

Nevertheless, trans activists remained wary of this victory given the legitimacy this legislation extends to CAMH, which has a long history of pathologizing transsexuality. Community members pointed to the ways that the gatekeeping role played by medical professionals at CAMH was mediated by morally regulatory practices. For example, trans-community members exchanged criticisms of an intake survey form that prospective participants of the gender program at CAMH were required to complete. This survey inquired repeatedly whether the individual used alcohol or other substances, had suffered depression, and had ever been arrested. Many members of a province-wide LGBTQ healthcare listserv easily identified these techniques of moral regulation as problematic, given that these stringent criteria for behavior would potentially exclude many people from consideration. Trans-community activists are attentive to the ways that oppression functions on multiple axes that further marginalize racialized, dis/abled, and impoverished segments of trans demographics (Jackson et al. 2006) as well as sex workers and others who are criminalized due to working in illegal economic sectors. The formation of transsexual subjectivities is mediated by bourgeois standards of morality that reinforce systems of power rooted in whiteness, middle-class professionalism, and ableism. Acceptance into the Gender Identity Program at CAMH will most likely be granted to individuals from privileged social locations who demonstrate, or have the potential to demonstrate, degrees of material success (Trans Health Lobby RHN Digest, 400).

Similar to deals with the corporate sector vis-à-vis trans employment, neoliberal entrepreneurial logic is a significant component of the bargains trans organizers unintentionally struck with the province of Ontario while trying to relist SRS. Neoliberal philosophy and policies have embedded rational choice and cost-benefit analysis within most social arenas. Trans health-care campaigns were not exempt from such reasoning, as organizers engaged with the administrations of the Conservative government and its Liberal successors. Given the complexity of politics and the multiplicity of interests of the diverse groups involved, various conceptualizations of health care operate simultaneously. Trans activists argue that SRS is a basic and fundamental right that ought to be publicly funded in the interest of equality and social justice. In presenting the case to the government for relisting SRS, lobby groups, community organizations, and professional allies emphasized the financial benefits to the province.

Many activists walk the tightrope concerning the very moral regulation and ability that they problematize in relation to gender identity clinics (GICs) by highlighting the ways that denial of such essential rights to health care roots many transsexuals firmly within "at-risk" or "vulnerable" populations. As articulated by such organizations as EGALE (a leading Canadian LGBT human rights organization), refusal to grant transsexual people access to medicalized transition procedures prolongs and increases the risk of alcohol and substance use, psychological trauma, such mental-health issues as anxiety and depression stemming from being "trapped in the wrong body," and high rates of suicide. These demands for publicly funded trans health care must be situated within neoliberalism and its erosion of social-welfare programs. Which would cost the province and taxpayers more—SRS, or hospitalization, treatment facilities, and other health-care costs as well as disability insurance, social assistance, and employment insurance payments? When analyzed in terms of neoliberalism, which locates the realization of freedom and equality through one's ability to participate in the free-market economy, it becomes clear that these nondiscriminatory rights are not rooted unequivocally in radically democratic or social-justice principles of equitable wealth redistribution. Instead, the public funding of SRS is marketed as an investment in the productive potential of candidates approved for such procedures. Although transitioning is not comprehended as the panacea to all struggles trans people must endure, it certainly will alleviate much suffering, freeing up physical, psychic, and social space for more creative and constructive pursuits, presumably within legal sectors of the economy and society.

When understood as such, it becomes evident that social recognition of trans people and our specific needs functions as a social contract governing the lives of trans people. Expectations of employability and work ethic have been a longstanding component of the programs run by GICs (Irving 2008). The "Real-Life Experience" (RLE) exercise (entrenched since the 1970s in the most commonly and widely practiced Standards of Care and only recently revised by the World Professional Association for Transgender Health) requires prehormonal and preoperative transsexuals to work, to attend school, and/or to volunteer as visible members of the sex with which they identify. The RLE makes explicit the fact that, following transition, transsexuals will have expectations to meet.

Couching arguments for medical transition in productive logic cannot be limited to medical and psychological gatekeepers situated within GICs. Trans organizers and allies reproduce the impetus toward productivity informing many contemporary approaches to health and wellness. The preoperative transsexual subject is often presented to government officials and to members of society either in terms of their productive potential or their past and present contributions to society. For example, a leading transsexual activist in Toronto lamented the government's decision to cut funding to SRS by stressing that

> as a transsexual woman attempting to get an university education and lead a productive life, I am saddened that the Ontario government no longer deems it necessary to fund the procedure that would complete my transition. . . . It imposes hardship and heartache on me and others in similar circumstances. (Egale 2003)

This sentiment is echoed by health-care professionals situated within alternative institutional locations, such as the Sherbourne Health Centre (SHC), that have stated commitments to social justice and anti-oppression praxis. The SHC's mandate is to treat low-income and street-active people within Toronto's downtown core. It also specializes in health-care provision and advocacy for LGBTIQQ communities. In a letter written to Alberta's Minister of Health and Wellness in response to the 2009 delisting of SRS in that province, the chief executive officer explains that SRS

> is a legitimate and necessary procedure . . . which relieves significant human suffering and enables the majority to live fulfilled and productive lives. . . . From a human rights perspective, a health perspective and even an economic perspective, many Canadian provinces and Western countries are recognizing the need to strengthen protections for transgendered communities and to improve their publicly funded health services. (Boggild 2009)

Given that subjectivity is formed through productive power relations that result from subordination, it is important to comprehend the constructions of "proper" transsexual subjects deserving of rights not only in terms of sex and gender non-normativity as a result of the binary system of sex/gender but also in terms of neoliberal logics of hyperexploitation and entrepreneurialism to facilitate an increase in wealth accumulation. When considered in terms of a social contract, what impact will relisting SRS as a fundamental right have on criminalized, dis/abled, unemployed, racialized, and colonized members of trans communities? What social expectations will continue to govern trans people?

Conclusion

The above considerations show that my student's initial question—what does the economy have to do with trans identities and organizing?—is daunting and should not be taken as rhetorical. Given that critical political economic approaches remain relatively underutilized by trans scholars and activists, providing a one-word response—"everything"—to such an inquiry as if it were obvious in no way addresses the complexity of the question. Critical approaches to political economy root the emergence of transsexual identities within the broad capitalist mode of production. Fostering flexible analytical categories to ensure their ability to explain adequately the relationship between non-normative sex/gender embodiments and expressions is necessary. Trans subjectivities that problematize the notion of personal identity and include relations of subordination are mediated by multiple systemic relations of power, which include class location, race, ability, and sexuality. Of equal importance, however, is the realization that trans subject formation not only is mediated by social relations of power but is in and of itself a social relation of power. As demonstrated, the formation of the proper, worthy, active, and valuable transsexual subject within neoliberal society plays a regulatory role. The very extension of life to transsexual individuals is determined through neoliberal regimes of wealth accumulation. It is within the enterprise society based on hyperindividualism, competitiveness, and freedom through market relations that contemporary transsexual subjects derive meaning. The good transsexual is a flexible, courageous, and physically/mentally and financially fit individual who displays productive potential. This is the sex/gender performance that will more than likely ensure success in winning human rights. The ways that the formation of transsexual subjectivity is intertwined with socioeconomic relations have profound impacts on theorizing trans identities, bodies, and resistance. Additionally, this often-unconscious relation is embedded within political organizing in ways that may thwart transgressive, radically democratic, and emancipatory political projects. For this reason, much more interdisciplinary research must be conducted in this area.

10

JULIA SERANO

Reclaiming Femininity

Over the last few years, my femme identity has very much informed the way that I relate to myself as a trans woman, as a queer woman, and as a feminist more generally. If you were to ask a hundred different femmes to define the word "femme," you would probably get a hundred different answers. Having said this, most femmes would no doubt agree that an important, if not central, aspect of femme identity involves reclaiming feminine gender expression, or "femininity." It is commonplace for people in the straight mainstream as well as within our queer and feminist circles to presume that feminine gender expression is more frivolous, artificial, impractical, and manipulative than masculine gender expression and that those of us who dress or act femininely are likely to be more tame, fragile, dependent, and immature than our masculine or "gender-neutral" counterparts.[1] By reclaiming femininity, those of us who are femme are engaged in a constant process of challenging these negative assumptions that are routinely projected onto feminine gender expression.

Although reclaiming femininity is an important part of our femme identities, the specific ways in which we engage in reclaiming, reappropriating, and reconceptualizing femininity differs from person to person based on our varied experiences, struggles, and histories. I have found that my life history as a transsexual woman has led to my having a somewhat different view of femininity and femme identity than that commonly held by the majority of cissexual femme women (i.e., femme women who have not had transsexual experience). In this piece, I explore some of these differences. My hope is that, rather than drawing a sharp distinction between trans femmes and cis femmes, what I have to say will make clear the many similarities that we share. And rather than disidentifying with my trans experience, it is my hope that cis femmes (and other readers) will draw parallels between my struggles and experiences and their own.

Many of my thoughts regarding the similarities and differences between cis and trans femmes grew out of my experience at the Femme 2006 Conference, which took place in San Francisco in August of that year. At the time, I was about three-quarters finished writing the book that would eventually become *Whipping Girl: A Transsexual Woman on Sexism and the Scapegoating of Femininity*.[2] My main purpose in writing the book was to debunk many of the myths and misconceptions that people have—both in the mainstream and within feminist and queer communities—about trans women and femininity. Focusing simultaneously on femininity and trans women was no accident. I had spent five years doing trans activism up to that point—conducting transgender 101 workshops, writing essays critiquing media depictions of trans people, and working to challenge the exclusion of trans women from lesbian and women's spaces. The one thing that came up over and over again was the way in which trans women and others on the trans-female/feminine spectrum (i.e., those of us who were assigned a male sex at birth but gravitate toward femaleness or femininity) receive the bulk of society's fascination, consternation, and demonization with regard to transgenderism. In contrast, people on the trans-male/masculine spectrum (i.e., people who were assigned a female sex at birth but gravitate toward maleness or masculinity) have remained relatively invisible. This disparity in attention suggests that those of us on the trans-female/feminine spectrum are culturally marked, not for failing to conform to gender norms, per se, but because of the specific direction of our gender transgression—that is, because of our feminine gender expression and/or our female gender identities. And although it has become common for people to use the word "transphobia" as a catch-all phrase to describe anti-trans sentiment, it is more accurate to view the discrimination and stigma faced by trans people on the trans-female/feminine spectrum in terms of trans-misogyny.

I have found that many people who have not had a trans-female or trans-feminine experience often have trouble wrapping their brains around the concept of trans-misogyny, so I offer the following two anecdotes to help illustrate what I mean by the term. Once, about two years ago, I was walking down the street in San Francisco, and a trans woman happened to be walking just ahead of me. She was dressed femininely, but not any more femininely than a typical cis woman. Two people, a man and a woman, were sitting on a door step, and as the trans woman walked by, the man turned to the woman he was sitting next to and said, "Look at all the shit he's wearing," and the woman he was with nodded in agreement. Now presumably the word "shit" was a reference to femininity—specifically, the feminine clothing and cosmetics the trans woman wore. I found this particular comment to be quite telling. After all, although cis women often receive harassing comments from strange men on the street, it is rather rare for those men to address those remarks to female acquaintances and for them to apparently approve of the remarks. Furthermore, if this same man were to have harassed a cis woman, it is unlikely that he would do so by referring to her feminine clothing and makeup as "shit." Similarly, someone who is on the trans-masculine spectrum could potentially be harassed, but it is unlikely that his masculine clothing would be referred to as "shit." Thus, trans-misogyny is informed by, yet distinct from, transphobia and misogyny, in that it specifically targets transgender expressions of femaleness and femininity.

The second example of trans-misogyny that I would like to share occurred at an Association for Women in Psychology conference I attended in 2007 (for those unfamiliar with that organization, it is essentially a feminist psychology conference). One psychologist gave a presentation on the ways in which feminism has informed her approach to therapy. During the course of her talk, she discussed two transgender clients of hers, one on the trans-masculine spectrum, the other on the trans-feminine spectrum. Their stories were very similar in that both had begun the process of physically transitioning but were having second thoughts about it. First, the therapist discussed the trans-masculine spectrum person, whose gender presentation she described simply as being very butch. She discussed this individual's transgender expressions and issues in a respectful and serious manner, and the audience listened attentively. However, when she turned her attention to the trans-feminine client, she went into a very graphic and animated description of the trans person's appearance, detailing how the trans woman's hair was styled, the type of outfit and shoes she was wearing, the way her makeup was done, and so on. This description elicited a significant amount of giggling from the audience, which I found to be particularly disturbing given the fact that this was an explicitly feminist conference. Clearly, if a male psychologist gave a talk at this meeting in which he went into such explicit detail regarding what one of his cis female clients was wearing, most of these same audience members as well as the presenter would surely (and rightfully) be appalled and would view such remarks to be blatantly objectifying. In fact, in both of these incidents I have described, comments that would typically be considered extraordinarily misogynistic if they were directed at cis women were not considered categorically inappropriate and offensive when directed at trans women.

As these anecdotes demonstrate, expressions of trans-misogyny do not merely focus on trans women's female gender identities, but, more often than not, they specifically target her feminine gender expression. Trans-misogyny is driven by the fact that in most U.S. contexts, feminine appearances are more blatantly and routinely judged than masculine ones. It is also driven by the fact that connotations such as "artificial," "contrived," and "frivolous" are practically built into our cultural understanding of femininity, and these same connotations allow masculinity to come off as invariably "natural," "sincere," and "practical" in comparison.

For example, when a woman wishes to charm or impress someone, she is often described as using her "feminine wiles." But when a man tries to charm or impress someone, nobody ever accuses him of using his "masculine wiles." Instead, he is simply seen as being himself. Most dictionaries define "wiles" as artifice, a device, trick, or stratagem meant to fool, trap, ensnare or entice. This is how people typically view feminine gender expression: as manipulative, insincere, and artificial.

There is a common, yet false, assumption that those feminists and queer women who favor trans-woman exclusion are primarily concerned with the fact that trans women were born male, that we have experienced male privilege, that we had or may still have penises, or that we may still have residual "male energy" (whatever the fuck that is). I would argue that the growing acceptance, and even celebration, of trans-male and trans-masculine folks within queer women's communities over the last decade demonstrates that this supposed fear of maleness and masculinity is largely a red herring. Rather, in my many encounters with cis feminists who are hesitant or resistant about including trans women's voices and issues within the feminist movement, almost invariably, the first thing they mention is what they consider to be our "over the top" or "exaggerated" feminine gender expression: the way we supposedly dress hyperfemininely, wear way too much makeup, and turn ourselves into "caricatures" of "real" women. Janice Raymond chided trans women for the fact that we supposedly "conform more to the feminine role than even the most feminine of natural-born women," and Robin Morgan claimed that by doing so, we "parody female oppression and suffering."[3]

Anyone who knows multiple actual trans women knows that this monolithic image of trans women as "hyperfeminine" is nothing more than a ruse, one that typically grows out of an uncritical acceptance of media depictions of trans women or out of stereotyping based on one or two trans women the person may have seen or met (and who were obvious as trans precisely because of their especially high femme presentation). Actual trans women vary greatly in their personal styles and gender expressions. Some are rather conventional in their femininity, while others are understated, and still others strive to be fabulously feminine. Some identify as femme dykes or femme tomboys. Other trans women are very androgynous in their manner of dress and gender expression, and still others dress and identify as butch. So what purpose does this monolithic image of trans women as hyperfeminine serve? Well, in a world where femininity is regularly disparaged as being manipulative and insincere, such images reinforce the popular cissexist assumption that our female gender identities are "fake" or "contrived" and therefore not to be taken seriously. Indeed, in the eyes of society, trans women are seen as doubly artificial, because we are trans and because we are feminine.

As I became more and more aware of the ways in which anti-feminine sentiment is used to undermine and to delegitimize trans women, the more I began to realize the ways in which I had unconsciously (and sometimes consciously) distanced myself from femininity in order to gain acceptance in the queer community. When I first began attending and performing spoken word at queer and feminist events back in 2002 and 2003, I definitely played down my femme side and played up my tomboy side. And you know what? It worked. I became relatively accepted in those circles. I honestly do not think that I would have been accepted so readily within San Francisco's queer and feminist communities if I had attended those first events dressed in an especially feminine manner.

This, of course, is not just a trans-woman issue; it is a femme issue. It is not just the heterosexist mainstream that promotes the idea that masculinity is strong and natural while femininity remains weak and artificial. In today's gay-male communities, masculinity is praised while femininity remains suspect. In today's queer-women's communities, masculinity is praised while femininity remains suspect. If people want to be taken seriously in these communities, then they will inevitably feel a certain pressure to conform to the communities' masculine-centric ideals. I cannot tell you how many of my cis queer female friends have shared with me stories similar to my own, of how they really tried to butch it up when they first came out as lesbians or as dykes, because they really wanted to be accepted and to be taken seriously.

As a trans woman, my attempt to distance myself from my own feminine expression was particularly poignant. After all, I had spent most of my life coming to terms with my feminine inclinations. As a kid, I repressed my feminine tendencies for fear of being called out as a sissy or fairy. As a young adult, I began to reclaim them, to feel empowered by them, and I lived openly as an unabashedly feminine boy for several years before my decision to transition. So it is sadly ironic that, after my transition, I felt the need to play down femininity once again to be taken seriously as a queer woman and a feminist.

It was through conversations with my femme-identified friends—some who were trans, but many of whom were cis—and their sharing with me their own struggles grappling with being feminine in a queer culture that is so masculine-centric that I began to embrace my femme identity around 2005. So when the Femme Conference came to San Francisco in 2006, and when I was invited to do spoken word at one of the performance events, I was ecstatic. For me, it represented a sort of publicly coming-out-as-femme moment. It was also important for me, because I was confident that trans women and femmes were natural allies. I believed this not only because of the overlap between these two communities (for example, such individuals as myself who identify as both trans women and femmes), but because of both groups' shared history of being considered suspect in lesbian communities because of our feminine gender expression. My belief that trans women and femmes were natural allies also stemmed from my own experiences in the San Francisco Bay Area, where I generally found that the cis queer women who were most willing to stand up for their trans sisters and to call their peers out on trans-misogyny were almost always femmes.

However, when I attended the conference, I found that my belief that trans women and femmes were natural allies was not shared by all the attendees, not by a long shot. So for me, the conference was a bit of an emotional roller-coaster ride. I want to share some of these moments, the good and the bad. My purpose for doing so is not to call anyone out or to make people feel defensive. Neither is this a critique of the conference itself, because I feel the organizers sincerely intended the space to be inclusive and welcoming of trans-feminine voices. Rather, I am sharing these moments with you in the hope that they might offer some insight into where trans women such as myself are coming from.

First, I felt love and appreciation among the artists with whom I shared the stage at the performance—especially my friends Meliza and Celestina, with whom I performed. Their love gave me the strength to do something that I had never done before: to perform for a predominantly queer women's audience while wearing makeup, heels, and a dress (and a rather slinky dress at that). I'm sure this may not sound like such a big deal to many femmes, but anyone who has been on the receiving end of as many trans-women-are-caricatures-of-real-women comments as I have would surely understand.

After we performed our piece, I was on cloud nine, excited by how well it went and how well it was received. But I was brought back down to Earth by a well-meaning audience member who stopped me to tell me that she enjoyed the piece. And before I could thank her, she added, "And you look so real. I never would have guessed." On the outside I smiled, but on the inside, all I wanted to do was cry.

Then, there were the events that occurred during a Femininities, Feminism, and Femmes panel that followed a film screening of the movie *FtF: Female to Femme* (and a number of other short films).[4] Many of the conference attendees seemed to love *FtF,* and I myself enjoyed much of the film—it included some excellent interviews, and I especially appreciated the fact that it depicted "femme" without automatically pairing it with "butch." But personally, I found it difficult to get around a recurring scene in the film (that was apparently meant to provide comic relief) that depicted a femme support group that was obviously meant to be parody of trans support groups. Having attended trans support groups myself, and having seen grown adults emotionally break down because for the first time in their lives they were sharing their cross-gender feelings with other people or because they had lost their jobs or families after deciding to transition, I found those scenes to be disturbing. To draw what I feel is an apt analogy, as someone who has survived an attempted date rape, I would be offended if someone were to parody a rape survivors' support group. Similarly, as someone who for much of my life would have rather been dead than have anyone else know about my transgender feelings, I found the parody of trans support groups to be offensive (despite the fact that it was surely not the film-makers' purpose to offend trans people).

Thankfully, the panel that followed the film was designed to present different perspectives within the femme community, and it included trans woman, artist, and activist Shawna Virago. Shawna brought up her similar feelings about the film, and how she felt that it invisibilized the cis privilege most of the conference attendees enjoyed. I was grateful that this perspective (which I shared) was voiced. It made me feel as though my own voice were included in the conversation.

But then, the first question immediately following the panelists' opening statements came from a cis woman who suggested that Shawna "didn't get" the film, that it was "just a spoof." She then added that she felt that Shawna's comments were "divisive." The word "divisive" is a red flag for me. I cannot begin to tell you how many times I have heard trans women, or allies of trans women, called "divisive" when we call out people on their transphobia or trans-misogyny. In contrast, cis queer women who make trans-misogynistic comments or who organize or attend queer women's spaces that exclude trans women are *never* called "divisive." The fact that acts that marginalize trans women are not typically described as being "divisive" implies that a presumed and unspoken "oneness" exists in queer women's communities that implicitly precludes trans women.

Anyway, the most difficult moment for me at Femme 2006 occurred during a keynote talk that I attended in which the speaker made three separate disparaging remarks about trans women. The first comment came out of the blue (as she was not discussing trans people or trans issues) when she referred to herself as a "bio-dyke" and defined that as someone who is born female and who is attracted to other women who are born female. (And by the way, can we please get over the word "bio"? I may be a trans woman, but the last time I checked, I was not inorganic or nonbiological in any way.) Anyway, I tried my best to ignore that remark. But then, a little later on in her talk, she made two more comments. The first was a rather confusing comment that seemed to legitimize queer women's fears of "accidentally" becoming attracted to a trans dyke—a sort of lesbian version of *The Crying Game* syndrome, I suppose. Shortly thereafter, she dusted off the thirty-year-old stereotype of the trans woman who "takes up too much space" at a lesbian meeting. This last comment was particularly triggering for me given the fact that (like virtually all queer women's events these days) this conference had a significant turnout of trans-male/masculine-spectrum folks (despite the fact that it was a femme-themed conference) and hardly any trans women in attendance. So for the speaker to suggest that trans women "take up too much space" in a community where we have almost no voice and are often explicitly unwelcomed was illogical and offensive.

My immediate impulse after hearing that comment—being the rebel-rouser that I am—was to begin to craft a biting response for the question-and-answer session that was to follow. But then I realized how pointless that would be, as I would be playing right into her stereotype of me as "taking up too much space." She had placed me in a double-bind. So, upset and without any other obvious recourse, I walked out of the session. I was not trying to make a statement or anything. I honestly just wanted to get as far away as possible. I wanted to go home.

During that long walk out of that large conference room, a couple things were going through my mind. First, I felt very alone. There was no evidence that the audience at large was bothered at all by these comments (although, after the fact, I found out that others were also disturbed). Second, the phrase "trans-woman exclusion"—which I had used countless times in my activism to change the policy at the Michigan Womyn's Music Festival and other women's events and spaces—suddenly popped into my head.[5] For all my work rallying against "exclusion," here I was, leaving a queer women's event that I was explicitly invited to. In a sense, I was excluding myself, not because of any policy but because I found the atmosphere and rhetoric in that room to be intolerable. I was leaving because I was made to feel as though I did not belong.

This latter form of trans-woman exclusion, driven not by any formal policy but by a more general sense of disregard or disrespect for trans women, typifies many queer women's events and spaces. Often, when trans women ask me when I am performing next and I tell them that it is at a queer women's event, they will tell me that they would rather not go, because they do not feel comfortable or safe in those spaces, or because they have been harassed or belittled at similar events before. In most cases, these women are sexually oriented toward women and identify as lesbian or bisexual themselves. But they want no part of queer women's events because of the unchecked trans-misogyny that is often pervasive there.

Anyway, I walked out of that talk, and it is very likely that I would not have come back to the conference had it not been for an amazing cis woman named Tara who followed me out. She stopped me in the lobby to tell me that she was embarrassed and disturbed by the speaker's comments, and she showed me much love and support in a discussion we shared just outside the session. She let me rant for a couple minutes about how upset I was over those comments, and she listened. And that was really what I needed right then: to be listened to. To be reminded that my voice, my thoughts, my feelings still counted, at least to somebody.

In a way, what happened at that keynote talk and at the panel after the *FtF* film screening, while frustrating and difficult for me, also had a silver lining. These events provoked discussions about trans-woman irrelevancy within queer women's communities—discussions that were long overdue. I do not think that such dialogue would have occurred at any other predominantly queer women's event. I believe it happened then and there precisely because it was a femme conference—because many femmes recognize trans women as being a vital part of the femme community.

Two years later, I was invited to give one of the keynote talks at the Femme 2008 Conference.[6] Because of my experience at the previous conference, I attended Femme 2008 with somewhat different expectations than I had before. For one thing, I no longer believed that femmes and trans women are "natural" allies. In fact, in retrospect, the very phrase "natural allies" strikes me as rather oxymoronic. Being an ally is not something that comes naturally. It requires work. To be an ally, you have to listen. You have to be willing to stand by your ally's side, even when it is not directly in your interest to do so.

I still believe that trans women and femmes make good potential allies, as we both face discrimination (in the straight mainstream and within our own LGBT communities) because of our feminine gender expression. And in similar (and sometimes different) ways, we are both working to reclaim femininity, to be empowered by our own feminine gender expression, despite the negative and inferior connotations the rest of the world projects onto us for it. And trans women and femmes share another important attribute: We are survivors. The rest of the world may assume we are weak and fragile because of our feminine inclinations, but in reality, living with other people's relentless misogynistic bullshit has made us tenacious bad-asses.

Although I feel that these shared experiences provide fertile ground upon which we can build an alliance, I also must recognize that many femme-identified folks do not view trans women as potential allies and do not see us as a part of their communities. Many femmes are indifferent toward trans women and our issues, and still others are downright antagonistic (as was evident at Femme 2006).

I have come to realize (and have written in *Whipping Girl*) that there tend to be two prevalent and very different attitudes regarding what queer communities should look like and whom they should include. The first—which is the one I favor—views queer community in terms of alliances built on shared experiences and interests. As a kinky femme-identified trans woman who just so happens to get it on with the ladies, I seek alliances with other women, with other femmes, with other transgender-spectrum folks, with others who engage in same-sex relationships or BDSM, and with fat, differently abled, and intersex folks who share the experience of being made to feel that their bodies are unworthy and inferior to those of other people. Furthermore, as someone who experiences marginalization because of my queerness and trans-ness, I also recognize the importance of creating and fostering alliances with people who are marginalized in other ways (for example, because of racism, classism, and so on). For me, community is not so much about surrounding myself with people who are "just like me" but about learning from and supporting others who share issues and experiences that are similar (yet somewhat different) from my own.

This alliance model exists in sharp contrast to the second view of queer communities, which is centered on sameness rather than difference and on insularity rather than openness. Many lesbian and gay communities are built according to this model, as are those segments of the queer community in which people must constantly tout their über-queer credentials less they be accused of being assimilationist or simply passé. Insular-focused queers typically insist that their own ideologies, values, expressions, and norms are not merely different from but superior to those who have more conventional genders and sexualities. And those gender and sexual minorities who do not quite conform to those community standards are typically seen as having no place within the community.

When I was first coming out as a dyke, I really wanted to fit in, to be accepted. I was really hoping that the dyke community would become a home for me. Unfortunately, it has not. Although I have met a lot of really great, amazing supportive women in those spaces, I have also had a lot of really sucky interactions with people who are either apathetic or antagonistic toward trans women. I have come to realize that I will never be fully accepted within lesbian or dyke circles because of the ways in which I differ from the majority: I am a trans woman, I am a femme, and I have recently come out as bisexual. In a world where many women define "lesbian" as being in opposition to maleness, in opposition to heterosexuality, and in opposition to femininity, I realize that I literally have three strikes against me. So I have instead decided to embrace the fact that I am lesbian kryptonite, as my existence blurs all those distinctions and calls into question all those oppositions. I no longer have any desire to try to gain inclusion or "acceptance" within lesbian or dyke-centric spaces. Fuck insular communities that are centered around any identity. I am no longer looking for a home; I am looking to make alliances.

Although many of us may call ourselves "femme," it is important for us to acknowledge that we are all socially situated in different ways, and this often results in each of us having our own perspectives on femininity and femme identity. Sometimes I find it difficult to talk about my very different history—specifically, the fact that I was socialized male (or, as I put it, forced against my will into boyhood)—because it is so often cited by trans-misogynistic women as evidence that I do not belong in lesbian or women's spaces, because I am not a "real" woman. But at the same time, I also feel that the most important conversations to engage in are often the ones that leave you most vulnerable. So in the last part of this essay, I throw all caution to the wind and talk about how my very different trans history has led to my having a very different perspective on femininity and femme identity than that held by many of my cis femme sisters.

It seems to me that for many cis femme dykes, a major issue that they must reconcile in their lives is the way their feminine expression seems to be at odds with their queer identity. This can lead to invisibility—that is, because they are feminine, they are often not read by others as queer. It can also result in having their queer and feminist credentials constantly called into question by those who view femininity as an artifact of compulsory heterosexuality and, therefore, inherently conformist. In an apparent attempt to challenge accusations that they are assimilationist or that they reinforce sexist stereotypes, many femmes have instead argued that their gender expression is transgressive, because it is employed toward queer ends, thus challenging heterosexism. Or they might argue that their gender expression is performative, or merely a performance, one that makes visible the ways in which gender itself is constructed. As Leah Lakshmi Piepzna-Samarasinha put it in her Femme 2008 keynote talk, this is the idea that femme gender expression is "ironic and campy."

Now I can certainly relate to the notion of feminine expression as performance. As someone who has to "dress down" for my day job, I know that when I do get the chance to dress up for an occasion, I have a definite sense of doing something different, of putting on a different exterior than I normally do. Having said that, even when I am at my most outwardly feminine, the feeling that my gender expression is a "performance" does not even come close to how contrived and self-conscious I felt back before my transition, when I had to wear male-specific clothing (e.g., putting on a suit and tie when attending a wedding). So although you can make the case that masculinity and femininity are "performances," for me, feminine expression feels way more natural. It resonates with my sense of self in a way that I do not really have words to describe. It just feels *right* to me, whereas masculine expression always felt wrong.

What also strikes me is the fact that, although being dressed up as a guy felt very artificial and contrived *to me,* other people tended to read my masculine presentation as natural. In contrast, when I am wearing feminine clothing, it may feel natural *to me,* but other people tend to see me as being "all dolled up." This touches on what I say earlier about "feminine wiles" and femininity's being seen as inherently artificial. In our culture, masculine expression seems to arise out of who one simply is, whereas feminine expression is always viewed as an act or a performance.

This is why I recoil from this idea of femme gender expression as "ironic and campy," as a form of drag or performance, because it plays into the popular assumption that femininity is artificial. I am particularly sensitive about this subject, because, as I mention earlier, others often view me as doubly artificial because I am trans *and* because I am feminine. The assumption that my gender is artificial or a performance is regularly cited by those who wish to undermine or to dismiss my female identity. I refuse to let anyone get away with the cissexist presumption that my gender must be a "performance" simply because I am a transsexual. And I similarly refuse to let anyone get away with the masculine-centric presumption that my gender must be a "performance" simply because I am feminine.

I also find the notion of femininity as performance to be somewhat disingenuous and oversimplistic. I mean, I can "perform" femininity. I can put on makeup, skirts, and heels. I can curtsy, throw like a girl, or bat my eyelashes if I want to. But performance does not explain why certain behaviors and ways of being come to me more naturally than others. The idea that femininity is *just* a construct or *merely* a performance is incompatible with the countless young feminine boys who are not self-conscious about their gender expressions, who become confused regarding why their parents become outraged at their behavior, or who do not understand why other children relentlessly tease them for being who they are. Many such children find their gender expression to be irrepressible, and they remain outwardly feminine throughout their lives despite all the stigmatization and male socialization to the contrary. Other femininely oriented male children learn to hide their feminine gender expressions to survive, but at a great cost.

I was one of the latter children. I know that for many cis queer women, femininity is something that others foist upon them, an unwanted burden, an expectation that they are unable or unwilling to meet. This is perhaps why so many cis lesbian feminists have gone to such great lengths to argue that femininity is artificial, a mere artifact of patriarchy. But for me, femininity was like ether or air—it was always there, just waiting for the chance to leak out of me. When I think about gender expression as being a "performance," I think about myself as a kid, watching my pronunciation of the letter "S" when I spoke to make sure it did not linger. "Performance" was fighting back the urge to be more animated with my hands when I talked, and learning never to use words like "adorable" or "cute" nonsarcastically. "Performance" was going to the barber to get my hair cut short like my parents wanted it, when what I really wanted was to let my hair grow long. Like I said, for me, masculinity always felt artificial, while femininity felt natural.

Natural. The word "natural" has become super-fucking-taboo in queer and feminist circles. Usually when I utter the word "natural" in such settings, I feel as though the queer-theory police will bust into the room at any minute and arrest me for being an essentialist. People are quick to toss around accusations of "essentialism" without really giving much thought to what that word actually means. An essentialist is someone who believes that all women are the same: We are all naturally feminine, we are all naturally attracted to men, and so forth. Essentialists view women who are not feminine or not exclusively attracted to men as unnatural, artificial.

I am not an essentialist (despite the fact that some have accused me of that). I do not believe that all women are the same; I believe that all women are different. I believe that women naturally fall all over the map with regard to gender expression and sexual orientation. I believe that there are no wholly "artificial" genders or sexualities. I believe that many of us experience natural inclinations or predispositions toward certain gendered and sexual behaviors. But these inclinations do not exist in a vacuum—rather they arise in a culture where gender and sexuality are heavily policed; where they are defined according to heterosexist, cissexist, transphobic, and misogynistic assumptions; and where they intersect with racism, classism, ableism, ageism, and other forms of oppression. I would argue that this view of gender and sexuality is not essentialist but holistic.

As I alluded earlier, it is common for people to have somewhat varied opinions regarding what the word "femme" actually means. For me, having a holistic view of gender and sexuality, I suggest that most of us who are femme share two things in common. First, we find that, for whatever reason, feminine gender expression resonates with us on deep, profound levels in inexplicable ways that are not easy to put into words. The second thing that we share is a sense of being different, perhaps because we are dykes or bisexual; perhaps because we are trans women or feminine men or fall somewhere else along the transgender spectrum; or perhaps because our bodies fall outside the norm in some way, because we are fat, differently abled, or intersex. Or perhaps we experience some combination of these or are different in some other way. Because of our differences, we each have to make sense of what it means to be feminine in a world where we can never achieve the conventional feminine ideal and where feminine gender expression and sexualities are plagued by misogynistic connotations. For me, that's what femme is: It's a puzzle we each have to solve. And because we are all different, we will each come up with a different solution, a different way of making sense of and expressing our femme selves.

One reason why I forward holistic views of gender and sexuality is because they allow us to finally put to rest "the femme question."[7] People who dismiss femininity—who consider it frivolous, vain, a patriarchal trap, a product of socialization, an artifact of the gender binary, or whatever—have been fucking with femmes for far too long. Their attempts to try to artificialize or to artifactualize our feminine gender expression (rather than accepting it as natural and legitimate) is the same sort of tactic that occurs when homophobes assume gay people are looking for an "alternative lifestyle" or just have not met the "right person" yet. It is the same bullshit that occurs when bisexuals are accused of being "confused" or of still having one foot in the closet, or when people assume that trans men transition to obtain male privilege or assume that trans women transition to fulfill some sort of bizarre sex fantasy. We should not have to explain why we are trans or why we are queer, and, by the same reasoning, we should not have to explain why we are feminine!

Once we accept that on some level feminine expression is natural, that for some of us—whether female, male, both, or neither—it resonates on a deeply profound level, then we can tackle the real problem: the fact that femininity is seen as inferior to masculinity both in straight settings and in queer and feminist circles. Once we accept the fact that femininity exists and needs no explanation, then we can focus on debunking the countless double standards, such as that masculinity is strong while femininity is weak, that masculinity is tough while femininity is fragile, that masculinity is practical while femininity is frivolous, that masculinity is active while femininity is passive, that masculinity is rational while femininity is overly emotional, and, of course, that masculinity is natural while femininity is artificial. Once we get beyond having to account for *why* we are feminine, then we can finally make the case that all the dismissive connotations and meanings that other people associate with feminine expression are merely misogynistic presumptions on their parts.

This is why I also take issue with the notion of framing "femme" as transgressive or subversive, because, unlike conventional femininity, it occurs within a queer context. This argument seems to buy into the assumption that expressions of femininity that do not occur in a queer context somehow reinforce the gender binary, heterosexism, the patriarchy, or what have you. And I think that is really fucked up! My mother is a heterosexual cis woman. My sisters are heterosexual cis women. As heterosexual cis women, they experience some privileges that I do not experience. They are accepted in the straight, mainstream more readily than I will ever be. But they are marginalized in their day-to-day lives because they are feminine. To argue that they are reinforcing the binary, or the patriarchy, or the hegemonic gender system, because they are conventionally feminine (as opposed to subversively feminine), essentially implies that they are enabling their own oppression. This is just another variation of the claim that rapists make when they insinuate that the women in question were "asking for it" because of what they were wearing or how they behaved. I understand why male rapists try to blame the victims in this way, but for the life of me, I cannot understand why we as feminists and queers buy into this same sort of mentality.

I'll be the first to admit that the expectation that all girls and women are, or should be, conventionally feminine marginalizes and injures many people. Those who are androgynous, or tomboys, or butches, or on the trans-masculine spectrum face disdain for their gender nonconformity. And many women who perhaps are naturally feminine are routinely made to feel embarrassed, ashamed, unworthy, and disempowered, because they do not quite meet society's practically unattainable standards of beauty. But the problem here is not femininity, but expectations. What we as feminists should be challenging is *compulsory* femininity rather than femininity itself.

If all we femmes have one thing in common, it is that we have had to learn to embrace our own feminine expressions while simultaneously rejecting other people's expectations of us. What makes femininity "femme" is not the fact that it is queer, transgressive, ironic, performative, or the complement of butch. No, what makes our femininity "femme" is the fact that we do it for ourselves. It is for that reason that it is so empowering. And that is what makes us so powerful.

As femmes, we can do one of two things with our power: We can celebrate it in secret within our own insular queer communities, patting ourselves on the back for being so much smarter and more subversive than our straight feminine sisters. Or we can share that power with them. We can teach them that there is more than one way to be feminine and that no style or expression of femininity is necessarily any better than anyone else's. We can teach them that the only thing fucked up about femininity is the dismissive connotations that other people project on it. But to do that, we have to give up the self-comfort of believing that our rendition of femme is more righteous, more cool, or more subversive than anyone else's.

Although I do not think that my femme expression or anyone else's femme expressions are in and of themselves subversive, I do believe that the ideas that femmes have been forwarding for decades: ideas about reclaiming femininity, about each person's taking the parts of femininity that resonate with her and leaving the rest, about being femme for ourselves rather than for other people, about the ways in which feminine expression can be tough and active and bad-ass and so on. These ideas are powerful and transformative and can truly change the world.

I think that it is great to celebrate femmes within our own queer communities, but we should not merely stop there. We need to share the idea of self-determined and self-empowered feminine expression, and the idea that feminine expression is just as legitimate and powerful as masculine expression, with the rest of the world. The idea that femininity is inferior and subservient to masculinity intersects with all forms of oppression and is (I feel) the single-most-overlooked issue in feminism. We need to change that, not only for those of use who are queer femmes but for our straight cis sisters who have been disempowered by society's unrealistic feminine ideals, for our gender-variant and gender-nonconforming siblings who face disdain for defying feminine expectations and/or who are victims of trans-misogyny, and also for our straight cis brothers, who have been socialized to avoid femininity like the plague and whose misogyny, homophobia, transphobia, and so on are driven primarily by their fear of being seen as feminine. Although I do not think that my femme expression is subversive, I do believe that, together as femmes, we have the power to truly change the world.

11

DEAN SPADE

What's Wrong with Trans Rights?

> Rights discourse in liberal capitalist culture casts as private potentially political contests about distribution of resources and about relevant parties to decision making. It converts social problems into matters of individualized, dehistoricized injury and entitlement, into matters in which there is no harm if there is no agent and no tangibly violated subject.
>
> —Wendy Brown, *States of Injury*

As the concept of trans rights has gained more currency in the last two decades, a seeming consensus has emerged about which law reforms should be sought to better the lives of trans people.[1] Advocates of trans equality have primarily pursued two law-reform interventions: antidiscrimination laws that list gender identity and/or expression as a category of nondiscrimination, and hate-crime laws that include crimes motivated by the gender identity and/or expression of the victim as triggering the application of a jurisdiction's hate-crime statute. Organizations like the National Gay and Lesbian Task Force (NGLTF) have supported state and local organizations around the country in legislative campaigns to pass such laws. Thirteen states (California, Colorado, Hawaii, Illinois, Iowa, Maine, Minnesota, New Jersey, New Mexico, Oregon, Rhode Island, Vermont, and Washington) and the District of Columbia currently have laws that include gender identity and/or expression as a category of antidiscrimination, and 108 counties and cities have such laws. NGLTF estimates that 39 percent of people in the United States live in a jurisdiction where such laws are on the books.[2] Seven states now have hate-crime laws that include gender identity and/or expression.[3] In 2009, a federal law, the Matthew Shepard and James Byrd, Jr., Hate Crimes Prevention Act, added gender identity and/or expression to federal hate-crime law. An ongoing battle regarding whether and how gender identity and/or expression will be included in the Employment Non-Discrimination Act (ENDA), a federal law that would prohibit discrimination the basis of sexual orientation, continues to be fought between the conservative national gay and lesbian organization, the Human Rights Campaign (HRC), legislators, and a variety of organizations and activists seeking to push an inclusive bill through Congress. Antidiscrimination bills and hate-crime laws have come to define the idea of "trans rights" in the United States and are presently the most visible efforts made by nonprofit organizations and activists working under this rubric.

The logic behind this law-reform strategy is not mysterious. Proponents argue that passing these laws does a number of important things. First, the passage of antidiscrimination laws can create a basis for legal claims against discriminating employers, housing providers, restaurants, hotels, stores, and the like. Trans people's legal claims when facing exclusion in such contexts have often failed in the past, with courts saying that the exclusion is a legitimate preference on the part of the employer, landlord, or business owner.[4] Laws that make gender identity/expression–based exclusion illegal have the potential to influence courts to punish discriminators and to provide certain remedies (e.g., back pay or damages) to injured trans people. There is also a hope that such laws and their enforcement by courts would send a preventative message to potential discriminators, letting them know that such exclusions will not be tolerated; these laws would ultimately increase access to jobs, housing, and other necessities for trans people.

Hate-crime laws are promoted under a related logic. Proponents point out that trans people have a very high murder rate and are subject to a great deal of violence.[5] In many instances, trans people's lives are so devalued by police and prosecutors that trans murders are not investigated or trans people's murderers are given shorter punishments than are typical in murder sentencing. Proponents believe that hate-crime laws will intervene in these situations, making law enforcement take this violence seriously. There is also a symbolic element to the passage of these laws: a statement that trans lives are meaningful, often described by proponents as an assertion that trans people are human. Additionally, proponents of antidiscrimination laws and hate-crime laws argue that the processes of advocating the passage of such laws, including media advocacy representing the lives and concerns of trans people and meetings with legislators to tell them about trans people's experiences, increase positive trans visibility and advance the struggle for trans equality. The data-collection element of hate-crime statutes, through which certain government agencies keep count of crimes that fall into this category, is touted by proponents as a chance to make the quantity and severity of trans people's struggles more visible.

The logic of visibility and inclusion surrounding antidiscrimination and hate-crime law campaigns is very popular, yet there are many troubling limitations to the idea that these two reforms compose a proper approach to problems trans people face in both criminal- and civil-law contexts. One concern is whether these laws actually improve the life chances of those who are purportedly protected by them. Looking at categories of identity that have been included in these kinds of laws over the last several decades indicates that these kinds of reforms have not eliminated bias, exclusion, or marginalization. Discrimination and violence against people of color have persisted despite law changes that declared it illegal. The persistent and growing racial wealth divide in the United States suggests that these law changes have not had their promised effects and that the structure of systemic racism is not addressed by the work of these laws.[6] Similarly, the twenty-year history of the Americans with Disabilities Act (ADA) demonstrates disappointing results. Courts have limited the enforcement potential of this law with narrow interpretations of its impact, and people with disabilities remain economically and politically marginalized by systemic ableism. Similar arguments can be made about the persistence of national origin discrimination, sex discrimination, and other forms of pervasive discrimination despite decades of official prohibitions of such behavior. The persistence of wage gaps, illegal terminations, hostile work environments, hiring/firing disparities, and bias-motivated violence for groups whose struggles have supposedly been addressed by antidiscrimination and hate-crime laws invites caution when assuming the effectiveness of these measures.

Hate-crime laws do not have a deterrent effect. They focus on punishment and cannot be argued to actually prevent bias-motivated violence. In addition to their failure to prevent harm, they must be considered in the context of the failures of our legal system and, specifically, the violence of our criminal punishment system. Antidiscrimination laws are not adequately enforced. Most people who experience discrimination cannot afford to access legal help, so their experiences never make it to court. Additionally, the Supreme Court has severely narrowed the enforceability of these laws over the last thirty years, making it extremely difficult to prove discrimination short of a signed letter from a boss or landlord stating, "I am taking this negative action against you because of your [insert characteristic]." Even in cases that seem as obvious as that, people experiencing discrimination often lose. Proving discriminatory *intent* has become central, making it almost impossible to win these cases when they are brought to court. These laws also have such narrow scopes that they often do not include action taken by some of the most common discriminators against marginalized people: prison guards, welfare bureaucrats, workfare supervisors, immigration officers, child-welfare workers, and others who have significant control over the lives of marginalized people in the United States. In a neoliberal era characterized by abandonment (reduction of social safety nets and infrastructure, especially in poor and people-of-color communities) and imprisonment (increased immigration- and criminal-law enforcement), antidiscrimination laws provide little relief to the most vulnerable people.

In addition to these general problems with law reforms that add gender identity/expression to the list of prohibited characteristics, trans litigants have run into specific challenges when seeking redress from discrimination under these laws. Even in jurisdictions where these laws have been put in place, trans litigants have lost discrimination cases about being denied access to sex-segregated facilities.[7] In the employment context, this often means that even when a worker lives in a jurisdiction where discriminating against trans people is supposedly illegal, denying a trans person access to a restroom that comports with their gender identity at work is not interpreted as a violation of the law. Of course, given the staggering unemployment of trans populations emerging from conditions of homelessness, lack of family support,[8] violence-related trauma, discrimination by potential employers, effects of unmet health needs, and many other factors,[9] even if the legal interpretations of trans people's restroom-access demands were better, they would not scratch the surface of trans poverty.[10] However, these interpretations in employment cases involving restrooms are particularly dangerous, because they can be applied by courts to other high-stakes settings where trans people struggle in systems that rely on sex segregation. Because trans people frequently face violence and discrimination in the context of sex-segregated spaces, such as shelters, prisons, and group homes, and because restroom access is often the most contentious issue between trans workers and their employers, these anti-trans legal interpretations take the teeth out of trans-inclusive laws and are examples of the limitations of seeking equality through courts and legislatures.

Critical race theorists have developed analyses about the limitations of antidiscrimination laws that are useful in understanding the ways these law reforms have and will continue to fail to deliver meaningful change to trans people. Alan Freeman's critique of what he terms the "perpetrator perspective" in discrimination law is particularly helpful in conceptualizing the limits of common trans-rights strategies.[11] Freeman's work looks at laws that prohibit discrimination based on race. He exposes how and why antidiscrimination and hate-crime statutes do not achieve their promises of equality and freedom for people targeted by discrimination and violence. Freeman argues that discrimination law misunderstands how racism works, which makes it fail to effectively address it.

Discrimination law primarily conceptualizes the harm of racism through the perpetrator/victim dyad, imagining that the fundamental scene is that of a perpetrator who irrationally hates people on the basis of their race and fires or denies service to or beats or kills the victim based on that hatred. The law's adoption of this conception of racism does several things that make it ineffective at eradicating racism and help it contribute to obscuring the actual operations of racism. First, it individualizes racism. It says that racism is about bad individuals who intentionally make discriminatory choices and must be punished. In this (mis)understanding, structural or systemic racism is rendered invisible. Through this function, the law can only attend to disparities that come from the behavior of a perpetrator who intentionally considered the category that must not be considered (e.g., race, gender, disability) in the decision he or she was making (e.g., hiring, firing, admission, expulsion). Conditions like living in a district with underfunded schools that "happen to be" 96 percent students of color,[12] having to take an admissions test that has been proven to predict race better than academic success,[13] or experiencing any of a number of disparities in life conditions (access to adequate food, health care, employment, housing, clean air and water) that we know stem from and reflect long-term patterns of exclusion and exploitation cannot be understood as "violations" under the discrimination principle, and thus remedies cannot be won. This narrow reading of what constitutes a violation and can be recognized as discrimination serves to naturalize and affirm the status quo of maldistribution. Antidiscrimination law seeks out aberrant individuals with overtly biased intentions.[14] Meanwhile, all the daily disparities in life chances that shape our world along lines of race, class, indigeneity, disability, national origin, sex, and gender remain untouchable and affirmed as nondiscriminatory or even as fair.

The perpetrator perspective also obscures the historical context of racism. Discrimination is understood as the act of taking into account the identity that discrimination law forbids us to take into account (e.g., race, sex, disability) when making a decision, and it does not regard whether the decision maker is favoring or harming a traditionally excluded group. In this way, the discrimination principle has been used to eviscerate affirmative action and desegregation programs.[15] This erroneously conceptualized "colorblindness" undermines the possibility of remedying the severe racial disparities in the United States that are rooted in slavery, genocide, land theft, internment, and immigration exclusion as well as racially explicit policies that historically and presently exclude people of color from the benefits of wealth-building programs for U.S. citizens, such as Social Security, land grants, and credit and other homeownership support.[16] The conditions that created and continue to reproduce such immense disparities are made invisible by the perpetrator perspective's insistence that any consideration of the prohibited category is equally damaging. This model pretends the playing field is equal, and thus any loss or gain in opportunity based on the category is harmful and creates inequality, again serving to declare the racial status quo neutral. This justification for systemic racism masquerading as a logic of equal opportunity gives rise to the myth of "reverse racism," a concept that misunderstands racism to suggest parallel meanings when white people lose opportunities or access through programs aiming to ameliorate impacts of racism and when people of color lose opportunities due to racism.

Discrimination law's reliance on the perpetrator perspective also creates the false impression that the previously excluded or marginalized group is now equal, that fairness has been imposed, and the legitimacy of the distribution of life chances restored. This declaration of equality and fairness papers over the inequalities and disparities that constitute business as usual and allows them to continue. Narrowing political-resistance strategies to seeking inclusion in antidiscrimination law makes the mistaken assumption that gaining recognition and inclusion in this way will equalize our life chances and allow us to compete in the (assumed fair) system. This often constitutes a forfeiture of other critiques, as if the economic system is fair *but for* the fact that bad discriminators are sometimes allowed to fire trans people for being trans.[17] Constituting the problem of oppression so narrowly that an antidiscrimination law could "solve" it erases the complexity and breadth of the systemic, life-threatening harm that trans resistance seeks to end.

Not surprisingly, the rhetoric accompanying these quests for inclusion often casts "deserving workers"—people whose other characteristics (race, ability, education, class) would have entitled them to a good chance in the workforce were it not for the illegitimate exclusion that happened.[18] Using as examples the least marginalized of the marginalized, so to speak, becomes necessary when issues are framed so narrowly that a person who faces intersecting vectors of harm would be unlikely to benefit from antidiscrimination law. This framing permits—and even necessitates—that efforts for inclusion in the discrimination regime rely on rhetoric that affirms the legitimacy and fairness of the status quo.

The inclusion focus of antidiscrimination law and hate-crime law campaigns relies on a strategy of simile, essentially arguing that "we are just like you; we do not deserve this different treatment because of this one characteristic." To make that argument, advocates cling to the imagined norms of the U.S. social body and choose poster people who are symbolic of U.S. standards of normalcy, whose lives are easily framed by sound bites that resound in shared notions of injustice. "Perfect plaintiffs" for these cases are white people with high-level jobs and lawful immigration status. The thorny issues facing undocumented immigrants; people experiencing simultaneous discrimination through, for example, race, disability and gender identity; or people in low-wage jobs where it is particularly hard to prove discrimination, are not addressed by antidiscrimination law. Laws created from such strategies, not surprisingly, routinely fail to protect people with more complicated relationships to marginality. These people, who face the worst economic vulnerability, are not lifted up as the "deserving workers" that antidiscrimination law advocates rally to protect.

Hate-crime laws are an even more direct example of the limitations of the perpetrator perspective's conception of oppression. Hate-crime laws frame violence in terms of individual wrongdoers. These laws and their advocates portray violence through a lens that oversimplifies its operation and suggests that the criminal-punishment system is the proper way to solve it. The violence targeted by hate-crime laws is that of purportedly aberrant individuals who have committed acts of violence motivated by bias. Hate-crime advocacy advances the fallacy that such violence is especially reprehensible in the eyes of an equality-minded state and thus must be punished with enhanced force. Although it is no doubt true that violence of this kind is frequent and devastating, critics of hate-crime legislation argue that hate-crime laws are not the answer. First, as mentioned above, hate-crime laws have no deterrent effect: People do not read law books before committing acts of violence and then choose against bias-motivated violence because it carries a harsher sentence. Hate-crime laws do not and cannot actually increase the life chances of the people they purportedly protect.

Second, hate-crime laws strengthen and legitimize the criminal-punishment system, a system that targets the very people these laws are supposedly passed to protect. The criminal-punishment system was founded on and constantly reproduces the same biases (racism, sexism, homophobia, transphobia, ableism, xenophobia) that advocates of these laws want to eliminate. This is no small point, given the rapid growth of the U.S. criminal-punishment system in the last few decades and the gender, race, and ability disparities in whom it targets. The United States now imprisons 25 percent of the world's prisoners, although it has only 5 percent of the world's population.[19] Imprisonment in the United States has quadrupled since the 1980s and continues to increase, despite the fact that violent crime and property crime have declined since the 1990s.[20] The United States has the highest documented rate of imprisonment per capita of any country.[21] A 2008 report declared that the United States now imprisons one in every one hundred adults.[22] Significant racial, gender, ability, and national-origin disparities exist in this imprisonment system. One in nine black men between the ages of twenty and thirty-four are imprisoned. Although men still vastly outnumber women in prisons, the rate of imprisonment for women is growing far faster, largely the result of sentencing changes created as part of the War on Drugs, including the advent of mandatory minimum sentences for drug convictions. An estimated 27 percent of federal prisoners are noncitizens.[23] Although accurate estimates of rates of imprisonment for people with disabilities are difficult to obtain, it is clear that the combination of severe medical neglect of prisoners, deinstitutionalization of people with psychiatric disabilities without the provision of adequate community services, and the role of drug use in self-medicating account for high rates.[24]

In a context of mass imprisonment and rapid prison growth targeting traditionally marginalized groups, what does it mean to use criminal punishment-enhancing laws to purportedly address violence against those groups? This point has been especially forcefully made by critics who note the origins of the contemporary lesbian and gay rights formation in antipolice activism of the 1960s and 1970s and who question how current lesbian and gay rights work has come to be aligned with a neoliberal "law and order" approach.[25] Could the veterans of the Stonewall and Compton's Cafeteria uprisings against police violence have guessed that a few decades later LGBT law reformers would be supporting passage of the Matthew Shepard and James Byrd, Jr., Hate Crimes Prevention Act, a law that provides millions of dollars to enhance police and prosecutorial resources? Could they have imagined that anyone would claim the police as protectors of queer and trans people against violence, while imprisonment and police brutality are skyrocketing? The neoliberal reframing of discrimination and violence that have drastically shifted and undermined strategies of resistance to economic exploitation and state violence produce this narrow law-reform agenda that ignores and colludes in the harm and violence faced every day by queer and trans people struggling against racism, ableism, xenophobia, transphobia, homophobia, and poverty.

These concerns are particularly relevant for trans people given our ongoing struggles with police profiling, harassment, violence, and high rates of youth and adult imprisonment. Trans populations are disproportionately poor because of employment discrimination, family rejection, and difficulty accessing school, medical care, and social services.[26] These factors increase our rate of participation in criminalized work to survive, which, combined with police profiling, produces high levels of criminalization.[27] Trans people in prisons face severe harassment, medical neglect, and violence in both men's and women's facilities. Violence against trans women in men's prisons is consistently reported by prisoners as well as by researchers, and court cases and testimony from advocates and formerly imprisoned people reveals trends of forced prostitution, sexual slavery, sexual assault, and other violence. Trans people, like all people locked up in women's prisons, are targets of gender-based violence, including sexual assault and rape, most frequently at the hands of correctional staff. Prisoners who are perceived as "too masculine" by prison staff at women's facilities are often at significantly increased risk of harassment and enhanced punishment, including psychologically damaging isolation, for alleged violations of rules against homosexual contact. These prisoners also face a greater risk of assault motivated by an adverse reaction to gender nonconformity.[28]

Because the criminal-punishment system itself is a significant source of racialized-gendered violence, increasing its resources and punishment capacity will not reduce violence against trans people. When advocates of hate-crime laws frame the criminal-punishment systems as a solution to the violence trans people face, they participate in the false logic that criminal punishment produces safety, when it is clear that it is actually a site of enormous violence. Criminal punishment cannot be the method we use to stop transphobia when the criminal punishment system is the most significant perpetrator of violence against trans people. Many commentators have used this support of the expansion of punishment regimes through the advent of hate-crime advocacy as an example of cooptation, where resistance struggles that have named certain conditions or types of violence come to be used to prop up the very arrangements that are harming the people who are resisting. A new mandate to punish transphobic people is added to the arsenal of justifications for a system that primarily locks up and destroys the lives of poor people, people of color, indigenous people, people with disabilities, and immigrants and that uses gender-based sexual violence as one of its daily tools of discipline against people of all genders.[29]

Much of the thinking behind the need for hate-crime and antidiscrimination legislation, including by advocates who recognize how limited these interventions are as avenues for increasing the life chances of trans people, is about the significance of having our experiences of discrimination and violence named in law. The belief that being named in this way has a benefit for the well-being of trans people has to be reexamined with an understanding that the alleged benefits of such naming provides even greater opportunity for harmful systems to claim fairness and equality while continuing to kill us. Hate-crime and antidiscrimination laws declare that punishment systems and economic arrangements are now non-transphobic, yet these laws not only fail to eradicate transphobia but also strengthen systems that perpetuate it.

This analysis illuminates how law-reform work that merely tinkers with systems to make them look more inclusive while leaving their most violent operations intact must be a concern of many social movements today. For example, prison abolitionists in the United States argue that the project of prison reform, which is usually aimed at reducing certain kinds of violence or unfairness in the prison system, has always functioned to maintain and to expand imprisonment.[30] Prison-reform efforts aimed at a reducing a variety of harms, such as gender and sexual violence, medical neglect and abuse, and overcrowding, to name but a few, have often been made by well-meaning people who wanted to address the horrors of prison life. But these reform efforts have been incorporated into the project of prison expansion, mobilized as rationales for building and filling more and more prisons. Abolitionists caution that a system designed from its inception as a technology of racialized control through exile and punishment will use any rationale necessary to achieve that purpose.

A recent example of particular interest to feminism and trans politics is the 2003 National Prison Rape Elimination Act (NPREA). Although it was passed in the name of preventing sexual assault, the NPREA has been used to further enforce and to increase penalties against prisoners for consensual sexual activity, including such activities as handholding. Abolitionist activists doing prisoner support work have pointed out that because some of the main tools the NPREA uses are punishment tools, those tools have become just another part of the arsenal used by punishment systems to increase sentences, to target prisoners of color and queer and trans prisoners, and to expand imprisonment. It is unclear whether the new rules have reduced sexual violence, but it *is* clear that they have increased punishment.[31] Activists considering using law reform as a tool, then, have to be extraordinarily vigilant to determine whether they are actually strengthening and expanding various systems' capacities to harm or whether our work is part of dismantling those capacities.[32]

In prison- and immigration-reform contexts, trans activists are raising concerns about the danger of dividing affected populations by mobilizing ideas about who constitutes a "deserving" or "undeserving" subject. Campaigns that focus on immigrants portrayed as "hard working" (racist, antipoor code for those who do not need support like public benefits or housing) and "law abiding" (not caught up in the criminal punishment system) or that frame immigration issues in terms of family unity relying on heteropatriarchal constructs, further stigmatize those who do not fit the "deserving" frame and create policies that only benefit a narrow swath of affected people. Similarly, campaigns about imprisonment that only focus on people convicted of nonviolent crimes, "political" prisoners, or people exonerated by the introduction of new evidence, risk refining the system in ways that justify and legitimize the bulk of its continued operation by eliminating its most obvious contradictions. Three concerns about law-reform projects permeate many sites of resistance. First, these projects change only what the law says about what a system is doing but not its actual impact. Second, they refine a system in ways that help it continue to target the most-vulnerable people while only partially or temporarily removing a few of the less vulnerable from its path. And finally, law-reform projects often provide rationales and justifications for the expansion of harmful systems.

Freeman's critique of the perpetrator perspective helps us understand how a discrimination-focused law-reform strategy that aims to prohibit the consideration of certain categories of identity in the context of certain decisions (who to hire, fire, evict, house, or assault) misconceives how the violences of racism, ableism, xenophobia, transphobia, sexism, and homophobia operate. Freeman's work shows how discrimination law fails to remedy the harms it claims to attend to and actually can empower systems that maldistribute life chances. Reconceptualizing the theory of power and struggle that underlies such law reforms allows us to turn our attention to other systems in law that produce structured insecurity and shortened life spans for trans people and consider alternative avenues of intervention.

Examining the operation of legal systems that administer life chances at the population level, such as welfare systems, punishment systems, health-care systems, and immigration systems, can expose how law operates to sort people into subpopulations facing different exposures to security and insecurity. Looking at sites of the legal administration of societal norms, we can see how certain populations come to have such pervasive experiences with both abandonment and imprisonment. From that vantage point, we can strategize about how to use legal reform tools as part of a broader strategy to dismantle capitalism's murderous structures while we build alternative methods of meeting human needs and organizing political participation. Because of the obvious failures of the most-popular contemporary law-reform strategies to address harms trans people are facing, trans experience can offer a location from which to consider the broader questions of the neoliberal cooptation of social movements through law reform and the institutionalization of resistance and from which to reframe the problems of violence and poverty that impact marginalized populations in ways that give us new inroads to intervention.

If we shift our framework from trans rights to critical trans resistance, we find ourselves with new analysis of the harms that people who defy gender norms face and new ideas for how we might dismantle systems that produce and enforce gender norms. Such a shift means that we move from demands for recognition and inclusion in law to demands for material changes to our lives. We recognize formal legal equality as a window dressing for harmful and violent political and economic arrangements (settler colonialism, white supremacy, capitalism, heteropatriarchy), and we come to understand that what we want and need will never be won through a legal system founded in and dedicated to preserving racialized-gendered property statuses. Our social movement strategies, then, become centered in mobilization, and our targets become the sites of violence we see producing trans death.

The demands for wealth redistribution, prison abolition, and an end to immigration enforcement that are emerging from trans communities suggest a critical trans politics guided by the urgent circumstances we face and a desire to center those living under the most severe forms of coercive violence as a guide for prioritization. The social-movement infrastructure we need to win these demands is far more participatory, democratic, and decentralized than what has emerged in law reform–centered rights-seeking formations. The loud concerns raised within social movements in the last decade about the roles nonprofitization and professionalization have played in containing and undermining transformative social change are useful to trans politics: We perceive the current push to institutionalize our work in those same hierarchical, elitist, undemocratic, and unaccountable forms to support the same narrow status-quo affirming agenda.[33] Across the United States, local communities are proposing and creating different tools, forms, and agendas to address these concerns and to innovate infrastructure for trans resistance. This resistance refuses to make itself legible in a neoliberal framework; to articulate demands for rights that reproduce racist, ableist, antipoor, xenophobic frameworks of deservingness and undeservingness; to sell off transformative goals for funding opportunities; or to endorse violent institutions for a chance at being nominally invited to be part of them. Co-developing this critical trans politics requires all of us to tap our creativity, imagination, bravery, compassion, humility, self-reflection, patience, generosity, and perseverance as we seek change deep enough to dismantle the violences that are foundational to our current conditions.

12

RYKA AOKI

When Something Is Not Right

"Hold on, hold—hold on! Something is not right here. Something is *not right!*"

It's March 2008, and I am in Greensboro, North Carolina, on tour with the Tranny Roadshow, a barnstorming transsexualgenderqueer vaudeville show/gender studies symposium coming soon to a liberal arts college near you.

It's past midnight, and we are returning to our hotel after preaching the Gospel of Gender Awareness, which for me essentially means convincing anyone who will listen that transwomen do more than inject ourselves with industrial silicone, blow wannabe frat boys in alleys for twenty bucks, and get beaten to death when a wannabe frat boy claims he was fooled by a chick with a dick—all while keeping the audience entertained and wanting more.

Anyone can be trans, or an activist, but to be on the Roadshow, you had better do a good Elvis. Jamez is an ex-Alaskan dog-musher/current Harvard Divinity student who plays the violin and recites poetry in a shaggy lion costume with floppy yarn mane. Kelly is a social worker and zine librarian who resembles nothing so much as a four-foot-ten Chuck Norris–channeling Hunter S. Thompson. When Red's not singing to straight hipsters about how irritating they are, she's a professional chef who rhapsodizes about the perfect gravy, homemade mayonnaise. Oh, and she has about a million viewers who follow her Weblog on YouTube. And then there's me, an Asian American English professor with an Ivy League MFA, who sings, "We're Off to See the Wizard!" while waving a floppy blue dildo with Styrofoam Muppet eyes.

Tonight we rocked the house. The queer kids seemed queerer—they applauded louder, flirted harder. Best of all, they bought more of our CDs and zines, which means I have enough money to pay the parking lot attendant when I get back to LAX. Even the faculty were cute, like that professor who tried to make small talk but was so nervous, as if unsure whether hitting on me made him gay. So it's all good as we enter the hotel. And then, suddenly, it's Another World.

The mid-city Clarion or Red Roof or Ramada is not like its brethren in New Orleans or Las Vegas, where you dump your bags in the your room and bust out into the night. Often, the local business hotel *is* the destination, where the lights are brightest, the music loudest, the prime rib primest, and where both traveler and local can count on air conditioning, clean restrooms, and a drink served in a tall, thin glass. If you live in the area, you can hook up with an interesting out-of-towner who will seduce you with sweet nothings and margaritas and then leave before you have the chance to forget his name.

Heck, even the local boys are trying to be just as anonymous as you, so as long as you understand this is a no-tell situation and you don't catch any icky diseases, having a place to dance, drink, flirt, and get a room at one convenient location sure as hell beats another night of watching *The Biggest Loser*.

Here in North Carolina, this hotel seems to be working perfectly, for as we exit the elevator and turn down the hallway, we encounter a blonde. Gloriously primped, hairsprayed, and a little old for that halter top, she's like that faded VHS of *Xanadu* I have somewhere in my closet. At her side is her friend, brunette, dressed similarly, but with decidedly less splendor. Together, they have bagged two big young bucks, with their obligatory baseball caps and baby-fat muscles that roll from their arms to their backs all the way up their necks. Back in high school, when I was a boy and on the wrestling team, I knew a couple of guys like this. They ate a lot of meat and would break things when they started swinging—think carnivorous wrecking balls.

Usually, a scene like this means Armageddon for a group of queers, but the women seem to be happy with their boys and the boys with their women, and all of them with their drinks. Besides, we're still goofy and glowing from our night. So we leave the couples to their breeding and continue down the hallway.

And it's just as we pass them that we hear, "Hold on, hold—hold on! Something is not right here. Something is *not right!*"

It's the blonde.

Shit. Like deer in headlights, we freeze. Bad move. In that moment, the blonde reaches out and *grabs my arm.*

"Hold on, *hold on!*" Now she's on the verge of yelling. "Let me look at you."

I try to pull away, but she tightens her grip. This is not good. Not good at all. Now I'm scared—I am in the South in a town I don't know, and someone has grabbed my arm. How could I have been so careless? I'm the only one wearing a skirt and makeup. Jamez and Kelly are in their typical sweater/sweatshirt and jeans, and Red, even onstage, is much more of an outdoorsy down vest–type girl. What's more, I'm the only Asian in the group, and probably the entire hotel.

"No, No *No*. Let *me* look at *you.*"

She moves up close to me, so close I smell the rum on her breath and see the smudges in her eyeliner. It's taking everything I have to hold myself steady, to try to focus. What to do? I can probably break her grip, but that will probably piss her off, and then the guys would jump in. . . . There's no way to escape without guaranteeing a scene. Crap. I try to breathe, to tell myself I can't faint now.

I look at her, at her electric-blue eye shadow, and try to think of something smart to say, something to help us get away, because we are about to be clocked as trans people, or at least I am, and with those big guys who are really big, and drinking, and in mating mode. . . . I need to think of something right now. But no words come. There's too much fear in me, and too much alcohol and pheromones in them. I am about to become a statistic. I swear if she calls me a drag queen, I'm going down fighting and say, "Look who's talking, bitch!"

I just hope I can make enough of a racket that my friends can get away . . . and that whatever they do, it won't hurt too much.

But then, her expression changes to a strange little smile and she says, "You are so beautiful." And her friend with the brown hair walks next to her and nods, and her eyes are caring and—why do they seem so . . . sad?

OK, this is weird. But it's not violent, and I'll take weird over violent any day.

I can even feel my hair relax. Blood rushes back to my arms and legs and I wobble, but the blonde holds me steady, and her grip is strong. I smile, ready to say thank you and continue on my way.

But then the blonde squeezes my arm even harder. She glares at my friends.

"*What* are you are gonna to do with *her*?"

Jamez and Kelly look like they've been punched in the gut. Each of them has worked for women's and queer rights. Now they've just been pegged as scraggly white guys coercing a lone woman, obviously not from around here, to their room.

Now we're fucked, not because they think we're transgender or queer but because they think we're *straight*. There is no way my friends can explain the mistake, because those guys are really big, and during this whole time they haven't stopped drinking.

"I *said, what* are you gonna do with *her*!?"

Louder this time. The blonde wants an answer. She lurches at the tallest person in our group, who happens to be Red. "Who are you?"

"I'm Red."

"I know you are." [Red's got red hair.] "But who *are* you?"

She's not talking to Red as a woman, but as yet another man. Red goes blank. I wince. It hurts when a trans woman is read as a man—it's happened to all of us. But here, for safety's sake, we were locked in our identities. Red's grungy flannel shirt is saving her right now. If she had been in a dress and not passed, that would have been ugly. So we leave it alone. Just as passing is saving me, not passing is saving her. All I can do is remember that Red, just as Jamez and Kelly and I have, has endured much worse.

The blonde turns to me. "Honey, you stay right here." As she says this, one of the wrecking balls sways over at Kelly, all just under five feet of him.

"You her boyfriend? Huh? Huh? Dude, they're trying to hit on your girlfriend."

In his big slow way, I think he's doing some sort of guy honor thing. Although now there's the prospect of another woman joining them, instead of punching his friend in the arm, he's warning Kelly that he is about to lose his girl. It's kind of sweet.

But the big guy, bless him, is wrong. Because the women aren't hitting on me. The brunette puts her hand on my shoulder, "Honey, you are so beautiful, you do *not* have to go through with this. *You don't have to do this.*" She says the last sentence as if I were a lost child at a Walmart.

The blonde nods. "You can stay with us. You can stay in our room tonight."

It's generous and terrifying at the same time, because during this whole encounter, she has not let go of my arm. The big guys wink and nudge. Jamez and Red make noises to leave. Suddenly, the blonde loses her patience and screams.

"*What are y'all going to do to her? Y'all gonna gang bang her?*" She is drunk and pissed and dangerous. The big guys spin around, literally heads to the wall.

"Uh, let's let the girls handle this," one of them mumbles.

Red and Jamez take this chance to dash down the hallway. Good move. Although I don't want to be left alone, I can't blame them.

Kelly, thank goodness, stays with me, as I tell the two women that we're just friends really, just friends, and we're so tired, please, we just need to sleep now. I am not sure of exactly what I babble, but eventually the blonde looks deeply into my eyes and says, "Honey, if you need anything, we're here for you. We're right here in this room and if you need us, you just come over here and we'll take care of you."

Finally, she releases my arm. I hug her, say thank you, and nod. Kelly waves. We walk down the hallway, and once we turn the corner, we giggle like idiots and dash to our room and bolt the door.

"Okay, now how many ways did they get *that* wrong!?"

Kelly and I are screaming. "Oh my God! We fucking almost *died*!" Fuck. I think need a drink. Shitfuckshitfuckshitfuck—

Slow down, breathe. . . .

I flop on my bed and stare at the ceiling. What the hell? And as I finally catch my breath, an even weirder thought comes to mind: In Greensboro, North Carolina, some straight white women, who obviously had other things going on, noticed what they thought was a vulnerable Asian girl from out of town and decided they were going to help.

How many people would let a moment like that go? I didn't look like them. I'm not white. I obviously wasn't a local. They could have just let me pass and kept the party going. Lots of us hip, enlightened, rainbow-fearing queers would have done just that.

They misread the situation about as completely as one can imagine, but at least they tried. They saw that something was not right, and they got involved, to help someone they did not know, simply because they thought I was in need.

Perhaps as they had been in need before—not only trans and queer women get abused. Would I have done the same for them? I'd like to think so. I hope I would have the compassion to say something.

Kelly's done with the bathroom, and as I finally wash off my makeup and pop out my contacts, I think of how perception can bring familiarity, antipathy, or violence. To be transgender means never quite knowing which reaction you're going to get, where, or from whom. You can be a sister one moment, then have a security guard stop you in the bathroom the next. In one store, the salesperson will smile and say welcome. In another, you'll get ugly stares and giggles.

Because they perceived me to be female, the women treated me with kindness. Had I really been in trouble, they might have saved my life. But if they had seen me as male, I'd have been dismissed as another potential threat. Does this make how they acted toward me any less remarkable?

I don't know. But I do know that it's really late and I am in Greensboro, North Carolina, preaching the gospel of gender awareness and there's another show tomorrow. And I need to sleep, and sleep comes best with a story where I can believe that even as race, gender, or culture, can seem insurmountable—that on some nights, one human can see another human, perceive that she is in need and, despite their differences, decide to be fierce and brave.

For now, that's good enough. No violence, no hate. Just weird. And I'll take weird over violent any day, or any night.

I hop into my bed, have one last laugh with Kelly, and finally turn off the lights.

A few weeks later, Jamez, Kelly, and I are touring with a different group of artists in Colorado. One of them is Linda, a seventy-eight-year-old harmonica player who transitioned from male to female at seventy-two. She needs someone to talk to. She needs to talk to me. And she needs to talk to me about transition.

This is the last thing I want. I don't want to hear about the five of her six now-grown children who don't talk to her. I don't want to hear about the grandchildren she may never see again, or the line-dance instructor at the senior center who said she was unwelcome because she is transgender. I don't want to hear that her closest companion is her dog, but that it's all "still worth it."

So when it comes time to drive from Denver to our show in Fort Collins, I pull Jamez aside and ask that I not ride with her. Some of my concern is valid; I don't like deep conversations, especially trans conversations, before a show. It gets rough hearing stories of senseless cruelty and injustice while rushing jet-lagged and jittery to a show that's happening in two hours. It can be difficult hearing about the sales clerk at the mall who kicks a trans woman out of her store, or, god forbid, another friend dying—all while hoping for a sound check, adjusting a set list, rehearsing lines, and preserving enough energy for a great performance.

But that's far from the whole story. In all my time with the Roadshow, I have never asked to not ride with someone before.

It's Linda. In Linda, I see a wobbly old trans woman who seems too much like someone I am terrified to become. Like many trans women, her speech seems both overbearing and tentative. Do I converse this way? She hadn't started hormones until later life; her hairline had receded. I touch my own hair, worried. She's still awkward with her makeup, and her thin body makes her hands look way too large; should I be wearing gloves? Her skin is crinkly and paper thin. My father's skin is like that. . . .

The irony is terrible. I am on tour specifically to tell auditoriums full of people that we need to be more accepting of everyone, regardless of how nonconforming they seem. I am here to tell audiences that trans people, and trans women in particular, should be treated as women, and no matter what their appearance, should be treated with dignity, acceptance, and respect. Yet here I am, unable to put my prejudices aside to ride with someone who simply wants a friend.

So I'm riding in the other car with Kelly. He's relating a funny story about the Denver Zine Library, and I am trying to smile, but I can't get past the fact that I totally, totally *suck*.

The trip to Fort Collins goes smoothly, as does the sound check. I scope out the stage, check the acoustics, and thank the performance gods that the sound person knows the difference between a quarter-inch cable and an XLR. However, as I go over my set list, I notice that Linda is sitting by herself on a little stool, looking fragile and nervous in a pink cowboy hat, with two shiny harmonicas and a bottle of water.

I don't know where it comes from, but somehow I retrieve enough sense to remember what it feels like to be alone, especially before a show. Somehow I shake some sense into my head, remember that she does not deserve to be treated poorly and that even if I can't be a decent human being, at least I should act like one. So I take a deep breath, walk over, and ask how she's feeling. I listen, as closely as I can, and tell her it's okay to be nervous, and that this audience is going to love her. I tell her, thank you for being so brave and how important it was for her to be part of the tour.

Of course, Fort Collins loves Linda's harmonica music. And they love Linda. Yes, it sounds like a cliché, but when you're queer, and especially trans, clichés where people are listening and clapping, instead of raping and killing . . . well, those are clichés that you keep.

Once the show is over, the Roadshow decides to cut loose at a gay cowboy bar in Denver. From Fort Collins to Denver, Linda and I compare harmonica styles. We share songs as well as stories. She tells me about her lives as a dancer, a dirt biker, a veteran. She builds custom dune buggies and says we should ride one day.

At the bar, Linda teaches me some dance where you kick or something, and I quickly realize in Los Angeles, I do too much driving and not enough walking.

After I bow out, totally winded, she outdances not only me but Kelly and a couple of pretty muscle boys as well. Watching her, I can't help but think that being true to one's self is a lot like navigating the dance floor. It's awkward and clumsy at first. But if you can keep going, one day your shoes break in, your legs stop shaking, you stop sweating like a pig, and a good song can reflect the beauty of your soul.

I am to leave the tour early for a speaking engagement in Chicago. When we return to our rooms, Linda says that she probably won't be able to wake up to see me leave for my morning flight. She looks like she's about to cry.

The next morning, as I pack my last items, harmonica music comes through my door. I peek into the hallway, and Linda is standing there, in her pink flannel nightgown. Her eyes are red, and she says that song was for you. Then she breaks down. Just sobbing. Deep shoulder-heaving sobs.

And when I hold her, all she can get say is, "Thank you for being my friend."

Once, I imagined my art was my savior. I hoped and believed my words could heal and elevate everything they touched. Poetry and music were sacred dialects through which I spoke to my ancestors and what kept me alive as I was growing up in an abusive home. My stage name, "de la Cruz," is both a tribute to art as an ideal vehicle to ask why the world is as it is, and a dedication that I will use my life to share the answers I find.

But poetry does not deliver salvation. When I think of my reaction when I first met Linda, I feel awful. I'd like to say that there was some misunderstanding, or that this superficial person wasn't really me. But it was.

I failed. I did exactly what I am trying to eliminate. I judged on appearance. I presumed. I was prejudiced. And I know that there is always that chance that I will get a little too high on my horse and fail again. I'll screw up. Again.

For me, this encounter and others like it keep me from vilifying people for slip-ups and ignorance. Whether someone misspeaks to me or misjudges me, if that person honestly is trying, I need to remember my own weakness, be humble, and forgive.

I can talk about being a dyke or being trans or being a POC, but no identity is enough. And no matter how transcendent a story or composition may seem, it is foolish to believe that I can separate my work from my prejudices and phobias.

It scares me that I might be so wrong about so many things . . . that all the patience, study, and lessons I acquire only guarantee that I shall make ever-more-thoughtful and eloquent mistakes.

Yet I am even more determined to listen, learn, and continue performing and writing. For as naive as it is to believe that transcendent art comes from transcendent people, it is unforgivable to let fear of failure stop work that, imperfect as it is, may on a good night reach out to others like a cussing, yet caring voice in a Greensboro hotel.

And, maybe some people will laugh at me, others will get pissed off with me, and others will whisper I must be drunk. But just like the blonde in the hallway, all haltered and hairsprayed and maybe a little more afraid and fucked up than she lets on, at least I am going to try to do the right thing. And even if I'm slurring my words and wearing way too much electric-blue eye shadow, when something is not right, I plan to write something, say something, to hold an arm tightly and try helping as best as I can.

Notes

INTRODUCTION

1. Simone de Beauvoir, *The Second Sex*.
2. Judith Butler, *Gender Trouble*; *Undoing Gender*; Riki Anne Wilchins, *Read My Lips*.
3. Examples include the British *Journal of Gender Studies* (1998), *Women's Studies Quarterly* (2008), *Hypatia* (2009), *Women and Performance* (2010), *Feminist Studies* (2011), and the *Journal of Gender and History* (2011). In 2006, the Center for Gender Studies at University of Chicago held a conference, "Trans/Forming Knowledge; The Implications of Transgender Studies for Women's, Gender, and Sexuality Studies." Stephen Whittle reflects on this evolution in "Where Did We Go Wrong? Feminism and Trans Theory: Two Teams on the Same Side?" *Transgender Studies Reader*, 194–202.
4. Leslie Feinberg, "A Movement Whose Time Has Come." Produced outside the academy, this pamphlet would later wind its way into the academy to become one of the canonical primary sources in the field of transgender history.
5. For example, Susan Stryker has defined transgender as *"the movement across a socially imposed boundary away from an unchosen starting place"* (italics in original). Stryker, *Transgender History*, 1.
6. This means that most trans people are not "counted" in certain medical statistics. According to statistics based on genital surgery, the incidence of transsexuality is between 1 in 10,000 and 1 in 30,000. This reflects the impossibility of gaining accurate statistics in part because what "counts" as transsexual surgeries varies wildly depending on definitions of male-to-female and female-to-male transitions and cultural and legal standards that vary across states and nations. Furthermore, trans-related surgery is a transnational practice (for financial, legal, and cultural reasons, many people seek surgeries outside their own countries), but global statistics do not exist.
7. Two registers of transphobia are so common that they are phrased as punctuation to a broader problem: "and they can't even get the pronouns right," and/or, "and there are no restrooms I can use." These are barometric and consequential, related to such material issues as expulsion from school, job loss, and the impossibility of functioning without use of a restroom. Efforts to acknowledge transgender existence in college classrooms must be mindful of context and the pressures gender-variant students may experience, particularly in light of the fact that the majority of trans* students are not out or visible as trans. Sometimes, intending to raise awareness, instructors will ask students to introduce themselves

and to share their preferred pronouns (e.g., "My name is Alex and I prefer 'they'"). This practice derives from support and/or activist groups that establish clear "safe-space" guidelines; the question allows participants to know and to refer to each other with identity-appropriate pronouns. But classrooms are not generally safe spaces. This practice requires trans* students to either come out or to participate in the further erasure of their gender identities. Precisely this dilemma may keep many trans students away from gender studies classes: Where gender is under greater scrutiny, trans people may feel themselves also to be under greater scrutiny. Simultaneously, they may be asked to take up a politicized mantle or to even become the teachers when they are simply trying to take a class. It is important to find ways to interrupt gender normativity that do not require trans* and gender-diverse students to come out, to silence themselves, or to do the teacher's work.

8. For example in Minnesota, one company effectively fired a trans woman by refusing to let her use the women's restroom and refusing to come up with any other "bathroom solution." The Minnesota Supreme Court ruled that this was not gender-identity discrimination, even though statewide nondiscrimination legislation includes gender identity. *Goins v. West Group* (Minn. 2001).

9. Sandy Stone, "The Empire Strikes Back: A Posttranssexual Manifesto," 230. Susan Stryker organized a conference at Indiana University commemorating the twentieth anniversary of Stone's article, "Postposttranssexual: Transgender Studies and Feminism," April 8-9, 2011, Bloomington, Indiana.

10. This line of questioning, owing in large part to French and Marxist theorists, such as Louis Althusser, Simone de Beauvoir, Monique Wittig, and Michel Foucault, critiques the belief that speaking (or coming out) as x constitutes liberation. In "The Evidence of Experience," historian Joan Scott critiques the extrapolation of personal experience into universal truths (which are always false) and authority; Gayatri Spivak, in "Can the Subaltern Speak," questions whether the structures that produce alterity and subalterity make it impossible to take up subalterity as a speaking position.

11. Susan Stryker, "(De)Subjugated Knowledges: An Introduction to Transgender Studies," *Transgender Studies Reader*, 12.

12. Janice Raymond, in *The Transsexual Empire: The Making of the She-Male*, specifically attacks Sandy Stone for her involvement in lesbian feminism during the 1970s as well as blaming transsexuality in general for sexism, misogyny, gender essentialism, antifeminism, violence against women ("women" defined by Raymond to exclude trans women), and the medical establishment's male dominance.

13. Christopher Moore, in *The Believers*, directed by Todd Holland; produced by Nicole Miller and Beth Burkhart (Frameline Films, 2006).

14. Ashley Moore, *The Believers*.

15. Bobby Jean Baker, *The Believers*.

16. These documentaries depart from the typical academic fare in that they consist entirely of trans* people authoring and authorizing themselves as indigenous knowers.

17. Monique Wittig, "One Is Not Born a Woman," in *The Straight Mind and Other Essays* (Boston: Beacon, 1992), 9-20; Adrienne Rich, "Compulsory Heterosexuality and Lesbian Existence" (orig. 1980, published in *Blood, Bread, and Poetry*; New York: Norton Paperback, 1994); Joan Nestle, *A Restricted Country* (New York: Firebrand, 1987); Gayle Rubin, "Of Catamites and Kings: Reflections on Butch, Gender, and Boundaries," in Joan Nestle, ed, *The Persistent Desire: A Femme-Butch-Reader* (Boston: Alyson, 1992), 466-482.

18. Sandy Stone, "The Empire Strikes Back"; Wendy Brown, "The Impossibility of Women's Studies" in *Edgework: Critical Essays on Knowledge and Politics* (Princeton, NJ: Princeton University, 2005), 116-135.

19. Dean Spade, "Transpolitics on a Neoliberal Landscape," delivered to Barnard College, February 9, 2009.
20. Susan Stryker, *Transgender Studies Reader*, 9.

CHAPTER 1

Epigraphs: Linda Tuhiwai Smith, *Decolonizing Methodologies: Research and Indigenous Peoples* (1999; repr., London: Zed Books, 2002), 183; Paulo Freire, *Pedagogy of the Oppressed* (1970; repr., New York: Continuum, 2003), 88.

1. Vic Muñoz, "Trapped in the Wrong Classroom: Making Decolonial Trans-Cultural Spaces in Women's Studies," *WSQ: Women's Studies Quarterly* 36, nos. 3–4 (Fall–Winter 2008): 300–301.

2. Paulo Freire, *Pedagogy of the Oppressed* (1970; reprint, New York: Continuum, 2003).

3. Susan Stryker, Paisley Currah, and Lisa Jean Moore, "Introduction: Trans-, Trans, or Transgender?" *WSQ: Women's Studies Quarterly* 36, nos. 3–4 (Fall–Winter 2008): 11–22. I use trans- and transing throughout this chapter instead of transgender and transsexual to situate my writing in alliance with what Stryker, Currah, and Moore beautifully articulate: "Neither '-gender' nor any of the other suffixes of 'trans-' can be understood in isolation—that the lines implied by the very concept of 'trans-' are moving targets, simultaneously composed of multiple determinants. 'Transing,' in short, is a practice that takes place within, as well as across or between, gendered spaces. . . . Those of us schooled in the humanities and social sciences have become familiar, over the last twenty years or so, with queering things; how might we likewise begin to critically trans our world" (13).

4. Linda Tuhiwai Smith, *Decolonizing Methodologies: Research and Indigenous Peoples* (1999; reprint, London: Zed Books, 2002), 183.

5. "Trapped in the wrong body" as a master narrative functions in many complex ways that I do not go into here but have elsewhere. In short, these five words are used to tell the whole story of being trans, even though it is clear that there is much more diversity to trans experiences.

6. Paulo Freire and Donaldo Macedo, "A Dialogue: Culture, Language, and Race," *Harvard Educational Review* 65, no. 3 (1995): 377–402.

7. I use the term "Boricua" instead of "Puerto Rican."

8. "The Onondaga People wish to bring about a healing between themselves and all others who live in this region that has been the homeland of the Onondaga Nation since the dawn of time. The Nation and its people have a unique spiritual, cultural, and historic relationship with the land, which is embodied in Gayanashagowa, the Great Law of Peace. This relationship goes far beyond federal and state legal concepts of ownership, possession or legal rights. The people are one with the land, and consider themselves stewards of it. It is the duty of the Nation's leaders to work for a healing of this land, to protect it, and to pass it on to future generations. The Onondaga Nation brings this action on behalf of its people in the hope that it may hasten the process of reconciliation and bring lasting justice, peace, and respect among all who inhabit the area." The land rights action petitions the federal court to declare that New York violated federal law when it took Onondaga Land. Onondaga Nation, www.onondaganation.org/land/complaint.html.

9. L. Laiana Wong, "Speaking Hawaiian in Hawaiian" (presentation, annual meeting of the American Educational Research Association, New York, 2008).

10. The Ponce Massacre, March 21, 1937. The national guard was ordered by the U.S.-appointed governor, General Blanton Winship, to shoot and to kill unarmed students who were marching peacefully, simply because the students were part of the Nationalist Party.

The marchers had obtained permits to march, but these were revoked under orders from the governor at the last minute. The students went on with the march. Twenty were killed and hundreds injured, including women and children.

11. Inés María Mendoza, "Testimony to the Hays Commission," in *Doña Inés María Mendoza y la batalla del idioma: Cartas 1937–1938*, ed. C. Natal Rosario (San Juan, Puerto Rico: Fundación Luis Muñoz Marín, 2004), 19.

12. Ibid., 20–21.

13. Indigenous people of Aotearoa/New Zealand.

14. White people in Aotearoa/New Zealand.

15. Alison Jones, "Ka whawhai tonu matou: The Interminable Problem of Knowing Others" (lecture, University of Auckland, October 24, 2007), available at www.education.auckland.ac.nz/webdav/site/education/shared/about/schools/tepuna/docs/Inaugural_Lecture.pdf.

16. Ibid., 3; emphasis in original.

17. Ibid., 7; emphasis in original.

18. Kuni Jenkins and Leonie Pihama, "Matauranga Wahine: Teaching Maori Women's Knowledge alongside Feminism," *Feminism and Psychology* 11, no. 3 (2001): 293–303.

19. Alison Jones, "Cross-cultural Pedagogy and the Passion for Ignorance," *Feminism and Psychology* 11, no. 3 (2001): 279–292.

20. For a thorough critique of "multicultural-education" paradigms from an Indigenous perspective, read the excellent and provocative article by Troy Richardson and Sofia Villenes, "'Other' Encounters: Dances with Whiteness in Multicultural Education," *Educational Theory* 50, no. 2 (2000): 255–273.

21. Jones, "Ka whawhai tonu matou"; emphasis in original.

22. See, for example, Elizabeth R. Cole, "Intersectionality and Research in Psychology," *American Psychologist* 64, no. 3 (2009): 170–180; Derald Wing Sue, Rosie P. Bingham, Lisa Porche-Burke, and Melba Vasquez, "The Diversification of Psychology: A Multicultural Revolution," *American Psychologist* 54 (1999): 1061–1069.

23. Gloria Anzaldúa, *Borderlands/La Frontera: The New Mestiza*, 2nd ed. (San Francisco: Aunt Lute Books, 1999).

24. Anzaldúa, *Borderlands/La Frontera*; Jones, "Ka whawhai tonu matou."

25. Freire, *Pedagogy of the Oppressed*; Maxine Greene, *The Dialectic of Freedom* (New York: Teachers College Press, 1998).

26. George Sefa Dei and Arlo Kempf, *Anti-colonialism and Education: The Politics of Resistance* (Rotterdam, The Netherlands: Sense Publishers, 2006).

27. Leonie Pihama, "Tihei Mauri Ora: Honouring Our Voices. Mana Wahine as a Kaupapa Maori Theoretical Framework" (Ph.D. diss., University of Auckland, 2001), available at www.kaupapamaori.com/theory/5/; Graham Smith, "Indigenous Struggle for the Transformation of Education and Schooling," (keynote address, Alaskan Federation and Natives [AFN] Convention, Anchorage, Alaska, 2003), available at www.kaupapamaori.com/theory/5/; Smith, *Decolonizing Methodologies*.

28. See the work and writings of Alison Jones from Aotearoa/New Zealand. See, for example, Jones, "Cross-cultural Pedagogy"; Jones, "Ka whawhai tonu matou."

29. As an example of not "seeing what is in plain sight" and instead is denied and forgotten, see "Sullivan/Clinton Campaign Then and Now," http://sullivanclinton.com.

30. Mendoza, "Testimony to the Hays Commission."

31. Greene, *The Dialectic of Freedom*, 3.

32. Karina L. Walters, Teresa Evans-Campbell, Jane M. Simoni, Theresa Ronquillo, and Rupaleem Bhuyan, "'My Spirit in My Heart': Identity Experiences and Challenges

among American Indian Two-Spirit Women," *Journal of Lesbian Studies* 10, nos. 1–2 (2006): 127.

33. Clive Aspin, "The Place of Takatāpui Identity within Māori Society: Reinterpreting Māori Sexuality within a Contemporary Context" (presentation, Competing Diversities: Traditional Sexualities and Modern Western Sexual Identity Constructions Conference, Mexico City, 2005), available at www.tpt.org.nz/downloads/takatapuiidentity.doc.

34. Fiona Meyer-Cook and Diane Labelle, "Namaji: Two-Spirit Organizing in Montreal, Canada," *Journal of Gay and Lesbian Social Services* 16, no. 1 (2004): 29–51; Lynn Stephen, "Sexualities and Genders in Zapotec Oaxaca," *Latin American Perspectives* 29, no. 2 (2002): 41–59.

35. Wesley Thomas and Sue-Ellen Jacobs, "'. . . And We Are Still Here': From Berdache to Two-Spirit People," *American Indian Culture and Research Journal* 23, no. 2 (1999): 91–107.

36. Sue-Ellen Jacobs, Wesley Thomas, and Sabine Lang, eds., *Two-Spirit People: Native American Gender Identity, Sexuality, and Spirituality* (Urbana: University of Illinois Press, 1997).

37. Walters et al., "'My Spirit in My Heart,'" 127.

38. Adrian A. Stimson, "Two Spirited for You: The Absence of 'Two Spirit' People in Western Culture and Media," *West Coast Line* 40, no. 1 (2006): 78.

39. Teresa Evans-Campbell, Karen I. Fredriksen-Goldsen, Karina L. Walters, and Antony Stately, "Caregiving Experiences among American Indian Two-Spirit Men and Women: Contemporary and Historical Roles," *Journal of Gay and Lesbian Social Services* 18, nos. 3–4 (2007): 75–92; Heather Adams and Layli Phillips, "Experiences of Two-Spirit Lesbian and Gay Native Americans: An Argument for Standpoint Theory in Identity Research," *Identity: An International Journal of Theory and Research* 6, no. 3 (2006): 273–291; Brian Joseph Gilley, "Making Traditional Spaces: Cultural Compromise at Two-Spirit Gatherings in Oklahoma," *American Indian Culture and Research Journal* 28 no. 2 (2004): 81–95; Shari Brotman, Bill Ryan, Yves Jalbert, and Bill Rowe, "Reclaiming Space–Regaining Health: The Health Care Experiences of Two-Spirit People in Canada," *Journal of Gay and Lesbian Social Services* 14, no. 1 (2002): 67–86; Walters et al., "'My Spirit in My Heart,'" 127.

40. Sally Roesh Wagner, *Sisters in Spirit: Haudenosaunee (Iroquois) Influence on Early American Feminists* (Summertown, TN: Native Voices, 2001).

CHAPTER 2

1. Judith Halberstam, *In a Queer Time and Place: Transgender Bodies, Subcultural Lives* (New York: New York University Press, 2005).

2. Joan Faber McAlister, "Lives of the Mind/Body: Alarming Notes on Tenure and Biological Clocks," *Women's Studies in Communication* 31, no. 2 (2008): 218–225.

3. Kris Varjas, Brian Dew, Megan Marshall, Emily Graybill, Anneliese Singh, Joel Meyers, and Lamar Birckbichler, "Bullying in Schools towards Sexual Minority Youth," *Journal of School Violence* 7, no. 2 (2008): 59–86.

4. American Psychiatric Association, *The Diagnostic and Statistical Manual of Mental Disorders*, 4th ed. (Arlington, VA: American Psychiatric Publishing, 1994).

5. Kelley Winters, *Gender Madness in American Psychiatry: Essays from the Struggle for Dignity* (Seattle, WA: BookSurge Publishing, 2008).

6. Transgender Theories, *FORUM with Michael Krasney*, KQED, August 22, 2007, www.kqed.org/.stream/anon/radio/forum/2007/08/2007-08-22b-forum.mp3.

7. Julia Serano, *Whipping Girl: A Transsexual Woman on Sexism and the Scapegoating of Femininity* (Emeryville, CA: Seal Press, 2007).

8. Harold Garfinkel, "Passing and the Managed Achievement of Sex Status in an 'Intersexed' Person," reprinted with commentary in Susan Stryker and Stephen Whittle (eds.), *The Transgender Studies Reader* (Boca Raton, FL: CRC Press, 2006), 58–93.

9. Bruce Bagemihl, *Biological Exuberance: Animal Homosexuality and Natural Diversity* (New York: St. Martin's Press, 1999).

10. Joan Roughgarden, *Evolution's Rainbow: Diversity, Gender, and Sexuality in Nature and People* (Berkeley: University of California Press, 2004).

11. Donna Haraway, "Situated Knowledges: The Science Question in Feminism and the Privilege of Partial Perspective," *Feminist Studies* 14, no. 3 (1998): 575–599.

12. Roughgarden, *Evolution's Rainbow*, 75–105.

13. Gerulf Rieger, Meredith Chivers, and Michael Bailey, "Sexual Arousal Patterns of Bisexual Men," *Psychological Science: A Journal of the American Psychological Society/APS* 16, no. 8 (2005): 579–584; Benedict Carey, "Straight, Gay, or Lying? Bisexuality Revisited," *New York Times*, July 5, 2005.

14. Robin Wilson and Paul Fain, "Lawrence Summers Quits as Harvard President in Advance of New No-Confidence Vote; Derek Bok to Step In," *Chronicle of Higher Education*, February 21, 2006.

15. Madeline Wyndzen, "A Personal and Scientific Look at a Mental Illness Model of Transgenderism," *American Psychological Association Division 44 Newsletter* (Spring 2004), www.genderpsychology.org/autogynephilia/apa_div_44.html.

16. Oscar Rios-Cardenas, M. Scarlett Tudor, and Molly R. Morris, "Female Preference Variation Has Implications for the Maintenance of an Alternative Mating Strategy in a Swordtail Fish," *Animal Behaviour* 74 (2007): 633–640.

17. Jessica Hoffman, "On Prisons, Borders, Safety, and Privilege: An Open Letter to White Feminists," *make/shift* 3 (2008), www.makeshiftmag.com.

18. Lisa Harney, "The Injurious Nature of Asserting Your Voice," *Questioning Transphobia*, November 14, 2008, www.questioningtransphobia.com/?p=807.

19. Lukas Tinbergen, "The Natural Control of Insects in Pinewoods: I. Factors Influencing the Intensity of Predation by Song Birds," *Archives Neerlandaises de Zoologie* 13 (1960): 265–343.

20. Kenji Yoshino, *Covering: The Hidden Assault on Our Civil Rights* (New York: Random House, 2006).

21. Serano, *Whipping Girl*.

22. Ben Berres, "Does Gender Matter?" *Nature* 442 (2006): 133–136.

23. Russ Lande, "Statistics and the Partitioning of Species Diversity, and Similarity among Multiple Communities," *Oikos* 76 (1996): 5–13.

24. Timothy F. H. Allen and Thomas W. Hoekstra, *Toward a Unified Ecology* (New York: Columbia University Press, 1992), 158–200.

CHAPTER 3

1. Wendy Brown, "The Impossibility of Women's Studies," in *Women's Studies on the Edge*, ed. Joan Wallach Scott (Durham, NC: Routledge, 2008), 17–38.

2. Andrea Smith, "Native Studies and Critical Pedagogy: Beyond the Academic-Industrial Complex," in *Activist Scholarship: Antiracism, Feminism, and Social Change*, ed. Julia Sudbury and Margo Okazawa-Rey (Boulder, CO: Paradigm Publishers, 2009), 37–54.

3. Ibid., 39–40.

4. As the strike unfolded and the institutional media machine was launched, it became very clear to many of us exactly what the product was and, hence, the educational-corporate complex: the "York U" corporate logo.

5. Susan Stryker, Paisley Currah, and Lisa Jean Moore, "Introduction: Trans-, Trans, or Transgender?" *WSQ: Women's Studies Quarterly* 36, nos. 3–4 (Fall–Winter 2008): 11–22.

6. Sandy Stone, "The Empire Strikes Back: A Posttranssexual Manifesto," in *Body Guards: The Cultural Politics of Gender Ambiguity*, ed. Julia Epstein and Kristina Straub (London: Routledge, 1991), 280–304.

7. Avery F. Gordon, *Ghostly Matters: Haunting and the Sociological Imagination* (Minneapolis: University of Minnesota Press, 2008).

8. Raymond Williams, *Marxism and Literature* (Oxford, UK: Oxford University Press, 1977).

9. *Trans Entities: The Nasty Love of Papí and Wil*, dir. Morty Diamond (Trannywood Productions, 2007).

10. Judith Butler, *Undoing Gender* (New York: Routledge, 2004), 100.

11. The concept of unmapping is one I borrow from Sherene H. Razack, where to unmap means to denaturalize not only social and physical geographies but also those relations of dominance dependent upon such naturalizations. See Razack, *Race, Space, and the Law: Unmapping a White Settler Society* (Toronto, Ontario: Between the Lines Press, 2002).

12. Carol Schick, JoAnn Jaffe, and Ailsa M. Watkinson, eds., *Contesting Fundamentalisms* (Halifax, Nova Scotia: Fernwood Publishing, 2004).

13. Stuart Hall, "Notes on Deconstructing 'The Popular,'" in *People's History and Socialist Theory*, ed. Raphael Samuel (London, UK: Routledge and Kegan Paul, Ltd., 1981), 227–240.

14. Robyn Wiegman, ed., "Introduction: On Location," in *Women's Studies on Its Own: A Next Wave Reader in Institutional Change* (Durham, NC: Duke University Press, 2002), 1–44.

15. Ibid., 9; emphasis in original.

16. Robyn Wiegman, ed., "The Progress of Gender: Whither 'Women'?" *Women's Studies on Its Own*, 106–140; emphasis in original.

17. Eve K. Sedgwick, *Epistemology of the Closet* (Berkeley: University of California Press, 1990).

18. Wiegman, "The Progress of Gender: Whither 'Women'?" 131; emphasis in original.

19. Ibid., 133.

20. Stryker, Currah, and Moore, "Introduction: Trans-, Trans, or Transgender?" 14.

21. Wiegman, "The Progress of Gender: Whither 'Women'?" 133.

22. Butler, *Undoing Gender*, 101.

23. Gordon, *Ghostly Matters*, 6.

24. Ibid., 6–7.

25. Ibid., 3.

26. Roland Barthes, quoted in Ibid., 7.

27. Ibid., 7.

28. For example, one of the most interesting and unintentional allegories of a *trans* modality appeared in the Hollywood movie *127 Hours* (Danny Boyle, dir.; Fox Searchlight Pictures, 2010). Nowhere near *trans,* if by that we mean minoritized as "transgender" or "transnational," the story of mountain climber Aron Ralston becomes allegorical of *trans*

as a critical mobility when he engages in the active labor of undoing physical coherence as he has known it to survive the impossible demands of materialization. The story is not just that he removes a core part of himself to achieve mobility but that he must, as it were, labor with the tools at hand to achieve nonprecarious personhood. *Trans* in this modality, then, refers not only to critical mobilities and crossings but also to the way that such "matter(s)" is enabled and dependent upon pre- and overdetermined assemblages, apparatus, and machineries that authorize personhood at any given historical moment in any given social formation (outside the film, these include state-authorized birth certificates, nationalization processes, passports, driver's licenses, and so on).

29. Gordon, *Ghostly Matters,* 8.

30. Bobby Noble, *Sons of the Movement: FtMs Risking Incoherence in a Post-Queer Cultural Landscape* (Toronto, Ontario: Canadian Scholars Press, 2006), 2–3.

31. Stryker, Currah, and Moore, 2008.

32. Leslie Heywood and Jennifer Drake, eds., *Third Wave Agenda: Being Feminist, Doing Feminism* (Minneapolis: University of Minnesota Press, 1997), 11.

33. Queer theory has not fared much better when it comes to circumventing the hegemonies of its own whiteness. Although individual white scholars of feminism and queer theory (and all points of convergence herewith) have attempted to take the measure of whiteness as what Audre Lorde (1984) named as a mythical norm of these identity/non-identity-based social movements, the coherency that marks their official narratives is one calibrated by what Baldwin has written as a whiteness "impaled on its history like a butterfly on a pin" (1985).

34. Robyn Wiegman, "Feminism, Institutionalism, and the Idiom of Failure," in *Women's Studies on the Edge,* ed. Joan Wallach Scott (Durham, NC: Routledge, 2008), 39–66.

35. As this collection goes to press, I am now cross-appointed faculty member, institutionally *transing* across the disciplines of Sexuality Studies, English, and Women's Studies.

36. Sharon Rosenberg, "At Women's Studies Edge: Thoughts toward Remembering a Troubled and Troubling Project of the Modern University," in *Troubling Women's Studies: Pasts, Presents and Possibilities,* ed. Ann Braithwaite, Susan Heald, Susanne Luhmann, and Sharon Rosenberg (Vancouver, British Columbia: Sumach Press, 2004), 195–239.

37. Cathy Caruth, *Unclaimed Experience: Trauma, Narrative and History* (Baltimore, MD: Johns Hopkins University Press, 1996), 6.

38. Rosenberg, "At Women's Studies Edge," 226.

CHAPTER 4

Epigraphs: Dana Leland Defosse, original call posted on http://groups.google.com/group/alt.transgendered/browse_thread/thread/69c04e35666a9a1b/69ebde0bf2af8dc6?lnk=st&q=cisgendered+dana+defosse&rnum=1&hl=en#69ebde0bf2af8dc6. Carl Buijs, "A new perspective on an old topic" (04/16/1996), posted on http://groups.google.com/group/soc.support.transgendered/msg/184850df15e48963?hl=en. Monica Roberts, "Cisgender Isn't an Insult," posted July 10, 2009, http://transgriot.blogspot.com/2009/07/cisgender-isn't-insult.html.

1. Across the United States and Canada, use of the terms "cisgender" and "cis" varies by location and the political orientation of any given community. Born within social-activist contexts, cisgender is not necessarily familiar to the majority of trans* people; moreover, the term is rarely used in the work of changing institutional policies.

2. Recorded quotes from students in the courses "Lesbian(?) Contexts," "Trans/Gender in Historical Perspective," and "Advanced Seminar in LGBT Studies," 2008, 2009, 2010.

3. Monica Roberts is one of very few people to bring up issues of race in connection to the term "cisgender," and she does so as an African American trans woman to make an analogy *rather than* to question whether cisgender itself may carry racist hierarchies: "I believe the people having a problem with the word are wailing in unacknowledged cisgender privilege. They are taken aback that there is a trans community term coined by trans people to describe them. [It's like] how many [white] peeps get upset and call me 'racist' over the 'vanilla flavored privileged' term I used to describe white privilege.... [T]hey call me 'racist' anytime I criticize the underlying structural assumptions that buttress whiteness" (from "Cisgender Isn't an Insult," posted July 10, 2009, http://transgriot.blogspot.com/2009/07/cisgender-isn't-insult.html).

4. Trans and gender-queer critique of cis has grown in the last two years, all in informal and unpublished venues. The term became the subject of Kate Bornstein's Twitter account for several days during and following my talk on cisgender at the Postposttranssexual Conference, in Bloomington, Indiana, in April 2011. From May 16 to 19, 2011, a member of the Trans-Academics listserv brought up the term and elicited more than sixty elaborate submissions in what became a conversation among twenty-eight different people.

5. Riki Anne Wilchins, *Read My Lips: Sexual Subversion and the End of Gender* (New York: Firebrand Books, 1997), 25.

6. By "Queer-Studies classroom," I mean environments in which gender, sex, and/or sexuality are explicitly engaged, regardless of discipline and not limited to university settings.

7. Holly Boswell, "The Transgender Alternative," *Chrysalis Quarterly* 1, no. 2 (Winter 1991–1992): 29–31.

8. We often ask what is being brought into or excluded from purview in (or despite) such titles as Gender and Women's Studies, LGBT Studies, Sexuality Studies, Gender Studies, and Queer Studies. The burgeoning field of Transgender Studies does not find a "natural" home in either Women's Studies or LGBT Studies. Wendy Brown, "The Impossibility of Women's Studies," in *Edgework: Critical Essays on Knowledge and Politics* (Princeton, NJ: Princeton University Press, 2005), 116–135; Susan Stryker, "Transgender Studies: Queer Theory's Evil Twin," *GLQ: A Journal of Lesbian and Gay Studies* 10, no. 2 (2004): 212–215; Gayle Salamon, *Assuming a Body: Transgender and Rhetorics of Materiality* (New York: Columbia University Press, 2010), 95–130.

9. Leslie Feinberg's extraordinarily influential 1992 pamphlet "Transgender Liberation: A Movement Whose Time Has Come" (New York: World View Forum) offers a Marxist and feminist analysis of (trans)gender oppression as the basis for forging a movement that linked, rather than separated, all manifestations of gender oppression and all marginalized communities and identities that are born of such oppression.

10. Paisley Currah, Jamison Green, and Susan Stryker, "The State of Transgender Rights in the United States of America" (paper prepared for the National Sexuality Resource Center, San Francisco, CA, 2008).

11. Susan Stryker, *Transgender History* (Berkeley, CA: Seal Press, 2008), 1.

12. The list of institutions that typically require sex/gender legibility and consistency is infinite. To mention a few here: social services, such as rape crisis centers, homeless shelters, and medical clinics; educational and job-training services; housing; employment; public accommodations, including restrooms; marriage; rights to custody of children;

inheritance; health insurance; incarceration in gender-appropriate facilities; and identity records (passport, driver's license, and so forth), all of which use legal gender for purposes of identification. See Paisley Currah, Richard Juang, and Shannon Minter, eds., *Transgender Rights* (Minneapolis: University of Minnesota, 2006); Dean Spade, "Documenting Gender," *Hastings Law Journal* 59, no. 4 (2007–2008): 731–841; Dean Spade, *Normal Life: Administrative Violence, Critical Trans Politics, and the Limits of Law* (Boston: South End, 2011); Currah, Green, and Stryker, "The State of Transgender Rights in the United States of America"; Viviane Namaste, *Sex Change, Social Change: Reflections on Identity, Institutions, and Imperialism* (Toronto, Ontario: Women's Press, 2005).

    13. Wilchins, *Read My Lips*, 33–40; Joanne Meyerowitz, *How Sex Changed: A History of Transsexuality in the United States* (London: Harvard University Press, 2002); Nikki Sullivan, "The Role of Medicine in the (Trans)Formation of 'Wrong' Bodies," *Body and Society* 14 (2008): 105–116; Dean Spade, "Mutilating Gender," in *The Transgender Studies Reader*, ed. Susan Stryker and Stephen Whittle (New York: Routledge, 2006), 315–332; Elizabeth Loeb, "Cutting It Off: Bodily Integrity, Identity Disorders, and the Sovereign Stakes of Corporeal Desire in U.S. Law," *WSQ: Women's Studies Quarterly* 36, nos. 3–4 (Fall–Winter 2008): 44–63.

    14. Emi Koyama (06/07/2002), posted on Koyama's blog site, http://eminism.org/interchange/2002/20020607-wmstl.html.

    15. This is true in academic contexts as well, as programs integrate gay and lesbian and queer studies but fail to integrate trans and bi studies. Robert McRuer has observed, "Queer theory and LGBT studies have arguably come together with disability studies more than many other 'identity'-based fields." And yet his version of "queer/disabled" history excises trans when he suggests that "gay liberation distanced from disability" by winning the removal of homosexuality from the *DSM III*. McRuer's formulation erases trans, but from a trans-conscious queer/disability perspective, there is no institution more consequential (not liberating) to trans lives than the *DSM*'s inclusion of Gender Identity Disorder as a mental illness. Robert McRuer, "Shameful Sites: Locating Queerness and Disability," in *Gay Shame*, ed. David Halperin and Valerie Traub (Chicago, IL: University of Chicago Press, 2009), 181–187. Cf. Shannon Price Minter, "Do Transsexuals Dream of Gay Rights? Getting Real about Transgender Inclusion," in *Transgender Rights*, 141–170; Sylvia Rivera, "Queens in Exile, the Forgotten Ones," in *Genderqueer: Voices from beyond the Binary*, ed. Joan Nestle, Riki Wilchins, and Clare Howell (Los Angeles: Alyson Books, 2002), 67–85; David Valentine, *Imagining Transgender: An Ethnography of a Category* (Durham, NC: Duke University Press, 2007); Aaron H. Devor and Nicholas Matte, "ONE Inc. and Reed Erickson: The Uneasy Collaboration of Gay and Trans Activism, 1964–2003," in *The Transgender Studies Reader*, 387–405.

    16. S. Bear Bergman and J. Wallace, "Open Log: IM on Identity," *Women and Environments* (Fall–Winter 2009): 5–8; Julia Serano, *Whipping Girl: A Transsexual Woman on Sexism and the Scapegoating of Femininity* (Emeryville, CA: Seal Press, 2007).

    17. Serano, 12 and 33, respectively. Serano's definition of cisgender depends on the definition of transgender, but Serano does not offer a definition of transgender. Transsexual has more distinct parameters, as experiencing one's self as one of the sex/genders of the male/female binary: specifically, the sex/gender that one was *not* assigned to be at birth. It is worth emphasizing that transsexuality does not depend on "living full time in" or transitioning to one's "subconscious sex," nor on surgical procedures, nor on social or legal confirmation of a status change; all those stereotypical markers of transsexuality require financial means and external circumstances that are not available to or chosen by many, if not most, people whose "physical and subconscious sex" is not "aligned."

18. Serano does not elaborate on the cisgender/cissexual distinction in her book as much as she has in personal conversation. *Whipping Girl* is not concerned with transgender, but, uniquely, its purpose is to see transsexuals "develop our own language and concepts that accurately articulate our unique experiences and perspectives and to fill in the many gaps that exist in both gatekeeper and transgender activist language" (162). Serano and others rightly critique the academic and social movements' prioritizing and privileging of transgender, gender queer, and gender fluidity at the expense of transsexual politics and existence. See also Jay Prosser, *Second Skins* (New York: Columbia University Press, 1998); Bobby Noble, *Sons of the Movement: FTMs Risking Incoherence on a Post-Queer Cultural Landscape* (Toronto, Ontario: Women's Press, 2006). Author interview, Julia Serano, Berkeley, CA, February 18, 2009.

19. Serano, *Whipping Girl,* 162–163.

20. One of Serano's interventions is to challenge naturalizing vocabularies, such as the very common tendency to refer to non-trans people as "biological" or "genetic" males and females. As Serano explains, "I usually interject that, despite the fact that I am a transsexual, I am not inorganic or nonbiological in any way. . . .When you break it down . . . it becomes obvious that the words 'biological' and 'genetic' are merely stand-ins for the word that people want to use: 'natural'" (174–175, and 161–193 *passim*). Serano and others critique the concept of "passing" for the way it implies that the trans person is doing the action while masking the fact that passing is about what other people—observers and interpreters—do. S. Bear Bergman, *The Nearest Exit May Be behind You* (Vancouver, British Columbia: Arsenal Press, 2009); Talia Mae Bettcher, "Evil Deceivers and Make-Believers: On Transphobic Violence and the Politics of Illusion," *Hypatia* 22, no. 3 (Summer 2007): 43–65.

21. People began protesting MWMF's anti-trans policies in 1992. Since then, Camp Trans has experienced major transformations in mission, demographics, and strategy.

22. Leslie Feinberg most forcefully articulated this in a speech delivered at Camp Trans in 1993 ("Building Bridges") and in an interview with Davina Anne Gabriel, "The Life and Times of a Gender Outlaw: Leslie Feinberg," *TransSisters: The Journal of Transsexual Feminism* (September–October 1993): 4–13.

23. Cf. Emi Koyama, "Whose Feminism Is It Anyway? The Unspoken Racism of the Trans Inclusion Debate" (first on http://eminism.org, now available in a collection of Koyama's transfeminist essays under same title); reprinted in *The Transgender Studies Reader,* 698–704.

24. Camp Trans Web site, www.camp-trans.org.

25. "Camp is first and foremost a place for people who wish to actively oppose policies which exclude trans women from 'women's-only' spaces, most specifically, Michigan Womyn's Music Festival."

26. First and last in the Exclusion list, respectively: "ANY person, no matter their gender, orientation, identity, or partnership status, who does not oppose (who either supports or does not have an opinion on) policies which exclude trans women from women's spaces, specifically Michigan Womyn's Music Festival"; and "Any person not dedicated to building a week-long community space where trans people are as free as possible from the repression and constraints placed upon them by the larger society."

27. *Defo0008* 04:40, 6 July 2006 (UTC), posted on http://en.wikipedia.org/wiki/Talk:Cisgender; emphasis added.

28. "Transgenderism is constituted as a paradox made up of equal parts of visibility and temporality." Judith Halberstam, *In a Queer Time and Place: Transgender Bodies, Subcultural Lives* (New York: New York University Press, 2005), 77. "We invite our readers

to recognize that 'trans-' likewise names the body's orientation in space and time; we ask them to . . . begin imagining these phenomena according to *different* spatio-temporal metaphors." Susan Stryker, Paisley Currah, and Lisa Jean Moore, "Introduction: Trans-, Trans, or Transgender," *WSQ: Women's Studies Quarterly* 36, nos. 3–4 (Fall–Winter 2008): 11–22; 13; emphasis added.

29. The emergence of the term "trans ally" as distinct from "LGBT ally" reflects the failure of "LGBT" organizations as well as most academic institutions to function as trans-inclusive entities; trans allyship specifically recognizes trans issues.

30. In response to growing social-movement visibility, trans-ally trainings are now offered in a host of educational contexts, including to social- and medical-service providers as well as student organizations and outreach groups on college campuses.

31. Vik DeMarco, "Ally Exceptionalism: Problems in Approaches to Allyship Trainings" (B.A. Honors Thesis, Gender and Women's Studies, University of Wisconsin Madison, 2010); Christoph Hanssmann, "Training Disservice: The Productive Potential and Structural Limitations of Health as a Terrain for Trans Activism," this volume, 112–132. On anti-oppressive education, cf. Kevin Kumashiro, "Toward a Theory of Anti-oppressive Education," *Review of Educational Research* 70, no. 1 (2000): 25–53.

32. See, e.g., Eli Clare, *Exile and Pride: Disability, Queerness, and Liberation* (Boston: South End Press, 1999); Susan Stryker, "We Who Are Sexy: Christine Jorgensen's Transsexual Whiteness in the Postcolonial Philippines," *Social Semiotics* 19 (2009): 79–91; Kenji Tokawa, "Why You Don't Have to Choose a White Boy Name to Be a Man in This World," in *Gender Outlaws: The Next Generation*, ed. Kate Bornstein and S. Bear Bergman (Berkeley, CA: Seal Press, 2010), 207–212; Zev Al-Walid, "Pilgrimage," in *Gender Outlaws*, 261–267; Dean Spade, "Compliance Is Gendered: Struggling for Gender Self-Determination in a Hostile Economy," in *Transgender Rights*, 217–240; Richard M. Juang, "Transgendering the Politics of Recognition," in *Transgender Rights*, 242–261; Koyama, "Whose Feminism Is It Anyway?"

33. Valentine, *Imagining Transgender*; Dean Spade, "Trans Law and Politics on a Neoliberal Landscape," *Temple Political and Civil Rights Law Review* 18, no. 2 (2009): 353–373; Spade, "Documenting Gender." Also cf. Cathy Cohen, "Punks, Bulldaggers, and Welfare Queens: The Radical Potential of Queer Politics?" in *Black Queer Studies*, ed. E. Patrick Johnson and Mae Henderson (Durham, NC: Duke University Press, 2005), 21–51.

34. In the interest of protecting people's anonymity, I do not cite the place, year, or names of people involved in this exchange. E-mail text used with its author's permission.

35. On the problems with such glosses, cf. Evan B. Towle and Lynn M. Morgan, "Romancing the Transgender Native: Rethinking the Use of the 'Third Gender' Concept," in *The Transgender Studies Reader*, 666–684.

36. Queer critique of neoliberal homonormativities offered by Lisa Duggan, *Twilight of Equality: Neoliberalism, Cultural Politics, and the Attack on Democracy* (Boston: Beacon Press, 2003); Jasbir K. Puar, *Terrorist Assemblages: Homonationalisms in Queer Times* (Durham, NC: Duke University Press, 2007).

37. The exact language is "in girls, rejection of urination in a sitting position," with no discussion of "boys'" urination preferences. The *DSM III* was the first to include Gender Identity Disorder (GID); subsequent editions include the same diagnostic criteria for childhood GID, although the *DSM IV* expanded the criteria. American Psychiatric Association, "Gender Identity Disorder in Children, 302.6," in *Diagnostic and Statistical Manual of Mental Disorders*, 3rd ed. (Washington, DC: American Psychiatric Association, 1980). In the late 1950s, physicians used "urinating in the standing position" as diagnostic proof that the sex of a gender-ambiguous subject under scrutiny was male. Harold Gar-

finkel, ed., "Passing and the Managed Achievement of Sex Status in an 'Intersexed' Person," in *Studies in Ethnomethodology* (Oxford, UK: Polity, 1967).

38. See, for example, Halberstam, *In a Queer Time and Place*; Prosser, *Second Skins*; Noble, *Sons of the Movement*; Kath Weston, *Render Me, Gender Me: Lesbians Talk Sex, Class, Color, Nation, Studmuffins* (New York: Columbia University Press, 1996).

39. On compulsory narrative and resistance to such, see Rachel Pollack, "Archetypal Transsexuality," *TransSisters: The Journal of Transsexual Feminism*, no. 9 (Summer 1995): 39–41; Sandy Stone, "The Empire Strikes Back: A Posttranssexual Manifesto," in *Body Guards: The Cultural Politics of Gender Ambiguity*, ed. Julia Epstein and Kristina Straub (London, UK: Routledge, 1991): 280–304; Lucas Cassidy Crawford, "Transgender without Organs? Mobilizing a Geo-affective Theory of Gender Modification," *WSQ: Women's Studies Quarterly* 36, nos. 3–4 (Fall–Winter 2008): 127–143; Nikki Sullivan, "Transmogrification: (Un)Becoming Other(s)," in *The Transgender Studies Reader*, 552–563; Judith Butler, "Doing Justice to Someone: Sex Reassignment and Allegories of Transsexuality," in *The Transgender Studies Reader*, 183–192; Wilchins, *Read My Lips*.

40. Defosse's entry goes on, "I think the use of cisgender also captures a subtle and nondualistic aspect of the issue at hand; cisgender reinforces and reflects itself, while transgender originates where cisgender begins but extends into a greater dimension by 'crossing over.'" *Defo0008* 04:40, 6 July 2006 (UTC), posted on http://en.wikipedia.org/wiki/Talk:Cisgender. Other subtle renderings of cisgender failed to take hold as well. For example, *unsigned* added to Defosse's comments, "I also coined cisgendered as a term around 1994 in publicity for the GLQSOC-L, the Gay, Lesbian, Queer Social Science listserv, to describe those who move from one mode of masculinity or femininity to another. This usage never caught on." *Unsigned 68.162.116.127* (talk) 00:12, 15 October 2007 (UTC), posted on http://en.wikipedia.org/wiki/Talk:Cisgender.

41. *Diagnosing Difference* critiques this medico-juridical hegemony. Dir. Annalise Ophelian (Floating Ophelia Productions, San Francisco, 2010).

42. Countless mainstream and trans* community news articles have conferred this title on Bowers.

43. Author interview with Dr. Marci Bowers, July 25, 2009, Trinidad, Colorado. Bowers has insisted on this point in numerous public interviews and documentaries as well.

44. Since the 1960s, trans* communities have debated umbrella categories, such as transgender. Inherent to the debate are strong feelings about activism and whether one should be "out" about one's trans* history. Stone, "The Empire Strikes Back"; Jamison Green, "Look! No, Don't! The Visibility Dilemma for Transsexual Men," in *The Transgender Studies Reader*, 499–508. Other aspects of the debate include boundary policing and the challenge of forming alliances among people with disparate proximities to the privileges accorded to normativity. As I write this article, this boundary policing has reached a pitch in some circles, even as it solidifies hierarchies and divisions. Critical of this trend, Jennifer Finney Boylan asked on Facebook whether people are really serious about doing away with the category transgender and whether the Gay and Lesbian Alliance Against Defamation (GLAAD) should therefore reconsider its recommendations to the Associated Press Style Guide regarding use of "transgender" as a blanket term; in response, Boylan received 103 comments (May 25, 2011). See also Mercedes Allen, "The Death of the 'Transgender' Umbrella," *The Bilerico Project*, June 1, 2011, www.bilerico.com/2011/06/the_death_of_transgender.php?sms_ss=facebook&at_xt=4de7025e1a73766d,1.

45. Serano rightly notes that many people whose gender identity is in congruence with the sex they were assigned at birth object to the suggestion that SRS, transition, and MTF identity can turn a male-bodied person into a woman. I am also aware that many

trans-identified people object to the erasure of transsexuality implied by the claim that Bowers is now a cisgender/cissexual women, because it buys into cis privilege. Both objections invest in a cis/trans binary that ultimately supports cis privilege. I prefer a trans* politics that does not reject trans identity but that also does not depend on possession and retention of *ur*-trans identity.

46. One of the best articulations of this, including a critique of the imperialism embedded in concepts of disability, is Michael Davidson, *Concerto for the Left Hand: Disability and the Defamiliar Body* (Ann Arbor: University of Michigan Press, 2008).

47. Cf. Tobin Siebers, *Disability Theory* (Ann Arbor: University of Michigan Press, 2008); Terry Galloway, "Tough," in *Gay Shame*, 196–200; Dominique Bednarska, "Passing Last Summer," in *Nobody Passes: Rejecting the Rules of Gender and Conformity*, ed. Mattilda Bernstein Sycamore (New York: Avalon, 2006), 71–82; Clare, *Exile and Pride*; Rosemary Garland-Thomson, *Extraordinary Bodies: Figuring Physical Disability* (New York: Routledge, 1996).

48. If, as Serano points out, all people engage in assumptions about others' sex/gender, it is also the case that most people, regardless of identity, assume that most other people are cis.

49. Anne Enke, *Finding the Movement: Sexuality, Contested Space, and Feminist Activism* (Durham, NC: Duke University Press, 2007).

50. Ellen Samuels, "My Body, My Closet: Invisible Disability and the Limits of Coming-Out Discourse," *GLQ: A Journal of Lesbian and Gay Studies* 9, nos. 1–2 (2003): 233–255.

51. This phrase comes from Elaine Ginsburg, ed., *Passing and the Fictions of Identity* (Durham, NC: Duke University Press, 1996), 4.

52. Trans and disability studies engage "masquerade" and the many meanings of "passing." Cf. Siebers, *Disability Theory*.

53. Samuels, 247. Samuels quotes Megan Jones, "'Gee, You Don't Look Handicapped . . .': Why I Use a White Cane to Tell People I'm Deaf," *Electric EDGE* (July–August 1997): "Many people are more comfortable relating to me and accommodating me if they can be absolutely certain that I am who I say I am, a deaf-blind person. And they are not absolutely certain that I am that person until I bump into a wall or shape my hands into what is to them an incomprehensible language. In other words, I must make myself completely alien to these people in order for them to feel that they understand me" (www.ragged-edge-mag.com/archive/look.htm).

54. Benjamin Singer, "From the Medical Gaze to Sublime Mutations: The Ethics of (Re)Viewing Non-normative Body Images," in *The Transgender Studies Reader*, 601–620; Sullivan, "The Role of Medicine in the (Trans)Formation of 'Wrong' Bodies."

55. A foundation of feminist, queer, and trans theory, Michel Foucault, *A History of Sexuality, Vol. 1: An Introduction* (New York: Vintage, 1990); Michel Foucault, *Discipline and Punish: The Birth of the Prison* (New York: Vintage, 1995); Judith Butler, *Gender Trouble: Feminism and the Subversion of Identity* (New York: Routledge, 1990).

56. Evelynn Hammonds, "Black (W)holes and the Geometry of Black Female Sexuality," *differences: A Journal of Feminist Cultural Studies* 6, nos. 2–3 (1994): 126–145.

57. LGBT Studies is not exempt from this tendency, although it is perhaps more common in conventional disciplines whose methodological, theoretical, and pedagogical practices depend on binary gender stability and normativity.

58. Stone, "The Empire Strikes Back," 231.

59. Thanks to Ellen Samuels for this image of paper suits. Carrie Sandahl makes paper suits of biocertification graphic in her performance piece "The Reciprocal Gaze," which she

discusses in "Ahh, Freak Out! Metaphors of Disability and Femaleness in Performance," *Theatre Topics* 9, no. 1 (1999): 11–30. Samuels discusses biocertification at length in *Fantasies of Identification: Disability, Gender, Race* (book manuscript in process).

60. Ryka Aoki, "When Something Is Not Right," this volume, 195–202.

CHAPTER 5

1. Paul Gibson, "Gay Male and Lesbian Youth Suicide," in *Report of the Secretary's Task Force on Youth Suicide*, Vol. 3, ed. Marcia R. Feinleib (Washington, DC: U.S. Department of Health and Human Services, January 1989). The George H. W. Bush administration attempted to suppress this report, but media leaked HHS's recommendations that mental health and youth services train their staff to be supportive on "gay issues," that schools protect gay youth from peer abuse and provide accurate information about homosexuality, and that families accept their children. For commentary on media amnesia about a hostile climate toward LGBT people, see Warren J. Blumenfeld, "The Media, Suicide, and Homophobia," October 2010, at www.campusprideblog.org/blog/warren-j-blumenfeld-media-suicide-and-homophobia. A media frenzy in Laramie, Wyoming, followed the murder of Matthew Shepard (1976–1998). In 1999, the award-winning movie *Boys Don't Cry* brought national attention to transphobia by depicting the 1993 rape and murder of Brandon Teena (1972–1993) in Humboldt, Nebraska, after a male acquaintance realized Teena was born labeled female. The Matthew Shepard and James Byrd, Jr., Hate Crimes Prevention Act passed into law in October 2009 over the objections of Focus on the Family leader James Dobson, who incorrectly claimed that the federal hate-crime law's unprecedented inclusion of LGBT people would bar religious people from speaking against homosexuality. A provision within the law protects homophobic and transphobic religious speech. Joseph Boven, "Matthew Shepard Hate Crimes Act Passes Despite GOP Opposition," *Colorado Independent,* October 9, 2009, http://coloradoindependent.com/39849/matthew-shepard-hate-crimes-act-passes-despite-gop-opposition. Social conservatives continue to propagate the lie that anti-harassment enforcement prevents freedom of religious belief in their efforts to prevent equal treatment in the military or anti-bullying education.

2. Russlynn Ali, "Dear Colleagues Letter," U.S. Department of Education Office for Civil Rights, October 26, 2010, www2.ed.gov/about/offices/list/ocr/letters/colleague-201010.html.

3. This work uses "trans" as an adjective instead of transsexual or transgender to avoid focus on whether one has used medical technology, to center individuals' self-identification, and to sidestep debate that is irrelevant here over whether medical technology changes sex or gender. People are designated as trans women or trans girls if they were labeled male at birth but know themselves to be women or girls and trans men or trans boys if they were labeled female at birth but know themselves to be men or boys. Pronouns to refer to people in their past remain consistent with their present identification. "Gender diverse" is used, because increasing numbers of students identify outside unchanging binary woman/man gender with such terms as androgynous, genderqueer, genderfluid, genderfucked, and so forth.

4. Joseph G. Kosciw, et al., *The 2009 National School Climate Survey: The Experience of Lesbian, Gay, Bisexual and Transgender Youth in Our Nation's Schools* (New York: Gay, Lesbian and Straight Education Network, 2010), 22, 18, www.glsen.org/binary-data/GLSEN_ATTACHMENTS/file/000/001/1675-5.PDF (accessed December 12, 2010). The 2009 survey included 409 (5.7 percent) students who identified as "Transgender" and 289 (4 percent) who identified as "Other Gender" (10).

5. Ibid., 26, 27.

6. Joseph G. Kosciw et al., *The 2007 National School Climate Survey: The Experiences of Lesbian, Gay, Bisexual and Transgender Youth in Our Nation's Schools* (New York: Gay, Lesbian and Straight Education Network, 2008), 81, www.glsen.org/binary-data/GLSEN _ATTACHMENTS/file/000/001/1290-1.pdf. The summarizing text gives the figures 85.1 percent, 49.5 percent, and 34.1 percent, but these reflect trans and gender-diverse students who report having experienced harassment or assault based on "Sexual Orientation *and* Gender/Gender Expression." When students experiencing harassment and assault based on "Gender/Gender Expression Only" are added, the above figures result. Unless otherwise specified, online references were accessed July 28, 2009.

7. Kosciw, *The 2009 National School Climate Survey*, 116.

8. Ibid., 88.

9. I advised the students to choose a pseudonym, so the results of the interviews would not identify them by name as trans in print (or online) and prevent them from being able to control who knows they are trans in the future.

10. In answer to my follow-up question, Mary agreed that she was at risk for suicide in her early teens.

11. Kosciw, *The 2009 National School Climate Survey*, 32.

12. Ibid., 38.

13. Ibid., 101–104; Kosciw, *The 2007 National School Climate Survey*, 68–69.

14. There has been a positive increase in legislation since 1999, when five states and the District of Columbia protected sexual orientation and one state protected gender identity or expression. By 2009, fifteen states covered sexual orientation, and twelve protected gender identity or expression. Kosciw, *The 2009 National School Climate Survey*, 4; Kosciw, *The 2007 National School Climate Survey*, 10, 17, 25, 30, 34, 38, 59, 68.

15. Kosciw, *The 2009 National School Climate Survey*, 46–48.

16. "Campus Pride Issues Warning Regarding the Princeton Review's Top 20 'Gay Community Accepted' College Ranking," www.campusprideblog.org/blog/campus-pride -issues-warning-regarding-princeton-review%E2%80%99s-top-20-%E2%80%9Cgay -community-accepted%E2%80%9D-colleg. For Campus Climate Index, see www.campus climateindex.org.

17. Since the early-twenty-first century, advocacy groups for trans children have approached school districts, published educational information, given interviews, and supported legal changes. For example, TransYouth Family Allies lists numerous print, radio, and television interviews along with resources for parents, educators, and health-care practitioners, and other services they provide; see www.imatyfa.org/index.html. Independent media and the Internet have allowed groups that advocate for trans children's rights to spread their message through such videos as the Portland, Oregon, TransActive video, *Transgender Children—Out of the Shadows*, October 2007, www.youtube.com/watch?v =w2EV3w2QxII. American Broadcast Company and National Public Radio aired two influential discussions about trans kids. ABC's *20/20* anchor Barbara Walters interviewed three families who were supporting their trans children's desire to live authentically in her April 2007 report. Walters exposed issues they faced and barriers to accommodations in school. Alan B. Goldberg, prod., "Born in the Wrong Body," http://abcnews.go.com/2020/ Story?id=3072518&page=1; Alan B. Goldberg and Joneil Adriano, "I'm a Girl," http:// abcnews.go.com/2020/story?id=3088298&page=1. Ira Glass documented two eight-year-old trans girls who met at a Gender Odyssey conference. Gender Odyssey held the first conference for parents of transgender children in Seattle in 2007. Ira Glass, prod., "Somewhere Out There," *This American Life*, episode 374, February 13, 2009, www.thisamerican life.org/Radio_Episode.aspx?sched=1283. Articles often continue to use the pronoun chil-

dren and their families reject. Patricia Leigh Brown, "Supporting Boys or Girls When the Line Isn't Clear," *New York Times,* December 2, 2006, www.nytimes.com/2006/12/02/us/02child.html?_r=2&oref=slogin; Hanna Rosin, "A Boy's Life," *The Atlantic,* November 2008, www.theatlantic.com/doc/200811/transgender-children.

18. Figures as of December 2010 at www.transgenderlaw.org/college/index.htm for Transgender Law and Policy Institute (TLPI). Proponents of hate-crime legislation point out that federal courts can sometimes bring justice where regional biases might lead to failure to prosecute or to convict criminals. Some debate exists about the efficacy of hate-crime laws and their contribution to a criminal-justice system that expresses bias against LGBT people and other minorities. See Sylvia Rivera Law Project, "SRLP Announces Nonsupport of the Gender Employment Non-discrimination Act! April 6, 2009," http://srlp.org/node/301.

19. Consortium of Higher Education Lesbian Gay Bisexual Transgender Resource Professionals, "Safe Zone: Frequently Asked Questions," www.lgbtcampus.org/old_faq/safe_zone_roster.html. For more information see Safe Zone Programs, "Resources for Safe Zone Programs," http://safezonefoundation.tripod.com/id27.html.

20. For anyone in the helping profession who deals with people in distress or who suffer from post-traumatic stress, *Trauma Stewardship* is a fantastic resource for avoiding secondary trauma by honoring others' suffering without internalizing their pain. Laura van Dernoot Lipsky and Connie Buck, *Trauma Stewardship: An Everyday Guide to Caring for Self While Caring for Others* (San Francisco: Berrett-Koehler, 2009).

21. The University of Michigan's policy link as of July 28, 2009, was www.itd.umich.edu/itpolicies/preferrednames.php, and under its FAQ, it explains that individuals can enter their preferred names into the system but that the legal names will continue to show up on the online directory unless the Accounts Office does a manual override; www.itd.umich.edu/itpolicies/preferrednamesFAQ.php. Brett Genny Janiczek Beemyn, "Ways that U.S. Colleges and Universities Meet the Day-to-Day Needs of Transgender Students," www.transgenderlaw.org/college/index.htm#practices (hereafter cited as Beemyn, "Ways").

22. Some of the universities with preferred gender options are Duke University, Oberlin College, Tufts University, the University of Hawaii, and the University of Oregon. Brett Genny Beemyn and Jessica Pettitt, "How Have Trans-inclusive Non-discrimination Policies Changed Institutions?" *GLBT Campus Matters,* June 2006 (hereafter cited as Beemyn, "How"), www.transgenderlaw.org/college/index.htm; Beemyn, "Ways."

23. Sample surgeons' letters can sometimes be found online through trans support groups, but access usually requires membership in the online group.

24. USSC, *Davis v. Monroe County Board of Education* (1999), 119 S. Ct. 1661.

25. Ali, 8.

26. Brett Genny Beemyn, "Making Campuses More Inclusive of Transgender Students," *Journal of Gay and Lesbian Issues in Education* 3, no. 1 (2005): 77–87, www.haworthpress.com/web/JGLED (hereafter cited as Beemyn, "Making").

27. New College of California has converted all its restrooms to gender-neutral ones. Many colleges explicitly list their gender-neutral restrooms on their Web sites. Beemyn, "Ways."

28. Beemyn, "How." These include the University of Maryland, Ohio State University, and the University of Oregon. Beemyn, "Ways."

29. Beemyn, "How." Jenna Johnson and Daniel de Vise, "At George Washington University, Coed Quarters Becoming Option for All," *Washington Post,* December 4, 2010, www.washingtonpost.com/wp-dyn/content/article/2010/12/03/AR2010120306648.html?wprss=rss_education&sid=ST2010120306862 (accessed December 13, 2010).

30. Texas Christian University's student paper, the *Daily Skiff*, printed a news article announcing the planned LGBT and allies dorm called DiverCity Q. Curtis Burrhus-Clay, "LGBT-themed Campus Living Community to Debut in the Fall," *Daily Skiff*, April 1, 2009, http://media.www.tcudailyskiff.com/media/storage/paper792/news/2009/04/01/News/LgbtThemed.Campus.Living.Community.To.Debut.In.The.Fall-3690200.shtml. Within the week, the *Dallas Morning News* published the news. Holly K. Hacker, "TCU to Provide Special Housing for Gay, Lesbian Students," *Dallas Morning News*, April 7, 2009, www.dallasnews.com/sharedcontent/dws/dn/latestnews/stories/040809dnmettcugay.3900227.html. A week later, national coverage by CBN and FoxNews announced that the university had cancelled the DiverCity Q plan. "Christian Univ. Pulls Plans for Gay Dorms," April 14, 2009, www.cbn.com/CBNnews/579943.aspx; "Texas Christian University Scraps Plans for Gay Student Housing," April 14, 2009, www.foxnews.com/story/0,2933,515661,00.html.

31. "National Student Genderblind Campaign Research Update—Summer 2008," www.genderblind.org/research.pdf.

32. Beemyn, "Making."

33. Beemyn reports that the following have trans-inclusive student insurance plans: "Emerson College; the University of California, Davis; the University of California, Irvine; the University of California, Riverside; the University of California, San Diego; the University of California, San Francisco; the University of California, Santa Barbara; the University of California, Santa Cruz; the University of Michigan; and the University of Vermont." Eight more college student health plans cover hormones only. Beemyn, "Ways."

34. Beemyn, "Making."

35. The positive write-up of the event in the student newspaper and heated debate in the comments indicate that this event encouraged discussion about transition. Dominique Beck, "Transgendered Activist Speaks at NT," *North Texas Daily*, April 17, 2009, http://media.www.ntdaily.com/media/storage/paper877/news/2009/04/17/ArtsLife/Transgendered.Activist.Speaks.At.Nt-3715265.shtml.

36. Kristen A. Renn and Brent L. Bilodeau, "Leadership Identity Development among Lesbian, Gay, Bisexual, and Transgender Student Leaders," *National Association of Student Personnel Administrators (NASPA) Journal* 42, no. 3 (2005): 342–367.

CHAPTER 7

1. Despite range and variation in name and content, I refer broadly to these throughout the essay as "trainings."

2. Bassichis and Spade 2007, 19–21; Davis et al. 2001; Feinberg 2001; Kelly 1992; Klamen, Grossman, and Kopacz 2000; Lombardi and Bettcher 2006; Meyer 2001, 857–858; Nangeroni 1998; Rondahl 2009; Shield 2007, 373–375.

3. U.S. Department of Health and Human Services 2009.

4. Lupton 1997.

5. DelVecchio-Good et al. 2003, 595.

6. Hanssmann, Morrison, and Russian 2008, 12.

7. Bockting and Avery 2005; Bockting, Robinson, and Rosser 1998; Kenagy 2005; Xavier et al. 2005. As I discuss later in the essay, this is quite significant, but it is notable that trainers and curriculum developers as a group tend to have access to more social, economic, and professional privilege than trans and gender-nonconforming people as a broad group.

8. Health-professional education also fails to attend to the health needs of LGBQ individuals, and although some of the underlying reasons for this may be similar, this essay

focuses on gaps in medical education with respect to trans and gender-nonconforming individuals.

9. Corliss, Shankle, and Moyer 2007.

10. Although it is beyond the scope of this essay to explore in detail, it is worth noting that the problematic folding of transgender into LGBQ movements has resulted in a conflation of these differing positions and a perceived escalated need to draw differences between them.

11. Waitzkin and Waterman 1974; Lowe and Reid 1999.

12. Spade 2006, 319.

13. Ibid., 329.

14. Cross et al. 1989, 13.

15. Betancourt et al. 2000.

16. Bhui, Warfa, Edonya, McKenzie, and Bhugra 2007.

17. Robert Wood Johnson Foundation, "State-Level Strategies to Address Health and Mental Health Disparities through Cultural and Linguistic Competency Training and Licensure: An Environmental Scan of Factors Related to Legislative and Regulatory Actions in States," a study conducted during 2007–2008, RWJF ID#59024. See also the National Center for Cultural Competence; resources and studies are all published through Washington, DC: Georgetown University Center for Child and Human Development, Georgetown University Medical Center, and accessible at http://nccc.georgetown.edu.

18. Degree of English proficiency is another central topic of cultural-competence trainings, which may be more useful in their focus on helping providers understand effective strategies for communication and ethical use of interpretation services. But these trainings, in their current manifestations, tend to conflate nation of origin and language with a static notion of culture, oftentimes problematically. And the logic in employing these trainings is generally financial, above all. "The idea behind the CLAS system is that better communication leads to better adherence to medications and lifestyle changes, which leads to improved health status, which leads to less use of emergent care services and less frequent hospitalizations." J. P. Fortier and D. Bishop, in *Setting the Agenda for Research on Cultural Competence in Health Care: Final Report,* ed. C. Brach (Rockville, MD: U.S. Department of Health and Human Services/Office of Minority Health and AHRQ, 2003).

19. Sakamoto 2007; American Academy of Orthopaedic Surgeons (AAOS) 2005; Jimenez and Lewis 2007. The AAOS resource is only one example of many cultural-competence tools for providers.

20. This concept was discussed by nursing professor Cheryl Pope in her plenary lecture at the 2009 Health Care Education Association Conference in Asheville, North Carolina. Her talk was titled "Approaches to Health Disparities and Social Determinants of Health for Health Care Educators."

21. Carpenter-Song, Nordquest Schwallie, and Longhofer 2007; Sakamoto 2007; Shaw 2005; Taylor 2003.

22. Sakamoto 2007, 108.

23. Pon 2009, 67.

24. Taylor 2003.

25. Crenshaw 1995.

26. Some cultural-competence approaches incorporate a broader analysis of individual service provision with relation to social structures, laws, policies, curricula, health standards, and guidelines. Although these are likely to be more effective, as they generally call for structural and policy shifts to support institutional change, they begin from a similar starting point: cultivating sensitivity and empathy, increasing comfort, and so forth.

Structural shifts are seen to come after, and as a result of, lengthy work of the part of individual service providers to decrease their degrees of prejudice.

27. Spade 2003.
28. Lev 2004; Spade 2003.
29. Spade 2009.
30. Although some trans activists have called for a depathologization and demedicalization of trans identities and a move toward self-determination through a consumer basis, this shift from a framework of medical management to capitalist wealth-based access is very problematic and limiting along lines of privilege. Depathologization is critical, but so is medical support and increased, rather than decreased, access to care. It may be worthwhile to pursue, in a different but related discussion, models of health that are not built solely on "curing or managing disease" but also and/or alternatively on "building sustainable lives" or as "fostering good and equitable health."
31. Spade 2007.
32. For example, people with disabilities frequently encounter barriers associated with their bodies or identities being medicalized; LGBQ people may have difficulty accessing quality care due to their gender presentations, even if they are not trans; uninsured or underinsured individuals often encounter comparable barriers to accessing affordable care; people of color are frequently stigmatized, essentialized, or both in the course of accessing care, and so on. When trans people inhabit any or a multitude of these categories, barriers to care are further exacerbated. The issue is not just to make medicine "friendlier" for trans and gender-nonconforming individuals; rather, there are important links within and between marginalized communities in accessing care.
33. Spade 2003; World Professional Association for Transgender Health 2001.
34. I am indebted to Dean Spade for describing the way this particular framing of trans identity not only pervades popular media representations of trans people but also shapes laws, medicine and psychiatry, and other institutionalized mobilizations of trans identity.
35. By this I mean narratives that align with the standard symptoms of Gender Identity Disorder as a psychiatric diagnosis: pervasive feelings of having the "wrong body" or "wrong genitalia," having behaved from a young age in ways that do not parallel conventional expectations of masculinity and femininity, and so forth. Although some trans people may have these experiences, they are certainly not universal. I question the dominance and lopsided credibility assigned to this particular set of experiences.
36. Irving 2008.
37. Namaste 2000.
38. This does not mean there has been a complete shift—much health and medical research concerning trans people is pointedly not a product of trans or trans-supportive communities or scholars—but the direction of the shift is significant.
39. Mananzala and Spade 2008.
40. Lev 2004.
41. In conversations about a shift away from solely disease-based medicine, it is critical to maintain the centrality of necessity and affordability, which at this historical moment are linked to private insurance and public medical benefits.
42. "Training" here is singular, because that is the most common structure of instruction in this case. This is part of the problem, as subsequent or ongoing sessions would allow for a return to challenging or problematic concepts and would allow for a degree of follow-up and reengagement that is not possible in a single session.
43. Hanssmann, Morrison, and Russian 2008.
44. Ibid., 10–14.
45. Ibid., 11.

46. Based on the content of the training, these skills included using appropriate pronouns, using preferred rather than legal names if these are different, communicating clearly during exams and keeping in mind possible challenges for patients that involve areas of the body that for some people may be alienating or stressful (breast and cervical exams for trans masculine individuals, prostate and testicular exams for trans feminine individuals, for example).
47. Spade 2009.
48. Valentine 2007, 235.
49. Ibid., 39.
50. This is a pervasive problem in the field of population health in general.
51. World Professional Association for Transgender Health 2001. This refers to the amount of time that an individual must live full-time in their desired gender role. Currently, psychotherapy can replace this phase in some cases, and other aspects of it have been relaxed. Regardless, it is still an element of the WPATH Standards of Care, even in its ratcheted-down form.
52. Meyer 2001.
53. Sakamoto 2007, 109.
54. Lurie 2009; Singer 2006.
55. Lurie 2005, 93–112.
56. Singer 2006.
57. Sylvia Rivera Law Project 2010.
58. TransJustice was originally housed in SRLP prior to its move to ALP.
59. Audre Lorde Project 2009.
60. Housing Works 2008; Queers for Economic Justice 2010.
61. Feldman et al. 2006.
62. Vancouver Coastal Health 2010.
63. Bauer et al. 2009; Clements-Nolle and Bachrach 2003; Minkler and Wallerstein 2003; Pinto, Melendez, and Spector 2008.
64. Wallerstein and Duran 2006.
65. Minkler and Wallerstein 2003; Wallerstein and Duran 2006.
66. Clements-Nolle and Bachrach 2003.
67. Chae and Walters 2009; Walters and Simoni 2002.
68. TransPULSE 2010.
69. Cisnormativity refers to the erasure of transgender realities and experiences and the culturally and institutionally reinforced assumption that people assigned male at birth become men and people assigned female at birth become women. It "disallows the possibility of trans existence or trans visibility. As such, the existence of an actual trans person within systems such as health care is too often unanticipated and produced a social emergency of sorts because both staff and systems are unprepared for this reality" (Bauer and Hammond et al. 2009).
70. This is an ambitious goal, and perhaps unrealistic to attain against such a starkly contrasting distribution of resources. Nevertheless, creative redistributions are possible and worthwhile to pursue. A variety of ongoing projects and groups, for example, support the possibility of leveraging academic resources for communities and creating increased accountability for academic researchers from within communities. Community Campus Partnerships for Health (CCPH) in an example of this, as is the Indigenous Wellness Research Institute (IWRI) and various other community-based and university-based organizations.
71. For example, see D. Spade, "Transformation: Three Myths Regarding Transgender Identity Have Led to Conflicting Laws and Policies That Adversely Affect Transgender

People," *Los Angeles Lawyer,* 2008. Legal strategies to increase rights and to establish laws that protect trans people from discrimination (such as the Employment Non-Discrimination Act, or ENDA) may be strategic and important in many ways. However, they also devote resources to establishing laws that are (a) difficult to enforce, and thus largely symbolic; and (b) primarily beneficial to trans and gender-nonconforming individuals who are employed, who are able to secure funds for legal representation, or who otherwise have the resources to access and to pursue such protections. A few organizations have done this work, but it has not been widely pursued, even by organizations that claim "transgender rights" and "trans health" as central to their work. Several graduate student unions (among them the University of Michigan, the University of California system, and the University of Washington), the Sylvia Rivera Law Project, and American Friends Service Committee (AFSC) have all worked to increase trans health-care access and insurance coverage within their institutions or organizations. AFSC subsequently published a thorough account of its process for other organizations interested in adding health coverage for trans employees into their insurance plans.

72. This relative silence is also the case from LGBQ groups and organizations. The disproportionate investment (financial and otherwise) in gay marriage has led to a state of affairs in which legal marriage serves as the frame of analysis for a multitude of issues affecting LGBQ communities. Thus, access to health insurance is frequently discussed as an issue that may be resolved by legalizing same-sex marriage, so an individual may gain access to a partner's insurance (assuming that at least one individual has insurance coverage). Universal health care has not been similarly pursued as a way to solve the health-care problem for mainstream LGBQ communities, perhaps because it does not serve to further the marriage agenda.

73. Ahmed and Swan 2006, 99.

74. This is a concept that draws from critical race theorists in critical legal studies, such as Angela Harris and Richard Delgado, as well as one that is indebted to Freirean notions of pedagogy. It is used in practice in a variety of settings, including a variety of training curricula developed by organizations and groups working at the intersections of race, gender and sexuality, class, disability, and other axes of marginalization. I first encountered this as an explicit framing in a training developed by members of Seattle's Communities against Rape and Abuse (CARA).

CHAPTER 8

Acknowledgments: This essay distills multiple conversations over a decade of attempting to unravel the evident links between an emerging trans politics and the border wars waged on undocumented migrants globally. I extend my thanks to Angela Mitropoulos, Dean Spade, Lauren Taylor, Hugh Farrell, Emmett Ramstad, Eric Stanley, and members of the "Queer Necropolitics" informal study group (Jin Haritaworn, Sima Shakhsari, Adi Kuntsman, Gina Velasco, and others) for inspiration, challenges, and talk. I also thank A. Finn Enke for so kindly and patiently continuing to insist that I should be in this book, despite numerous deadline defaults.

1. For a critique of this tendency, see Afsaneh Najmabadi, "Transing and Transpassing across Sex-Gender Walls in Iran," *WSQ: Women's Studies Quarterly* 36, nos. 3–4 (2008): 23–42.

2. Also see the Israeli film *Paper Dolls (Bubot Niyar),* dir. Tomer Heymann, 2006.

3. In this chapter, I use the term "gender variant" to designate persons who do not conform to the logic that one must remain the gender assigned at birth for the duration of one's life or that gender can be only male or female. This avoids deploying identity catego-

ries, such as transgender or transsexual, with which many gender-variant people disidentify and that tend to be used in a universalizing manner.

4. Paisley Currah, "The Transgender Rights Imaginary," in *Feminist and Queer Legal Theory: Intimate Encounters, Uncomfortable Conversations,* ed. Martha Fineman, Jack E. Jackson, and Adam P. Romero (London, UK: Ashgate, 2009), 245–258.

5. On the appropriation of the border metaphor, see Aren Aizura, "Of Borders and Homes: The Imaginary Community of (Trans) Sexual Citizenship," *Inter-Asia Cultural Studies* 7, no. 2 (2006): 289–309; Nael Bhanji, "Diasporic Trans/scriptions: Home, Transsexual Citizenship, and Racialized Bodies," in *Transgender Migrations: The Bodies, Borders and (Geo) Politics of Transition,* ed. Trystan Cotton, 157–175 (New York: Routledge, 2011).

6. See, for example, Nan Seuffert, "Reflections on Transgender Immigration," *Griffith Law Review* 18, no. 3 (2009): 428–452; John A. Fisher, "Sex Determination for Federal Purposes: Is Transsexual Immigration Via Marriage Permissible under the Defense of Marriage Act," *Michigan Journal of Gender and Law* 10 (2003–2004): 237–268. An exception is Pooja Gehi, "Struggles from the Margins: Anti-immigrant Legislation and the Impact on Low-Income Transgender People of Color," *Women's Rights Law Report* 30 (2008): 315–346.

7. On modulation as a technique of societies of control, see Gilles Deleuze, "Postscript on the Societies of Control," *October* 59 (1992): 3–7.

8. Dean Spade, "Trans Law and Politics on a Neoliberal Landscape," *Temple Political and Civil Rights Law Review* 18, no. 2 (2009): 354.

9. Ibid., 368.

10. On biopolitics, see Michel Foucault, "From the Power of Sovereignty to Power over Life," in *Society Must Be Defended: Lectures at the College de France 1975–1976,* ed. Mauro Bertani and Alessandro Fontana (New York: Picador, 2003), 239–264. On the overuse of biopolitics, see Melinda Cooper, Anna Munster, and Andrew Goffey, "Biopolitics, for Now," *Culture Machine* 7 (2005), www.culturemachine.net/index.php/cm/article/view/24/31 (accessed June 20, 2009).

11. For example, although the U.S.-Mexico border is the locus of the xenophobic specular imaginary of U.S. nationalism, the border between Guatemala and Mexico is heavily policed by numerous formal and informal law-enforcement agencies. The European Union's Schengen Treaty designates all the E.U. countries as one supranational territory that outsources detention camps for undocumented migrants to nations on the borders of Europe placed in high-flow locations, such as Morocco, Tunisia, Turkey, Croatia, and so forth.

12. These institutions include the United Nations High Commission for Refugees and the International Organization for Migration. On regimes of mobility control, I cite Dimitris Papadopoulos, Niamh Stephenson, and Vassilis Tsianos, *Escape Routes: Control and Subversion in the 21st Century* (London, UK: Pluto Press, 2008), 162; but also see the work of Angela Mitropoulos.

13. Angela Mitropoulos, "Halt, Who Goes There?" in *City-State: A Critical Reader on Surveillance and Social Control,* ed. Louise Boon-Kuo and Gavin Sullivan (Sydney, Australia: UTS Community Law and Legal Research Centre, 2002), 73.

14. Angela Mitropoulos, "The Materialization of Race in Multiculture," *darkmatter* 2 (February 23, 2008), www.darkmatter101.org/site/2008/02/23/the-materialisation-of-race-in-multiculture (accessed January 3, 2011). On the Schmittian exception, see Carl Schmitt, *Political Theology: Four Chapters on the Concept of Sovereignty,* trans. George Schwab (Chicago, IL: University of Chicago Press, 1985).

15. See "Letter to the DREAM Movement: My Painful Withdrawal of Support for the DREAM Act," http://antifronteras.com/2010/09/18 (accessed October 5, 2010).

16. "Maintaining Awareness Regarding Al-Qaeda's Potential Threats," Department of Homeland Security, September 4, 2003, www.dps.state.vt.us/homeland/library_aware.htm.

17. United Kingdom Lesbian and Gay Immigration Group online forum, www.uklgig.org.uk/phpBB/viewtopic.php?f=4&t=2228&hilit=transgender (accessed April 13, 2011).

18. Immigration Equality and the Transgender Law Center, *Immigration Law and the Transgender Client*, section 1.2.4.1, www.immigrationequality.org/template3.php?pageid=1135 (accessed November 3, 2011).

19. Ibid., section 1.2.4.

20. Ibid., section 1.2.4.1.

21. Yates Memo Regarding Transgender Immigration Applicants, http://immigrationequality.org/uploadedfiles/Microsoft Word-App(2).pdf (accessed February 21, 2011).

22. The U.S. Defense of Marriage Act (1996) stipulates that marriage is between a man and a woman.

23. *Immigration Law and the Transgender Client*, section 1.2.4.1.

24. The preoccupation with romantic heterosexual coupledom as the only legitimate idea of family worthy of immigration sponsorship has been critiqued by many, including Eithne Luibhéid, who points out how U.S. immigration control has historically served as a mechanism for "constructing, enforcing and normalizing dominant forms of heteronormativity" and simultaneously casting a variety of non-heteronormative bodies as threats. See Eithne Luibhéid "Sexuality, Migration, and the Shifting Line between Legal and Illegal Status," *GLQ: A Journal of Lesbian and Gay Studies* 14, nos. 2–3 (2008): 296.

25. *Immigration Law and the Transgender Client*, section 4.6.6.

26. Ibid.

27. A critical dissection of the stereotype of trans people as "deceivers" can be found in Talia Mae Bettcher, "Evil Deceivers and Make-Believers: On Transphobic Violence and the Politics of Illusion," *Hypatia* 22, no. 3 (Summer 2007): 44–65.

28. Karma Chávez, "Border (In)Securities: Normative and Differential Belonging in LGBTQ and Immigrant Rights Discourse," *Communication and Critical/Cultural Studies* 7, no. 2 (2010): 141.

29. Ibid., 142.

30. For the term "entrepreneurial subject," I am indebted to Wendy Brown's essay "Neo-liberalism and the End of Liberal Democracy," *Theory and Event* 7, no. 1 (2003), in Wendy Brown, *Edgework: Critical Essays on Knowledge and Politics* (Princeton, NJ: Princeton University Press, 2005), 37–59

31. Luibhéid, "Sexuality, Migration, and the Shifting Line between Legal and Illegal Status," 307.

32. Queers for Economic Justice, "Queers and Immigration: A Vision Statement," *Scholar and Feminist Online* 6, no. 3 (2008), www.barnard.edu/sfonline/immigration/qej_01.htm (accessed May 13, 2011).

33. Chávez, "Border (In)Securities," 147.

34. Ibid., 148.

35. Sylvia Rivera Law Project, http:/slrp.org/about (accessed January 1, 2011).

36. Jasbir Puar, *Terrorist Assemblages: Homonationalism in Queer Times* (Durham, NC: Duke University Press, 2007), 206.

37. See Brian Massumi, *Parables for the Virtual: Movement, Affect, Sensation* (Durham, NC: Duke University Press, 2002), 2–3.

38. A more insightful critique of Transgender Day of Remembrance than I have room for here is Sarah Lamble's "Retelling Racialized Violence, Remaking White Innocence: The Politics of Interlocking Oppressions in Transgender Day of Remembrance," *Sexuality Research and Social Policy: Journal of NSRC* 5, no. 1 (March 2008): 24–42.

39. Neferti Tadiar, "Towards a Vision of Sexual and Economic Justice," *Scholar and Feminist Online* 7, no. 3 (2009), www.barnard.edu/sfonline/sexecon/print_tadiar.htm (accessed March 4, 2011).
40. Ibid., 3.
41. Yann Moulier-Boutang and Stany Grelet, "The Art of Flight: An Interview with Yann Moulier-Boutang," *Rethinking Marxism* 13, no. 3–4 (2001): 227.
42. Paolo Virno, "Virtuosity and Revolution: The Political Theory of Exodus," in *Radical Thought in Italy: A Potential Politics,* ed. Michael Hardt and Paolo Virno (Minneapolis: University of Minnesota Press, 1996), 189.
43. Papadopoulos, Tsianos, and Stephenson, *Escape Routes,* 220.

CHAPTER 10

1. An extensive critique of such presumptions about femininity can be found in Julia Serano, *Whipping Girl: A Transsexual Woman on Sexism and the Scapegoating of Femininity* (Emeryville, CA: Seal Press, 2007).
2. Ibid.
3. Janice G. Raymond, *The Transsexual Empire: The Making of the She-Male* (Boston: Beacon Press, 1979), 79; Robin Morgan, *Going Too Far* (New York: Random House, 1977), 180.
4. More information about *FtF: Female to Femme* can be found at www.altcinema.com/ftf.html.
5. For more information about the Michigan Womyn's Music Festival's trans woman–exclusion policy, see Serano, *Whipping Girl,* 233–245; Julia Serano, "Rethinking Sexism: How Trans Women Challenge Feminism," *AlterNet.org,* August 5, 2008, www.alternet.org/reproductivejustice/93826.
6. This essay is a revised version of the keynote talk I presented at Femme 2008.
7. Joan Nestle, ed., "The Femme Question," *The Persistent Desire: A Butch Femme Reader* (Boston: Alyson Publications, 1992), 138–146. The specific "femme question" that I am referring to here (and one that Nestle discusses in her piece) is the tendency of the straight mainstream as well lesbian and feminist communities to construct the existence of femmes as a problem and to project disparaging ulterior motives onto femmes.

CHAPTER 11

1. This text of this chapter is excerpted from my book *Normal Life: Administrative Violence, Critical Trans Politics and the Limits of Law* (Brooklyn, NY: South End Press, 2011).
2. National Gay and Lesbian Task Force, "Jurisdictions with Explicitly Transgender-Inclusive Non-Discrimination Laws," (2008), http://thetaskforce.org/downloads/reports/fact_sheets/all_jurisdictions_w_pop_8_08.pdf (accessed November 27, 2010).
3. National Center for Transgender Equality, "Hate Crimes," 2008, www.nctequality.org/Hate_Crimes.asp.2008 (accessed January 4, 2009).
4. See *Ulane v. Eastern Airlines,* 742 F.2d 1081 (7th Cir. 1984), where the Seventh Circuit Court of Appeals found that a transwoman who was dismissed from her job as an airline pilot was not protected under the sex-discrimination clause of Title VII of the Civil Rights Act of 1964, holding that "Title VII does not protect transsexuals"; and *Oiler v. Winn Dixie, Louisiana Inc.,* No.Civ.A. 00-3114, 2002 WL 31098541 (E.D.La. Sept. 16, 2002), where the U.S. District Court for the Eastern District of Louisiana found that a man who was fired from his job for occasionally cross-dressing outside work was not protected

under Title VII sex discrimination, even though his behavior had nothing to do with his job performance.

5. Rebecca L. Stotzer, "Gender Identity and Hate Crimes: Violence against Transgender People in Los Angeles County," *Sexuality Research and Social Policy: Journal of NSRC* 5, no. 1 (March 2008), http://nsrc.sfsu.edu/sexuality_research_social_policy.

6. Angela P. Harris, "From Stonewall to the Suburbs? Toward a Political Economy of Sexuality," *William and Mary Bill of Rights Journal* 14, no. 4 (April 2006): 1539–1582.

7. See *Goins v. West Group*, 619 N.W.2d 424 (Minn. App. Ct. 2000), where the Minnesota Supreme Court held that employers may restrict restroom and locker-room access based on birth sex; and *Hispanic Aids Forum v. Estate of Bruno*, 16 Misc.3d 960, 839 N.Y.S.2d 691 (N.Y. Sup., 2007), where a New York Supreme Court judge ruled in favor of a nonprofit organization that was facing eviction based on its failure to comply with a landlord's demands that it disclose the birth sex of its clients, holding that the physical anatomy of trans people is not relevant to gender identity. In *Ettsity v. Utah Transit Authority*, 502 F.3d 1215 (10th Cir. 2007), the Tenth Circuit held that a trans woman bus driver who was fired because she used women's restrooms as needed at various stops on her bus route was not protected by Title VII's prohibition against sex discrimination and gender stereotyping.

8. A recent survey of 6,450 transgender and gender-nonconforming people in the United States found that 57 percent had experienced significant family rejection. Jamie M. Grant, Lisa A. Mottet, and Justin Tanis, *Injustice at Every Turn: A Report of the National Transgender Discrimination Survey*, Executive Summary (Washington, DC: National Gay and Lesbian Task Force and National Center for Transgender Equality, 2011), www.thetaskforce.org/downloads/reports/reports/ntds_summary.pdf.

9. The same study found that 19 percent of transgender and gender-nonconforming people had been refused medical treatment due to their gender, 28 percent had postponed medical care when they were sick or injured due to discrimination, and 48 percent had postponed care when they were sick or injured because they could not afford it. The study also found that respondents reported a rate of HIV infection more than four times the national average, with rates higher among trans people of color. Grant, Mottet, and Tanis, *Injustice at Every Turn*.

10. The study also confirmed that trans people live in extreme poverty. Respondents were nearly four times more likely to have a household income of less than $10,000 per year compared to the general population. Grant, Mottet, and Tanis, *Injustice at Every Turn*.

11. Alan David Freeman, "Legitimizing Racial Discrimination through Anti-discrimination Law: A Critical Review of Supreme Court Doctrine," in *Critical Race Studies: The Key Writings That Formed the Movement*, ed. Kimberlé Crenshaw, Neil Gotanda, Garry Peller, and Kendall Thomas (New York: New Press, 1996), 29–45.

12. See *San Antonio Independent School District v. Rodriguez*, 411 U.S. 1 (1973), where the U.S. Supreme Court held that the severe imbalance in a school district's funding of its primary and secondary schools based on the income levels of the residents of each district is not an unconstitutional violation of Equal Protection rights under the Fourteenth Amendment.

13. David M. White, "The Requirement of Race-Conscious Evaluation of LSAT Scores for Equitable Law School Admission," *Berkeley La Raza Law Journal* 12, no. 2 (Fall 2001): 399; Susan Sturm and Lani Guinier, "The Future of Affirmative Action: Reclaiming the Innovative Ideal," *California Law Review* 84, no. 4 (July 1996): 953.

14. Freeman, "Legitimizing Racial Discrimination through Anti-discrimination Law."

15. *Milliken*, 418 U.S. 717; 87 *Parents Involved in Community Schools*, 551 U.S. 701.

16. Mazher Ali, Jeanette Huezo, Brian Miller, Wanjiku Mwangi, and Mike Prokosch, *State of the Dream 2011: Austerity for Whom?* (Boston: United for a Fair Economy, 2011), www.faireconomy.org/files/State_of_the_Dream_2011.pdf.

17. Dan Irving, "Normalized Transgressions: Legitimizing the Transsexual Body as Productive," *Radical History Review,* no. 100 (Winter 2008): 38–59.

18. Ibid. Several significant famous trans discrimination cases follow this pattern, with media and advocates portraying the assimilable characteristics of the trans person to emphasize his or her deserving nature. One example is the highly publicized case of Diane Schroer, who won a lawsuit after she lost a job at the Library of Congress when disclosed her trans identity. *Time* magazine described her as

> an ex-Special Forces colonel . . . Schroer was a dream candidate, a guy out of a Tom Clancy novel: he had jumped from airplanes, undergone grueling combat training in extreme heat and cold, commanded hundreds of soldiers, helped run Haiti during the U.S. intervention in the '90s—and, since 9/11, he had been intimately involved in secret counterterrorism planning at the highest levels of the Pentagon. He had been selected to organize and run a new, classified antiterror organization, and in that position he had routinely briefed Defense Secretary Donald Rumsfeld. He had also briefed Vice President Cheney more than once. Schroer had been an action hero, but he also had the contacts and intellectual dexterity to make him an ideal congressional analyst.

Schroer's public persona as a patriot and terrorist-fighter was used by advocates to promote the idea of her deservingness in ways that those concerned about the racist, anti-immigrant, imperialist War on Terror might take issue with. Critics have similarly pointed out dynamics of deservingness that determine which queer and trans murder victims become icons in the battle for hate-crime legislation. White victims tend to be publicly remembered (e.g., Harvey Milk, Brandon Teena, Matthew Shepard), their lives memorialized in films and movies (*Milk, Boys Don't Cry, Larabee*), and laws named after them (Matthew Shepard Local Law Enforcement Enhancement Act). The names of these white victims and the struggles for healing and justice on the part of their friends and family are in greater circulation than victims of color through media and nonprofit channels, even though people of color lose their lives at higher rates. Sanesha Stewart, Amanda Milan, Marsha P. Johnson, Duanna Johnson, Ruby Ordeñana are just a few of the trans women of color whose murders have been mourned by local communities but mostly ignored by media, large nonprofits, and lawmakers.

19. Roy Walmsley, *World Prison Population List,* 7th ed. (London, UK: International Centre for Prison Studies, 2005).

20. U.S. Department of Justice, "Key Crime and Justice Facts at a Glance," 2009, www.ojp.usdoj.gov/bjs/glance.htm.

21. Walmsley, *World Prison Population List.*

22. The PEW Center on the States, *One in 100: Behind Bars in America 2008,* 2008, www.pewcenteronthestates.org/uploadedFiles/8015PCTS_Prison08_FINAL_2-1-1_FOR WEB.pdf.

23. Government Accounting Office, "Information on Criminal Aliens Incarcerated in Federal and State Prisons and Local Jails," Congressional briefing, March 25, 2005, http://gao.gov/new.items/d05337r.pdf.

24. Lauraet Magnani and Harmon L. Wray, *Beyond Prisons: A New Interfaith Paradigm for Our Failed Prison System,* A Report by the American Friends Service Committee, Criminal Justice Task Force (Minneapolis, Minnesota: Fortress Press, 2006).

25. Anna M. Agathangelou, D. Morgan Bassichis, and Tamara L. Spira, "Intimate Investments: Homonormativity, Global Lockdown, and the Seductions of Empire," *Radical History Review*, no. 100 (Winter 2008): 120–143; Morgan Bassichis, Alex Lee, and Dean Spade, "Building an Abolitionist Trans Movement with Everything We've Got," in *Captive Genders: Transembodiment and the Prison Industrial Complex*, ed. Nat Smith and Eric A. Stanley (Oakland, CA: AK Press, 2011); Magnani and Wray, *Beyond Prisons*; Kristina Wertz and Masen Davis, "When Laws Are Not Enough: A Study of the Economic Health of Transgender People and the Need for a Multidisciplinary Approach to Economic Justice," *Seattle Journal of Social Justice* 8, no. 2 (Spring–Summer 2010): 467–489.

26. Dean Spade, "Documenting Gender," *Hastings Law Journal* 59, no. 4 (2008): 731; Chris Daley and Shannon Minter, *Trans Realities: A Legal Needs Assessment of San Francisco's Transgender Communities* (San Francisco: Transgender Law Center, 2003).

27. Joey L. Mogul, Andrea J. Ritchie, and Kay Whitlock, *Queer (In)Justice* (Boston: Beacon Press, 2011).

28. D. Morgan Bassichis, *"It's War in Here": A Report on the Treatment of Transgender and Intersex People in New York State Men's Prisons* (New York: Sylvia Rivera Law Project, 2007), http://srlp.org/files/warinhere.pdf; Alexander L. Lee, *Gendered Crime and Punishment: Strategies to Protect Transgender, Gender Variant and Intersex People in America's Prisons* (pts 1 and 2), Gender Identity Center *Trans in Prison Journal* (Summer 2004), Gender Identity Center *Trans in Prison Journal* (Fall 2004) (old issues of the journal can be requested through the Gender Identity Center of Colorado, Gender Identity Center Trans in Prison, and an earlier version of this paper is available at www.justdetention.org/pdf/nowheretogobutout.pdf); Christopher D. Man and John P. Cronan, "Forecasting Sexual Abuse in Prison: The Prison Subculture of Masculinity as a Backdrop for 'Deliberate Indifference,'" *Journal of Criminal Law and Criminology* 92, no. 1 (2001): 127; Alex Coolman, Lamar Glover, and Kara Gotsch, *Still in Danger: The Ongoing Threat of Sexual Violence against Transgender Prisoners* (Los Angeles: Stop Prisoner Rape and the ACLU National Prison Project, 2005), www.justdetention.org/pdf/stillindanger.pdf; Janet Baus and Dan Hunt, *Cruel and Unusual* (New York: Reid Productions, 2006).

29. Bassichis, Lee, and Spade, "Building an Abolitionist Trans Movement with Everything We've Got"; Agathangelou, Bassichis, and Spira, "Intimate Investments"; Dean Spade and Craig Willse, "Confronting the Limits of Gay Hate Crimes Activism: A Radical Critique," *Chicano-Latino Law Review* 21, no. 2 (Spring 2000): 38; Sarah Lamble, "Retelling Racialized Violence, Remaking White Innocence: The Politics of Interlocking Oppressions in Transgender Day of Remembrance," *Sexuality Research and Social Policy: Journal of NSRC* 5, no. 1 (March 2008): 24–42.

30. Angela Y. Davis, *Are Prisons Obsolete?* (New York: Seven Stories Press, 2003).

31. Gabriel Arkles's scholarship has explored how rules that purport to protect prisoners from sexual violence are frequently used to punish consensual sexual or friendship relationships, to prohibit masturbation, and to target queer and gender-nonconforming prisoners. The existence of such rules can also increase risks of sexual behavior and create opportunities for blackmail and abuse by corrections officers. See letter from Chase Strangio and Z. Gabriel Arkles to Attorney General Holder, May 10, 2010, page 9, http://srlp.org/files/SRLP%20PREA%20comment%20Docket%20no%20OAG-131.pdf; Gabriel Arkles, *Transgender Communities and the Prison Industrial Complex*, lecture at Northeastern University School of Law, February 2010. Arkles offers as an example of this type of problematic policymaking Idaho's Prison Rape Elimination Provision (Control No. 325.02.01.001, 2004, www.idoc.idaho.gov/policy/int3250201001.pdf), which includes a prohibition on "male" prisoners having a "feminine or effeminate hairstyle." E-mail from Gabriel Arkles, February 21, 2011 (on file with the author).

32. Further controversy has emerged around the NPREA since the Department of Justice proposed national standards "for the detection, prevention, reduction, and punishment of prison rape, as mandated by" the NPREA, which exclude immigration facilities. See National Juvenile Defender Center and the Equity Project, Transgender Law Center, Lambda Legal Education and Defense Fund, National Center for Lesbian Rights, American Civil Liberties Union, Sylvia Rivera Law Project, National Center for Transgender Equality, "Protecting Lesbian, Gay, Bisexual, Transgender, Intersex, and Gender Nonconforming people from Sexual Abuse and Harassment in Correctional Settings," Comments Submitted in Response to Docket No. OAG-131; AG Order No. 3244-2011 National Standards to Prevent, Detect, and Respond to Prison Rape April 4, 2011, 47–48 (on file with the author); Human Rights Watch, ACLU Washington Legislative Office, Immigration Equality, Just Detention International, National Immigrant Justice Center, National Immigration Forum, Physicians for Human Rights, Prison Fellowship, Southern Center for Human Rights, Texas Civil Rights Project, Women's Refugee Commission, "US: Immigration Facilities Should Apply Prison Rape Elimination Act Protections: Letter to U.S. President Barack Obama," February 15, 2011, www.hrw.org/es/news/2011/02/15/us-immigration-facilities-should-apply-prison-rape-elimination-act-protections.

33. See INCITE! Women of Color against Violence, ed., *The Revolution Will Not Be Funded: Beyond the Non-profit Industrial Complex* (Cambridge, MA: South End Press, 2007); Dean Spade and Rickke Mananzala, "The Non-profit Industrial Complex and Trans Resistance," *Sexuality Research and Social Policy: Journal of NSRC* 5, no. 1 (March 2008): 53–71.

Bibliography

Adams, Heather, and Layli Phillips. "Experiences of Two-Spirit Lesbian and Gay Native Americans: An Argument for Standpoint Theory in Identity Research." *Identity: An International Journal of Theory and Research* 6, no. 3 (2006): 273–291.
Agathangelou, Anna M., D. Morgan Bassichis, and Tamara L. Spira. "Intimate Investments: Homonormativity, Global Lockdown, and the Seductions of Empire." *Radical History Review*, no. 100 (Winter 2008): 120–143.
Ahmed, Sara, and Elaine Swan. "Doing Diversity." *Policy Futures in Education* 4, no. 2 (2006): 96–100.
Aizura, Aren. "Of Borders and Homes: The Imaginary Community of (Trans) Sexual Citizenship." *Inter-Asia Cultural Studies* 7, no. 2 (June 2006): 289–309.
Ali, Mazher, Jeanette Huezo, Brian Miller, Wanjiku Mwangi, and Mike Prokosch. *State of the Dream 2011: Austerity for Whom?* Boston: United for a Fair Economy, 2011. Available at www.faireconomy.org/files/State_of_the_Dream_2011.pdf.
Allen, Timothy F. H., and Thomas W. Hoekstra. *Toward a Unified Ecology*. New York: Columbia University Press, 1992.
Al-Walid, Zev. "Pilgrimage." In *Gender Outlaws: The Next Generation*. Edited by Kate Bornstein and S. Bear Bergman, 261–267. Berkeley, CA: Seal Press, 2010.
American Academy of Orthopaedic Surgeons. *Cultural Competency Challenge*. Rosemont, IL: American Academy of Orthopaedic Surgeons, 2005.
American Psychiatric Association (APA). "Gender Identity Disorder in Children, 302.6." In *The Diagnostic and Statistical Manual of Mental Disorders*. 3rd edition. Washington, DC: APA, 1980.
———. *The Diagnostic and Statistical Manual of Mental Disorders*. 4th edition. Arlington, VA: American Psychiatric Publishing, 1994.
Anzaldúa, Gloria. *Borderlands/La Frontera: The New Mestiza*. 2nd edition. San Francisco: Aunt Lute Books, 1999.
Aspin, Clive. "The Place of Takatāpui Identity within Māori Society: Reinterpreting Māori Sexuality within a Contemporary Context." Paper presented at the Competing Diversities: Traditional Sexualities and Modern Western Sexual Identity Constructions Conference, Mexico City, 2005. Available at www.tpt.org.nz/downloads/takatapui identity.doc.
Audre Lorde Project. *TransJustice*. 2009. Available at http://alp.org/tj.
Bagemihl, Bruce. *Biological Exuberance: Animal Homosexuality and Natural Diversity*. New York: St. Martin's Press, 1999.

Bassichis, D. Morgan. *"It's War in Here": A Report on the Treatment of Transgender and Intersex People in New York State Men's Prisons.* New York: Sylvia Rivera Law Project, 2007. Available at http://srlp.org/files/warinhere.pdf.

Bassichis, Morgan, Alex Lee, and Dean Spade. "Building an Abolitionist Trans Movement with Everything We've Got." In *Captive Genders: Transembodiment and the Prison Industrial Complex.* Edited by Nat Smith and Eric A. Stanley, 15–40. Oakland, CA: AK Press, 2011.

Bauer, Greta R., Rebecca Hammond, Robb Travers, Matthias Kaay, Karin M. Hohenadel, and Michelle Boyce. "'I Don't Think This Is Theoretical; This Is Our Lives': How Erasure Impacts Health Care for Transgender People." *Journal of the Association of Nurses in AIDS Care* 20, no. 5 (September–October 2009): 348–361.

Baus, Janet, and Dan Hunt. *Cruel and Unusual.* New York: Reid Productions, 2006.

Bednarska, Dominique. "Passing Last Summer." In *Nobody Passes: Rejecting the Rules of Gender and Conformity.* Edited by Mattilda Bernstein Sycamore, 71–82. New York: Avalon, 2006.

Beemyn, Brett Genny. "Making Campuses More Inclusive of Transgender Students." *Journal of Gay and Lesbian Issues in Education* 3, no. 1 (2005): 77–87. Available at www.haworthpress.com/web/JGLED.

———. "Ways that U.S. Colleges and Universities Meet the Day-to-Day Needs of Transgender Students." Available at www.transgenderlaw.org/college/index.htm#practices.

Beemyn, Brett Genny, and Jessica Pettitt. "How Have Trans-inclusive Non-discrimination Policies Changed Institutions?" *GLBT Campus Matters,* June 2006

The Believers. Dir. Todd Holland. DVD. Frameline Films, 2006.

Bergman, S. Bear. *The Nearest Exit May Be behind You.* Vancouver, British Columbia: Arsenal Press, 2009.

Bergman, S. Bear, and J. Wallace. "Open Log: IM on Identity." *Women and Environments* (Fall–Winter 2009): 5–8.

Berres, Ben. "Does Gender Matter?" *Nature* 442 (2006): 133–136.

Betancourt, Joseph, Alexander R. Green, J. Emilio Carillo, and Commonwealth Fund. *Cultural Competence in Health Care: Emerging Frameworks and Practical Approaches.* New York: Commonwealth Fund, 2000.

Bettcher, Talia Mae. "Evil Deceivers and Make-Believers: On Transphobic Violence and the Politics of Illusion." *Hypatia* 22, no. 3 (Summer 2007): 43–65.

Bhanji, Nael. "Diasporic Trans/scriptions: Home, Trans-sexual Citizenship, and Racialized Bodies." In *Trans Gender Migrations: The Bodies, Borders and (Geo) Politics of Transition.* Edited by Trystan Cotton, 157–175. New York: Routledge, 2011.

Bhui, Kamaldeep, Nasir Warfa, Patricia Edonya, Kwame McKenzie, and Dinesh Bhugra. "Cultural Competence in Mental Health Care: A Review of Model Evaluations." *BMC Health Services Research* 7 (2007).

Bockting, Walter O., and Eric Avery. *Transgender Health and HIV Prevention: Needs Assessment Studies from Transgender Communities across the United States.* New York: Haworth Medical Press, 2005. Available at www.loc.gov/catdir/toc/ecip0513/2005015577.html.

Bockting, Walter O., Bryan E. Robinson, and B. R. Simon Rosser. "Transgender HIV Prevention: A Qualitative Needs Assessment." *AIDS Care* 10, no. 4 (August 1998): 505–525.

Boggild, Suzanne. Letter to Canadian Minister of Health and Wellness. April 16, 2009. Available at www.sherbourne.on.ca/PDFs/SherbourneHealthLetter.PDF.

Boswell, Holly. "The Transgender Alternative." *Chrysalis Quarterly* 1, no. 2 (Winter 1991–1992): 29–31.

Brake, Deborah. *Getting in the Game: Title IX and the Women's Sports Revolution.* New York: New York University Press, 2010.
Broadus, Kyler. "The Evolution of Employment Discrimination Protection for Transgendered People." In *Transgender Rights.* Edited by Paisley Currah, Richard M. Juang, and Shannon Minter, 93–101. Minneapolis: University of Minnesota Press, 2006.
Brodie, Janine. "Citizenship and Solidarity: Reflections on the Canadian Way." *Citizenship Studies* 6, no. 4 (2002): 377–394.
Brotman, Shari, Bill Ryan, Yves Jalbert, and Bill Rowe. "Reclaiming Space–Regaining Health: The Health Care Experiences of Two-Spirit People in Canada." *Journal of Gay and Lesbian Social Services* 14, no. 1 (2002): 67–86.
Brown, Wendy. "The American Nightmare: Neoliberalism, Neoconservatism and De-Democratization." *Political Theory* 34, no. 6 (December 2006): 690–715.
———, ed. "The Impossibility of Women's Studies." In *Edgework: Critical Essays on Knowledge and Politics,* 116–135. Princeton, NJ: Princeton University, 2005.
———, ed. "Neo-liberalism and the End of Liberal Democracy." In *Edgework: Critical Essays on Knowledge and Politics,* 37–59. Princeton, NJ: Princeton University, 2005.
———. "Suffering the Paradox of Human Rights." In *Left Legalism/Left Critique.* Edited by Wendy Brown and Janet Halloway, 420–434. Durham, NC: Duke University Press, 2002.
Browning, Gary K., and Andrew Kilimister. *Critical and Post-critical Political Economy.* Basingstoke, UK: Palgrave Macmillan, 2006.
Butler, Judith. "Doing Justice to Someone: Sex Reassignment and Allegories of Transsexuality." In *The Transgender Studies Reader.* Edited by Susan Stryker and Stephen Whittle, 183–192. New York: Routledge, 2006.
———. *Gender Trouble: Feminism and the Subversion of Identity.* New York: Routledge, 1990.
———."Merely Cultural." *New Left Review,* no. 227 (January–February 1998): 33–44.
———. *The Psychic Life of Power: Theories of Subjectivity.* Stanford, CA: Stanford University Press, 1997.
———. *Undoing Gender.* New York: Routledge, 2004.
Buzuvis, Erin E. "Transgender Student-Athletes and Sex-Segregated Sport: Developing Policies of Inclusion for Intercollegiate and Interscholastic Athletics." *Seton Hall Journal of Sports and Entertainment Law* 21 (2011): 1–59.
Cahn, Susan. *Coming on Strong: Gender and Sexuality in Twentieth-Century Women's Sport.* New York: Free Press, 1994.
Cameron, Loren. *Body Alchemy: Transsexual Portraits.* San Francisco: Cleis Press, 1996.
Carey, Benedict. "Straight, Gay, or Lying? Bisexuality Revisited." *New York Times,* July 5, 2005.
Carpenter, Linda Jean, and R. Vivian Acosta. *Title IX.* Champaign, IL: Human Kinetics, 2004.
Carpenter-Song, Elizabeth A., Megan Nordquest Schwallie, and Jeffrey Longhofer. "Cultural Competence Reexamined: Critique and Directions for the Future." *Psychiatric Services (Washington, D.C.)* 58, no. 10 (October 2007): 1362–1365.
Caruth, Cathy. *Unclaimed Experience: Trauma, Narrative and History.* Baltimore, MD: Johns Hopkins University Press, 1996.
Cayleff, Susan E. *Babe: The Life and Legend of Babe Didrikson Zaharias.* Urbana: University of Illinois Press, 1995.
Chae, David H., and Karina L. Walters. "Racial Discrimination and Racial Identity Attitudes in Relation to Self-Rated Health and Physical Pain and Impairment among Two-Spirit American Indians/Alaska Natives." *American Journal of Public Health* 99, no. 1 (2009): S144.

Chambers, Barbara L. "Transsexuals in the Workplace, a Guide for Employers." In *Gender Expressions*. Available at www.ren.org/tswork.pdf.

Chávez, Karma. "Border (In)Securities: Normative and Differential Belonging in LGBTQ and Immigrant Rights Discourse." *Communication and Critical/Cultural Studies* 7, no. 2 (2010): 136–155.

Chen, Anthony S. "Lives at the Center of the Periphery, Lives at the Periphery of the Center: Chinese American Masculinities and Bargaining with Hegemony." *Gender and Society* 13, no. 5 (October 1999): 584–607.

Clare, Eli. *Exile and Pride: Disability, Queerness, and Liberation*. Boston: South End Press, 1999.

Clements-Nolle, Kristen, and Ari Bachrach. "Community-Based Participatory Research with a Hidden Population: The Transgender Community Health Project." In *Community-Based Participatory Research for Health*. Edited by Meredith Minkler and Nina Wallerstein, 332–347. San Francisco: Jossey-Bass, 2003.

Cohen, Cathy. "Punks, Bulldaggers, and Welfare Queens: The Radical Potential of Queer Politics?" *Black Queer Studies*. Edited by E. Patrick Johnson and Mae Henderson, 21–51. Durham, NC: Duke University Press, 2005.

Cole, Elizabeth R. "Intersectionality and Research in Psychology." *American Psychologist* 64, no. 3 (2009): 170–180.

Connell, R. W., and Julian Wood. "Globalization and Business Masculinities." *Men and Masculinities* 7, no. 4 (April 2005): 347–364.

Coolman, Alex, Lamar Glover, and Kara Gotsch. *Still in Danger: The Ongoing Threat of Sexual Violence against Transgender Prisoners*. Los Angeles: Stop Prisoner Rape and the ACLU National Prison Project, 2005. Available at www.justdetention.org/pdf/stillindanger.pdf.

Corliss, Heather, Michael Shankle, and Matthew Moyer. "Research, Curricula, and Resources Related to Lesbian, Gay, Bisexual, and Transgender Health in U.S. Schools of Public Health." *American Journal of Public Health* 97, no. 6 (2007): 1023–1027.

Crawford, Lucas Cassidy. "Transgender without Organs? Mobilizing a Geo-affective Theory of Gender Modification." *WSQ: Women's Studies Quarterly* 36, nos. 3–4 (Fall–Winter 2008): 127–143.

Crenshaw, Kimberlé. "Mapping the Margins: Intersectionality, Identity Politics, and Violence against Women of Color." In *Critical Race Theory: The Key Writings That Formed the Movement*. Edited by Kimberlé Crenshaw, Neil Gotanda, Gary Peller, and Kendall Thomas, 357–383. New York: New Press, 1995.

Cross, Terry L., B. J. Bazron, K. W. Dennis, and M. R. Isaacs. *Towards a Culturally Competent System of Care: A Monograph on Effective Services for Minority Children Who Are Severely Emotionally Disturbed*. Washington, DC: CASSP Technical Assistance Center, Georgetown University Child Development Center, 1989.

Currah, Paisley. "The Transgender Rights Imaginary." In *Feminist and Queer Legal Theory: Intimate Encounters, Uncomfortable Conversations*. Edited by Martha Fineman, Jack E. Jackson, and Adam P. Romero, 245–258. London, UK: Ashgate, 2009.

Currah, Paisley, Richard Juang, and Shannon Minter, eds. *Transgender Rights*. Minneapolis: University of Minnesota, 2006.

Currah, Paisley, and Dean Spade. "The State We're In: Locations of Coercion and Resistance in Trans Policy, Part 1." *Sexuality Research and Social Policy* 4, no. 4 (December 2007): 1–6.

Daley, Chris, and Shannon Minter. *Trans Realities: A Legal Needs Assessment of San Francisco's Transgender Communities*. San Francisco: Transgender Law Center, 2003.

Davidson, Michael. *Concerto for the Left Hand: Disability and the Defamiliar Body.* Ann Arbor: University of Michigan Press, 2008.

Davis, Angela Y. *Are Prisons Obsolete?* New York: Seven Stories Press, 2003.

Davis, Kate, Joel Harrison, Robert Eads, Lola Cola, Q-Ball Productions, Docurama, and New Video Group. *Southern Comfort.* United States: Docurama, 2001.

De Beauvoir, Simone. *The Second Sex.* New York: Vintage, 1989.

Deleuze, Gilles. "Postscript on the Societies of Control." *October* 59 (1992): 3–7.

DelVecchio-Good, Mary-Jo, Cara James, Byron Good, and Anne Becker. "The Culture of Medicine and Racial, Ethnic, and Class Disparities in Health Care." In *The Culture of Medicine and Racial, Ethnic, and Class Disparities in Health Care.* Edited by Brian D. Smedley, Adrienne Y. Stith, Alan R. Nelson, and the Institute of Medicine (U.S.). Committee on Understanding and Eliminating Racial and Ethnic Disparities in Health Care, 594–625. Washington, D.C.: National Academy Press, 2003.

DeMarco, Vik. "Ally Exceptionalism: Problems in Approaches to Allyship Trainings." B.A. Honors Thesis, Gender and Women's Studies, University of Wisconsin, Madison, 2010.

Devor, Aaron H., and Nicholas Matte. "ONE Inc. and Reed Erickson: The Uneasy Collaboration of Gay and Trans Activism, 1964–2003." In *The Transgender Studies Reader.* Edited by Susan Stryker and Stephen Whittle, 387–405. New York: Routledge, 2006.

Diagnosing Difference. Dir. Annalise Ophelian. DVD. Floating Ophelia Productions, San Francisco, 2010.

du Gay, Paul. "Representing Globalization: Notes on the Discursive Orderings of Economic Life." In *Without Guarantees.* Edited by Paul Gilroy, Lawrence Grossberg, and Angela McRobbie, 113–125. London, UK: Verso, 2001.

Duggan, Lisa. *Twilight of Equality: Neoliberalism, Cultural Politics, and the Attack on Democracy.* Boston: Beacon Press, 2003.

Egale. "De-listing of Sex Reassignment Surgery (SRS) an Injury to Public Health: Access to SRS by Transsexuals Is Crucial to Ensuring Full Dignity and Participation" [press release].

Engels, Friedrich. "Polemic against Economic Determinism." In *Dynamics of Social Change: A Reader in Marxist Social Science.* Edited by Howard Selsam, David Goldway, and Harry Martel. New York: International Publishers, 1983.

Enke, Anne. *Finding the Movement: Sexuality, Contested Space, and Feminist Activism.* Durham, NC: Duke University Press, 2007.

Evans-Campbell, Teresa, Karen I. Fredriksen-Goldsen, Karina L. Walters, and Antony Stately. "Caregiving Experiences among American Indian Two-Spirit Men and Women: Contemporary and Historical Roles." *Journal of Gay and Lesbian Social Services* 18, nos. 3–4 (2007): 75–92.

Feinberg, Leslie. *Transgender Liberation: A Movement Whose Time Has Come.* New York: World View Forum, 1992.

———. *Transgender Warriors: Making History from Joan of Arc to Dennis Rodman.* Boston: Beacon Press, 1996.

———. "Trans Health Crisis: For Us It's Life or Death." *American Journal of Public Health* 91, no. 6 (2001): 897–900.

———. *Trans Liberation: Beyond Pink or Blue.* Boston: Beacon Press, 1998.

Feldman, Jamie L., and Joshua Goldberg. Transgender Primary Medical Care Suggested Guidelines for Clinicians in British Columbia. Vancouver, BC: Canadian Rainbow Health Coalition, Transcend Transgender Support and Education Society, and Vancouver Coastal Health, 2006.

Festle, Mary Jo. *Playing Nice: Politics and Apologies in Women's Sports.* New York: Columbia University Press, 1996.

Fisher, John A. "Sex Determination for Federal Purposes: Is Transsexual Immigration Via Marriage Permissible under the Defense of Marriage Act." *Michigan Journal of Gender and Law* 10 (2003–2004): 237–268.

Freire, Paulo. *Pedagogy of the Oppressed*. 1970; reprint, New York: Continuum, 2003.

Freire, Paulo, and Donaldo Macedo. "A Dialogue: Culture, Language, and Race." *Harvard Educational Review* 65, no. 3 (1995): 377–402.

Foucault, Michel. *The Birth of Biopolitics: Lectures at the College de France 1978–1979*. Edited by Michel Senellart. New York: Palgrave Macmillan, 2008.

———. *Discipline and Punish: The Birth of the Prison*. New York: Vintage, 1995.

———. "From the Power of Sovereignty to Power over Life." In *Society Must Be Defended: Lectures at the College de France 1975–1976*. Edited by Mauro Bertani and Alessandro Fontana, 239–264. New York: Picador, 2003.

———. *A History of Sexuality, Volume One: An Introduction*. New York: Vintage, 1990.

———. "The Subject and Power." In *Power: The Essential Works of Foucault, 1954–1984*. Volume 3. Edited by James Faubion, 326–348. New York: New Press, 2001.

Freeman, Alan David. "Legitimizing Racial Discrimination through Anti-discrimination Law: A Critical Review of Supreme Court Doctrine." *Critical Race Studies: The Key Writings That Formed the Movement*. Edited by Kimberlé Crenshaw, Neil Gotanda, Garry Peller, and Kendall Thomas, 29–45. New York: New Press, 1996.

Gabriel, Davina Anne. "The Life and Times of a Gender Outlaw: Leslie Feinberg." *TransSisters* (September–October 1993): 4–13.

Galloway, Terry. "Tough." In *Gay Shame*. Edited by David Halperin and Valerie Traub, 196–200. Chicago, IL: University of Chicago Press, 2009.

Garfinkel, Harold, ed. "Passing and the Managed Achievement of Sex Status in an 'Intersexed' Person." In *Studies in Ethnomethodology*. Upper Saddle River, NJ: Pearson Education, 1967, 116–185.

Garland-Thomson, Rosemary. *Extraordinary Bodies: Figuring Physical Disability*. New York: Routledge, 1996.

Gehi, Pooja. "Struggles from the Margins: Anti-immigrant Legislation and the Impact on Low-Income Transgender People of Color." *Women's Rights Law Report* 30 (2008): 315–346.

Gehi, Pooja S., and Gabriel Arkles. "Unraveling Injustice: Race and Class Impact of Medicaid Exclusions of Transition-Related Health Care for Transgender People." *Sexuality Research and Social Policy* 4, no. 4 (December 2007): 7–35.

Gerber, Ellen W., Jan Felshin, and Waneen Wyrick. *The American Woman in Sport*. Reading, MA: Addison-Wesley, 1974.

Gibson, Paul. "Gay Male and Lesbian Youth Suicide." *Report of the Secretary's Task Force on Youth Suicide*. Edited by Marcia R. Feinleib. Washington, DC: U.S. Department of Health and Human Services, January 1989.

Gilley, Brian Joseph. "Making Traditional Spaces: Cultural Compromise at Two-Spirit Gatherings in Oklahoma." *American Indian Culture and Research Journal* 28, no. 2 (2004): 81–95.

Ginsburg, Elaine, ed. *Passing and the Fictions of Identity*. Durham, NC: Duke University Press, 1996.

Gordon, Avery F. *Ghostly Matters: Haunting and the Sociological Imagination*. Minneapolis: University of Minnesota Press, 2008.

Government Accounting Office. "Information on Criminal Aliens Incarcerated in Federal and State Prisons and Local Jails." Congressional briefing, March 25, 2005. Available at http://gao.gov/new.items/d05337r.pdf.

Green, Jamison. "Look! No, Don't! The Visibility Dilemma for Transsexual Men." In *The Transgender Studies Reader*. Edited by Susan Stryker and Stephen Whittle, 499–508. New York: Routledge, 2006.

Greene, Maxine. *The Dialectic of Freedom*. New York: Teachers College Press, 1998.

Griffin, Pat. *Strong Women, Deep Closets: Lesbians and Homophobia in Sport*. Champaign, IL: Human Kinetics, 1998.

Griffin, Pat, and Helen J. Carroll. *On the Team: Equal Opportunities for Transgender Student-Athletes*. National Center for Lesbian Rights and the Women's Sports Foundation, 2010. Available at www.nclrights.org/site/DocServer/TransgenderStudentAthleteReport.pdf?docID=7901.

Halberstam, Judith. *In a Queer Time and Place: Transgender Bodies, Subcultural Lives*. New York: New York University Press, 2005.

Hall, Stuart. "Notes on Deconstructing 'The Popular.'" In *People's History and Socialist Theory*. Edited by Raphael Samuel, 227–240. London, UK: Routledge and Kegan Paul, 1981.

Hammonds, Evelynn. "Black (W)holes and the Geometry of Black Female Sexuality." *differences: A Journal of Feminist Cultural Studies* 6, no. 2–3 (1994): 126–145.

Hanssmann, Christoph, Darius Morrison, and Ellery Russian. "Talking, Gawking, or Getting It Done: Provider Trainings to Increase Cultural and Clinical Competence for Transgender and Gender-Nonconforming Patients and Clients." *Sexuality Research and Social Policy* 5, no. 1 (2008): 5–23.

Haraway, Donna. "Situated Knowledges: The Science Question in Feminism and the Privilege of Partial Perspective." *Feminist Studies* 14, no. 3 (1998): 575–599.

Harney, Lisa. "The Injurious Nature of Asserting Your Voice." *Questioning Transphobia*, November 14, 2008. Available at www.questioningtransphobia.com/?p=807.

Harris, Angela P. "From Stonewall to the Suburbs? Toward a Political Economy of Sexuality." *William and Mary Bill of Rights Journal* 14, no. 4 (April 2006): 1539–1582.

Hartman, Yvonne. "In Bed with the Enemy: Some Ideas on the Connections between Neo-liberalism and the Welfare State." *Current Sociology* 53, no. 1 (January 2005): 57–73.

Harvey, David. *A Brief History of Neoliberalism*. Oxford, UK: Oxford University Press, 2005.

Hewitt, Paul. *Self-Made Man: The Diary of a Man Born into a Women's Body*. London, UK: Headline, 1996.

Heywood, Leslie, and Jennifer Drake, eds. *Third Wave Agenda: Being Feminist, Doing Feminism*. Minneapolis: University of Minnesota Press, 1997.

Hirshman, Jo. "TransAction: Organizing against Capitalism and State Violence in San Francisco." *Socialist Review* 28, no. 3 (2001): 69–80.

Hoffman, Jessica. "On Prisons, Borders, Safety, and Privilege: An Open Letter to White Feminists." *make/shift* 3 (2008). Available at www.makeshiftmag.com.

Hogshead-Makar, Nancy, and Andrew Zimbalist, eds. *Equal Play: Title IX and Social Change*. Philadelphia, PA: Temple University Press, 2007.

Housing Works. 2008. Available at http://housingworks.org/.

Human Rights Campaign Foundation. *Transgender Issues in the Workplace: A Tool for Managers*. 2004. Available at www.utexas.edu/student/cec/diversity/TransgenderWorkplace.pdf.

Hutchins, Jessica, and Clive Aspin, eds. *Sexuality and the Stories of Indigenous People*. Wellington, Aotearoa, New Zealand: Huia Publishers, 2007.

INCITE! Women of Color against Violence, ed. *The Revolution Will Not Be Funded: Beyond the Non-Profit Industrial Complex*. Cambridge, MA: South End Press, 2007.

Irving, Dan. "Normalized Transgressions: Legitimizing the Transsexual Body as Productive." *Radical History Review*, no. 100 (Winter 2008): 38–59.

———. "The Self-Made Man as Risky Business: A Critical Examination of Gaining Recognition for Trans Rights through Economic Discourse." *Temple Political and Civil Rights Law Review* 18, no. 2 (Spring 2009): 375–395.

Jackson, Beth, Andrea Daley, Dick Moore, Nick Mulé, Lori Ross, and Anna Travers. "Whose Public Health? An Intersectional Approach to Sexual Orientation, Gender Identity and the Development of Public Health Goals for Canada." Discussion Paper of the Ontario Rainbow Health Partnership Project, January 2006. Available at http://www.rainbowhealthnetwork.ca/files/whose_public_health.pdf.

Jacobs, Sue-Ellen, Wesley Thomas, and Sabine Lang, eds. *Two-Spirit People: Native American Gender Identity, Sexuality, and Spirituality*. Urbana: University of Illinois Press, 1997.

Jenkins, Kuni, and Leonie Pihama. "Matauranga Wahine: Teaching Maori Women's Knowledge alongside Feminism." *Feminism and Psychology* 11, no. 3 (2001): 293–303.

Jimenez, Ramon, and Valerae Lewis. *Culturally Competent Care Guidebook*. Rosemont, IL: American Academy of Orthopedic Surgeons, 2007.

Jones, Alison. "Cross-cultural Pedagogy and the Passion for Ignorance." *Feminism and Psychology* 11, no. 3 (2001): 279–292.

———. "Ka whawhai tonu matou: The Interminable Problem of Knowing Others." Lecture, University of Auckland, October 24, 2007. Available at www.education.auckland.ac.nz/webdav/site/education/shared/about/schools/tepuna/docs/Inaugural_Lecture.pdf.

Juang, Richard M. "Transgendering the Politics of Recognition." In *Transgender Rights*. Edited by Paisley Currah, Richard Juang, and Shannon Minter, 242–261. Minneapolis: University of Minnesota, 2006.

Kelly, C. E. "Bringing Homophobia out of the Closet: Antigay Bias within the Patient-Physician Relationship." *Pharos of Alpha Omega Alpha–Honor Medical Society. Alpha Omega Alpha* 55, no. 1 (1992): 2–8.

Kenagy, Gretchen. Transgender Health: Findings from Two Needs Assessment Studies in Philadelphia. *Health and Social Work* 30, no. 1 (February 2005): 19–26.

Kessler, Suzanne, and Wendy McKenna. *Gender: An Ethnomethodological Approach*. Chicago, IL: University of Chicago Press, 1978.

Khosla, Dhillon. *Both Sides Now: One Man's Journey through Womanhood*. New York: Penguin, 2006.

Klamen, Debra L., Linda S. Grossman, and David R. Kopacz. "Medical Student Homophobia." *Journal of Homosexuality* 37, no. 1 (1999): 53–63.

Kosciw, Joseph G., Elizabeth M. Diaz, and Emily A. Greytak. "Executive Summary." *The 2007 National School Climate Survey: Key Findings on the Experiences of Lesbian, Gay, Bisexual and Transgender Youth in Our Nation's Schools*. New York: Gay, Lesbian and Straight Education Network, 2008. Available at www.glsen.org/binary-data/GLSEN_ATTACHMENTS/file/000/001/1306-1.pdf

———. *The 2009 National School Climate Survey: The Experience of Lesbian, Gay, Bisexual and Transgender Youth in Our Nation's Schools*. New York: Gay, Lesbian and Straight Education Network, 2010. Available at www.glsen.org/binary-data/GLSEN_ATTACHMENTS/file/000/001/1675-5.PDF.

Koyama, Emi. "Whose Feminism Is It Anyway? The Unspoken Racism of the Trans Inclusion Debate." In *The Transgender Studies Reader*. Edited by Susan Stryker and Stephen Whittle, 698–704. New York: Routledge, 2006.

Kumashiro, Kevin. "Toward a Theory of Anti-oppressive Education." *Review of Educational Research* 70, no. 1 (2000): 25–53.

Lamble, Sarah. "Retelling Racialized Violence, Remaking White Innocence: The Politics of Interlocking Oppressions in Transgender Day of Remembrance." *Sexuality Research and Social Policy: Journal of NSRC* 5, no. 1 (March 2008): 24–42.

Lande, Russ. "Statistics and the Partitioning of Species Diversity, and Similarity among Multiple Communities." *Oikos* 76 (1996): 5–13.

Lawrence, Marta. *Transgender Policy Approved.* September 13, 2011, NCAA.org. Available at www.ncaa.org/wps/wcm/connect/public/NCAA/Resources/Latest+News/2011/September/Transgender+policy+approved.

Lee, Alexander L. *Gendered Crime and Punishment: Strategies to Protect Transgender, Gender Variant and Intersex People in America's Prisons.* Parts 1 and 2. Gender Identity Center *Trans in Prison Journal* (Summer 2004), Gender Identity Center *Trans in Prison Journal* (Fall 2004).

Lev, Arlene Istar. *Transgender Emergence: Therapeutic Guidelines for Working with Gender-Variant People and Their Families.* New York: Haworth Clinical Practice Press, 2004.

Loeb, Elizabeth. "Cutting It Off: Bodily Integrity, Identity Disorders, and the Sovereign Stakes of Corporeal Desire in U.S. Law." *WSQ: Women's Studies Quarterly* 36, nos. 3-4 (Fall–Winter 2008): 44–63.

Lombardi, Emilia, and Talia Bettcher. "Lesbian, Gay, Bisexual, and Transgender/Transsexual Individuals." In *Social Injustice and Public Health.* Edited by Barry S. Levy and Victor W. Sidel, 130–144. New York: Oxford University Press, 2006.

Lowe, Gary R., and P. Nelson Reid. *The Professionalization of Poverty: Social Work and the Poor in the Twentieth Century.* New York: Aldine de Gruyter, 1999.

Luibhéid, Eithne. "Sexuality, Migration, and the Shifting Line Between Legal and Illegal Status." *GLQ: A Journal of Lesbian and Gay Studies* 14, no. 2-3 (2008): 289–315.

Lupton, Deborah. 1997. "Foucault and the Medicalization Critique." In *Foucault, Health and Medicine.* Edited by Alan R. Petersen and Robin Bunton, 94–110. London, UK: Routledge.

Lurie, Samuel. "Identifying Training Needs of Health Care Providers Related to Treatment and Care of Transgendered Patients: A Qualitative Needs Assessment Conducted in New England." *International Journal of Transgenderism* 8, nos. 2-3 (2005): 93–112.

———. *Transgender Awareness Training and Advocacy.* 2009. Available at www.tgtrain.org/index.html.

Magnani, Lauraet, and Harmon L. Wray. *Beyond Prisons: A New Interfaith Paradigm for Our Failed Prison System, a Report by the American Friends Service Committee, Criminal Justice Task Force.* Minneapolis, Minnesota: Fortress Press, 2006.

Man, Christopher D., and John P. Cronan. "Forecasting Sexual Abuse in Prison: The Prison Subculture of Masculinity as a Backdrop for 'Deliberate Indifference.'" *Journal of Criminal Law and Criminology* 92, no. 1 (2001): 127–186.

Mananzala, Rickke, and Dean Spade. "The Nonprofit Industrial Complex and Trans Resistance." *Sexuality Research and Social Policy* 5, no. 1 (2008): 53–71.

Marx, Karl. "Theses on Feuerbach." In *The Marx-Engels Reader.* Edited by Robert Tucker, 143–145. 2nd edition. New York: W. W. Norton, 1978.

McAlister, Joan Faber. "Lives of the Mind/Body: Alarming Notes on Tenure and Biological Clocks." *Women's Studies in Communication* 31, no. 2 (2008): 218–225.

McBride, Stephen, and John Shields. *Dismantling a Nation: The Transition to Corporate Rule in Canada.* 2nd edition. Halifax, Nova Scotia: Fernwood Press, 1997.

McDonagh, Eileen, and Laura Pappano. *Playing with the Boys.* New York: Oxford University Press, 2008.

McDowell, Linda. "Masculinity, Identity and Labour Market Change: Some Reflections on the Implications of Thinking Relationally about Difference and the Politics of Inclusion." *Geografiska Annaler* 86, no. B1 (2004): 45–56.

McRuer, Robert. "Shameful Sites: Locating Queerness and Disability." In *Gay Shame*. Edited by David Halperin and Valerie Traub, 181–187. Chicago, IL: University of Chicago Press, 2009.

Mendoza, Inés María. "Testimony to the Hays Commission." In *Doña Inés María Mendoza y la batalla del idioma: Cartas 1937–1938*. Edited by C. Natal Rosario, 19. San Juan, Puerto Rico: Fundación Luis Muñoz Marín, 2004.

Meyer, I. H. "Why Lesbian, Gay, Bisexual, and Transgender Public Health?" *American Journal of Public Health* 91 (2001): 856–859.

Meyer-Cook, Fiona, and Diane Labelle. "Namaji: Two-Spirit Organizing in Montreal, Canada." *Journal of Gay and Lesbian Social Services* 16, no. 1 (2004): 29–51.

Meyerowitz, Joanne. *How Sex Changed: A History of Transsexuality in the United States*. London, UK: Harvard University Press, 2002.

Minkler, Meredith, and Nina Wallerstein. *Community-Based Participatory Research for Health*. San Francisco: Jossey-Bass, 2003.

Minter, Shannon Price. "Do Transsexuals Dream of Gay Rights? Getting Real about Transgender Inclusion." In *Transgender Rights*. Edited by Paisley Currah, Richard M. Juang, and Shannon Minter, 141–170. Minneapolis: University of Minnesota Press, 2006.

Mitropoulos, Angela. "Halt, Who Goes There?" *City-State: A Critical Reader on Surveillance and Social Control*. Edited by Louise Boon-Kuo and Gavin Sullivan, 73–74. Sydney, Australia: UTS Community Law and Legal Research Centre, 2002.

Mogul, Joey L., Andrea J. Ritchie, and Kay Whitlock. *Queer (In)Justice*. Boston: Beacon Press, 2011.

Morgan, Robin. *Going Too Far*. New York: Random House, 1977.

Moulier-Boutang, Yann, and Stany Grelet. "The Art of Flight: An Interview with Yann Moulier-Boutang." *Rethinking Marxism* 13, no. 3–4 (2001): 227–235.

Muñoz, Vic. "Trapped in the Wrong Classroom: Making Decolonial Trans-cultural Spaces in Women's Studies." *WSQ: Women's Studies Quarterly* 36, nos. 3–4 (Fall–Winter 2008): 300–301.

Najmabadi, Afsaneh. "Transing and Transpassing across Sex-Gender Walls in Iran." *WSQ: Women's Studies Quarterly* 36, nos. 3–4 (Fall–Winter 2008): 23–42.

Namaste, Viviane. *Invisible Lives: The Erasure of Transsexual and Transgendered People*. Chicago, IL: University of Chicago Press, 2000.

———. *Sex Change, Social Change: Reflections on Identity, Institutions, and Imperialism*. Toronto, Ontario: Women's Press, 2005.

Nangeroni, Nancy. *GenderTalk* (radio show), no. 181 (November 25, 1998). Available at www.gendertalk.com/radio/programs/150/gt181.shtml.

National Center for Cultural Competence. *Final Report: State-Level Strategies to Address Health and Mental Health Disparities through Cultural and Linguistic Competency Training and Licensure: An Environmental Scan of Factors Related to Legislative and Regulatory Actions in States*. Washington, DC: Georgetown University Center for Child and Human Development, Georgetown University Medical Center, 2008.

National Center for Transgender Equality. "Hate Crimes." 2008. Available at www.nctequality.org/Hate_Crimes.asp.2008.

National Gay and Lesbian Task Force. "Jurisdictions with Explicitly Transgender-Inclusive Non-discrimination Laws." 2008. Available at http://thetaskforce.org/downloads/reports/fact_sheets/all_jurisdictions_w_pop 8_08.pdf.

Nestle, Joan, ed. "The Femme Question." In *The Persistent Desire: A Butch Femme Reader*, 138–146. Boston: Alyson Publications, 1992.

Noble, Jean Bobby. *Sons of the Movement: FTMs Risking Incoherence on a Post-Queer Cultural Landscape*. Toronto, Ontario: Women's Press, 2006.

Papadopoulos, Dimitris, Niamh Stephenson, and Vassilis Tsianos. *Escape Routes: Control and Subversion in the 21st Century*. London, UK: Pluto Press, 2008.

The PEW Center on the States. *One in 100: Behind Bars in America 2008*. 2008. Available at www.pewcenteronthestates.org/uploadedFiles/8015PCTS_Prison08_FINAL_2-1-1_FORWEB.pdf.

Pihama, Leonie. "Tihei Mauri Ora: Honouring Our Voices. Mana Wahine as a Kaupapa Maori Theoretical Framework." Ph.D. diss., University of Auckland, 2001. Available at www.kaupapamaori.com/theory/5/.

Pinto, Rogério M., Rita Melendez, and Anya Spector. "Male-to-Female Transgender Individuals Building Social Support and Capital from within a Gender-Focused Network." *Journal of Gay and Lesbian Social Services* 20, no. 3 (2008): 203–220.

Pollack, Rachel. "Archetypal Transsexuality." *TransSisters: The Journal of Transsexual Feminism*, no. 9 (Summer 1995): 39–41.

Pon, G. "Cultural Competence as New Racism: An Ontology of Forgetting." *Journal of Progressive Human Services* 20 (2009): 59–71.

Prosser, Jay. *Second Skins*. New York: Columbia University Press, 1998.

Puar, Jasbir. *Terrorist Assemblages: Homonationalism in Queer Times*. Durham, NC: Duke University Press, 2007.

Queers for Economic Justice. "Queers and Immigration: A Vision Statement." *Scholar and Feminist Online* 6, no. 33 (2008). Available at http://q4ej.org/tag/welfare-justice-campaign.

Raymond, Janice G. *The Transsexual Empire: The Making of the She-Male*. Boston: Beacon Press, 1979.

Razack, Sherene H. *Race, Space and the Law: Unmapping a White Settler Society*. Toronto: Between the Lines Press, 2002.

Read, Jason. *The Micro-politics of Capital: Marx and the Prehistory of the Present*. New York: State University of New York Press, 2003.

Renn, Kristen A., and Brent L. Bilodeau. "Leadership Identity Development among Lesbian, Gay, Bisexual, and Transgender Student Leaders." *National Association of Student Personnel Administrators (NASPA) Journal* 42, no. 3 (2005): 342–367.

Richardson, Troy, and Sofia Villenes. "'Other Encounters': Dances with Whiteness in Multicultural Education." *Educational Theory* 50, no. 2 (2000): 255–273.

Rieger, Gerulf, Meredith Chivers, and Michael Bailey. "Sexual Arousal Patterns of Bisexual Men." *Psychological Science: A Journal of the American Psychological Society/APS* 16, no. 8 (2005): 579–584.

Rios-Cardensa, Oscar, M. Scarlett Tudor, and Molly R. Morris. "Female Preference Variation Has Implications for the Maintenance of an Alternative Mating Strategy in a Swordtail Fish." *Animal Behaviour* 74 (2007): 633–640.

Rivera, Sylvia. "Queens in Exile, the Forgotten Ones." In *Genderqueer: Voices from beyond the Binary*. Edited by Joan Nestle, Riki Wilchins, and Clare Howell, 67–85. Los Angeles: Alyson Books, 2002.

Robert Wood Johnson Foundation. *State-Level Strategies to Address Health and Mental Health Disparities through Cultural and Linguistic Competency Training and Licensure: An Environmental Scan of Factors Related to Legislative and Regulatory Actions in States*. Study conducted during 2007–2008, RWJF ID#59024.

Rondahl, Gerd. "Students' Inadequate Knowledge about Lesbian, Gay, Bisexual and Transgender Persons." *International Journal of Nursing Education Scholarship* 6, no. 1 (April 2009): 1–15.

Rose, Nikolas. "Governing the Enterprising Self." In *The Values of the Enterprise Culture: The Moral Debate*. Edited by Paul Heelas and Paul Morris, 141–164. New York: Routledge, 1992.

Rosenberg, Sharon. "At Women's Studies Edge: Thoughts toward Remembering a Troubled and Troubling Project of the Modern University." In *Troubling Women's Studies: Past, Presents and Possibilities*. Edited by Ann Braithwaite, Susan Heald, Susanne Luhmann, and Sharon Rosenberg, 195–239. Vancouver, British Columbia: Sumach Press, 2004.

Roughgarden, Joan. *Evolution's Rainbow: Diversity, Gender, and Sexuality in Nature and People*. Berkeley: University of California Press, 2004.

Rubin, Henry. *Self-Made Men: Identity and Embodiment amongst Transsexual Men*. Nashville, TN: Vanderbilt University Press, 2003.

Saad-Filho, Alfredo, and Deborah Johnston. *Neoliberalism: A Critical Reader*. London, UK: Pluto Press, 2005.

Sakamoto, Izumi. "An Anti-oppressive Approach to Cultural Competence." *Canadian Social Work Review* 24, no. 1 (2007): 105–114.

Salamon, Gayle. *Assuming a Body: Transgender and Rhetorics of Materiality*. New York: Columbia University Press, 2010.

Samuels, Ellen. "My Body, My Closet: Invisible Disability and the Limits of Coming-Out Discourse." *GLQ: A Journal of Lesbian and Gay Studies* 9, nos. 1–2 (2003): 233–255.

Sandahl, Carrie. "Ahh, Freak Out! Metaphors of Disability and Femaleness in Performance." *Theatre Topics* 9, no. 1 (1999): 11–30.

Schick, Carol, JoAnn Jaffe, and Ailsa M. Watkinson, eds. *Contesting Fundamentalisms*. Halifax, Nova Scotia: Fernwood Publishing, 2004.

Schmitt, Carl. *Political Theology: Four Chapters on the Concept of Sovereignty*. Translated by George Schwab. Chicago, IL: University of Chicago Press, 1985.

Scott, Joan. "The Evidence of Experience." *Critical Inquiry* 17, no. 4 (Summer 1991): 363–387.

Sedgwick, Eve K. *Epistemology of the Closet*. Berkeley: University of California Press, 1990.

Sefa Dei, G., and A. Kempf. *Anti-colonialism and Education: The Politics of Resistance*. Rotterdam, The Netherlands: Sense Publishers, 2006.

Serano, Julia. "Rethinking Sexism: How Trans Women Challenge Feminism." *AlterNet.org*, August 5, 2008. Available at www.alternet.org/reproductivejustice/93826.

———. *Whipping Girl: A Transsexual Woman on Sexism and the Scapegoating of Femininity*. Emeryville, CA: Seal Press, 2007.

Seuffert, Nan. "Reflections on Transgender Immigration." *Griffith Law Review* 18, no. 3 (2009): 428–452.

Shaw, Susan J. "The Politics of Recognition in Culturally Appropriate Care." *Medical Anthropology Quarterly* 19, no. 3 (2005): 290–309.

Shield, Sonja. "The Doctor Won't See You Now: Rights of Transgender Adolescents to Sex Reassignment Treatment." *New York University Review of Law and Social Change* 31 no. 2 (2007): 361–433.

Siebers, Tobin. *Disability Theory*. Ann Arbor: University of Michigan Press, 2008.

Singer, Benjamin. "From the Medical Gaze to Sublime Mutations: The Ethics of (Re)Viewing Non-normative Body Images." In *The Transgender Studies Reader*. Edited by Susan Stryker and Stephen Whittle, 601–620. New York: Routledge, 2006.

Skeggs, Beverly. *Class, Self, Culture*. London, UK: Routledge, 2004.
Smith, Andrea. "Native Studies and Critical Pedagogy: Beyond the Academic-Industrial Complex." In *Activist Scholarship: Antiracism, Feminism, and Social Change*. Edited by Julia Sudbury and Margo Okazawa-Rey, 37–54. Boulder, CO: Paradigm Publishers, 2009.
Smith, Graham. "Indigenous Struggle for the Transformation of Education and Schooling." Keynote Address, Alaskan Federation and Natives (AFN) Convention, Anchorage, Alaska, 2003. Available at www.kaupapamaori.com/theory/5/.
Smith, Linda Tuhiwai. *Decolonizing Methodologies: Research and Indigenous Peoples*. 1999. Reprint, London, UK: Zed Books, 2002.
Spade, Dean. "Compliance Is Gendered: Struggling for Gender Self-Determination in a Hostile Economy." In *Transgender Rights*. Edited by Paisley Currah, Richard M. Juang, and Shannon Minter, 217–240. Minneapolis: University of Minnesota Press, 2006.
———. "Documenting Gender." *Hastings Law Journal* 59, no. 4 (2008): 731–841.
———. "Mutilating Gender." In *The Transgender Studies Reader*. Edited by Susan Stryker and Stephen Whittle, 315–332. New York: Routledge, 2006.
———. *Normal Life: Administrative Violence, Critical Trans Politics and the Limits of Law*. Brooklyn, NY: South End Press, forthcoming.
———. "Trans Law and Politics on a Neoliberal Landscape." *Temple Political and Civil Rights Law Review* 18, no. 2 (2009): 353–373.
Spade, Dean, and Rickke Mananzala. "The Non-profit Industrial Complex and Trans Resistance." *Sexuality Research and Social Policy: Journal of NSRC* 5, no. 1 (March 2008): 53–71.
Spade, Dean, and Craig Willse. "Confronting the Limits of Gay Hate Crimes Activism: A Radical Critique." *Chicano-Latino Law Review* 21, no. 2 (Spring 2000): 38–52.
Spivak, Gayatri. "Can the Subaltern Speak?" *Marxism and the Interpretation of Culture*. Edited by Cary Nelson and Larry Grossberg, 271–316. Chicago: University of Illinois Press, 1988.
Stephen, Lynn. "Sexualities and Genders in Zapotec Oaxaca." *Latin American Perspectives* 29, no. 2 (2002): 41–59.
Stimson, Adrian A. "Two Spirited for You: The Absence of 'Two Spirit' People in Western Culture and Media." *West Coast Line* 40, no. 1 (2006): 69–119.
Stone, Sandy. "The Empire Strikes Back: A Posttranssexual Manifesto." In *Body Guards: The Cultural Politics of Gender Ambiguity*. Edited by Julia Epstein and Kristina Straub, 280–304. London, UK: Routledge, 1991.
Stotzer, Rebecca L. "Gender Identity and Hate Crimes: Violence against Transgender People in Los Angeles County." *Sexuality Research and Social Policy: Journal of NSRC* 5, no. 1 (March 2008): 43–52.
Stryker, Susan. "(De)Subjugated Knowledges: An Introduction to Transgender Studies." In *The Transgender Studies Reader*. Edited by Susan Stryker and Stephen Whittle, 1–18. New York: Routledge, 2006.
———. *Transgender History*. Berkeley, CA: Seal Press, 2008.
———. "Transgender Studies: Queer Theory's Evil Twin." *GLQ: A Journal of Lesbian and Gay Studies* 10, no. 2 (2004): 212–215.
———. "We Who Are Sexy: Christine Jorgensen's Transsexual Whiteness in the Postcolonial Philippines." *Social Semiotics* 19 (2009): 79–91.
Stryker, Susan, Paisley Currah, and Lisa Jean Moore. "Introduction: Trans-, Trans, or Transgender?" *WSQ: Women's Studies Quarterly* 36, nos. 3–4 (Fall–Winter 2008): 11–22.

Sturm, Susan, and Lani Guinier. "The Future of Affirmative Action: Reclaiming the Innovative Ideal." *California Law Review* 84, no. 4 (July 1996): 953.

Sue, Derald Wing, Rosie P. Bingham, Lisa Porche-Burke, and Melba Vasquez. "The Diversification of Psychology: A Multicultural Revolution." *American Psychologist* 54 (1999): 1061–1069.

Sullivan, Nikki. "The Role of Medicine in the (Trans)Formation of 'Wrong' Bodies." *Body and Society* 14 (2008): 105–116.

———. "Transmogrification: (Un)Becoming Other(s)." In *The Transgender Studies Reader*. Edited by Susan Stryker and Stephen Whittle, 552–563. New York: Routledge, 2006.

Sylvia Rivera Law Project. *Training and Reference Materials*. 2010. Available at http://srlp.org/resources/trainingmaterials.

Taylor, Janelle. "Confronting 'culture' in medicine's 'culture of no culture.'" *Academic Medicine: Journal of the Association of American Medical Colleges* 78, no. 6 (2003): 555–559.

Thomas, Wesley, and Sue-Ellen Jacobs. "'. . . And We Are Still Here': From Berdache to Two-Spirit People." *American Indian Culture and Research Journal* 23, no. 2 (1999): 91–107.

Tinbergen, Lukas. "The Natural Control of Insects in Pinewoods: I. Factors Influencing the Intensity of Predation by Song Birds." *Archives Neerlandaises de Zoologie* 13 (1960): 265–343.

Tokawa, Kenji. "Why You Don't Have to Choose a White Boy Name to Be a Man in This World." In *Gender Outlaws: The Next Generation*. Edited by Kate Bornstein and S. Bear Bergman, 207–212. Berkeley: Seal Press, 2010.

Towle, Evan B., and Lynn M. Morgan. "Romancing the Transgender Native: Rethinking the Use of the 'Third Gender' Concept." In *The Transgender Studies Reader*. Edited by Susan Stryker and Stephen Whittle, 666–684. New York: Routledge, 2006.

TransPULSE. 2010. Available at www.transpulse.ca.

Trensniowski, Alex. "He's Having a Baby." *People,* April 14, 2008, 54–60

U.S. Department of Health and Human Services. *Shortage Designation: HPSAs, MUAs and MUPs in Health Resources and Services Administration*. 2009. Available at http://bhpr.hrsa.gov/shortage/muaguide.htm.

U.S. Department of Justice. "Key Crime and Justice Facts at a Glance." 2009. Available at www.ojp.usdoj.gov/bjs/glance.htm.

Valentine, David. *Imagining Transgender: An Ethnography of a Category*. Durham, NC: Duke University Press, 2007.

Vancouver Coastal Health. *Transgender Health Program*. 2010. Available at http://transhealth.vch.ca/resources/careguidelines.html.

Van Dernoot Lipsky, Laura, and Connie Buck. *Trauma Stewardship: An Everyday Guide to Caring for Self While Caring for Others*. San Francisco: Berrett-Koehler, 2009.

Varjas, Kris, Brian Dew, Megan Marshall, Emily Graybill, Anneliese Singh, Joel Meyers, and Lamar Birckbichler. "Bullying in Schools towards Sexual Minority Youth." *Journal of School Violence* 7, no. 2 (2008): 59–86.

Virno, Paolo. "Virtuosity and Revolution: The Political Theory of Exodus." In *Radical Thought in Italy: A Potential Politics*. Edited by Michael Hardt and Paolo Virno, 13–37. Minneapolis: University of Minnesota Press, 1996.

Wagner, Sally Roesh. *Sisters in Spirit: Haudenosaunee (Iroquois) Influence on Early American Feminists*. Summertown, TN: Native Voices, 2001.

Waitzkin, Howard, and Barbara Waterman. *The Exploitation of Illness in Capitalist Society*. Indianapolis, IN: Bobbs-Merrill, 1974.

Wallerstein, Nina, and Bonnie Duran. "Using Community-Based Participatory Research to Address Health Disparities." *Health Promotion Practice* 7, no. 3 (2006): 312–323.

Walmsley, Roy. *World Prison Population List.* 7th edition. London, UK: International Centre for Prison Studies, 2005.

Walters, Karina, and Jane Simoni. "Reconceptualizing Native Women's Health: An 'Indigenist' Stress-Coping Model." *American Journal of Public Health* 92 (2002): 520–524.

Walters, Karina L., Teresa Evans-Campbell, Jane M. Simoni, Theresa Ronquillo, and Rupaleem Bhuyan. "'My Spirit in My Heart': Identity Experiences and Challenges among American Indian Two-Spirit Women." *Journal of Lesbian Studies* 10, nos. 1–2 (2006): 125–149.

Walworth, Janis. *Transsexual Workers: An Employers Guide.* Los Angeles: Center for Gender Sanity, 1998.

Weiss, Jillian T. *Transgender Workplace Diversity: Policy Tools, Training Issues and Communication Strategies for HR and Legal Professionals.* Charleston, SC: BookSurge Publishing, 2007.

Wertz, Kristina, and Masen Davis. "When Laws Are Not Enough: A Study of the Economic Health of Transgender People and the Need for a Multidisciplinary Approach to Economic Justice." *Seattle Journal of Social Justice* 8, no. 2 (Spring–Summer 2010): 467–489.

Weston, Kath. *Render Me, Gender Me: Lesbians Talk Sex, Class, Color, Nation, Studmuffins.* New York: Columbia University Press, 1996.

White, David M. "The Requirement of Race-Conscious Evaluation of LSAT Scores for Equitable Law School Admission." *Berkeley La Raza Law Journal* 12, no. 2 (Fall 2001): 399.

Whittle, Stephen. *Employment Discrimination and Transsexual People.* Available at www.gires.org.uk/assets/employment-dis-full-paper.pdf.

———. "Where Did We Go Wrong? Feminism and Trans Theory: Two Teams on the Same Side?" In *The Transgender Studies Reader.* Edited by Susan Stryker and Stephen Whittle, 194–202. New York: Routledge, 2006.

Wiegman, Robyn. "Feminism, Institutionalism, and the Idiom of Failure." In *Women's Studies on the Edge.* Edited by Joan Wallach Scott, 39–66. Durham, NC: Routledge, 2008.

———, ed. "Introduction: On Location." *Women's Studies on Its Own: A Next Wave Reader in Institutional Change,* 1–44. Durham, NC: Duke University Press, 2002.

———, ed. "The Progress of Gender: Whither 'Women'?" *Women's Studies on Its Own: A Next Wave Reader in Institutional Change,* 106–140. Durham, NC: Duke University Press, 2002.

Wilchins, Riki Anne. *Read My Lips: Sexual Subversion and the End of Gender.* New York: Firebrand Books, 1997.

Williams, Raymond. *Marxism and Literature.* Oxford, UK: Oxford University Press, 1977.

Wilson, Robin, and Paul Fain. "Lawrence Summers Quits as Harvard President in Advance of New No-Confidence Vote; Derek Bok to Step In." *Chronicle of Higher Education,* February 21, 2006.

Winters, Kelley. *Gender Madness in American Psychiatry: Essays from the Struggle for Dignity.* Seattle, WA: BookSurge Publishing, 2008.

Wong, Laiana. "Speaking Hawaiian in Hawaiian." Presentation at the annual meeting of the American Educational Research Association, 2008.

World Professional Association for Transgender Health. *WPATH Standards of Care.* Available at www.wpath.org/publications_standards.cfm.

Wyndzen, Madeline. "A Personal and Scientific Look at a Mental Illness Model of Transgenderism." *American Psychological Association Division 44 Newsletter* (Spring 2004). Available at www.genderpsychology.org/autogynephilia/apa_div_44.html.

Xavier, Jessica, Marilyn Bobbin, Ben Singer, and Earline Budd. "A Needs Assessment of Transgendered People of Color Living in Washington, DC." *International Journal of Transgenderism* 8, nos. 2–3 (2005): 31–47.

Yoshino, Kenji. *Covering: The Hidden Assault on Our Civil Rights.* New York: Random House, 2006.

Contributors

Aren Z. Aizura is the Mellon Postdoctoral Associate at the Institute for Research on Women and Department of Gender and Women's Studies at Rutgers University, New Brunswick, New Jersey. His research focuses on how biopolitical technologies of race, gender, transnationality, medicalization, and political economy shape and are shaped by transgender and queer bodies. His journal articles have appeared in *Asian Studies Review, Inter-Asia Cultural Studies,* and *Medical Anthropology: Cross-Cultural Studies in Health and Illness*; book chapters are included in *Queer Bangkok* (2011) and *Transgender Migrations: The Bodies, Borders, and Politics of Transition* (2011). He is the co-editor with Susan Stryker of the forthcoming *Transgender Studies Reader*, Volume 2.

Ryka Aoki de la Cruz is a professor of English at Santa Monica College and author of *Seasonal Velocities: Poems, Stories and Essays.* She has been featured at the National Queer Arts Festival, the National Gay and Lesbian Theatre Festival, and many others. Two of her compositions were adopted as official "Songs of Peace" by the American Association of Hiroshima-Nagasaki A-Bomb Survivors. She has been honored by the California State Senate for her work with Trans/Giving, Los Angeles's only art/performance series dedicated to trans, genderqueer, and intersex artists. She was formerly head judo coach at the University of California, Los Angeles, and Cornell University.

A. Finn Enke is an associate professor in the Departments of Gender and Women's Studies and History, as well as director of LGBT Studies at the University of Wisconsin, Madison. Enke is the author of *Finding the Movement: Sexuality, Contested Space, and Feminist Activism* (2007). Work in progress includes *Gender Changes: Transfeminist Activism from the 1960s to the New Millennium.*

Kate Forbes is a former assistant professor of science, mathematics, and technology at State University of New York Empire State College in Syracuse. She now works for a private IT firm. In her spare time, she blogs at Shakesville.com and at her personal blog (acuntofonesown.org), writes, and plays roller derby.

Pat Griffin is a professor emerita in the Social Justice Education Program at the University of Massachusetts, Amherst, and the former director of It Takes a Team! Education Campaign for Lesbian, Gay, Bisexual, Transgender Issues in Sport, an initiative of the Women's Sports Foundation. She is author of *Strong Women, Deep Closets: Lesbian and Homophobia in Sports* (1998) and co-editor of *Teaching for Diversity and Social Justice: A Sourcebook for Teachers and Trainers*, second edition (2007). In 2007, Dr. Griffin was named one of the top one hundred sport educators in the United States by the Institute for International Sport. She played basketball and field hockey and swam at the University of Maryland. She coached high school basketball, field hockey, and softball in Montgomery County, Maryland, and coached swimming and diving at the University of Massachusetts–Amherst.

Christoph Hanssmann recently began a Ph.D. program in sociology at the University of California–San Francisco. His Master's degree work in public health at the University of Washington focused on health in marginalized communities and community-based participatory research. He worked as a health educator at Seattle Children's Hospital and has been involved in a variety of community organizing and training projects, many of which focused on issues concerning transgender, gender-nonconforming, and LGBQ communities in the context of social, economic, racial, and health justice. He is also engaged in building frameworks for research, advocacy, and training that increase communities' self-determination and access to resources.

Dan Irving is an assistant professor teaching within the Sexuality Studies and Human Rights programs in the Institute of Interdisciplinary Studies at Carleton University, Ottawa. He has published in *Radical History Review* and *Temple Political and Civil Rights Law Review*.

Vic Muñoz is professor of psychology and gender studies at Wells College, Aurora, New York. Dr. Muñoz teaches in women's and gender studies, psychology, and First Nations and indigenous studies and is the author of *Where "Something Catches": Work, Love, and Identity in Youth* (1995).

Bobby Noble is associate professor of English and sexuality studies at York University, Toronto. Through cultural studies, he analyzes contemporary constructions of sex, sexuality, bodies, race, gender, and masculinity as well as transgender and transsexual identities in culture and social movements. Dr. Noble has published numerous articles as well as two monographs: *Masculinities without Men?* (2004) and *Sons of the Movement: FTMs Risking Incoherence on a Post-*

Queer Cultural Landscape (2006). He is also co-editor of *The Drag King Anthology* (2003), a Lambda Literary Finalist.

Clark A. Pomerleau is an assistant professor of history at the University of North Texas. Dr. Pomerleau teaches women's, gender, and sexuality history. Current research covers second-wave feminisms, feminist masculinities, the significance of gender-role stereotypes in post–World War II U.S. society, and American social-justice movements. Published works include articles in *Women's Studies Quarterly* and the *Journal of Homosexuality*. His current book in progress focuses on a feminist community education collective as a lens providing new perspective on activism in the 1970s–1980s.

Julia Serano is a writer, performer, and activist. She is the author of *Whipping Girl: A Transsexual Woman on Sexism and the Scapegoating of Femininity* (2007), a collection of personal essays that reveal how misogyny frames popular assumptions about femininity and shapes many of the myths and misconceptions about transsexual women. Her other writings have appeared in anthologies (including *Gender Outlaws: The Next Generation*; *Word Warriors: 30 Leaders in the Women's Spoken Word Movement*; and *Yes Means Yes: Visions of Female Sexual Power and a World without Rape*) and in feminist, queer, pop culture and literary magazines and websites (such as *Bitch*, AlterNet.org, *Out*, Feministing.com, and *make/shift*) and have been used as teaching materials in gender studies, queer studies, psychology, and human sexuality courses in colleges across North America. Dr. Serano also works as a researcher in the field of developmental and evolutionary biology at the University of California, Berkeley.

Dean Spade was a Williams Institute Law Teaching Fellow at the University of California, Los Angeles, Law School and Harvard Law School prior to joining the faculty of Seattle University. In 2002, he founded the Sylvia Rivera Law Project (www.srlp.org), a nonprofit law collective that provides free legal services to transgender, intersex, and gender-nonconforming people who are low-income and/or people of color. While working at SRLP, he taught classes focusing on sexual orientation, gender identity, and law at Columbia and Harvard law schools. Current research interests include the impact of the War on Terror on transgender rights, the bureaucratization of trans identities, and models of nonprofit governance in social movements. He is the author of *Normal Life: Administrative Violence, Critical Trans Politics and the Limits of Law* (2011).

Index

ableism, 23, 186; subjectivities and, 166
academic-industrial complex, 46. *See also* the academy
academy, the: activism and scholarship in, 128–131, 223n70; biases within, 37–42; coming out in, 37; commodification of knowledge and, 46, 51–52, 56; corporatization of, 46; covering and, 41–43; diversity in, 40, 42–43, 130; gender transition and, 36–37, 43–44; medical research and, 37–40; "queer time" and, 36–37; women's studies and, 36–38, 44. *See also* higher education
access: anti-discrimination laws and, 185, 190–191; to employment, 87, 190–191; gender/sex nonconformity and, 64, 212–213nn17–18, 222n32; to health care, 37–38, 93–95, 113–118, 124, 129–130, 165–167; to information and resources in higher education, 86–88; as lens in health provider training, 127; neoliberalism and individualism and, 155, 157–158; to transition procedures, 130, 155; violence and health care, 113; whiteness and, 64
activism: capitalism and, 159; cisgender genealogy and, 62–63; employment and, 159–161; feminism and, 47; health care and sex reassignment surgery and, 155, 164, 166–167; health provider training and, 120, 124; immigration reform and, 192; multi-issue organizing and, 127; policies in higher education and, 81; programming in higher education and, 86; rights and law reform and, 184–185
adolescent development, 28–29
Ahmed, Sara, 130
Allums, Kye, 98, 106
allyship: cis and performance of, 62; in education, 68–69, 86–88; policing and, 71, 76–77. *See also* health provider training
ally training, 86–88; transphobia in, 68–69

American Educational Research Association, 2008 Conference, 24
American Journal of Public Health, 113
American Psychiatric Association, 38, 71
Americans with Disabilities Act (ADA), 186
anti-colonial. *See* decolonization
anti-discrimination law: access to employment and housing and, 185; criminal punishment system and, 186; critical race theory and, 187; discriminatory intent and, 186; in higher education, 86–87, 90–91, 95–96; immigration law and, 135–136; neoliberalism and, 186; people of color and, 185–186; perpetrator perspective and, 187–189, 193; racism and, 185, 187–188; restrooms and, 92, 96, 187; secondary education and, 85; transphobia and, 191; trans rights and, 184–185; visibility and, 185–186
Anzaldúa, Gloria, 29
Aoki, Ryka, 77
Arkle, Gabriel, 230n31
Association for Women in Psychology 2007 Conference, trans-misogyny and, 172
asylum, 135, 137, 139–140
athletes, intersex and transgender, 100–101, 110–111
athletics: femininity and, 98, 101–102; gender binary in, 98–101, 104, 106–108, 110–111; gender identity and, 98–99, 110; gender verification in, 103–104, 107–108; heteronormativity and, 98–99, 101–102; International Olympic Committee criteria, 104–105; masculinity and, 101–102, 107; policies in, 98–99, 103–106, 110–111; privilege in, 101, 111; sexism in, 109; sex reassignment surgery and the International Olympic Committee, 104–105, 108; sex segregation in, 100–101, 108–109; Title IX, 100, 108–110; whiteness and women in, 101–102
Audre Lorde Project (ALP), 127
"autogynephilia," 38

binary. *See* gender binary
biomedicine. *See* medical establishment
biopolitics, 136–137
Board of Immigration Appeals, 142
Body Alchemy: Transsexual Portraits, 163
borderlands, 29
borders: appropriation of, 135; capitalism and, 155; mobility and, 135–136
Boricuas, 24, 27–28
Bornstein, Kate, 84
Bowers, Marci, 73–74
branding, of trans subjects, 160–161
Brown, Wendy, 54, 184
Buijs, Carl, 60
Butler, Judith, 49, 53, 62, 153, 156, 165

Cameron, Loren, 163–164
Camp Trans: critiques of racism in, 66–67; inclusion/exclusion policies and, 66–67; self-identification and, 66
Campus Climate Index, 85
Campus Pride, 85
capitalism: activism and, 159; borders and, 155; educational-industrial complex and, 46, 52, 54; employment and, 159–160; individualism and, 157; knowledge commodification and, 46; law reform and, 193; subjectivities and, 153–156, 168–169
Caruth, Cathy, 59
Cayuga Indian Nation Land Claim, 26
Cayuga Nation territory, 24, 30
Center for Addictions and Mental Health (CAMH) Gender Identity Clinic, 166
Chavez, Karma, 144, 146
Childhood Gender Identity Disorder, 71
cisgender: activism and, 62–63; allyship and, 62, 68; critical race theory and, 64; feminism and, 64; gender normativity and, 62, 69–70, 73, 75–76, 129, 215n44, 223n69; genealogy of, 60–61, 63; as racialized, 62; trans* identity and, 62; transphobia and, 68. *See also* cissexuality
cisnormativity. *See* cisgender; gender normativity
cissexuality: access to medical treatment and narratives of, 38–39; privilege of, 64–66, 69–70, 76–77, 212–213nn17–18
cis/trans binary, 64, 66–67; neoliberalism and, 65, 76–77. *See also* gender binary
citizenship: performance of, 144–145; reproduction of, 144–145; rights of, 134
class, hierarchies of, 64, 66–67, 70, 75–76
classism, Camp Trans critiques of, 66–67
classrooms, as historical spaces, 24
Coalición de Derechos Humans (CDH), 145–146
college. *See* higher education
colonialism: decolonization and, 26; education and, 24–29; forgetting and, 27–29; trans subjectivity and, 164
colonization: gender and, 23–24, 28; gender and trans- and women's studies and, 29–32; space and, 24, 26–28; Sullivan-Clinton Campaign and, 30. *See also* decolonization
colonizing, 26, 32
coming out, 66, 69, 76, 86, 97; the academy and, 37
community-based participatory research, 128
Compton's Cafeteria, 190
Contesting Fundamentalisms, 50
counseling, in higher education, 93–94, 96
covering, the academy and, 41–43. *See also* passing
criminal punishment system: bias and marginalization within, 189–190; gender-based violence in, 191, 230n31; hate-crime law and, 189–190; National Prison Rape Elimination Act and, 192, 230n31, 231n32; transphobia and, 191; violence and, 189–190; War on Drugs and, 190
crisis hotlines, 93–94
critical political economy, 153, 158
critical race theory: anti discrimination law reform and, 187; cisgender and, 64
critical trans resistance, 164–168, 193–194
cultural competence model: critique of, 117, 120–121; in medical education, 115–121, 124–127, 129–131
Currah, Paisley, 46–47, 56, 63, 134, 158
Cusanelli, Katelynn, 95

data, versus theory, 36
Day of Silence, 84
decolonization: 23–26, 31–32; dialectic of freedom and, 32; educators and, 24, 29–31; gender/sovereignty and, 23–24, 32; language recovery and, 32; pedagogy of, 23–24; transing- and, 23–24, 28–32. *See also* colonization
Defense of Marriage Act, 142
Defosse, Dana Leland, 60–61, 68, 215n40
DelVecchio-Good, Mary-Jo, 114
DeMarco, Vik, 68
Department of Education, 30, 81, 91
Department of Homeland Security, 143–144
Department of Justice: Board of Immigration Appeals and, 142; National Prison Rape Elimination Act and, 192, 231n32. *See also* criminal punishment system
detention camps, 137
The Diagnostic and Statistical Manual of Mental Disorders, 4th ed., 71; medical establishment and, 38–39
Didrikson, Babe, 102
dis/ability: discrimination and Title IX and, 108; narratives in medical education and, 120; rights, cisgender and, 64
dis/ability studies: queer theory and, 212n15; temporality and, 74; transgender studies and, 74
disciplining. *See* policing

Index

discrimination: covering as, 41–42; in higher education, 81; individualism and, 157–158, 162; law reform and, 192–193; neoliberalism and, 157–158; secondary education and, 85; sex segregation and, 187; Title X and, 81, 108. *See also* anti-discrimination law
discriminatory intent, 186
diversity, in the academy, 40, 42–43, 130
Division of Institutional Equity and Diversity, 87
dorms: gender neutral policies in, 93, 96; safety and single-sex accommodation in, 92–93
Drake, Jennifer, 56
DREAM Act, 138
DSM, 71; medical establishment and, 38–39
dysphoria, 46

economy, 148, 153–156, 158–160, 164, 166–169
education: allyship in, 68–69; Indigenous peoples and, 24; Maori, 26, 29, 31; Puerto Rican colonial policy and, 24–25. *See also* educators; higher education
educational-corporate complex, 46, 52, 54. *See also* academic-industrial complex; the academy
educators, decolonial, 24, 29
emergency funding, 86
"The Empire Strikes Back: A Posttranssexual Manifesto," 48
employment: access to, 87; activists and, 160–161; anti-discrimination laws and access to, 185, 190–191; branding for, 154, 160–161; capitalism and, 159; criminalized, 154–155, 166, 190–191; Employment Non-Discrimination Act and, 184; rights to, 154, 159
Employment Non-Discrimination Act (ENDA), 184
erasure, 70
essentialism, 181
exodus, 150

Family, Unvalued: Discrimination, Denial, and the Fate of Binational Same-sex Couples Under U.S. Law, 144–146
Feinberg, Leslie, 113, 158
feminine gender expression. *See* femininity
femininity: athletics and, 98, 101–102; compulsory, 183; dismissal of, 42–43; invisibility and queer identity and, 179; myths about trans women and, 170–171; neoliberalism and, 162; as performance, 179–180; reclaiming, 170; scientists and the academy and, 34, 39–43; trans-misogyny and, 171–172, 174
feminism: activism and, 47; cisgender use and, 64; fundamentalism and, 52; historicity of, 51, 54; identity politics and, 46, 48, 76–77; institutionalized, 57; knowledge production in, 53, 57; "radical," 47; temporality of, 51, 53–54; trans-national theory and, 57; wave-frameworks of, 56; women's studies and, 53–54. *See also* transfeminism

feminist studies, colonization and, 28–30
femme, identity, 170, 174, 179. *See also* femininity
Femme 2006 Conference, 170, 174, 176, 178
Femme 2008 Conference, 177, 179
Foucault, Michel, 75–76, 136, 156–157
Freeman, Alan, 187, 193
Frye, Phyllis, 159
FtF: Female to Femme, 175
FTMi, 159
fundamentalism, 52

Gay, Lesbian, and Straight Education Network (GLSEN), 82, 84
gender binary: athletics and, 98–101, 104, 106–108, 110–111; enforced by women's studies, 57; in health care, 125–126; hierarchies of, 69; neoliberalism and, 168; passing and, 65–66, 213nn19–20; trans- studies and, 158
gender confirmation surgery. *See* sex reassignment surgery
gender expression. *See* gender identity
gender identity: ally training and, 68–69; anti-discrimination law and, 186; athletics and, 98–99, 110; Employment Non-Discrimination Act and, 184; hate-crime law and, 184; higher education and, 86; policing in medical establishment, 114, 116, 118, 131; policing in secondary education, 81–82; political economy and, 153; subjectivity and, 156; universalism and, 52; violence in criminal punishment system and, 191
Gender Identity Disorder, 83, 126, 222n35; Non-disordered Gender Complexity as alternative to, 126
gender normativity, cisgender and, 62, 69–70, 73, 75–76, 129, 215n44, 223n69
Gender Outlaw, 84
Gender Recognition Act (GRA), U.K. civil partnership laws and, 138–139
gender/sovereignty, 23–24, 31–33; Native communities and cultural spaces and, 23, 31
Gender Spectrum, 99
gender studies: colonization and, 23, 29; policing and, 76; politics of gender transgression and, 128; trans* academics and inclusion in, 36–38; women's studies and, 52
gender transition: the academy and, 36–37, 43–44; health care reform and, 129; medico-juridical determination of, 64, 73; mental health and, 167. *See also* sex reassignment surgery
gender verification, athletics and, 103–104, 107–108
Godsey, Keelin, 106
Gordon, Avery, 48, 54–55
Green, Jamison, 63
Greene, Maxine, 30–31

Halberstam, Judith, 36, 158, 160
Hammonds, Evelyn, 76
Hanssmann, Christoph, 68
harassment: by health care providers, 94; in higher education, 81, 91; neoliberalism and, 157–158; reporting, 84; in restrooms, 92; in secondary education, 83–84
Haritaworn, Jin, 128
Harry Benjamin International Gender Dysphoria Association (HBIGDA), 128
hate-crime law: deserving narratives in, 188–189, 192, 229n18; gender identity and, 184; immigration law and, 135–136; perpetrator perspective and, 189; policies in higher education and, 86; transphobia and, 191; trans rights and, 184–185; violence and sentencing and, 185, 189; visibility and, 185–186
Haudenosaunee, 24, 26, 30
Hays Commission, 24–25
health advocates, 112, 119
health care: access to, 37–38, 93–95, 113–118, 124, 129–130, 165–167; gender binary within, 125–126; harassment by providers of, 94; in higher education, 87, 93–95; narratives and, 38–39, 119–121, 222n35; needs assessment studies in, 115; sex/gender self-determination and access to transition procedures as, 155, 164–167; sex reassignment surgery and, 155, 164–165; single-sex accommodations in, 92; social justice and, 168; violence and access to, 113. *See also* medical treatment
health provider training, 112, 115–116; activism and, 112; evaluation of, 121, 126; innovation in, 125, 129; limits of, 116–117, 119–120, 123; Lurie's "Revolutionary Gender Model" of, 125–126; narratives in, 115–116, 119–121; privilege in, 124. *See also* medical education
heteronormativity: athletics and, 98–99, 101–102; immigration law and, 143
heterosexism, 23–24, 31, 179, 182
Hewitt, Paul, 163
Heywood, Leslie, 56
hierarchies: binary gender, 64, 66, 68–69; race and class, 67, 70, 211n3; visibility and, 75–76
higher education: access to resources in, 86–87; activism in, 95–96; ally training in, 86–87; anti-discrimination policy in, 86–87, 90–91, 95–96; emergency funding in, 86; faculty diversity in, 40, 42–43; gender identity and, 86; harassment in, 81, 91; hate-crime policy in, 86; homophobia in, 85; LGBT groups in, 95; mentoring in, 95–96; names in, 87–90; policies for students and employees in, 81, 90; privilege in, 35; programming in, 95–96; sex reassignment surgery and, 90; Title IX in, 81, 91; transphobia and, 85
HIV/AIDS, 96, 127, 146, 158, 228n9
homelessness, 127, 158, 162, 187

homonationalist, 144–145
homophobia: hate-crime law and, 189–190; in higher education, 85; restrooms and, 92
HONOR project, 129
horizontal oppression, 40
hormone therapy: access in higher education to, 93–94, 96; International Olympic Committee policy and, 104–105; medical establishment and, 165
housing: anti-discrimination laws and access to, 185; in higher education, 93, 96. *See also* dorms
Housing Works, 127
humanism, 51
human rights: immigration and, 142; neoliberalism and, 157, 169; sex/gender self-determination and, 165; sex reassignment surgery and, 165
Human Rights Campaign, 184
Hunter, Tyra, 113

identity politics, 46, 71, 75–76; feminism and, 46, 48; neoliberalism and, 154
Imagining Transgender, 122
immigration: criminalization of, 144–145; gender variant and queer narratives of, 133–134, 136, 149; human rights advocacy and, 142; imperceptible politics and, 150; legibility and, 137–138, 141; mobility and, 135–137, 149–150; narratives in medical education and, 120; National Prison Rape Elimination Act and, 192, 231n32; passing and, 143–144; queer rights and, 145–146; sexuality and, 145; surveillance and, 142–143, 145; transphobia and, 144; undocumented, 137–138; in the United Kingdom, 138–139; visa categories and, 137
Immigration and Naturalization Service (INS), 142–143
Immigration Equality, 134, 139–140, 143–144
immigration law: anti-discrimination and hate-crime law and, 135–136; asylum and, 135, 137, 139–140; heteronormativity and, 143–144, 192; intersectionality and, 135, 145–148; neoliberalism and, 134–136, 140, 145, 147; reform of, 192; refugee category and, 140; surgical gender status and, 142–144; visibility and, 134, 148–149
Immigration Law and the Transgender Client, 134–135, 139–143, 145, 148
imperceptible politics, 150
imperialism, 24; trans subjectivity and, 164
"imposter syndrome," 36
indigeneity: education and, 24–26, 29–31; gender identity and, 31; rights and, 28; traditional knowledge and, 26, 32
Indigenist LGBT research, 31
Indigenous Peoples of the Pacific Special Interest Group (IPP-SIG), 24

individualism, 157–158, 162, 169
interdisciplinarity, 50, 55–56
International Association of Athletics Federation (IAAF), 104, 108
International Congress on Gender Identity and Human Rights, 134
International Olympic Committee (IOC), 103–108; transgender athlete policy, 104–105
intersectionality, 44; immigration law and, 135; poverty and immigration and, 147; race and, 147; transgender rights imaginary and, 146–147; women's studies and, 44
intersexuality, 100; athletics and, 98–100
invisibility, femininity and, 179. *See also* visibility
Iran, gender reassignment in, 133

Jacobs, Sue-Ellen, 31
Jenkins, Kuni, 25–26
Jones, Alison, 25–26

Kantaras, Michael, 163
Kholsa, Dhillon, 163
knowledge, production and commodification of, 46, 51–53, 56–57
Koyama, Emi, 64–65

Ladies Professional Golf Association, 103
language: binarized systems of, 49; gender policing of, 77
language recovery, decolonization and, 32
Laub, Dori, 59
law reform, 184–187, 190–194. *See also* anti-discrimination law; hate-crime law
Lawson, Lana, 98, 103
Lev, Arlene Istar, 121
"level playing field," myth of, 98, 103, 106–108, 111
LGBT groups, in higher education, 95
LGBT studies, policing and, 76
locker rooms, single sex-accommodation in, 92
Luibhéid, Eithne, 145
Lurie, Samuel, 125

Maori: educators, 26, 29; Maori-as-, 25; women, 26
Marfan syndrome, 107
Marsden, Samuel, 25
Marx, Carl, 155, 159
masculinity: athletics and, 101–102, 107; neoliberalism and, 155, 161–164; trans-misogyny and, 174, 182–183
Massumi, Brian, 147
materialism, 155
Matthew Shepard and James Byrd, Jr. Hate Crimes Prevention Act, 184, 190
Matthew Shepard Local Law Enforcement Enhancement Act, 229n18

medical community. *See* medical establishment
medical education: activism and, 120, 131–132; alternative models of, 121, 126; cultural competence models in, 115–121, 124–127, 129–131; curriculum in, 114–116, 123, 125; intake forms in, 118, 123; sexism in, 118; terminology in, 119, 121–122, 126–127; WPATH standards of care and, 123, 223n51. *See also* health provider training; medical establishment
medical establishment: *DSM*, 4th ed., and, 38; gender identity and, 114, 118; gender reassignment in Iran and, 133; hormone therapy and, 165; knowledge production in, 116; pathologization in, 115, 118, 126, 131; policing in, 116, 118, 131; sexism in, 118–119; transphobia in, 118
medical treatment: narratives and access to, 38–39, 119, 121; self-determination in, 131. *See also* health care; medical establishment
medico-juridical determination, 64, 73. *See also* medical establishment
Mendoza, Inés María, 24–25
mental health: health care in higher education and, 93–95; neoliberalism and, 167
mentoring, in higher education, 96
Michigan Womyn's Music Festival, 66–67, 176
migration. *See* immigration
misogyny, 171–172
Mitropoulos, Angela, 137
mobility: borders and, 135–136; control of, 136–137; exodus and, 149–150
Moore, Lisa Jean, 46–47, 56
Morgan, Robin, 173
Moulier-Boutang, Yann, 149–150
movement, as commerce, 137. *See also* mobility
MTV Real World: Brooklyn, 95
multicultural education, critique of, 26

Namaste, Vivian, 120, 128
names, 87–90, 96
narratives: access to health care and, 64, 119, 121, 222n35; cissexual, 38–39; cis/trans, 71, 73, 75–76; feminist, 53, 56, 58; in health provider training, 115–116, 119–121; trans rights, 154, 162
National Center for Lesbian Rights, 110
National Coalition for LGBT Health, 124
National Collegiate Athletic Association (NCAA), 105–106
National Gay and Lesbian Task Force (NGLTF), 184
National Prison Rape Elimination Act (NPREA), 192, 231n32
National Student Genderblind Campaign, 93
Native communities: sexualities and gender identities and, 31–32. *See also* indigeneity; *names of specific tribes*

neoliberalism: anti-discrimination laws and, 186; cis/trans binary and, 76–77, 168; citizen construction and, 154; discrimination and, 157–158; economic growth and, 156–157; employment and, 157–159; femininity and, 162; human rights and, 157, 169; immigration law and, 134–136, 140, 145, 147; individualism and, 157–158, 162; law reform and, 193; masculinity and, 155, 161–164; mental health and, 167; police and violence and, 190; self-determination and, 155, 158; sex reassignment surgery and, 166–168; subjectivities and, 154, 156–157, 168–169; violence and harassment and, 157–158
non-discrimination policy. *See* anti-discrimination law
Non-disordered Gender Complexity, alternative to Gender Identity Disorder, 126

Olympics, 102. *See also* athletics
Onandaga, 24, 29, 30, 205n8
Ontario Health Insurance Plan (OHIP), sex reassignment surgery and, 155, 164, 166, 168
On the Team: Equal Opportunities for Transgender Student Athletes, 110
othering, 125, 130
"outing," 89

Pakeha, educators, 25–26, 29, 31
Panopticon, 75–76
passing: access and whiteness and, 64; airport security and, 149; cissexual privilege and, 65–66, 76, 213nn19–20; immigration and, 143–144, 149; normative hierarchies and, 74–76; policing and, 74–75; safety and, 197. *See also* covering
pathology: depathologization of, 222n30; trans* in medical establishment as, 39, 63, 118–120, 126, 131, 154, 166
pedagogy, transing-, 23–24, 33
people of color: anti-discrimination law reform and, 185–186; narratives in medical education and, 120; Native LGBT people and, 23–24, 32–33; trans-, 23–24, 29, 32–33; Trans-Justice and, 127
performance art, 201
permanent residency petitions, 140, 142–143, 145, 148
perpetrator perspective, 187–189, 193
Personal Responsibility and Work Opportunity Act, 164
Piepzna-Samarasinha, 179
Pihama, Leonie, 26
policing: gender and women's studies and, 76; gender identity, 81–82, 116, 118, 131; language and, 77; passing and, 74–76
Pon, G., 117
Ponce Massacre, 24, 205n10
post-traumatic stress syndrome, 83

poverty: anti-discrimination law reform and, 187, 228nn8–10; employment access and, 190–191; intersectional politics and immigration and, 147
prejudice: institutional power and, 117–118; in medical research, 38–40
Press, Irina, 102
Press, Tamara, 102
primary data: in a secondary-source world, 37–38; theory and, 36
prison. *See* criminal punishment system
privilege: in athletics, 101, 111; cissexual, 64–66, 69–70, 76–77, 212–213nn17–18; in health care, 122, 124, 220n7
programming: in higher education, 95–96; limits of, 95; transphobic violence and, 95
psychology, 28–29, 32
Puar, Jasbir, 146–147

queer communities, 129, 171, 178, 183; trans misogyny in, 173, 177–178
Queer Liberation Front, 83
queer rights, immigration and, 145–146
Queers and Immigration: A Vision Statement, 145
Queers for Economic Justice, 127, 145–146
queer studies, 62, 135, 211nn6–7, 212n15
queer theory, disability studies and, 212n15
"queer time," 36–37

race: binary gender and hierarchies of, 49, 66–67; cisgender and, 62, 64; cultural competence models and, 117; intersectional politics and, 147
racism: anti-discrimination law reform and, 185, 187–188; Camp Trans and critiques of, 66–67; decolonizing and, 23, 31; Title IX and, 108. *See also* discrimination
Raymond, Janice, 173
Real Life Experience (RLE), 167. *See also* real-life test
real-life test, 123, 131, 223n51
refugees, 140; narratives and, 120
research: in the academy, 37–40; when subject becomes researcher, 37–38
restrooms: anti-discrimination policy and, 96; violence, harassment, and single-sex accommodation in, 92
Richards, Renée, 102–103
rights: citizenship, 134; indigenous and trans/queer, 24; land, 23–24, 27–30
Roberts, Monica, 60, 62, 68, 211n3
Rosenberg, Sharon, 58
Rubin, Henry, 163

Safe Zone, 86–88, 95
Sakamoto, Izumi, 125
Samuels, Ellen, 75
SB590 law, Indiana, 138

Index

Schroer, Diane, 229n18
scientists: bias and privilege and, 37–42; femininity and the academy and, 34, 39–43
search image, 41
secondary education: anti-discrimination laws in, 85; harassment and violence in, 81–85; policing gender in, 81–82; sexual assault in, 83; transphobia in, 85
self-authorizing. *See* self-determination
self-determination: access to transition procedures and, 130, 155; gender/sovereignty and, 32; human rights and, 165; neoliberalism and, 155, 158, 165
Semenya, Caster, 98, 104, 108
separate but equal, 108
Serano, Julia, 42, 65–66, 76, 212n17, 213nn18–20, 215n45, 216n48
sexism: in athletics, 109; hate-crime law and, 189, 193; in medical establishment, 118–119
sex reassignment surgery (SRS): activism and, 166; class politics of, 49; counseling and, 93–95; higher education and, 87, 90; human rights and, 165; immigration law and, 142–144; International Olympic Committee policy and, 104–105, 108; neoliberalism and, 166–168; publicly funded health care for, 155, 164–165; social justice and, 168; worker productivity and, 160–161. *See also* gender transition
sex segregation: in athletics, 100–101, 108–109; discrimination and, 187
sexual assault: criminal punishment system and, 191; National Prison Rape Elimination Act and, 192, 231n32; secondary education and, 83
sexual harassment, 85. *See also* harassment; sexual assault
sex verification, athletics and, 103–104, 107–108
sex workers, 166
Shakhsari, Sima, 133
Shepard, Matthew, 81
Sherbourne Health Center, 168
Singer, Ben, 125–126
single-sex accommodations, 92
Smith, Andrea, 46
Smith, Linda Tuhiwai, 23
social justice, 23, 39, 40, 111, 167
Sons of the Movement, 56
Southern Comfort, 113
space(s): cis, effected through, 68, 213–214n28; dis/ability studies and, 74; feminist and trans classrooms as historical, 24; gender orientation in, 73–74; gender/sovereignty, 23, 31; identity categories and, 74–75; as market, 137; of production and consumption, 153; "queer time" and, 36–37; trans- cultural and decolonial, 24; trans entities within feminist, 50–51; visibility and right to occupy, 75; whiteness and colonial, 59
Spade, Dean, 70, 128, 135–136, 158, 163
sports. *See* athletics

Stimson, Adrian A., 32
Stone, Sandy, 48, 76
Stonewall, 190
Stryker, Susan, 46–47, 56, 63, 128, 160, 203n3
subjectivity: branding and, 160; capitalism and, 153–156, 168–169; colonialism/imperialism and, 164; employment rights and, 154; feminism and, 56; gender identity and, 156; neoliberalism and, 154; trans, 154; transsexuality and, 160–161, 165–166; whiteness and, 57–58
substance abuse, violence and, 85
suicide, risk of, 83, 93–94
Sullivan-Clinton Campaign, 30
surveillance: biometric, 138; immigration and, 137, 142–143, 145; the Panopticon and, 75–76. *See also* policing
Sylvia Rivera Law Project (SLRP), 126–127, 146

Tadiar, Neferti, 148
Takatapui, 31
Teena, Brandon, 81
temporality: cis, effected through, 68, 73–74, 213–214n28; dis/ability and, 74; of feminism, 51; "queer time" and, 36–37
This Bridge Called My Back, 57
Thomas, Wesley, 31
Title IX: athletics and, 100, 108–110; higher education and, 91; racial and disability discrimination and, 108; sex discrimination and, 81
Toronto Star, 161
Tranny Roadshow, 195, 200
Trans 101. *See* allyship; health provider training
trans* academics, inclusion in gender studies, 37–38
Transcend Transgender Support and Education Society, 127
trans entities, 48–51, 54, 57–59
Trans Entities: The Nasty Love of Papí and Wil, 48–49
transfeminism, 48, 53; women's studies and, 46–50
Transgender Day of Remembrance (TDOR), 95, 147
Transgender Law Center, 134, 139–140, 143
transgender-rights imaginary, 134, 146, 149–150
transgender studies. *See* trans- studies
Transgender Tapestry, 159
TransGriot, 60, 62, 68
trans* identity, political category of, 62. *See also* gender identity
trans illiteracy, in women's studies, 50
TransJustice, 127
trans-misogyny: alliances and, 174, 177; essentialism and, 181; femininity and, 182; masculinity and, 174, 182; misogyny and transphobia and, 171–172; queer communities and, 177–178; trans-woman exclusion and, 176–177

transnationality, 136; feminism and, 57
transphobia: allies and, 71; ally training and, 68–69; anti-discrimination law and, 189–191, 193; cis and, 68; in the criminal punishment system, 191; effects of, 129, 223n69; hate-crime law and, 191; in higher education, 85, 92, 95; immigration and, 144; in medical establishment, 118; secondary education and, 85; trans-misogyny and, 171–172
Trans Pulse project, 129
trans rights: activists and non-profits and, 184–185; law reform and, 184–185, 193–194; narratives, 154, 162; National Gay and Lesbian Task Force and, 184; "Western" models for, 133–134
transsexuality: cissexual privilege and passing and, 65–66, 213nn19–20; employment marketing and, 154, 160–161; masculinity and, 163; pathologizing, 166; subjectivity and, 160–161, 165–166
Transsexual Workers: An Employment Guide, 160
transsomatechnics, 164
trans- studies: colonization and, 29; dis/ability studies and, 74; gender binary and, 158; medical education and, 124; women's studies and, 48
trans theory. *See* trans- studies
trans-woman exclusion, 176–177
TransX, 135
Troubling Women's Studies, 58
"two spirit," 31–32; use in classrooms, 70; use in health provider training, 129

Undoing Gender, 49
unemployment, 158–159, 162, 187. *See also* employment
United Citizens for Equality, Cayuga Indian Nation Land Claim and, 27, 30
United Kingdom Lesbian and Gay Immigration Group (UKLGIG), 138–139, 148
Uniting American Families Bill, 140
universalism, 52
university. *See* higher education
U.S.A. Track and Field, 104–105
U.S. Citizenship and Immigration Services, 141–142
U.S. Department of Education Office for Civil Rights, 81, 91
U.S. Department of Homeland Security, 138
U.S. Golf Association, 105
U.S. Tennis Association, 102

Valentine, David, 70, 122–123
Vancouver Coastal Health (VCH), 124; Trans Care Project of, 127

violence, 199; access to health care and, 113; anti-discrimination law and, 185–186, 190; criminal punishment system and, 186, 191–192; of feminist occlusions, 48; hate-crime law and, 189–190; in higher education and, 95; National Prison Rape Elimination Act and, 192, 231n32; neoliberalism and, 157–158; perpetrator perspective and, 189; police and neoliberalism and, 193; resistance to, 127; restrooms and, 92; in secondary education, 81–85; substance abuse and suicide risk and, 85
Virago, Shawna, 175
visas, 137
visibility: anti-discrimination and hate-crime law and, 185–186; immigration law and, 134; normativity and politics of, 74–75; right to occupy spaces and, 75; trans and intersex athletics and, 100. *See also* passing

Walters, Karina L., 31
Walworth, Janis, 160–161
War on Drugs, 190
Washington State Interscholastic Activity Association (WIAA), 105
Weiss, Jillian T., 159
whiteness: access and passability and, 64; cisgender and studies of, 64; colonial spaces and, 28–30, 59; subjectivity and, 57–58, 166; trans erasure and, 70–71; women in athletics and, 101–102
white students: adolescent development and, 28–30; cisgender identification and, 62
Wiegman, Robyn, 51–54, 58
Wilchins, Riki, 62
Williams, Raymond, 48
Wingspan, 145–146
Women's Sports Foundation, 110
women's studies: the academy and, 36–28, 44, 47; colonization and, 23, 29–30; feminism in, 53–54; gender studies and, 52; historical production of, 52; institutionalization of, 54; intersectionality and, 44; knowledge production and commodification in, 46, 51–52, 56; policing and, 76; race and gender binary in, 57; transfeminism and, 46–50; trans illiteracy in, 50; trans- studies and, 48
Women's Studies on Its Own, 51
Women's U.S. Open, 102
Wong, Laiana, 24, 26
World Professional Association for Transgender Health (WPATH), 123–124, 128, 223n51

xenophobia, 146, 189, 190, 193

Yoshino, Kenji, 41